Personal Insurance: Life, Health, and Retirement

Personal Insurance: Life, Health, and Retirement

G. Victor Hallman, Ph.D., J.D., CPCU, CLU
Lecturer—Insurance Department
The Wharton School of the University of Pennsylvania

Karen L. Hamilton, Ph.D., CPCU
Director of Curriculum
American Institute for CPCU

First Edition • 1994

American Institute for CPCU
720 Providence Road, Malvern, Pennsylvania 19355-0770

First Edition • July 1994

Library of Congress Catalog Number 94-71922
International Standard Book Number 0-89463-066-0

Printed in the United States of America

Foreword

The American Institute for Chartered Property Casualty Underwriters and the Insurance Institute of America are independent, nonprofit, educational organizations serving the needs of the property and liability insurance business. The Institutes develop a wide range of programs—curricula, study materials, and examinations—in response to the educational requirements of various elements of the business.

The American Institute confers the Chartered Property Casualty Underwriter (CPCU®) professional designation on those who meet the Institute's experience, ethics, and examination requirements.

The Insurance Institute of America offers associate designations and certificate programs in the following technical and managerial disciplines:

Accredited Adviser in Insurance (AAI®)
Associate in Claims (AIC)
Associate in Underwriting (AU)
Associate in Risk Management (ARM)
Associate in Loss Control Management (ALCM®)
Associate in Premium Auditing (APA®)
Associate in Management (AIM)
Associate in Research and Planning (ARP®)
Associate in Insurance Accounting and Finance (AIAF)
Associate in Automation Management (AAM®)
Associate in Marine Insurance Management (AMIM®)
Associate in Reinsurance (ARe)
Associate in Fidelity and Surety Bonding (AFSB)
Associate in Insurance Services (AIS)
Certificate in General Insurance
Certificate in Supervisory Management

Certificate in Introduction to Claims
Certificate in Introduction to Property and Liability Insurance
Certificate in Business Writing

The Institutes began publishing textbooks in 1976 to help students meet the national examination standards. Since that time, we have produced more than eighty individual textbook volumes. Despite the vast differences in the subjects and purposes of these volumes, they all have much in common. First, each book is specifically designed to increase knowledge and develop skills that can improve job performance and help students achieve the educational objectives of the course for which it is assigned. Second, all of the manuscripts of our texts are widely reviewed before publication, by both insurance business practitioners and members of the academic community. In addition, all of our texts and course guides reflect the work of Institute staff members. These writing or editing duties are seen as an integral part of their professional responsibilities, and no one earns a royalty based on the sale of our texts. We have proceeded in this way to avoid even the appearance of any conflict of interests. Finally, the revisions of our texts often incorporate improvements suggested by students and course leaders.

We welcome criticisms of and suggestions for improving our publications. It is only with such constructive comments that we can hope to improve the quality of our study materials. Please direct any comments you may have on this text to the Curriculum Department of the Institutes.

Norman A. Baglini, Ph.D., CPCU, CLU
President and Chief Executive Officer

Preface

CPCU 2 provides information and fosters learning that is valuable to CPCU candidates on both a professional level and a personal level. Many insurance professionals deal with personal insurance and help their clients to better insure and more appropriately manage their personal loss exposures. Information in this textbook will prepare CPCU candidates for these current professional demands. In addition, CPCU candidates must manage and insure their own personal loss exposures, and the CPCU 2 text can be of great aid in that area as well.

Personal financial planning is an important aspect of personal risk management—in fact, it is the most important aspect according to many insurance and financial planning professionals. CPCU candidates must be aware of the issues and products involved in personal financial planning for both professional and personal reasons. This knowledge helps them, as professionals, to better understand and more appropriately treat their clients' personal loss exposures. As individuals and family members, they must also handle their own financial planning effectively.

Personal Insurance: Life, Health, and Retirement is one of the texts used for the CPCU 2 curriculum because it deals with the treatment of personal nonproperty-liability loss exposures with much emphasis on personal financial planning. The text covers health insurance, life insurance, investment planning, retirement planning, estate planning, and business continuation planning.

Many reviewers contributed a substantial amount of time and effort to develop a text that is accurate, up to date, and readable. The following reviewers' constructive comments and suggestions are greatly appreciated:

John A. Anderson
Director of Compliance
American General

James E. Brennan, CPCU, CLU, CIC
Academic Advisor for the Professional Insurance Program
Lecturer, Finance and Insurance
University of Connecticut

Bradley J. Borg, CPCU
Principal
The Minneapolis Agency, Inc.

Debra B. Copeland, CPCU, CLU
Principal
Van Zandt, Emrich, & Cary, Inc.

Angela S. Grodanz, CPCU
General Accident

Bruce A. Hill, CLU
Assistant Professor of Insurance
Eastern Kentucky State University

Charles Morgan, J.D., CPCU, ARM, CLU
Zurich-American Insurance Group

Jeane O'Connell, CPCU, CLU, ChFC
Owner
Jeane O'Connell—Tax & Financial Services

Victor A. Puelo, Jr.
Assistant Professor of Insurance
Appalachian State University

Fred Tillman, Ph.D., ChFC
Professor of Risk Management and Insurance
Georgia State University

David S. Tubolino
Assistant Vice President—Sales Management
Amerisure Co.

Special thanks also go to Michael W. Elliott, Assistant Vice President, American Institute for CPCU; Karen K. Porter, Assistant Director of Curriculum, American Institute for CPCU; and Lowell S. Young, Director of Curriculum, American Institute for CPCU.

Our goal is to help develop an understanding of this material that will sufficiently prepare CPCU candidates for the future. In order to reach this goal, we must pay close attention to reader responses. Your comments regarding this text are welcome and extremely valuable. In preparation for the next edition, we need any suggestions or advice you might offer. Please call or write to us, at the American Institute for CPCU, and give your input.

G. Victor Hallman
Karen L. Hamilton

Contributing Authors

The American Institute for CPCU and the authors of this text acknowledge, with deep appreciation, the work of the following contributing authors:

Edward E. Graves, CLU, ChFC
Associate Professor of Insurance
The American College

Claude C. Lilly III, Ph.D., CPCU, CLU
Professor of Risk Management and Insurance
Florida State University

William J. Ruckstahl, CLU, ChFC
Associate Professor of Finance
The American College

Glenn L. Wood, Ph.D., CPCU, CLU
Professor of Finance
California State University—Bakersfield

Contents

Chapter 1

Private Health Benefits

The personal risk management process can be applied to health exposures. Health exposures such as physical injury, illness, and disability can be identified and evaluated in terms of medical expenses for the individual and his or her family members, loss of income through disability of income earners, and, more recently, custodial care expenses for the individual or family members because of inability to perform the normal activities of daily living. Various alternatives can be considered for treating these loss exposures, such as the following:

- Loss control (maintaining a proper diet, keeping physically fit, and not smoking, as examples)
- Avoidance (such as not participating in dangerous sports)
- Retention (using deductibles in medical expense coverage and elimination periods in disability income coverage or accumulating an emergency reserve for noninsured medical expenses and shorter, temporary periods of disability)
- Loss financing through insurance (acquiring medical expense coverage, disability income insurance, and long-term care insurance)
- Noninsurance transfers (such as an employer's paying an employee's costs of counseling to handle stress)

Individuals evaluate these alternatives in light of their families' situations and select the best alternatives to meet their health exposures. Just as with other personal exposures, for many individuals loss control and avoidance help to reduce or prevent health exposures, and insurance is the best risk financing measure to deal with health exposures.

Private health insurance is offered through private entities such as insurance companies. It may be written on an individual or a group basis. If written on an individual basis, the underwriter considers the risk characteristics of the individual, such as the person's age, gender, and health. If written on a group basis, the underwriter considers the group characteristics that affect risk, including the size and average age of the group. (However, for small groups, usually under twenty-five members, the underwriter may also consider individual characteristics.) Public health benefits, such as Medicare and Medicaid, are also available to many individuals since they are provided by federal and state governments and governmental agencies.

This chapter discusses the various types of private health insurance policies that are available and the private health benefits providers. Chapter 2 deals with group and individual differences, public health benefits, and cost containment issues.

Health Insurance Policies

Health insurance policies (both individual and group) provide basically two types of coverage—(1) medical expense and (2) disability income. Both deal with financial losses resulting from sickness or accidental injury. In addition, health insurance may provide dental benefits and various other kinds of health insurance coverages. Finally, long-term care (LTC) coverage is one of the fastest growing areas of health insurance.

Medical Expense Insurance

Medical expense insurance is generally written as either basic medical expense contracts or major medical contracts. Both types deal with medical expenses that arise when an insured becomes ill or is accidentally injured.

Eligibility

Most medical expense contracts are written to cover not only the named insured, but also eligible family members. Many state insurance regulations dealing with individual and family policies specify that a contract may cover an individual or two or more eligible family members, including the policyholder's spouse and dependent children under the age of nineteen and any other individuals dependent on the policyholder. Some states have increased the age limit on children to twenty-five if the children are attending school on a full-time basis.

Individuals can be added to a medical expense insurance policy after it has been issued. The individual often must first submit an application and show that he or she meets the insurer's underwriting requirements. Then, after any additional premium is paid, coverage is provided.

Newborn children are automatically covered under many contracts. The insurer must usually be notified of the birth within a short period of time, usually thirty days.[1] Furthermore, an additional premium is usually required, beginning in the month directly following a child's birth. However, if a premium is already being paid for children, some contracts do not require the payment of any additional premium since the same dependent child charge applies regardless of the number of children covered.

Types of Coverage

Medical expense contracts customarily provide one or more of the following coverages:

- Hospital expense benefits
- Surgical expense benefits
- Physicians nonsurgical expense benefits

Hospital Expense Benefits

Hospital expense benefits are provided for specified *inpatient* (care received while hospitalized for at least one night) and *outpatient* (care received while at a hospital for one day at a time without an overnight stay) medical care expenses incurred as a result of treatment received in a hospital. Benefits generally consist of (1) charges for room and board (if any) and (2) charges for necessary services and supplies (so-called **ancillary services**), such as fees for lab work or the cost of traction.

Room and Board   The room and board component may be reimbursed up to a specified maximum daily benefit, such as $250, or it may be paid in full. In either case, the daily benefit is usually related to the semiprivate (shared) room and board charges in the geographic area where the group is located—the **usual, customary, and reasonable (UCR)** cost of semiprivate room and board accommodations. Intensive care room and board is often limited to two to three times the daily semiprivate limit. Typical maximum periods for continuous hospital confinement, during which benefits are payable, are 60, 90, 120, or 365 days. For example, an insurer might pay for up to 365 days of semiprivate hospital room and board charges on the basis of the UCR charges for such room and board.

Ancillary Services   The amount paid for necessary ancillary services is generally limited in one of three ways, although other variations are possible:

1. For each confinement a specified dollar maximum, which is usually a multiple of the room and board daily benefit (for example, twenty times the daily room and board benefit).

2. A specified dollar maximum plus a certain percentage of charges in excess of that maximum, with or without an overall maximum being applied (such as the first $1,000 of charges in full, plus 75 percent of the next $2,000 of these charges).

3. Full payment for the period during which room and board benefits are payable. Under this approach, reimbursement for hospital extras is usually without a separate limit but is subject to the maximum number of confinement days under the plan.

The coverage definition of ancillary services varies. One health insurance publication lists forty-five types of benefits. Some of the ancillary services categories found in hospital expense benefits include those in the following list:

*   General nursing care
*   Up to one-half the daily room and board benefit for convalescent or nursing home confinement
*   Drugs and medicine requiring a written prescription of a physician
*   Radiology
*   Microscopic or laboratory tests
*   Anesthetics and their administration
*   Casts, splints, trusses, braces, and crutches
*   Initial emergency transportation from where the sickness was contracted or the injury occurred to the nearest hospital

Maternity Benefits   Maternity benefits can be included, usually for an additional premium, as a hospital expense benefit, but with individual health insurance, maternity coverage may be too expensive relative to the benefits. (In other words, the premiums paid to the insurer may equal the amount of benefits received from the insurer.) Women who are likely to use the coverage will purchase it, resulting in adverse selection. Insurers may guard against adverse selection with the *ten-month rule*, which excludes coverage for births within ten months of the policy inception. The ten-month rule and adverse selection are not of as much concern under group contracts as they are for individual contracts because insurers are able to obtain a spread of loss exposures. (Insurers usually spread loss exposures under individual contracts by pooling or grouping them.) In any event, under the 1978 amendments to Title VII of the Civil Rights Act of 1964 (and under certain state nondiscrimination laws as well), the definition of disability or sickness includes maternity, and thus benefits must be provided for pregnancies on the same basis as they are provided for other disabilities covered under an employer's medical expense plan for its employees.

In nonemployment-related individual contracts, maternity benefits can be a stated amount, such as $1,000, or the regular policy coverage for room and board and miscellaneous expenses may apply. Regardless of the method of providing coverage, benefits are payable for pregnancies that commence after the person has been covered under the policy for a certain time, usually thirty days, to lessen adverse selection.

Surgical Expense Benefits

Surgical expense benefits are provided for the cost of operations and surgical procedures. While surgical expense coverage may be defined by means of a schedule that contains a list of operations and the amount that the insurer will pay for each, this coverage often is provided on the basis of the UCR charges for surgical procedures without a specified schedule.

Nonscheduled Benefits   Under a nonscheduled approach, reimbursement is based on the UCR charge for the procedure performed. The policy simply states that the insurer will pay no more than the UCR charge for a surgical procedure.

This concept has been replaced in some areas by the use of **diagnosis related groups (DRGs)** (medical conditions that recognize age, sex, and other health determinants that can affect the costs of treatment). DRGs are established by the federal government under the Medicare program. A DRG establishes the maximum the government—and the insurer that includes DRGs in the surgical expense policy—will pay for a procedure.

Scheduled Benefits   Many different schedules for surgical expenses are used by insurance companies, with three basic differences:

1. The amount insurance companies allow for each procedure
2. The overall maximum benefit for multiple procedures
3. The relative or proportionate value of the procedures listed in the schedule to each other

A sample schedule is shown in Exhibit 1-1. The insurer, for example, will pay no more than $5,500 for surgery to bypass a single coronary artery. For operations not listed on a schedule, an insurance company will pay an amount based on the severity of the operation and the relation of this severity to the

Exhibit 1-1
Schedule of Surgical Procedures With Dollar Limits

Procedure	Dollar Value	Procedure	Dollar Value
General Surgery		**Neurosurgery**	
Appendectomy	$1,150	Cranioplasty	$3,115
Hernia	1,085	Craniotomy	3,760
Mastectomy	1,500	Neuroplasty	1,050
Vasectomy	450	**Orthopedic Surgery**	
Cardiology		Total knee arthroscopy	3,695
Aortic aneurysm repair	3,500	Total hip arthroscopy	3,875
Triple coronary bypass	8,000	**Obstetrics/Gynecology**	
Single coronary bypass	5,500	Ceasarean section	2,200
Insert pacemaker	980	Total hysterectomy	2,450

maximum amount paid in the schedule of operations. For example, a double coronary bypass may be scheduled at $7,000, since it is not as severe or expensive a procedure as a triple bypass but is more extensive a procedure than a single bypass.

Sometimes an individual has multiple surgical procedures performed at the same time. If only one incision is necessary for several surgical procedures, some insurers will pay up to the policy limits applicable to the most expensive of these procedures. When more than one incision is required, the coverage for the most expensive incision may be paid; additionally, 50 percent of the amount of coverage for every other incision may be payable.

Instead of using stated dollar amounts in a schedule of operations, an insurer may place various *unit values* on each operation; that is, the insurer uses a **relative value schedule**. The value of a unit is indicated in the policy declarations. The amount of coverage available for a specific type of surgery can be determined by multiplying the number of units for that procedure times the value of a unit. The relative values, that is, the number of units, reflect the complexity and time required to perform the surgical procedure, while the value of each unit should be a function of geographic area price levels.

Exhibit 1-2 shows a surgical schedule with unit values. It specifies six units of coverage for an appendectomy. The policy values each unit of coverage at $200. The total amount of insurance protection coverage would be $1,200 (6 x $200). Because of price level changes, the value of each unit might be changed to $215 by endorsement, in which case the insurer would pay $1,290 (6 x $215) for the surgical procedure.

Exhibit 1-2
Schedule of Surgical Procedures With Unit Values

Procedure	Unit* Value	Procedure	Unit* Value
General Surgery		**Neurosurgery**	
Appendectomy	6.00	Cranioplasty	15.50
Hernia	5.50	Craniotomy	19.00
Mastectomy	7.50	Neuroplasty	5.25
Vasectomy	2.25	**Orthopedic Surgery**	
Cardiology		Total knee arthroscopy	18.50
Aortic aneurysm repair	17.50	Total hip arthroscopy	19.50
Triple coronary bypass	40.00	**Obstetrics/Gynecology**	
Single coronary bypass	25.50	Ceasarean section	11.00
Insert pacemaker	5.00	Total hysterectomy	12.25

*Each unit is worth $200.

Physicians Nonsurgical Expense Benefits

Physicians nonsurgical expense benefits might provide for both in-hospital and home visits by a physician as well as visits by a patient to a physician's office. Policies may provide that this benefit contains limitations on the amount payable per visit or per day. There usually is a limitation on the number of visits per period of illness. Any excess charges may be absorbed by the insured, as illustrated in the following scenario, or may be covered under a supplemental major medical plan.

For example, suppose Sarah developed a severe case of pneumonia. During Sarah's hospitalization, her doctor visited her twice a day for two weeks. Each visit cost $50. Sarah had a medical expense policy that provided $40 for each in-hospital visit subject to a maximum of twenty visits. The amount of coverage provided by Sarah's physicians expense policy is $800, as calculated in Exhibit 1-3.

Exhibit 1-3
Physicians Expense Benefit Illustration

Visits	Doctor's Charge	Insurer Paid	Sarah Paid
1-20	$1,000	$800	$200
21-28	400	0	400
Total	$1,400	$800	$600

Basic Medical Expense Policy

A **basic medical expense policy**, sometimes called a **hospital-surgical policy**, provides a list of specific benefits for expenses incurred when a covered person is ill *and* in the hospital. The policy lists the types of items for which it will pay and also the maximum amounts that it will pay. For example, separate coverages and amounts might be provided for hospital room and board, miscellaneous hospital expense, pregnancy-related expenses, surgery, physicians' nonsurgical services, extended care facility room and board, and outpatient diagnostic laboratory and X-ray expense.

Any basic medical expense policy must be examined carefully to ascertain what coverage it provides. The amount of protection provided for each category of expense benefit varies substantially among contracts. Variations also exist regarding the specific types of medical services covered in each category.

Catastrophic or Major Medical Expense Policy

Catastrophic insurance policies or **major medical expense insurance policies** were designed to provide broad coverage with high limits protecting against large, unpredictable, and unbudgetable medical care expenses. Catastrophic or major medical expense insurance policies may be purchased in addition to a basic medical expense policy, in which case they relate to the basic policy in much the same way that an umbrella liability policy relates to basic liability coverages. Alternatively, catastrophic or major medical expense policies can be purchased in lieu of a basic policy. The insured then pays all basic medical expenses but is insured for very high expenses.

Maximum Benefit

Catastrophic policies or major medical policies normally contain an aggregate ceiling that can range from $25,000 to an unlimited amount. Some policies have internal limits, such as a maximum rate per day for hospital room and board or a surgical schedule.

Deductibles

Catastrophic or major medical contracts usually are written with a deductible. Deductibles can range from as low as $100 to $10,000 or more. However, the frequency with which deductibles are applied varies. They may be paid once per calendar year or once per occurrence. Policies often provide that if two or more family members are involved in the same accident or are injured in the same event, then only one deductible amount applies for that occurrence. Moreover, many policies stipulate that the deductible amount need be paid only once for each period of hospital confinement, even if the confinement is not continuous over a certain time period. For example, many policies require that another deductible be paid if more than six months have elapsed since the last hospital confinement for the same illness or injury, and if, during the time between confinements, the insured can return to full and normal activities.

Suppose Breck, who is covered by a major medical policy with the six-month period just described, has cancer. He was hospitalized three times in the same year for treatment: January 15 to February 7, March 1 to March 20, and October 30 to November 14. Between the March and October-November confinements, Breck was able to resume all of his normal activities. He will be required to pay his deductible twice during the year—once for the January-February and March visits, since only three weeks passed between hospitalizations, and another for the October-November visit, since more than six months elapsed between March 20 and October 30 *and* since he was able to return to full and normal activities. If Breck had been unable to resume his normal activities in between the last two hospitalizations, he would have only had to pay one deductible.

On the other hand, some insurers may use a three-month period rather than a six-month period, and some insurers do not make the various periods dependent on an individual's returning to full and normal activity.

In lieu of a deductible per period of confinement, some contracts have an annual deductible based on either a calendar year or a policy year. A **calendar-year deductible** has to be satisfied once during any calendar year. A **policy-year deductible** has to be satisfied during every twelve-month period following the anniversary of the policy.

Coinsurance

Most catastrophic policies and major medical policies contain a **coinsurance clause**, which stipulates that the insurer will pay only a specified percentage, such as 80 percent, of the eligible (covered) expenses in excess of the deductible and the insured will retain the remaining portion of the loss. For example, assume that a policy covering a $10,000 loss is written with a $1,000 deductible and an 80 percent coinsurance provision. The insurer would pay only $7,200 of the claim, as calculated in Column A of Exhibit 1-4. The purpose of the coinsurance clause is to encourage insureds to minimize costs.

However, many insurers today provide that after a fixed-dollar amount of medical expenses is incurred, usually above the deductible, by the insured, such as $2,500, the coinsurance clause does not apply and the insurer will pay 100 percent of the remaining covered expenses. This is referred to as a **stop-**

loss limit. It requires the insured to bear some of his or her medical expenses but does not allow the insured to become financially distressed. Continuing the example illustrated in Exhibit 1-4, after considering the coinsurance clause and the deductible, the insured is still responsible for $2,800. If there is a $2,500 stop-loss limit on the policy, the stop-loss limit is not reached because the amount for which the insured is responsible above the deductible is only $1,800. Thus the insured must pay the $1,000 deductible and the $1,800, or $2,800, as shown in Column B of Exhibit 1-4. However, if the claim is for $15,000, the insured will pay $3,500.

Exhibit 1-4
Coinsurance and Stop-Loss Limit Calculation

	A	B
Policy Deductible	$ 1,000	$ 1,000
Coinsurance Provision	80%	80%
Stop-Loss Limit	$ 2,500	$ 2,500
Amount of Loss	$10,000	$15,000
Less Deductible	1,000	1,000
Amount Subject to Coinsurance	$ 9,000	$14,000
Coinsurance Provision	0.80	0.80
Insurer's Share of Loss	$ 7,200	$11,200
Insured's Share of Loss	$9,000 – $7,200 = $1,800	$14,000 – $11,200 = $2,800
Stop-Loss Limit	$2,500	$2,500
Excess Over Stop-Loss Limit	no excess	$ 300
Amount Covered by Insurance	**$7,200**	$11,200 + $300 = **$11,500**
Amt. Retained by Ins.	$10,000 – $7,200 = **$2,800**	$15,000 – $11,500 = **$3,500**

Comprehensive Major Medical Policies

Comprehensive major medical expense policies that combine the features of basic medical and major medical expenses insurance in a single contract are a popular type of medical expense coverage. A comprehensive medical policy satisfies most medical insurance needs since it covers nearly all types of medical expenses incurred in or out of a hospital. It also typically contains a relatively small deductible and a high maximum benefit limit.

Under a comprehensive major medical policy, the deductible is reasonably low (for example, $250-$500), but there is a coinsurance provision (typically 80 percent). The comprehensive major medical policy may take one of several forms. One provides for an initial "across-the-board" deductible; thereafter, all covered medical care expenses are reimbursed at 80 percent up to the plan's overall maximum benefit. Another type pays 100 percent of the eligible hospital expenses up to a maximum benefit level; thereafter, an 80 percent coinsurance clause becomes applicable. Under this same type of plan, the initial deductible is applicable either to surgical or other covered medical expenses followed by 80 percent coinsurance, and the entire plan is subject to an overall maximum benefit. Comprehensive plans may include a stop-loss feature similar to that discussed earlier under major medical insurance; that is, after the insured has incurred out-of-pocket expenses totaling a certain amount, the plan will reimburse benefits at 100 percent for the balance of the calendar year.

Prescription drugs are often treated separately. A separate deductible may apply for prescription drugs or a **flat dollar copayment** (under which the insured pays a specified amount each time a prescription is filled), such as $3 per prescription, may be required. In some cases, in order to receive prescription coverage, generic drugs must be prescribed if available. Other policies simply exclude prescription coverage. If an insured desires protection against the cost of prescription drugs, an endorsement must be added to his or her policy and an additional premium must be paid.

Other Policy Types

Many variations of medical expense insurance exist. For example, some insurers offer a package of health insurance protection composed of basic medical expense and major medical expense benefits. When this is done, a deductible must usually be paid by an insured between the hospital expense coverage and the major medical coverage. This deductible, which is called a **corridor deductible**, may not be as large as the flat deductible normally contained in a major medical policy written separately. In addition, if a medical expense is not covered by the basic coverages but is covered by the major medical benefits, the insured may have to pay a deductible before the major medical policy will provide coverage. The corridor deductible and the major medical deductible are illustrated in Exhibit 1-5.

Medical Expense Insurance Policy Exclusions

Medical expense insurance policy exclusions serve the same purposes as property and liability insurance policy exclusions. For example, they protect the insurer against catastrophes such as wars in which large numbers of insureds might be injured, and they prevent duplicate coverage. Other exclusions keep premiums down by excluding coverage for losses that could be reasonably handled as ordinary expenses by the insured. Some of the exclusions an insured might find in a medical expense insurance contract are listed below. (These would probably not all be found in the same policy.)

Exhibit 1-5
Illustration of Corridor Deductible

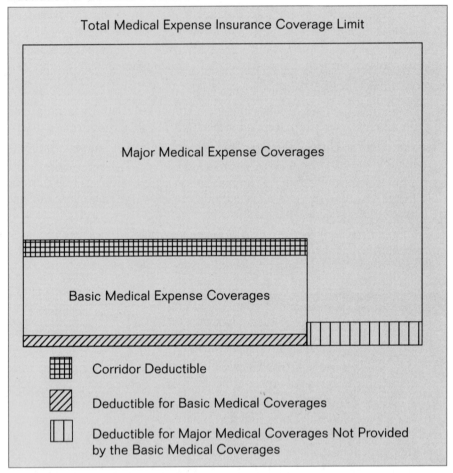

- War or any act of war; while on active duty in military, naval, or air forces of any country or international authority; while participating in riot, insurrection, or rebellion
- Care outside of U.S. or Canada
- Loss covered under workers compensation or employers liability act
- Medical care, services, or supplies paid for by national, state, or local government or agency thereof
- Alcoholism, drug addiction
- Cosmetic surgery except that necessitated by injuries
- Eyeglasses and eye refractions

- Hearing aids or the process of fitting them
- Transportation, except local ambulance service, to or from hospital
- Custodial care

Disability Income Insurance

Disability income insurance is designed to replace a portion of the income a worker loses when he or she becomes unable to work as the result of an accident or sickness. Many people do not purchase disability income insurance because (1) they think the cost is too high, (2) they think they will never be disabled, or (3) they are not aware of the importance of such coverage. The disability exposure is very significant. At younger ages, disability is more likely to occur than death. If disability does occur, it lasts for at least a couple of years, on average.

Types of Benefits

A disability income policy may include coverage for loss of income only or might include several other benefits as well. It might stipulate that the periodic benefit is a proportion of an insured's income before disablement, such as 66 $^2/_3$ percent of an individual's monthly wage up to a stated maximum dollar limit (such as $5,000 per month). This is the approach commonly followed in group long-term disability income coverage (group LTD). On the other hand, policies may state the benefit as a specified dollar amount per week or month of disability. This is normally done in individual policies. Unlike the wages they replace, disability income benefits are not subject to income taxes if the premiums were paid with after-tax dollars.

Total Disability

To receive total disability benefits, an insured must be totally disabled. However, the term **total disability** can be defined in two ways.

A typical contemporary definition of total disability provides that at the beginning of a period of total disability and until disability income benefits are paid for a specified period, the insured is eligible for total disability benefits if he or she is unable to engage in his or her own occupation. After such a period, the insured will be considered totally disabled only if he or she is unable to engage in any gainful occupation for which he or she is reasonably fitted by education, training, or experience with consideration given to the insured's previous earnings level. The specified period varies among insurers and may be two, three, or four years, as examples.

However, some policies may permit the insured to recover benefits for total disability as long as he or she is unable to engage in the "substantial and material" duties of his or her own occupation and has a loss of income. This is sometimes called an "own occ" definition and is the most liberal to the insured.

An example may help to stress the differences in the definitions of total disability. Ivan is a sculptor. He is involved in an auto accident that causes him to lose the use of his right hand, and he can no longer make sculptures. According to the "own occ" definition, Ivan is totally disabled because he cannot engage in his own occupation. However, if the "no gainful employment" definition is considered, Ivan is not totally disabled because he may be able to find work as a college professor.

Partial Disability

In some situations, a disabled insured may be unable to return to work on a full-time basis or to work at full capacity for a temporary period of time. This contingency is referred to as **partial disability** and is handled by **partial disability coverage**. Some contracts provide benefits for partial disability in addition to benefits for total disability. Thus, if an insured is partially disabled—or is totally disabled for a time and then partially disabled for a while before reaching full recovery—his or her disability income policy will (subject to policy limits) continuously cover his or her loss of income until he or she is fully recovered. The amount of the partial disability payment is often a pro rata percentage (measured by the amount of income lost and time away from work) of the total disability benefit. Partial disability benefits are payable for a shorter period than total disability benefits.

Residual Disability

In some cases, the insured is left with a diminished working capacity and suffers a permanent reduction in earnings even though he or she is not totally disabled. This is referred to as **residual disability**, and **residual disability coverage** addresses this situation. Residual disability coverage applies when an insured returns to work at a reduced income following a period of total disability. Benefits are payable in proportion to the reduction in the insured's earnings before the onset of total disability. Residual disability coverage is usually only limited by the maximum benefit period of the basic plan.

Residual disability and partial disability coverages are usually not provided in the same contract because of their close similarity.

Accidental Death, Dismemberment, and Loss of Sight

Many disability policies also provide scheduled benefits for accidental death or dismemberment or for loss of sight that occurs within a certain time after an accident. The highest benefit is paid for loss of life or loss of two or more limbs. This maximum amount, known as a **principal sum**, is set out in a schedule. Normally, the coverage for lesser injuries is a percentage of the principal sum. Exhibit 1-6 illustrates a possible schedule of benefits for accidental death, dismemberment, and loss of sight.

Exhibit 1-6
Accidental Death, Dismemberment, and Loss of Sight Schedule

For loss of:	
Life	The principal sum
Both hands or both feet or sight of both eyes	The principal sum
One hand and one foot	The principal sum
One hand or foot and sight of one eye	The principal sum
One arm or leg	Two-thirds the principal sum
One hand or foot	One-half the principal sum
Sight of one eye	One-third the principal sum

Waiver of Premium

Some disability income policies contain a provision that waives the payment of premiums while the insured is disabled. The typical waiver of premium provision states that, if total disability continues uninterrupted for a specified period (usually ninety days), subsequent premiums are waived during the continuing period of disability. The insured must pay any premiums due during the specified period. Once the period is satisfied, the waiver becomes retroactively effective and any premiums paid during the waiting period are refunded to the disabled insured. The insured has no obligation to pay back the waived premiums, but must resume the normal payment of premiums after recovering. (The same kind of waiver-of-premium feature is available in many life insurance policies.)

Rehabilitation

Many insurance companies encourage insureds to participate in a rehabilitation program without jeopardizing their disability payments. The insurer reimburses the disabled insured for expenses incurred while participating in a rehabilitation program approved by the insurance company. Rehabilitation benefits may be payable in addition to monthly disability indemnity benefits.

Other Optional Benefits

The insured may choose to include one or both of the following benefits for an additional premium:

- **Cost-of-living provision.** This provision increases the benefit payable by a factor for inflation in an effort to keep the disability income benefit at a reasonable level when needed.

- **Guaranteed insurability provision.** This provision, also referred to as the **additional purchase guarantee,** allows an insured to periodically increase the benefits payable as his or her income increases over time, without having to prove that he or she still meets the insurer's underwriting standards.

Key Coverage Provisions

Several significant provisions, which may affect the scope of coverage, are found in disability income contracts. They are discussed below.

Waiting or Elimination Periods

Most disability income policies have a time deductible known as an **elimination period** or a **waiting period.** This period encompasses the time between the disabling injury or sickness and the start of the disability income benefits. For example, a contract may contain a thirty-day waiting period for disability caused by injury or sickness. Benefits would not begin until the injured or sick individual had been disabled for thirty days. Generally, the lower the premium, the longer the waiting period.

Waiting periods under a disability policy achieve results similar to those achieved by a deductible for property insurance. Small losses are retained by the insured; larger, more severe losses are transferred to the insurer.

Because increasing the waiting period typically reduces the premium, individuals and families whose emergency funds are adequate to absorb a substantial income loss might choose a longer waiting period. Before choosing a longer elimination period, however, the purchaser should consider the possible impact of income lost during the waiting period.

Notice of Claim

In addition to a requirement that an insured must notify the insurer of the beginning of a loss, some disability income policies contain a provision that requires an insured to prove periodically (for example, every six months) that he or she is still disabled. This is generally accomplished by a report from a doctor.

Recurrent Disability

Several periods of disability may be considered as the same disability if they occur in succession. A typical disability policy clause reads as follows:

> If, within 6 months of a period of total disability due to injury or sickness for which monthly indemnity has been payable. . . , the Insured sustains a subsequent period of disability from the same or related cause or causes, such subsequent period shall be considered a continuation of the prior period of total disability and indemnified as such.

> If, however, following a period of total disability, the Insured is engaged in his occupation, or any gainful occupation or employment for which he is qualified by reason of his education, training or experience, and has performed all the important duties for 6 months or more, such subsequent period of disability resulting from the same or related cause or causes shall be considered as new disability resulting from sickness. . . .

An individual could be disabled because of a back injury for six months. If that individual returned to work for one month and was then disabled again because of the same back injury, an insurer whose policy had a recurrent disability provision like the one above would treat the two occurrences as the same disability. The benefits already paid would be applied against any limitation on total benefits, but no new elimination period would be imposed.

Relation of Earnings to Insurance

To discourage abuse, and to support the principle of indemnity, individual disability income policies sometimes include a provision known as the **relation of earnings to insurance** clause. This provision bars an insured from collecting benefits in excess of his or her salary despite the number of contracts owned. Specifically, one provision states:

> If the total monthly amount of loss of time benefits promised for the same loss under all valid loss of time coverages upon the insured, whether payable on a weekly or monthly basis, shall exceed the monthly earnings of the insured at the time disability commenced or his average monthly earnings for the period of two years immediately preceding the disability for which claim is made, whichever is the greater, the insurer will be liable only for such proportionate amount of such benefits under this policy as the amount of such earnings or such average monthly earnings of the insured bears to the total amount of monthly benefits for the same loss under all such coverage upon the insured at the time such disability commences. . . .

Generally, this provision cannot act to reduce coverage below $200 per month or the sum of the coverages in all policies, whichever is less. A pro rata return of premium is made for the portion of the coverage not collected. The following example demonstrates how this relation of earnings to insurance provision reduces the coverage. Becky has two disability income policies issued by different insurers. One policy has a $1,000 per-month benefit, while the other has a $600 per-month benefit. Becky's current monthly salary is $1,100, but her average monthly salary for the past two years has been $1,180. If Becky becomes disabled, each insurer would pay the monthly amount shown as follows:

Insurer A: $\dfrac{\$1,180}{\$1,600}$ x $1,000 = $ 737.50

Insurer B: $\dfrac{\$1,180}{\$1,600}$ x $ 600 = $ 442.50

Total paid by Insurer A Insurer B   = $1,180.00

As an aspect of financial underwriting for individual disability income poli-cies, insurers will not issue disability income coverage for more than a certain percentage of an individual's monthly wage, in recognition of the facts that (1) disability benefits will be received income-tax free if the premiums were paid with after-tax dollars, (2) the insured does not incur the normal costs associated with working, and (3) the insurer wants the insured to have a financial incentive to remain at or to return to work. The underwriting rules are the main weapon of an insurer against overinsurance in individual disabil-ity income insurance. Group underwriters are generally not concerned about any individual disability income policies an insured may have. In addition, group disability income policies may not require a reduction in income benefits by income amounts received from individual disability income poli-cies.

Long-Term Care

Long-term care (LTC) insurance was not generally available until the mid-1980s. However, in the 1990s it has evolved to the point at which it is a significant insurance product, sold as individual and group insurance.

Long-term care insurance may be defined as follows:

> any policy or rider advertised, marketed, offered or designed to provide coverage for not less than twelve consecutive months for each covered person on an expense incurred, indemnity, prepaid or other basis; for one or more necessary or medically necessary diagnostic, preventive, therapeutic, rehabilitative, maintenance or personal care services, provided in a setting other than an acute care unit of a hospital. . . .[2]

Need for Coverage

The interest in this coverage becomes obvious when the following statistics are examined:

- The over-sixty-five population in the United States is expected to have grown at an annual rate of 18.5 percent between 1985 and 1995, while the rest of the population will have grown at a 7.5 percent rate.[3] This trend will be further influenced by the "baby boomer" population as it reaches later life by the year 2000.
- Nearly 40 percent of those over sixty-five will spend some time in a nursing home.[4]
- At any given time, about 4.5 percent of people over sixty-five reside in nursing homes and another 12.2 percent are disabled and live in the community.[5]
- Over the course of a year, about 1.7 million people spend time in nursing homes.[6]
- More than 50 percent of nursing home expenses are paid by the recipients or their families—often young adults supporting elderly parents.[7]
- One year in a nursing home typically costs from $25,000 to $30,000.[8]

Long-term care expenses are typically not covered by Medicare or by private medical expense insurance. Medicare pays only a very small portion of nursing home bills, and private medical expense coverage and Medicare often exclude custodial care and most other long-term care expenses. Medicaid pays around 42 percent of the nation's nursing home bill, but people must first "spend-down" virtually all their assets to qualify for Medicaid.[9] **Spend-down** means to literally use up or spend all assets in an effort to fall below the level of wealth that eliminates eligibility for certain welfare benefits. For example, in Pennsylvania, before Medicaid (called Medical Assistance in Pennsylvania) will cover a person's nursing home costs, the following requirements must be satisfied:

- Excluding the person's home, his or her assets must be valued below $2,400 (or $2,000 in some cases).
- The person may not be an insured under a life insurance policy with more than a $1,500 death benefit.
- Within the preceding thirty months, the person may not have sold or given away any asset that would otherwise cause him or her to be ineligible without receiving its fair market value in return.

Obviously the choice to spend-down is a difficult and often painful decision. However, it is not always the best choice because some nursing homes do not accept Medicaid recipients. Furthermore, the eligibility requirements for Medicaid benefits may change.[10]

LTC insurance provides a means to preserve the assets of individuals who require long-term care, as well as the assets of their families. The market for

LTC insurance is limited by health (those who are already disabled are generally not eligible), age (to some extent), and the cost of long-term care. LTC insurance is primarily purchased by the elderly, although a trend is occurring, especially with group insurance, toward purchase at younger ages. According to one report, individual LTC insurance purchasers were an average of seventy-two-years old; the average age of persons buying group association plans was sixty-nine; and the average age of employees purchasing group coverage was forty-three.[11]

Policy Features

Currently issued LTC policies often include several kinds of covered services for which they will pay promised daily benefits, such as the following:

- Skilled nursing facility care
- Intermediate nursing facility care
- Custodial nursing facility care
- Other custodial facility care
- Home health care
- Adult day care
- Respite care for those caring for an incapacitated person

Modern policies often include a wide range of these services, and many advisers have suggested that this is beneficial for the consumer. Some policies, however, still provide only nursing home coverage.

The LTC insurance buyer usually has several options involving dollar limits, benefit period, and elimination periods applicable to nursing home coverage:

- Dollar limits are typically expressed as a daily benefit ranging from $40 to $120 or more per day.
- The benefit period ranges from one year to lifetime, with two-to-four years being the most popular range of choices.
- Waiting periods typically involve 0, 20, 30, 60, 90, 100, or 180 days.

Although dollar benefits are often expressed in terms of daily benefits, some policies provide a maximum benefit of the dollar limit times the duration, subject to a daily maximum dollar limit. For example, $100 per day for five years may actually mean a maximum benefit of $182,500, which can be used no more rapidly than $100 per day.[12]

Home-care coverage may involve a fixed daily dollar amount or a maximum dollar per hour of service, and possibly a lifetime maximum. The duration of home-care coverage may be shorter than for nursing home plans, and the daily dollar benefit may be only a percentage (such as 50 percent) of the regular policy benefit.

Other policy features commonly found include the following:

- **Inflation protection**—Either the right to periodically buy additional benefits at the then-current price based on the insured's then-current age without proof of insurability, or an inflation-guard type of approach whereby the daily benefit increases at an annual rate—typically 5 percent noncompounding. The inflation protection, which substantially increases the premium, may be discontinued at a certain age or after a certain period of time.

- **Waiver of premium**—While benefits are being paid, premiums are waived. However, in many cases, the premiums are waived only after a time period (usually several months) is satisfied.

- **Nonforfeiture benefits**—More common in group than in individual policies, nonforfeiture benefits are provided when an insured cancels his or her existing health coverage. For example, reduced paid-up insurance—which covers similar health exposures to those named in the original policy with lower limits but does not require additional premium payments—may be an option after the policy has been in force for a certain number of years. Another choice may be a return of premiums, which pays the insured a lump-sum amount based on the premiums paid for the coverage, less the dollar amount of claims paid to date. Policies with these types of nonforfeiture options naturally require higher premiums.

Coverage Triggers

A critical policy provision that involves the conditions that determine who is eligible to receive benefits may be referred to as a **coverage trigger**. Early policies required a prior hospital stay. This rather restrictive condition has been prohibited in some states. Other conditions include care ordered by a doctor (a liberal provision) or "medically necessary for sickness or injury" (a somewhat subjective standard). The most common coverage trigger in modern LTC policies involves the so-called **activities of daily living (ADLs)**. A person qualifies for LTC coverage if he or she is unable to perform a specified number (such as two or three) of a list of ADLs contained in the policy. Such ADLs typically include the following:

- Bathing
- Dressing
- Eating

- Using the toilet
- Walking
- Maintaining continence
- Taking medicine
- Transferring from bed to chair

Underwriting

LTC policies are normally subject to individual underwriting that screens applicants on the basis of several factors, including age, medical condition, and medical history. These underwriting factors often prevent persons in bad health from obtaining LTC insurance. The screening process may be more extensive for individual policies than for policies issued on a group basis. Insurers do not normally require a physical examination, but rather rely on the applicant's statements and an attending physician's statements concerning the applicant's health in the application for LTC insurance.

Premiums

Most LTC policies are written with level, entry-age premiums. LTC policies are often **guaranteed renewable**—that is, the policies cannot be canceled by the insurer on the basis of a change in the insured's health. The premium level itself depends on the age of the insured and the size and duration of the benefit, as well as the elimination period and any options such as inflation protection. Premiums may vary substantially from insurer to insurer. For example, consider the premium quotes listed in Exhibit 1-7. For the same type of LTC policy, annual premiums for a fifty-five-year-old range from $320 to $1,230. Annual premiums for a sixty-five-year-old range from $680 to $2,242.

Exhibit 1-7
Premium Quotes for Long-Term Care Insurance

	Age 55	Age 60	Age 65
Company A	$ 320.00	$ 500.00	$ 680.00
Company B	330.80	463.10	727.70
Company C	404.00	724.00	1,282.00
Company D[2]	1,230.00	1,711.00	2,242.00

[1] Annual premiums for $100-per-day benefit for a nonsmoker with a 0-day elimination period and a two-year benefit period.

[2] The premiums for this company's policies reflect a twenty-day elimination period.

Chuck Jones, "Find the Right LTC Insurance for Your Clients," *LAN,* May 1993, pp. 103-118.

Dental Care Expense Insurance

Before 1970, few employees had group dental care expense insurance. Since then, the number of individuals covered under group dental plans has risen rapidly. Roughly 100 million people in the United States have some form of dental coverage.

Dental insurance coverage can be provided (1) under an integrated plan in which the dental expenses are blended into the covered expenses of a major medical benefit plan, or (2) under a nonintegrated plan on either a scheduled or a nonscheduled basis. Generally, dental plans are separate from other medical expense coverages and may be unique in certain respects. Some of the features or concepts underlying dental plans often are an emphasis on preventive care, the need to deal with deferred or elective procedures (such as orthodontia), lower maximum limits and possibly lower deductibles, more emphasis on predetermination of benefits, special eligibility requirements, and possibly more emphasis on the use of alternative procedures. Most dental expense coverages have common provisions such as coinsurance, calendar-year or policy-year maximums on all dental services, and separate maximum limits and coinsurance requirements on certain kinds of services (such as orthodontia). For example, a policy may cover 100 percent of preventive services such as semiannual cleanings; 80 percent of minor or major work such as fillings, crowns, and root canals; and 50 percent of orthodontia services.

Dental plans tend to be used extensively when they are first adopted. Probably the implementation of a plan encourages people to have all their dental problems corrected—problems that had not been treated because of high dental costs. Once this period of "catch-up" dental care has run its course, a dental plan's experience should be stabilized.

Miscellaneous Health Insurance Coverages

Some insurance contracts cover only a portion of the expenses or disabilities that have been discussed. Others are designed to meet a specialized need. Several of the more common contracts are discussed in this section.

Dread Disease Policies

A few insurers specialize in policies that cover only specific illnesses such as cancer, meningitis, rabies, and multiple sclerosis.

Cancer policies constitute a large segment of the dread disease policy market. In addition to limiting coverage to only the one disease, they may have internal limits per benefit period in addition to an aggregate benefit limit. Benefits are normally paid in addition to any other coverage an insured may have.

Dread disease policies are highly controversial. Several states (Connecticut, Maine, Massachusetts, New Jersey, and New York) restrict their use. Many insurance advisers suggest that insureds should be careful not to concentrate on purchasing coverage for a limited group of dread diseases, at possibly a relatively high cost in relation to the real benefits secured, without having adequate health insurance protection for the less dramatic but equally expensive general health exposures.

Hospital Indemnity Policies

A hospital indemnity contract (or hospital income contract) pays an individual only while he or she is hospitalized. Despite its name, a hospital indemnity policy is a **valued contract** (a policy that pays the stated amount of the benefits regardless of the amount of loss) rather than a contract of indemnification. The benefit is normally stated in terms of a flat amount per day, week, or month. However, an individual receives a benefit for every day he or she is confined to a hospital. For example, a hospital indemnity policy that provides $1,500 per month pays $50 ($1,500/thirty days in a month) for each day of hospital confinement.

The benefits under a hospital indemnity policy can be used to supplement gaps in a medical expense contract, to provide extra income during a period of hospitalization, or to handle miscellaneous expenses such as child care. However, a hospital indemnity contract does not eliminate the need for a disability or medical expense policy. The hospital indemnity contract pays a fixed daily benefit only while an insured is in the hospital. A disability income policy pays benefits if an insured is disabled, even if an individual is not hospitalized. A medical expense policy pays for specific charges, both in and out of the hospital, that often exceed the amount of coverage available under a hospital indemnity contract. Consequently, these coverages offer an insured broader insurance protection than a hospital indemnity policy.

Hospital indemnity policies have been used in the past to supplement Medicare benefits. However, under new federal-state regulations for Medicare supplements, only certain policies can now be used for this purpose, and hospital indemnity policies do not qualify as one of the approved Medigap policies, discussed below.

Medigap Coverage

Many of the elderly are concerned about often substantial expenses not paid by Medicare (discussed in Chapter 2). For example, there is an initial deductible, a daily hospital charge for stays of more than sixty days, a requirement that Medicare recipients pay 20 percent of doctor bills, and no coverage for private duty nurses, dental care, foreign health care (care provided outside the United States), and prescription drugs while not in the hospital. Also, if a person does not have the physician's coverage offered under Medicare, he or she has to pay 100 percent of the doctor bills. To satisfy the need created by such "gaps" in Medicare benefits, many companies developed so-called "Medigap" policies.

In the past, insurers offered the public a large number and variety of policies designed to supplement Medicare. Some of these policies were criticized in terms of their cost and benefits provided, and some people argued that the very diversity of available coverages resulted in confusion and, possibly, in duplicative coverage.

As a result, the federal Omnibus Budget Reconciliation Act of 1990 and state legislation and regulations now apply to the sale of Medigap policies. Ten standard Medigap policies have been approved for sale to the public under the terms of this federal law. All ten standard plans must contain a basic core of benefits plus one or more of a list of additional optional benefits. Of course, the more optional benefits provided, the higher the premium for the particular standard plan. The potential insured can select the standard plan he or she desires, from among the ten, and feels he or she can afford. An insurer does not have to sell all, or even any, of these standard Medigap plans, but it usually cannot offer any different Medicare supplement plans without the approval of federal and state authorities.

Other Miscellaneous Health Coverages

In addition to the coverages just described, there are a variety of other health coverages in the marketplace, including travel accident policies and credit disability insurance.

Travel Accident Policies

A traveler can purchase accidental death and dismemberment insurance to pay for losses incurred while on a trip. Normally, this coverage insures against injury incurred on a plane, train, or other common carrier, but protection can be purchased to cover any type of transportation. Coverage may also be provided on a twenty-four-hour basis while the insured is traveling. In recent years this coverage has often been included as an additional benefit of credit cards or club memberships.

Credit Disability Insurance

Credit disability coverage provides disabled debtors with the funds necessary to meet loan obligations. The coverage is frequently sold in conjunction with mortgages, installment loans, and charge accounts, and, if bought through the lender, may be relatively expensive. It can be written on either an individual or a group basis.

Health Insurance Policy Provisions

In the early 1950s, the National Association of Insurance Commissioners (NAIC) formulated a model Uniform Individual Accident and Sickness Policy Provisions Law, which listed a number of provisions the commissioners felt should be included in each health insurance policy. The model legislation also contained a list of optional policy provisions that could be used in a health insurance policy. All states have promulgated laws that incorporate at least some of the recommendations of the NAIC.

Standard Mandatory Health Insurance Policy Provisions

The following provisions are required to be included in individual health insurance policies by statute in most states. States often have less stringent requirements for group health insurance policies, but they generally *require* at least three or four of the following provisions.

Entire Contract

All health insurance policies contain an entire contract provision, which stipulates that the policy, along with attached endorsements and the application, constitutes the entire contract between the insurer and the insured. The policy cannot be changed unless the change is approved by an executive officer of the insurance company. Even then, the change is not effective until the policy itself has been endorsed to reflect the modification.

Time Limit on Certain Defenses

Health insurance contracts have a time limit on certain defenses provision. This provision limits to two or three years the time during which an insurer can rescind or void a policy because of misstatements in the application that are incorrect or can omit information that was material to the underwriting decision. (Information is **material** if, had the insurer been aware of it, the policy would not have been issued or would have been issued at a higher premium or with more limited coverage.)

However, if the misstatements were fraudulent, the time limit does not apply. Attempts to defraud an insurance company result in a rescission of the policy at any time.

Grace Period

Health insurance contracts contain a grace period applicable to all renewal premiums. If premiums are paid after the due date, but within the grace period, coverage remains in effect. For most policies, the grace period lasts thirty days beyond the date the premium is due. For example, if the policy premium is due on January 1, under the grace period provision, the insured's coverage will continue until January 31. If the insured does not pay the premium on or before January 31, the coverage will lapse.

Reinstatement

Reinstatement allows an insured who has let his or her policy lapse due to nonpayment of premium to reactivate the same coverage. Although lapsed property and liability policies often can be reinstated only at the insurer's discretion, health insurance contracts contain a provision permitting the insured to reinstate a policy under other circumstances.

Most health insurance reinstatement provisions stipulate that, if no application for reinstatement is required and an insured pays the premium, the policy is automatically reinstated. When an application is required and the insured replies and pays the premium, a conditional receipt is issued. The policy is reinstated when the application is approved by the insurer. If the insurer does not notify the insured of disapproval within forty-five days of the date of the conditional receipt, the policy is automatically reinstated. Coverage for losses from accidental injury begins again on the date of reinstatement, but coverage for losses resulting from sickness usually does not start for ten days following the date of reinstatement.

The amount paid to reinstate a policy can be applied to previous unpaid premiums that span a period of no more than sixty days before reinstatement. The sixty-day provision may be eliminated from contracts in which the insured has the right to continue the policy until age fifty or, if issued after age forty-four, for at least five years from the date of issue.

Notice of Claim, Claim Forms, and Proof of Loss

In many cases, health insurers ask insureds to refrain from processing medical and prescription claims until their deductible has been satisfied. At that time, all the claims may be sent to the insurer. However, other insurers require the insured under a health insurance policy to notify the insurer within twenty days after a claim arises, barring unusual circumstances that preclude notification. After notification, the insurer must furnish the insured with proof of loss forms within fifteen days. The insured must fill out and return these forms to the insurer within ninety days of the accident or illness. If the insurer fails to provide the proof of loss forms within fifteen days after notification of the claim by the insured, the insured's ninety-day obligation is waived.

If an insured does not furnish written proof of loss within the time required, coverage for that claim is suspended unless circumstances acceptable to the insurer prevented notification within the allotted time. An overall limitation of one year to file written proof of loss applies unless an insured lacks the legal capacity to do so.

For example, Marian incurred numerous medical bills during a seven-day stay in the hospital. Marian's hospital expense policy gave her twenty days from the time she entered the hospital to notify her insurer about her loss, unless she had a valid reason why she could not. Instead of waiting twenty days, Marian notified her insurer about the claim three days after she left the hospital, but the notification took six days to reach the insurer. From the time the insurer received notice of the claim, the insurer had fifteen days to get the claim forms to Marian, but in this case, the insurer took only five days. Marian then had sixty-nine days (90–7–3–6–5) to file a written proof of loss.

Time of Payment of Claim

If a claim does not require periodic payments, then the covered claim is paid in entirety when the written proof of loss is received by the insurer. When benefits are payable on a periodic basis, such as those payable under a disability income contract, the payments are made on whatever basis is stipulated in the contract. For example, benefits could be paid monthly under a disability income contract. If an insured is deceased, any remaining benefits are paid to either the insured's designated beneficiary or the estate.

Legal Actions

The policy's legal actions provision prohibits any action against the insurer for sixty days after written proof of loss has been furnished. This is designed to allow the insurer adequate time to process the claim. This section also contains a statute of limitations provision that prevents the insured from bringing action against the insurer more than three years after written proof should have been furnished.

Physical Examinations and Autopsy

To protect against fraudulent claims, the insurer may have a physician examine an insured "as often as it may reasonably require" while a claim is being processed. However, the insurer may not use this provision to harass an insured. An insurer could not require an insured to have a physical examination weekly or even monthly without a valid reason.

When death benefits are payable under a health insurance policy, the insurer may have a right to have an autopsy performed, barring a state statute to the contrary. This latter provision avoids any conflict between state statutes and the insurance policy.

Change of Beneficiary

Some health insurance policies provide death benefits. When this is the case, an insured may change a beneficiary designation.

Optional Provisions

While the preceding provisions may be required by state statute, the use of the following provisions is *optional with insurers*. If an insurer elects to use these provisions but not their exact wording, the substitute wording must be at least as favorable to the insured as that found in these provisions, as determined by the insurance commissioner in each state. Most insurance contracts contain one or more of these optional provisions.

Misstatement of Age

If an insured has misstated his or her age, the policy is adjusted to reflect the correct age—which can benefit either the insurance company or the insured. If the age of an insured is understated, the premium being paid may be inadequate. If the age is overstated, the premium may be more than adequate. On discovering a discrepancy between the insured's stated age and actual age, the insurer adjusts the amount of coverage and pays benefits equal to what would have been purchased with the premium had the insured's correct age been known.

Unpaid Premium

Conceivably, because of the grace period, an insured could be eligible for insurance benefits without having paid the current premium. An insurance company can include a provision that permits it to reduce any benefit payment by any amount of premium due and unpaid at the time of the loss.

Cancellation

Insurers sometimes reserve the right to cancel a policy. Specifically, the insurer might incorporate the following provision into the policy:

The insurance company may cancel this policy at any time by written notice delivered to the insured, or mailed to his last address as shown by the records of the insurer, stating when, not less than five days thereafter, such cancellation shall be effective; and after the policy has been continued beyond its original term, the insured may cancel this policy at any time by written notice delivered or mailed to the insurer, effective upon receipt or on such later date as may be specified in such notice. In the event of cancellation, the insurer will return promptly the unearned portion of any premium paid. If the insured cancels, the earned premium shall be computed by the use of the short-rate table last filed with the state official having supervision of insurance in the state where the insured resided when the policy was issued. If the insurer cancels, the earned premium shall be computed pro rata.

Cancellation of a policy does not prejudice any outstanding claims. However, as a practical matter, cancellation provisions are almost never used in individual health insurance policies today.

Conformity With State Statutes

Most insurers stipulate that when there is a conflict between the policy and the statutes of the state in which a contract is issued, the policy is automatically amended "to conform to the minimum requirements of such statutes."

Illegal Occupation

Insurers may include a provision that eliminates coverage for individuals engaged in illegal occupations.

Intoxicants and Narcotics

An insurer may exclude losses that result from an insured's being intoxicated or under the influence of narcotics unless the intoxicant or narcotic is administered on the advice of a physician.

Policy Inspection

Most states now require that individual health insurance contracts contain a policy inspection provision that is known alternatively as the "policy examination" provision, the "refund upon examination" provision, or the "free policy examination" provision, but that is most commonly referred to as the "ten-day free look." It gives the insured an opportunity to examine a policy for ten days (or more in some states; Florida, for example, requires a "twenty-day free look") without being obligated to keep it and with full premium refund available. A comparable provision is not generally found in property and liability contracts.

Preexisting Conditions Clause

Preexisting conditions are physical conditions that affect an individual's health and for which treatment has been rendered before the inception of the health insurance policy. Preexisting conditions clauses limit coverage in individual health insurance contracts and sometimes in group policies covering smaller groups. For example, preexisting conditions may not be covered until after a specific period of time (such as six months, two years, or five years) has elapsed. An alternative sometimes used is to limit coverage on all preexisting conditions until the policy has been in effect for a specified period (for example, twelve months). However, if the condition recurs during this period, the condition continues to be excluded from coverage. (Some policies may allow coverage for the condition to resume once the insured has not been affected by it for a specified period.) In lieu of a specific preexisting condition provision, contracts may limit—through policy definitions or insuring agreements—coverage for any injury or sickness that manifests itself before the effective date of the policy. As an example, one health insurance policy defines sickness or disease in this way:

> Sickness or disease which first manifests itself while the Coverage Provision under which claim is made is in force for the Insured Person whose sickness is the basis of claim and which results in loss to which such Coverage Provision applies.

In some group policies, particularly those covering larger groups, preexisting conditions are automatically covered. Other group policies may require a preexisting provision only for new employees.

Providers of Health Benefits

A variety of private providers of medical expense health benefits exist. They include insurance companies, Blue Cross and Blue Shield plans (the "Blues"), health maintenance organizations (HMOs), and preferred provider organizations (PPOs). One of the characteristics of this field is the diversity of these providers of benefits.

Insurance Companies

Insurance companies provide the majority of group and individual medical expense and disability income benefits. Most of the health insurance benefits provided by insurance companies are sold by life insurance companies. However, property and liability insurers and monoline health insurers also write some health benefits.

Health insurance written by insurance companies traditionally *reimbursed* the insured for the cost of covered medical expenses. The insured first received necessary medical treatment and paid for it, and then submitted a claim to the insurer. The insurer would then reimburse the insured for the covered costs of medical treatment. Most insurance companies continue to focus on reimbursement benefits; however, the insured may not be required to pay at the time of medical treatment. For example, many medical care providers file the claim with the insurer on behalf of the insured and bill the insured for any amounts the insurance company does not pay.

Some insurance companies have established contracts with medical care providers that set the cost for specific treatments. The insured covered by such a policy goes to a provider with whom the insurer has contracted and receives any necessary treatments. The medical care provider then makes a claim to the insurer at the agreed-upon cost, and the insurer makes payment solely to the medical care provider. This is referred to as a **service plan** and has traditionally been offered by Blue Cross/Blue Shield as discussed below.

Blue Cross/Blue Shield

Traditionally, Blue Cross/Blue Shield (the "Blues") have been essentially regionally operated *noninsurance* companies that help individuals and groups finance their medical expenses. Blue Cross/Blue Shield have provided health *services* rendered to their **subscribers** (members covered by the Blues) through contractual arrangements with hospitals (Blue Cross) and participating physicians (Blue Shield) while insurance companies reimbursed the insured for covered medical expenses. However, the traditional distinctions between reimbursement and service benefits have become blurred for reasons that will be explained. Competition today between the "Blues" and insurance companies often centers on price and service rather than on benefits.

Traditionally, Blue Cross plans provided hospitalization benefits, while Blue Shield plans provided physician expense benefits. The Blue Cross idea started in 1929 in Texas when a group of schoolteachers agreed to pay Baylor University Hospital in advance for up to twenty-one days of semiprivate hospital care each year. The idea of prepaying medical care expense benefits spread rapidly. Instead of limiting coverage to one hospital, however, some plans developed in the early 1930s offered subscribers a choice of hospitals on a community-wide basis. The communities that first established community plans include Sacramento, California; Washington, D.C.; Newark, New Jersey; and New York City. In 1939, the Blue Cross symbol was adopted by the prepayment plans that had been developed, and these plans became known as Blue Cross plans.[13]

Blue Cross plans have a counterpart in the physician expense area—Blue Shield plans. Blue Shield plans, like Blue Cross plans, permit consumers to prepay the costs of medical care expenses (for example, physicians in-hospital; home and office visits; surgery; and radiation treatments). Most Blue Cross/ Blue Shield plans operate on a nonprofit basis, and the two organizations are generally separate. However, they work cooperatively in many areas, such as major medical plans.

Blue Cross/Blue Shield have traditionally operated on a service basis (although some plans do operate on an indemnity basis). They have agreed to provide services rather than dollar amounts of coverage. For example, Blue Cross would agree to provide so many days of hospital care in a member hospital (one with which the plan has a contractual arrangement) for subscribers, rather than pay for so many days of care in an accredited hospital. However, Blue Cross/Blue Shield plans have been modified so that some coverage is offered on a reimbursement basis, but a large portion of the coverage is still written on a service basis.

While Blue Cross and Blue Shield started out as separate programs, the lines of demarcation are no longer clear. The lack of distinction between the two programs is the result of several factors. First, each plan began to offer some coverages provided by the other plan. For example, some Blue Cross plans have marketed some physician coverage. Second, in some states the Blue Cross and Blue Shield plans have joined forces in marketing coverage—sharing office space, conducting joint enrollments, and using joint billing. Additionally, they have joined forces to offer major medical coverages and have cooperated in administering some government programs. This joint activity has progressed to the point that some Blue Cross and Blue Shield plans have merged.

The activities of Blue Cross/Blue Shield are coordinated at the national level through the Blue Cross/Blue Shield Association. This organization acts as a clearinghouse for the individual plans. The geographic area covered by individual Blue Cross/Blue Shield plans varies. Some plans cover one or more states. Others cover only a portion of a state.

Managed Health-Care Delivery and Reimbursement Systems

Providers of health-care services and consumers have sought alternative health-care delivery systems—that is, they have attempted to develop a "managed" approach to health care. The need for managed health-care delivery and reimbursement systems has arisen because of the increasing cost of providing medical expense benefits and the increasing demand for medical care services. In addition, the health insurance system does not meet the needs of some segments of the United States population.

Traditional health insurance plans reimbursed patients and selected health-care providers, but did not actually provide care. On the other hand, the Blues have traditionally arranged to provide health-care services to their insureds. Two alternative systems are the health maintenance organization (HMO) and the preferred provider organization (PPO).

- HMOs differ from traditional group health insurance in that they both finance and provide health-care services. An **HMO** is an organization that brings together various medical care providers for the purpose of servicing the medical needs of its participants.

- A PPO is a vehicle for financing health care, *not* providing health care. A **PPO** is a contractual agreement between a health-care purchaser, like an employer or insurer, and a health-care provider. Under most of these contracts, the providers agree to deliver health-care services for fees negotiated in advance.

Health Maintenance Organizations

Health maintenance organizations (HMOs) have been in existence for many years. An HMO prototype, the Ross-Loos Clinic, was developed in 1929 in Los Angeles. The Kaiser Foundation initiated a health maintenance organization type of operation in Oakland, California, in 1942. The Health Insurance Plan of Greater New York has been in operation since 1947 and functions in a way similar to an HMO. While HMOs have been in existence for many years, the health maintenance organization movement was given impetus in 1973 when Congress passed the *Health Maintenance Organization Act.*

Under an HMO plan, individuals pay a periodic fixed cost for comprehensive health-care services. For this payment, the plan participants are guaranteed specific health-care services through the health-care providers that are members of the HMO. Thus, participants in an HMO must often restrict their choice of physicians and other health-care providers to those who are members of the particular HMO. The types of services provided under an HMO plan might include any of the following:

- Physician services
- Hospital services
- Emergency health-care services
- Outpatient care services

- Diagnostic laboratory services
- Home health-care services
- Preventive health-care services

A major objective of an HMO is to reduce medical care expenses by increasing the use of preventive health services. Most insurance company and Blue Cross/Blue Shield plans have not stressed preventive health-care services. Instead, they are designed to pay for health-care services only after an accident or illness has occurred. HMOs are designed to maintain a person's health as well as render medical care when an illness or injury is not prevented.

Basic HMO Models

There are three basic types of HMO structures.

- The **staff practice** HMO operates with a staff of professionals who provide medical care services. Generally, all the plan doctors are located in a common facility and are salaried employees of either the medical group or the HMO.
- The **group practice** HMO is like a staff practice. There is usually one site where all of the doctors are located. The difference is that the facilities of the group practice are usually owned by the doctors, not the HMO.
- Under an **individual practice association (IPA)**, individual physicians or small groups of physicians are members of the HMO plan. The physician works out of his or her own office, but contracts with the HMO to serve plan participants. Under this concept, the physician who provides the health services is paid a flat fee, or **capitation fee**, for each member of the group. The physician is not paid a fee for each service. It is argued that this approach discourages physicians from providing unnecessary medical treatment. On the other hand, critics have suggested that it may also discourage physicians from providing necessary services for which no additional fee may be charged.

Services Provided

HMOs furnish basic health services to the enrollees without any limitation on costs, health status, or time. **Basic health services** include the following:

1. Physician services (including consultant and referral services by a physician)
2. Outpatient services and inpatient hospital services
3. Medically necessary outpatient and inpatient emergency health services
4. Short-term (not to exceed twenty visits), outpatient evaluative, and crisis intervention mental health services

5.   Medical treatment or referral services for the abuse of or addiction to alcohol or drugs

6.   Diagnostic laboratory and diagnostic and therapeutic radiologic services

7.   Home health services

8.   Preventive health services, including voluntary family planning services, dental care for children, and children's eye examinations conducted to determine the need for vision correction[14]

An HMO may offer the following additional **supplementary health services** for a separate premium:

1.   Services of facilities for intermediate and long-term care

2.   Vision care not included as a basic health service

3.   Dental services not included as a basic health service

4.   Mental health services not included as a basic health service

5.   Long-term physical medicine and rehabilitative services (including physical therapy)

6.   The provision of prescription drugs as part of the delivery of a basic health service or a supplemental health service provided by the health maintenance organization[15]

Dual Choice Requirement

The federal HMO Act of 1973, as amended, requires the offering of certain HMO options under certain conditions to the employees of an eligible employer. This is referred to as the **dual choice requirement** of the HMO Act. This law stipulates that an employer of twenty-five or more employees, if requested by a qualified HMO, must offer its employees the option of taking health maintenance coverage rather than other insurance protection. When more than one type of HMO exists in the employer's area, employees must be offered the option of selecting at least one individual practice association (IPA) plan and at least one staff *or* group practice plan. If an employer has employees located in different geographical areas, employees in each area have to be offered the dual choice using HMOs in their geographical area.

Under the 1988 amendments to the HMO Act of 1973, the federal dual choice requirement will be repealed as of October 24, 1995. Naturally, however, employers may continue to voluntarily offer HMOs to their employees after that date. In fact, the popularity of HMOs has been gaining with employers and employees even though some people object to the narrower choices of doctors and hospitals frequently offered by HMOs. Also, some state dual choice requirements may still be effective after 1995.

Preferred Provider Organizations

While HMOs have been growing in importance, another approach to providing health care on a group basis has developed. This approach is called **preferred provider organizations,** or PPOs.

Under a PPO plan, health-care providers and employers or insurers negotiate to set the fees to be charged to employees and their dependents who use the PPO services. The plan then provides additional benefits for the covered persons who use the services of the health-care providers that have entered into the PPO arrangement—the "preferred" providers. Thus, these preferred health-care providers are assured of a large volume of business, and employers are able to decrease health-care costs.

An example would be an agreement between a group of doctors in a city and a major employer under which employees or their dependents will not be charged more than a certain amount for a routine office visit and employees will be encouraged to use these doctors. The plan, for example, might provide 90 percent coverage if one of these doctors is used but only 75 percent coverage if another doctor is used.

PPOs are normally not used by themselves, but are used in conjunction with an existing plan provided by an insurance company, the Blues, or an employer on a self-funded basis. As just noted, employees typically have a financial incentive to choose a PPO whenever a medical service is sought. However, there may be no explicit requirement that the preferred provider be used. On the other hand, a variation of the regular PPO is what has been termed a **point of service plan.** This approach operates much like a regular PPO, except that covered persons channel their medical care through so-called **primary care physicians** (or **gatekeepers**) who serve as the insureds' personal physicians. These physicians refer insureds to other medical professionals as they deem necessary. Thus, the PPO has greater control over such medical care decisions and hence costs. This "gatekeeper" concept is like that used in HMOs in which choice of providers is limited.[16]

Advantages and Disadvantages of HMOs and PPOs

Cost saving is a principal reason given for developing HMOs and PPOs. For example, a group practice HMO may rely on economies of scale to see that resources are used efficiently. HMOs also rely on prevention to keep costs down, and they can maintain tight controls on the types of tests and procedures that are performed—again keeping costs down. Likewise, PPOs or HMOs can keep costs down by establishing prices for services, in advance, that are less than the usual fee for the same service.

Other presumed advantages include the following:

- Broader coverage with emphasis on preventive care.
- Less administrative work.
- Coordinated services at one location (for some HMOs and PPOs).
- Lower hospitalization rates.
- For HMOs, low cost-sharing or no cost-sharing (deductibles and coinsurance) by covered persons. Most PPOs are still subject to deductibles, coinsurance, and stop-loss provisions.

Possible disadvantages to HMOs and PPOs also exist. Some insureds do not like being required to use the services of a specific medical facility. Many insureds have family physicians with whom they have a comfortable and familiar relationship. If these physicians are not members of the HMO or PPO, insureds must switch to a new physician to avoid coverage problems and penalties. Furthermore, some people believe that HMO and PPO physicians treat patients impersonally. Appointments appear overbooked so that the doctor may see a patient for only a few minutes. No time is spent building a relationship with patients. Other possible disadvantages include geographical limitations and the fact that HMOs and PPOs are often not backed by state guaranty plans like those covering insurance companies.

Summary

Every person faces sickness- and injury-related exposures. These exposures can give rise to personal losses from medical expenses incurred and loss of earned income from disability. They can also result in the need for long-term care, which is mainly insured through long-term care (LTC) insurance.

Medical expense coverage may be provided through a basic medical expense contract or a catastrophic contract or major medical expense contract. Both provide hospital expense benefits, surgical expense benefits, and physician expense benefits. A basic contract lists specific benefits that are paid when an insured is in the hospital. A catastrophic contract or major medical expense contract provides broad coverage with high limits, protecting against large, unpredictable expenses. Insurers also offer comprehensive medical policies, which combine features of basic and major medical expense coverage.

Disability income insurance is designed to replace income that is lost when a worker is unable to work. Many disability policies cover total and partial or residual disability; accidental death, dismemberment, and loss of sight; and rehabilitation benefits.

In addition to standard medical expense and disability income insurance, there are specialized health insurance coverages. These include dental care benefits; dread disease, hospital indemnity, and travel accident policies; credit disability insurance; and Medigap coverage.

Health benefits have traditionally been available through insurance companies and Blue Cross/Blue Shield. However, two alternative health-care systems, HMOs and PPOs, are also available. HMOs and PPOs differ from traditional group health insurance in that they both finance and provide health-care services.

Chapter Notes

1. Failure to notify the insurer may cause the child to be subject to individual medical underwriting standards. If the child is not in good health, it is possible that coverage for the child may be declined at a later time.
2. NAIC Long-Term Care Insurance Model Act—January 1991.
3. Joanne S. Morrissey, "Long-Term Care or Long-Term Disaster?" *National Underwriter*, Life & Health/Financial Services, June 25, 1990, p. 39.
4. Marc A. Cohen, et al., *Long-Term Care Financing Proposals: Their Costs, Benefits and Impact on Private Insurance*, Health Insurance Association of America, January 1991, p. 3.
5. Cohen et al., p. 8.
6. Cohen et al., p. 9.
7. Cohen et al., p. 3.
8. Gary L. Corliss, "The Evolution of Long Term Care Insurance," *Resource*, vol. 16, no. 2, February 1991, p. 12.
9. Cohen et al., p. 3.
10. Blue Cross Special Report, "The New Look at Long-Term Care" (1991), p. 34.
11. Susan Van Gelder and Diane Johnson, *Long-Term Care Insurance: A Market Update*, Health Insurance Association of America, January 1991, p. 7.
12. Neal Slafsky, "Carving a Niche in the LTC Market," *Best's Review*, March 1991, p. 35.
13. Blue Cross Association, "Questions and Answers About the Blue Cross Organization," mimeograph, 1984, p. 1.
14. 39 Fed. Reg. 37311, 1973.
15. 39 Fed. Reg. 37311, 37312, 1973.
16. The term "point of service plan" is also used to refer to HMO plans or options that allow covered persons to go outside the HMO network of medical care providers but at an increased cost to those covered persons who choose to do so. These plans are also called "open-ended HMOs" and are becoming increasingly popular.

Chapter 2

Health Benefit Sources and Issues

A wide variety of sources of health benefits are available to the public. There are, of course, the coverages provided through various kinds of property and liability policies, such as medical payments benefits and liability coverages in liability insurance policies and no-fault auto coverages in some states. Aside from these property and liability coverages, however, the main sources of health benefits for the public are group health insurance; individual health insurance; and social health programs, including Social Security, Medicare, and workers compensation.

One of the burning issues in the health-care field is how to contain or control the rapidly rising costs of health care in the United States. For many years, health-care costs have generally been rising considerably faster than the general rate of inflation in the United States. Therefore, some of the health-care cost containment measures used by insurers, employers, and others are discussed in this chapter.

Finally, some of the major reforms that have been proposed for the health-care system of the United States are briefly outlined at the end of the chapter.

Group Health Insurance

One of the main ways of providing health benefits is through the **group insurance** mechanism. Here the benefits are provided to the members of an identifiable group under a group insurance contract or arrangement. In group insurance, the underwriting and rating is normally based on the group itself rather than on the individuals in the group.

Most private health insurance in the United States is provided as group insurance, usually covering the employees of a single employer or of multiple employers but also covering other eligible kinds of groups. In fact, nearly 90 percent of health benefits are paid under group policies. Group benefits are written by insurance companies, Blue Cross/Blue Shield, and HMOs and PPOs, and are self-funded by employers.

Sponsoring Groups

Many types of groups or organizations may purchase or sponsor group insurance protection. Sponsoring groups may be solely responsible for paying the insurance premiums (a **noncontributory plan**), covered group members may pay a share of the plan's costs (a **contributory plan**), or covered group members may pay the entire cost. In addition to individual employers, which are by far the most important, the major groups include employer associations, other associations or organizations, labor unions, and creditors.

Associations or organizations such as the CPCU Society, the American Bar Association, and the American Medical Association sponsor group coverages for their members. This is often called association group coverage. The participation of members of the organization is solicited by mass merchandising—such as mass mailing. The insurance is considered one of the benefits of belonging to the group and therefore helps the organization obtain and retain members. Generally, these are "member pay all" plans.

Labor unions can purchase coverage for their members. A trust fund is established, and premiums are paid into the trust. The trustee has responsibility for purchasing the insurance protection.

Creditors may purchase group insurance protection on their debtors. The laws of most states stipulate that, if the coverage is noncontributory, it must be provided for *all* debtors. If the coverage may be purchased as an option by the debtor, it is provided only on those individuals who elect it.

Employer associations might purchase group coverage for the employees of all the employers that are members of the association. Frequently, the associations are comprised of smaller firms joining together to obtain a better negotiating position when seeking insurance protection. The major problem with this type of arrangement from an employer's perspective is that the individual employer loses flexibility in selecting coverage since the same protection is generally provided for the entire employers' association group. The group plan may or may not be contributory.

Employers in some situations have joined together to provide health-care benefits for their employees. One method by which employers can do this is the **multiple employer welfare arrangement** or **MEWA**. (Benefits other than for health care can also be offered.) The type of multiple employer welfare arrangement used most often is the **multiple employer trust (MET)**, which can be fully insured, partially insured, or completely self-funded.

- Benefits under a **fully insured MET** are provided by an insurance carrier. The insurer sells the insurance coverage to the MET, not to the employers. A fully insured MET is usually administered by the insurer providing the coverage. However, the MET can be run by a **third-party administrator (TPA)**. A TPA is an independent entity that collects premiums, handles claims, prepares administrative reports, maintains the records, and in the case of a fully insured plan, purchases the insurance coverage.

- A **partially insured MET** self-funds a portion of the risk of paying benefits, but purchases insurance coverage to transfer some of the risk to an insurance company, in order to limit its losses. An example would be an MET that retains the first $100,000 of each loss but purchases excess coverage for each loss in excess of $100,000. The partially insured MET is usually operated by a third-party administrator.

- An MET that is **completely self-funded** assumes all risks of paying benefits. As in partially insured METs, a third-party administrator handles the operations of the MET.

While it may be desirable to put employers who are in the same business into an MET, this is not always done. Many METs are operated on a sound basis, but there have been a significant number of MET insolvencies. In the case of such insolvencies, employees may not be paid for their medical expenses, and employers may lose their premium payments.

Selecting Group Health Benefits

Someone in each type of group coverage has the responsibility for selecting the specific benefits to be provided. Many factors affect this decision, including the following:

- *Cost.* The cost of benefits will have a significant impact on the selection of benefits. For example, if an employer pays the entire cost, the benefits are constrained by the funds allocated by the employer. However, if employees contribute to the cost of a group policy, the combined employer-employee contribution could provide a better health insurance package than that available under a noncontributory plan.

- *Union contract requirements.*   When the benefits for employees are established through labor negotiations, the benefit levels will have to meet the limits negotiated under the union contract. Cost is still a consideration, even though the benefit levels have been established by a collective bargaining agreement.

- *Income of group members.*   The financial position of the group members sometimes dictates the types of benefits made available under group coverage. For example, if the members have low incomes, they may be more interested in basic medical expense coverage than in catastrophic health insurance protection. Also, low-income individuals might prefer limited benefits under a noncontributory plan rather than broader benefits under a contributory plan.

- *Specific need.*   In some cases, a specific type of benefit is needed, and the process of selecting coverage is simple. For example, group disability income coverage on a creditor's debtors with monthly debt payments should provide benefits equal to the amount of the monthly payment.

When the benefit selection process is difficult, the individual or organization selecting benefit levels may solicit recommendations from several sources. An agent or broker selling the coverage can help select the appropriate policies and place the business with an insurer. Most insurance companies have group sales representatives who work with agents and brokers in designing appropriate coverage. Some brokerage firms are large enough to have employees who work full time to assist in the development and design of group benefit packages. Further, a number of employee benefit consulting firms are active in assisting employers, unions, and others in selecting, designing, and containing (restricting) the costs of health benefits as well as other employee benefits.

In group insurance, the role of an agent or broker encompasses more than selling the coverage and aiding in the selection of benefits. The agent or broker also gathers data on the group, recommends whether the plan should be contributory or noncontributory as well as other specifications regarding coverage, and searches for the best protection at the lowest cost.

Medical Expense Insurance

A large portion of the employee benefit dollar is used to purchase or provide medical expense protection. Groups can obtain coverage for hospital, surgical, physicians, and miscellaneous expenses, as discussed in Chapter 1. Group insurance may provide basic hospital-surgical-medical benefits, catastrophic or major medical benefits, or comprehensive medical benefits.

Employers can provide group medical care expense benefits through several medical care delivery or financing systems, such as the following:*

- Private insurance companies
- Blue Cross/Blue Shield plans
- Health maintenance organizations (HMOs)
- Preferred provider organizations (PPOs)
- Self-funding

Disability Income Plans

When deciding what group disability income benefits to provide, an employer should examine all sources of income that would be available to a disabled employee. Disability coverage, if not designed properly, could give an employee the opportunity to make more money while disabled than while actively employed. A prudent employer integrates group disability insurance benefits with other programs to reduce malingering. For example, group disability insurance benefits are typically integrated with the disability benefits provided by Social Security.

Group disability income protection may be either short term or long term. The following brief examination of group coverages emphasizes the distinctive features of group disability income protection.

Short-Term Disability Income Plans

Many employees are covered by short-term disability income insurance. In addition, a number of employers provide short-term income benefits through arrangements referred to as "sick leave" or "salary continuation plans."

Short-Term Disability Insurance Group short-term disability income contracts are designed to replace loss of income resulting from injury or sickness. Generally, the contracts do not cover disabilities caused by occupational injury or sickness. Thus, the coverage complements workers compensation benefits.

The usual group short-term disability income benefit payment periods are thirteen to fifty-two weeks, with twenty-six weeks being the most common. Most plans have at least a seven-day waiting period for sickness, but they may have a shorter waiting period for disabilities caused by accidents because absences for accidents are less frequent and generally are not within the control of the employee. Thus, if a plan has no waiting period for accidents and a seven-day waiting period for sickness, benefit payments would begin on the first day of an accident-related disability and on the eighth day of a disability because of sickness. Plans often are written to provide benefits that begin with the first day of a hospital confinement even if it occurs during the benefit waiting period.

Five states and Puerto Rico have mandatory temporary disability income programs for nonoccupational injuries. In these states, employers must set benefit levels in group short-term disability income policies equal to or greater than the requirements of the state programs.

Group short-term disability income benefits are paid either on the basis of a fixed schedule or as a percentage of salary. In the latter case, a percentage of between 50 and 66 $^2/_3$ percent up to a specified dollar maximum is common.

A few employers provide coverage under a group short-term disability income policy for all types of disability, occupational *and* nonoccupational. In this case, the coverage is coordinated with workers compensation and is referred to as twenty-four-hour coverage.

Short-term coverage normally is used as the first level of disability income protection. Some employers provide long-term disability income group coverage to supplement the short-term protection, or they provide salary continuation programs that are supplemented by group coverage.

Sick Leave or Salary Continuation Plans   Insurance is not the only means of replacing income. The first portion of a disability income benefit package may consist of a **sick leave plan** or a **salary continuation plan**. Under such plans, an employee continues to receive all or a portion of his or her salary after becoming disabled. A benefit formula may or may not be used. When a benefit formula is applied, an employee, while disabled, receives an amount equal to a percentage of his or her salary prior to the time of the disability. The amount of disability income may vary directly with the employee's length of service.

Generally, sick leave and salary continuation plans are not designed for long periods of disability. They should compensate the employee for loss of income because of short-term disability and are designed to be used instead of group short-term disability income policies.

Long-Term Disability Income Insurance

A group long-term disability (LTD) policy is designed to provide benefits for an extended period of time. Many policies provide disability income benefits for an insured until the normal retirement age.

Usually, group LTD benefits are provided for all types of disability (occupational and nonoccupational), subject to a waiting period. However, the coverage is integrated with workers compensation in that the group policy provides that any workers compensation benefit payable is deducted from the LTD benefit otherwise payable. If there is an underlying short-term disability income policy or salary continuation plan, the waiting period in the long-term policy should be coordinated with the period of coverage under the short-term policy or the salary continuation plan so that no gap exists between the underlying plan and the long-term program. For example, if the LTD benefit is subject to a twenty-six-week waiting period, the short-term policy or salary continuation plan should pay benefits for twenty-six weeks.

The benefit levels under a group long-term disability income contract are determined by schedule or by taking a fixed percentage of the insured's salary up to a stated dollar limit. The long-term contract may also include *rehabilitation benefits* in an effort to return a disabled employee to the job market. For example, if the rehabilitation effort fails, the benefits for the disabled employee are not reduced. If the insured is rehabilitated, disability payments are eliminated. The rehabilitation benefit has two advantages. First, it provides funds to help the disabled worker become employable. Second, if the cost of the rehabilitation effort for employees as a whole is less than the reduction in disability payments, the premium for group coverage will be lower.

The definition of disability in short-term contracts usually is restricted to disabilities that prevent the insured from working at his or her own occupation. Generally, the definition of disability under a group long-term disability income policy for the first one to five years covers an insured if he or she cannot perform the regular duties of his or her occupation. After the one- to five-year period, a more stringent definition is used (that is, the insured must be unable to engage in any gainful occupation for which the insured is reasonably suited by education, training, or experience).

Integration With Other Plans

In addition to integrating salary continuation plans and workers compensation with group coverage, an employer should also consider benefits provided under the federal Social Security Act, statutory temporary nonoccupational disability benefits, and any disability income payments contained in any employer-sponsored group insurance or pension plan. Some pension plans also provide disability payments. Pension plan benefits are described in greater detail in Chapters 6 and 7.

Other Benefits

Group health plans can also provide a variety of benefits other than those just described. Such benefits may include prescription drug coverage (often called "free-standing" plans because prescription drugs may be covered under hospital plans and under major medical plans), dental coverage, vision care coverage, hearing care coverage, extended care facility coverage, home health-care coverage, and hospice coverage, among others. As with prescription drug coverage, many of these can be provided separately or as part of major medical coverage.

Finally, a few employers may offer their employees and eligible dependents group LTC coverage, as described in Chapter 1. However, currently this is normally on an employee-pay-all basis at the employee's election.

Underwriting Group Health Insurance

Many factors must be considered by an underwriter deciding whether or not to insure a group. As noted earlier, the basic concept of true group underwriting is quite different from that of individual underwriting. *In group underwriting, the underwriter looks at the characteristics of the group as a whole rather than at those of each individual within the group.*

While some underwriting criteria may vary to some degree from insurer to insurer, the following criteria are generally considered by nearly every group underwriter. A discussion of some of these criteria follows.

Group Size

Underwriters are usually concerned about the number of individuals participating in a group plan. Generally, a large group results in a diversity of exposure units and therefore controllable adverse selection and a stable loss pattern. Further, if a group is sufficiently large, it may be *experience rated*—that is, the group's rates are based at least in part on its own loss experience. If a group is not large enough to be experience rated, the insurance company will pool the group with other similar groups for rating purposes. In this case, each group pays rates based on the overall experience of the combined groups, often called *pooling* or *pooled rates*. Many companies are beginning to use a combination of experience rates and pool rates. For example, if experience is better or worse than the pool average, the pool rate may be modified for the experience of the group. If a group is small (less than twenty-five members), individual underwriting of the members is usually applied to varying degrees.

Group Characteristics

An underwriter is interested in the characteristics of the group. For example, the age of the individuals in the group has a direct bearing on the group's overall utilization of health insurance coverages as well as utilization of specific health insurance benefits. An older group might not use pregnancy benefits but would have larger disability income and medical expense claims than a younger group. In addition, the underwriter may want to know the ratio of males to females, since women normally have a higher frequency of medical and disability insurance claims than men.

Groups containing many seasonal workers may pose special problems for underwriters, particularly in the area of short-term disability. Employees who work for only a portion of the year may have a higher rate of disability claims than those who work year-round. In this area, this adverse selection can significantly increase costs.

Experience

Underwriters are always interested in the reason that a particular group is purchasing insurance. If a group is seeking insurance protection for the first time, the underwriter will want to know whether the need for group insurance protection has resulted from dramatic changes in the health of individuals within the group.

If the group is changing insurers, the underwriter will want to know why. A group may change insurers because its loss experience is poor and its rates have increased. An insurance company writing a new policy may be able to eliminate the effects of the poor experience of a group by modifying the coverage or by imposing a waiting period or making other plan design changes. However, many states now have "takeover laws" that do not allow conditions of the new policy to be more restrictive than those under the prior plan when switching carriers.

Policyholders

Group health insurance generally is written to provide benefits on a nonoccupational basis (because workers compensation laws address occupational injuries). However, an underwriter has several reasons to be concerned about who the group policyholder will be. First, in employee groups, the type of policyholder usually indicates the type of employment. For employer-employee groups in certain industries, the underwriter might not be eager to provide insurance protection because of the physical environment in which employees must work. For example, employees in foundries or mines are susceptible to respiratory ailments.

The policyholder is important from another perspective. If the policyholder is in an industry that will continue to grow, then the underwriter can anticipate a flow of new members into the group. However, if the industry is diminishing, the underwriter can anticipate increasing losses because the average age of the group will increase.

Finally, the group's industry might be subject to latent diseases that can increase losses—for example, asbestosis. The underwriter needs to be aware of this in order to charge an adequate rate for the adverse selection that might arise.

Plan Design

An important health insurance underwriting goal is that benefits for injury or sickness do not result in financial gain to any covered person or in unnecessary benefits. Methods of achieving this goal include deductibles, waiting periods, selection of coverages and units, coinsurance, and coordination of benefits. When a plan offers benefits that exceed needs, higher than average losses can be expected.

Adverse Selection

To avoid adverse selection, an underwriter requires in a contributory plan that a substantial portion of the group (usually at least 50 to 75 percent, depending on the size of the group) participate in a group insurance plan. In a noncontributory plan, 100 percent of the eligible group normally would participate since the employees are not paying any part of the cost of the plan. In addition, the underwriter should know whether any employee classes are excluded from the contract. The group policyholder could attempt to put members who should have a low incidence of claims under one contract and all others under a second contract. By obtaining a representative proportion of the entire group, an underwriter can avoid this type of adverse selection.

Premium Payment

Generally, underwriters prefer group contracts in which the policyholder absorbs some or all of the cost of the plan. This will increase participation in the group contract. If no employer contribution is made, employee participation might not be sufficient to overcome the impact of adverse selection. However, despite this general principle, employee-pay-all coverage can be used for group insurance, especially for supplemental coverages such as dental, vision, and hearing.

Administration

Implementing a group insurance contract is a complex process. The underwriter is interested in knowing how much expense will have to be incurred in order to put a group insurance policy on the insurance company's books. If above-average administrative costs will be necessary, the contract might not be desirable from a profit perspective.

The underwriter also wants to be sure that there is a stable and efficient administrative unit to administer the group plan. In this sense, an employer (in employer-employee groups) is generally considered an ideal administrative unit.

Persistency of the Group Coverage

Sometimes, the group policyholder obtains a new group contract on a regular basis (that is, the coverage will be put out for bid every one or two years). This situation can be undesirable from an underwriting perspective. The underwriter might not have an opportunity to recoup administrative costs involved in writing group coverage if a contract is terminated. These expenses include the development of booklets or certificates for employees, the establishment of group insurance administration procedures to deal with a specific group, the issuance of the group insurance policy, and the servicing of the plan of benefits.

Statutory Constraints

Underwriters must consider statutory constraints on the issuance of group insurance coverages. Most state statutes stipulate (1) what constitutes an eligible group, (2) what minimum number of employees can be covered under a group plan, (3) what organizations can be issued group insurance protection, (4) what class of individuals can be covered, and (5) what types of coverage can be provided.

Important Group Policy Provisions

A group health insurance policy, unlike an individual health insurance policy, might not be required by state law to contain a large number of standard policy provisions because groups are usually in better negotiating positions for benefits than individuals are. However, all states have the right to reject a group policy if their regulatory agency believes the policy can easily be misrepresented. Policies also can be turned down if they are unfair, unjust, inequitable, misleading, deceptive, or contrary to public policy.

The discussion of policy provisions that follows concentrates on provisions that are important both to the employer and to the employee. The form of these provisions will vary significantly, and it becomes the responsibility of the employer to ascertain whether a group health insurance contract provides the protection that is most beneficial to his or her employees.

Payment of Premiums

A group health insurance policy specifies dates on which premium payments are due. The *employer* is responsible for forwarding the premium to the insurance company. In noncontributory plans, premium payment is a simple process because the employer pays the entire cost of the program. Under contributory or employee-pay-all plans, part or all (respectively) of the cost is recovered from individually covered employees through payroll deductions. The employer is responsible for remitting the premium, including the employee's share, to the insurer.

Eligible Employees

A group health insurance policy contains provisions stating the eligibility requirements for employees. Frequently, an eligible employee is one who works full time, although some plans also cover certain part-time employees, depending on the employer's policies in this area. For example, a group insurance policy may stipulate that all employees who work thirty hours or more per week are eligible. Other eligibility requirements are also determined by the employer.

Dependent Coverage

Group health insurance policies always cover employees, but coverage does not necessarily extend to dependents. Most employers do, however, permit coverage for dependents.

- When the employer pays the entire premium, the individual employee does not participate in the decision of whether dependent coverage will be provided.

- If a plan is contributory, an employee pays for some or all of the cost to dependents. In such cases, the employee may not want to insure family members who are eligible for coverage under other plans.

The definition of an eligible dependent varies from contract to contract. A typical provision reads as follows:

> Dependent shall mean the spouse of an employee or retired employee and an unmarried child who is a registered full-time student under 23 years of age including: (A) an adopted child and (B) a stepchild, foster child, or other child who is in regular parent-child relationship and (C) any such child, regardless of age, who lives with or whose care is provided by an employee or annuitant on a regular basis if such child is mentally retarded or physically incapacitated to such an extent as to be dependent upon the employee or retired employee for care or support.

Conversion

Group hospital, surgical, and medical or group major medical insurance policies may contain a provision explaining how an employee can convert the group coverage to individual coverage if he or she should leave the group. In fact, a number of states now require that a conversion privilege be offered to terminating employees and their dependents for medical expense coverage upon termination of coverage under a group plan. A conversion privilege is important to an employee who quits and goes to work for another employer that does not have group coverage or to an employee who is unemployed for an extended period of time. The provision is also important to an employee who is not in good health at the time of the conversion. The conversion privilege permits the employee to obtain insurance protection when it might not be available in the regular health insurance market.

An employee is allowed to convert to a policy that may have insurance protection equal to or less than the insurance protection provided in the group policy. For this coverage, the employee often pays a premium greater than that paid by the employee and the employer under the group policy. The increased cost results from the presumption that the insurer is no longer able to insure a large number of people under one policy and thereby obtain administrative cost savings and because those who convert their coverage often do so because they are in ill health. The latter situation results in adverse selection.

Extension of Benefits

An employer may find it desirable to change insurers, or a health insurer may decide that it does not want to renew a policy. When a contract is terminated, some employees may be collecting benefits under the health insurance contract. To protect these employees, the extension of benefits provision guarantees an employee receiving benefits that those benefits will not be cut off immediately because of a change in insurers or a termination of the policy. When a group policy is replaced, the new policy usually covers all of the employees covered by the previous policy if they are currently receiving benefits. A new policy may include a provision, however, that claims arising from preexisting conditions are not covered during the first twelve months.

Consolidated Omnibus Budget Reconciliation Act of 1985 (COBRA)

Congress has been concerned about the situation in which employees and their dependents may cease to be eligible for any group medical expense coverage for a variety of reasons. To help deal with this problem, Congress included in COBRA certain continuation requirements for group health plans of most employers. An employer must comply with these provisions if the employer has twenty or more employees. (Governmental plans and church plans are excluded from COBRA's requirements.) An employer that fails to comply with COBRA is subject to certain excise taxes, unless the employer did not know, and could not reasonably have known, of the noncompliance.

This law requires employers to allow employees and certain dependents (called **qualified beneficiaries**) to keep group medical expense coverage if a **qualifying event**—such as the termination of employment, the death of the employee, or the separation or divorce of an employee and his or her spouse—occurs. However, the employees or dependents can be required to pay as much as 102 percent of the cost for the coverage. This is usually a desirable opportunity for employees because group premiums are generally favorable even if 102 percent of the amount is required.

An employer does not have to continue the group coverage indefinitely. Time limits are established for each type of qualifying event. For example, if the employee is terminated, coverage must be offered to the employee and dependents for up to eighteen months (plus an additional eleven months for those disabled at termination). However, if the employee dies, coverage must be extended to his or her dependents for thirty-six months. In any case, the employee or dependent, not the employer, pays for the coverage.

Employers are required to notify employees and their dependents when they qualify for the coverage extension. The employee and dependents then have sixty days to decide whether to take the extended coverage.

Under certain circumstances, coverage may cease before the time limits cited above. For example, coverage ceases under the following circumstances:

- The employer no longer provides coverage for *any* employees.
- The premium is not paid by a qualified beneficiary.
- A qualified beneficiary is covered under another group plan (unless the other group health plan contains a preexisting condition exclusion or limitation that affects the qualified beneficiary).
- A qualified beneficiary becomes eligible for Medicare.

Retirement

Many employers are concerned about providing health coverage for their retired workers and perhaps their dependents—coverage that would supplement Medicare. The problem with doing this is that a large unfunded liability may be created. As a result, employers may not be able to meet their retiree health coverage obligations and retirees may not receive retirement health benefits.

Since 1993, the Financial Accounting Standards Board (FASB) has required employers to recognize their accrued annual costs and balance sheet liabilities (and offsetting assets) for accounting purposes for postretirement benefits other than pensions. The main such postretirement benefit for many employers is retiree health (medical expense) benefits.

Coordination of Benefits

In group medical expense contracts, a method available to employers and insurers for reducing any overlap in insurance benefits is the **coordination of benefits (COB)**. This is a method of coordinating benefits payable under more than one group health insurance plan so that the covered person's benefits from all the plans do not exceed 100 percent (or, alternatively, 80 percent or more) of his or her "allowable" medical expenses, while at least maintaining the minimum level of benefits of the secondary plan.

COB provisions stipulate that, when two group policies cover the same individual, one of the policies will provide primary coverage and the other policy will serve as excess coverage. The usual COB provision (as adopted by many states) stipulates that any other plan without the COB provision is primary, and that any plan with it is secondary. If more than one plan has a COB provision, the following priorities are established:

- An employee's plan pays before the plan of the employee's spouse.

- A dependent child whose parents are not separated or divorced is covered by the plan of the parent whose birthday occurs earliest in the year. If the parents have the same birthday, the plan in force the longest is primary. (This is called the "birthday rule.")

- A dependent child whose parents are separated or divorced is covered first by the plan of the parent who has custody of the child. The child would next be covered under the plan of the stepparent married to the parent having custody. The plan of the parent who does not have custody of the child would pay last. (If a court stipulates a different order of payment, the court decree is followed.)

- A policy that covers a worker who has retired or been laid off pays after a plan covering the worker as an active employee.

While coordination of benefits provisions are designed to bar the family from profiting from payment under two group policies, a chance still exists that family members may collect more in benefits than they are required to pay in medical care expenses. For example, other kinds of medical benefits, such as auto medical payments coverage, are not included in the coordination of benefits provisions. Therefore, if the family has medical payments coverage under a personal auto policy, its members may be able to collect more in benefits than they actually have to pay in medical care costs. However, this situation may change since some states have revised their laws relating to coverage for auto accident claims and some group policies exclude coverage or provide for subrogation in such cases. In other instances, group medical benefits may be excess to auto medical payments or no-fault benefits.

Certificates

Insurance companies issuing group policies are usually required to provide certificates of insurance to members of the group. The individual certificate should include a summary of the essential features of the insurance coverage, including not only a description of the coverage, but also an explanation about how claims are filed. Today, many insurers have switched to the combined *certificate/booklet approach*, in which a certificate summarizes the essential features and the booklet provides more comprehensive information concerning the group coverages.

Miscellaneous Provisions

Group insurance policies may contain other provisions that affect an insured. There will be provisions stipulating how an insured should file a claim. Normally, this type of provision will include statements on the maximum permissible amounts of time before (1) the insurer must be notified of the loss, (2) the insurer must forward claim forms, and (3) the insured must submit the claim forms.

The contract may contain a provision stipulating that the insurer has the right and opportunity to have an insured examined as often as may reasonably be required to determine whether or not a claim is valid. Frequently, this provision is used in disability income contracts.

The contract may have a provision giving the insurer the right to have an autopsy performed in the case of death. This provision is not permitted under some state laws and therefore cannot be included in all group policies.

Finally, there may be provisions relating to the period during which an action can be brought against the insurer. Policies that contain this type of provision generally bar legal action against the insurer until at least sixty days after proof of loss has been filed in accordance with the policy requirements. There is also a maximum time after which suits cannot be filed against the insurer. Frequently, this upper limit is two or three years.

Advantages and Disadvantages of Group Health Insurance Coverage

Group health coverage has advantages and disadvantages for both group members and employers or sponsors. These are discussed below.

Advantages for Group Members

Compared to individual health insurance, group health coverage can be advantageous to members of a group in a number of ways, including the following:

1. Since a group rate is used, coverage should be less expensive for older or less healthy group members than if those covered members purchased individual health insurance protection.
2. Those who are not in good health can often obtain insurance as part of a group when they might not be able to do so on an individual basis.
3. The amount of premium, if any, paid by the employer reduces the cost to employees.
4. The employer's contribution is not treated as taxable income to the employees.

Advantages for Employers

Providing group health coverage can be advantageous to an employer in at least three ways:

1. It can give an employer a competitive edge in hiring employees.
2. An employer who provides an extensive group health insurance program need not be concerned about employees facing financial ruin because of extended periods of illness.
3. An employer may deduct any premiums paid for group insurance as a necessary and reasonable business expense.

Disadvantages

Despite the advantages of group insurance coverage, there are some disadvantages. If a younger employee is a member of a group consisting of older employees and the group is rated on its experience, he or she may find that group coverage is more expensive than individual protection. This situation can occur in declining industries or in industries that consistently use older workers.

Another possible disadvantage of group coverage is the protection gap that might occur when an employee changes employers or is laid off. The new employer might not have any group health coverage, the coverage might be less extensive than that of the former employer, or a waiting period might apply under the new employer's coverage. In the case of layoff, no coverage might be available after any COBRA continuation period ends. Of course, employees and their covered dependents often have conversion rights under their prior employer's group health contract, and employees and certain covered dependents also have important group coverage continuation rights under COBRA.

Other Considerations

Other considerations and funding vehicles have become quite important with regard to group health plans and particularly in connection with group medical expense plans. In fact, at least for larger employers, self-funding has become the predominant method for providing group medical expense benefits to their employees.

Self-Funding Arrangements

With a traditional insurance plan, the insurer, in exchange for a premium, (1) bears the cost of health-care claims and (2) administers the program. Many employers are attempting to reduce employee benefit costs by paying their employee health-care costs directly rather than insuring them. There are four basic ways that such a plan can be implemented:

1. *An employer can fund the entire health exposure and provide its own administrative functions.* This is relatively unusual.

2. *An employer can fund the entire exposure and purchase the services of some third party to provide administrative services.* The employer still has unlimited liability for health-care expenses, but it hires someone (an insurance company or another firm) to handle claims and other administrative duties. Such services are provided on an **administrative services only (ASO)** basis.

3. *An employer can fund the exposure up to a certain limit and provide its own administrative services.* The employer administers the program, but purchases excess insurance coverage. This coverage, known as **stop-loss protection**, limits the amount of loss the employer has to absorb per covered person, or family, or per occurrence each year (often called specific stop-loss insurance), or the aggregate amount of loss the employer has to absorb for all covered persons per year (often called "aggregate stop-loss insurance").

4. *An employer can fund the exposure up to a certain limit and hire a third party to provide administrative services.* This situation combines the purchase of excess insurance with an ASO arrangement. Since many ASO providers also are insurers, combining stop-loss coverage and a service arrangement can be convenient. This is a common approach to self-funding group medical expense benefits.

Employers can use voluntary employees' beneficiary associations (VEBAs) to self-fund employee benefit plans. VEBAs, or 501(c)(9) trusts, are generally tax-exempt trusts that provide life, health, and other benefits to covered employees and their dependents. Employers can also use certain so-called modified insurance arrangements for their group medical expense exposure under which they may have some of the advantages of self-funding (such as greater cash flow or retention of reserves for the employer and/or savings in premium taxes), but still have insured arrangements in varying degrees. Some examples of such "modified insurance arrangements" for group medical expense plans are minimum premium plans, retrospective insurance arrangements, premium-lag arrangements, reserve-reduction arrangements, and cost-plus arrangements.

Thus, it can be seen that employers can retain the risk (engage in self-funding or partial self-funding) in a variety of ways with regard to their group medical expense benefits. In fact, as noted at the beginning of this discussion, a strong trend toward such full or partial retention arrangements for group medical expense benefits has been occurring for some time to reduce the employers' health care and to improve their control over health benefit administration. Insurers have recognized and adapted to this trend by developing and offering their group customers (typically employers) ASO arrangements, excess or stop-loss insurance, and various modified insurance arrangements, as well as their traditional fixed premium and experience rated group products. With this complexity of financing arrangements, it is sometimes difficult for the courts and regulators to decide what is "self-funding" or "self-insured" and what is not. The issue of shifting of risk to a third-party carrier (for example, an insurer or HMO) may be an important factor in such a case or decision.

Integrated Health-Care System

Employers are constantly seeking ways to control the cost of providing medical expense benefits for employees. No one type of medical-care delivery system is ideal for every situation. Although an indemnification plan may be effective in one area, an HMO may be more effective in another. The result is a move toward the concept of an **integrated health-care system.**

Such a system comprises more than one means of health-care service delivery. For example, it could comprise an HMO, a PPO, and a traditional insurance company (or the Blues). Benefits would often vary, depending on the component used by an employee. In essence, the employee is provided with a choice in selecting a medical-care delivery system. This trend toward integrated systems has been given impetus by the development of HMOs, PPOs, and other types of health-care delivery systems by insurers, the Blues, and HMO organizations.

This development has been an important trend by employers in recent years. Because employee contributions are usually tied to the cost of the chosen health plan, employees tend to opt for the plan that provides the best benefit-cost relationship. Benefit plans compete and the costs drop, thus reducing the employers' costs as well.

Blanket Accident and Sickness Insurance

Employee groups are normally covered under group insurance policies. However, other kinds of groups (and occasionally employee groups) may be covered under blanket accident and sickness insurance. A **blanket policy** covers all members of a defined group. Certificates may be issued to members of the group. Members of the group are automatically covered.

As a rule, blanket coverages are more limited than group insurance coverages. For example, blanket policies provide limited forms of insurance protection, such as accidental death and dismemberment.

Most state laws stipulate the types of groups eligible for such coverage. For example, as allowed in many states, most blanket accident and sickness policies are issued to any of the following groups:

- A college, school, or a school board to cover students, teachers, or employees
- Any religious, charitable, recreational, educational, or civic organization, or branch thereof, to cover any group of members or participants exposed to specified hazards involved in operations sponsored or supervised by the organization
- A sports team, camp, or sponsor thereof, to cover members, campers, employees, officials, or supervisors[1]

Since blanket policies cover an entire group and not individual members of a group, an insured individual may not be required to complete an enrollment card.

Some states require some standard policy provisions in blanket contracts. These provisions are confined to explaining procedures for filing a claim, conditions under which legal action can be brought, and the definition of an entire contract.

Franchise Health Insurance

Franchise coverage is another method of providing health insurance coverage to a group. The major difference between franchise coverage and group and blanket coverage is that franchise coverage is provided by individual contracts, while group and blanket coverages are provided under a master policy.

Under a franchise arrangement, coverage is issued to those members of an employee group or association who desire the insurance. Members are issued individual policies and are responsible for remitting the insurance premium to the employer or to the association that, in turn, pays the premium to the insurance company.

Franchise coverage can be advantageous to individuals who do not qualify for true group insurance. Even small franchise groups may save the insurer some administrative costs because a single premium is remitted by the employer or association. These savings can be passed along to insureds. More liberal underwriting rules may be applied to individual policies issued on a franchise basis than for comparable regular individual policies.

Other Business Uses of Health Insurance

Disability income insurance can be used to meet certain business-related needs, such as meeting business overhead expenses during disability, funding a buy-sell agreement, or providing for expenses caused by the disability of a key employee.

Business Overhead Expenses

Individuals who become disabled might not only suffer a loss of income but might also incur a loss because of continuing business expenses. This situation frequently arises among self-employed persons, such as doctors, lawyers, accountants, insurance agents, and other independent business and professional people.

To meet the needs of these individuals, insurance companies have developed business overhead expense disability policies, which pay for continuing business expenses such as rent, utility bills, taxes, fees, dues, cost of goods, equipment, fixtures, products of the business, depreciation, salaries, water, telephone, laundry, and postage. These policies pay only for those expenses that are actually incurred by an individual during a specified period of disability. Thus, if an insured is an equal partner in a company, only that individual's proportionate share of expenses can be insured subject to the maximum benefit stated in the policy. An insurance company will not be responsible for expenses that were not incurred regularly before the disability.

The definition of disability used in most business overhead expense policies is "regular and own occupation." Premiums are income tax deductible, and the insured must treat any payments under the contract as income. Most policies are written with a short (less than two years) maximum benefit period. Normally, if a person remains disabled for a long period of time, his or her business will be sold or dissolved.

Buy-Sell Agreements

Covering overhead expenses is not the only way disability insurance can be used in a business or professional relationship. It may also be used to help fund a buy-sell agreement among partners in a partnership and among stockholders in closely-held corporations.

Under a disability buy-sell agreement, the business owners agree that, if one owner is disabled, he or she will be paid a disability benefit under a regular disability income policy. If it appears that the disabled owner will not return to work, the agreement compels the other owners (or the business entity) to purchase the disabled owner's share of the business by making periodic payments. Disability income insurance is used to provide funds with which to make these payments. Such disability buyout coverages might also provide for lump-sum payments under certain conditions. Insured buy-sell agreements are discussed in greater detail in Chapter 8.

Key Employee Disability Income Insurance

Another business use of disability income insurance involves the purchase (by an employer) of a disability income policy on a *key employee* (an employee without whom the business would suffer—for example, a salesperson responsible for generating 30 percent of company sales). If the employee becomes disabled, benefits are paid to the employer and can be used to hire someone to continue the key employee's activities.

Individual Health Insurance

We now turn from the principles of group health insurance and consider the underwriting of individual health insurance. The terms and conditions for the renewability (or continuation) of individual health policies are also discussed in this portion of the chapter.

Individual Underwriting Factors

To determine the acceptability of and to properly assign the premium for any individual medical expense or disability income applicant, an underwriter may require information regarding the applicant's age, sex, health history and physical condition, character traits, and occupation and avocation. This information can be obtained through several sources, including the application for the insurance, an inspection report, and possibly a physical examination.

Age

Age is an important criterion, not only in setting rates, but also in determining whether coverage will be issued. Most insurers have a different rate for every age for medical expense and disability income coverage, instead of a rate for age brackets. Therefore, there are rates for ages thirty-five, thirty-six, thirty-seven, thirty-eight, and thirty-nine, instead of using the same rate for ages thirty-five through thirty-nine.

Beyond age sixty-five, morbidity increases rapidly, and insurers may limit their policies so that they cannot be renewed beyond that age. This has been true especially since the advent of Medicare. For example, a policy might have a maximum issue age of sixty and terminate at age sixty-five to tie in with the normal retirement age of sixty-five and eligibility for Medicare. However, some policies are still available to people age sixty-five and older.

Sex

Experience reveals that males have lower morbidity than females. As a result, rates for women might be higher than rates for men. However, some states do not permit differentiating rates according to sex.

Health History and Physical Condition

A person who has, or has had, a condition that could contribute to future injuries or sicknesses is considered impaired. Applicants are categorized depending on the degree to which their past and present physical profile deviates from that of unimpaired applicants.

After all underwriting information has been reviewed, a decision is made as to the acceptability or insurability of the applicant. The underwriter has the following general choices:

- *Standard issue.* The applicant's health is acceptable to the underwriter, and the company's standard coverage is issued.

- *Modified coverage.* The more common modifications include offering a different policy form, reducing benefits, attaching riders that exclude coverage for some health conditions, or some combination of these. For example, a policy that excludes benefits for health-care expenses resulting from tuberculosis can be issued to an individual currently suffering from tuberculosis. This exclusion can be permanent or can apply only to a fixed period of time, for example, five years. The latter approach is used when the underwriter feels that the increased exposure will be eliminated within the designated time period. If a complete recovery occurs, the exposure is not greater for the applicant than for any other person, and the rating on modification in coverage can be removed.

- *A rated policy.* A rated policy takes into account the increased risk of the applicant by charging higher than standard premiums.
- *Declined applicant.* The applicant's health is not acceptable, even under modified coverage. The applicant is refused coverage.

Character Traits

Underwriters attempt to avoid providing coverage for individuals with undesirable character traits, such as suicidal tendencies, since they are more susceptible to conflict, mental problems, and undesirable health characteristics. Furthermore, they might be more inclined to file fraudulent claims.

Occupation and Avocation

An individual's occupation and avocation (hobbies) can have an impact on his or her exposure to accidents, and to a lesser degree, to sickness. Most insurers grade the exposures presented by different occupational and avocational categories. As the exposure increases, the rates are increased. Because of the greater accident exposure, a construction worker, for example, is more likely to be disabled than an accountant. Therefore, higher rates are charged for a disability income contract issued on the construction worker. The same can be said of a person who flies a plane or drives a race car as a hobby. Some occupations, such as underground mining, are so hazardous that insurers are unwilling to issue health or disability insurance at all.

Sources of Information

Underwriters have a number of potential sources from which they can gather data for evaluating an applicant. The primary source of information is the application. It contains information about the applicant's current health, health history, family health history, and habits.

The producer is another source of information. He or she performs the first level of underwriting, and most applications provide space for the producer's evaluation of the applicant.

The underwriter can also get information from doctors who have treated the applicant and from hospitals in which the applicant has been a patient. The underwriter's primary source for the names of doctors and hospitals is the application provided by the prospective insured.

Other sources of information include investigative reports and physical examinations by physicians or paramedical personnel. These reports may provide information that the application did not reveal.

Underwriting Evaluation

After an underwriter has gathered the information, it must be evaluated. This evaluation considers the important individual underwriting factors just discussed. Then, the underwriter can apply one or more of the general underwriting choices or actions noted previously.

With regard to underwriting individual and small group (where some individual underwriting may be done because the group is not large enough for group underwriting principles to apply completely) health insurance, it should be noted that state regulation might affect the underwriting practices that can be followed by insurers. In the state of New York, for example, since 1993, health insurers (including insurance companies, Blue Cross/Blue Shield, and HMOs and PPOs) must accept all individual and small group (from three to fifty lives) applicants for medical expense insurance without regard to their health history or current health status and at rates that do not vary by age, sex, occupation, or health status under the controversial Community Rating and Open Enrollment Law of New York.

This law also requires health insurers to charge all insureds in the same general geographic area the same premium rate for medical expense insurance. This is referred to as **community rating**. Some adjustment provisions in the law are designed to assist insurers that have covered a disproportionate number of undesirable risks.

Terms of Renewability and Rating

All states have laws specifying that individual health insurance policies must indicate on what basis the insured can continue the contract. The provisions relating to renewability can be divided into several categories. The first category includes those contracts that are renewable at the option of the insurer and those that are conditionally renewable. The second category includes guaranteed renewable policies, and the third category is composed of noncancelable and guaranteed renewable (noncancelable) contracts. Some contracts are written for a specific period and consequently are not renewable. Travel accident insurance for a specific trip is an example.

Renewable at the Option of the Insurer and Conditionally Renewable

The first renewability provision—**renewable at the option of the insurer**—is the least expensive and the least desirable from the insured's perspective. It restricts cancellation to the renewal date of the policy. This approach is much less used today than was the case in past years and is prohibited in many states.

The second approach in this general category is **conditionally renewable** policies. These policies are generally renewable from policy period to policy period by the insured, but under certain conditions the insurer can refuse such renewals. This approach is commonly used in association group or franchise cases. For example, in association group cases, an insurer might be able to refuse renewal if the insured person ceases to be a member of the association, if the insured ceases to be actively engaged in the occupation, or if the insurer refuses to renew all policies issued to members of the particular group.

Guaranteed Renewable

While an insurer has the right to change the premium rate of **guaranteed renewable** contracts for whole classes of insureds, an insured is promised that his or her coverage cannot be canceled or not renewed during the guaranteed period. Following the passage of the Medicare program, nearly all insurance companies reduced the period during which their individual medical expense policies were guaranteed renewable to age sixty-five. However, some insurers issue policies that are renewable until the first renewal date following the insured's eligibility for Medicare.

Noncancelable and Guaranteed Renewable

Policies that are **noncancelable and guaranteed renewable ("noncan")** give insureds the greatest amount of protection since an insurer not only cannot cancel the policy or refuse renewal until a stipulated time but also cannot change the premium rates. The term "noncancelable" may be used in conjunction with the phrase "guaranteed renewable," such as "noncancelable and guaranteed renewable to age sixty-five." Premiums for noncancelable policies are generally higher than for comparable coverage on only a guaranteed renewable basis.

Social Health Programs

To this point, the text has focused on health insurance available to individuals and families from private sources. Health insurance is also available to individuals and families through social health insurance programs—most notably Social Security and Medicare and workers compensation.

Social Security and Medicare

Several programs run by the federal government provide benefits that affect the health insurance coverage and financial planning of individuals. The coverages found in the *Old Age, Survivors, Disability, and Health Insurance Program* (OASDHI or "Social Security" and "Medicare") provide retirement, disability, survivors (death) and medical expense benefits. A basic understanding of these governmental programs is essential if one is to select appropriate individual insurance coverages and employee benefits.

Many people think that OASDHI applies only to retired people, but OASDHI is more than an income support program for the elderly. It is also a support program for disabled workers and their families, and survivors of deceased workers. Social Security provides three basic types of cash benefits—old age, survivors, and disability. Medicare provides basic hospital insurance benefits (Part A) and supplementary medical insurance (Part B) for most persons age sixty-five and over and for certain other categories of beneficiaries.

Characteristics of OASDHI

OASDHI is characterized by several factors, which are discussed below.

Compulsory

Except for Medicare Part B, participation in OASDHI is compulsory for all workers in covered employment, and almost all employment is now "covered." A voluntary program would attract a disproportionate number of older or unhealthy individuals and would not meet the social objective of providing benefits to a substantial majority of the population. Furthermore, the compulsory feature makes the program large, thereby providing administrative economies and actuarial advantages.

Medicare Part B is voluntary. Workers eligible for Medicare Part A can also elect to be insured under Medicare Part B.

Minimum Floor of Income

OASDHI provides retirees with a floor of protection. It is designed to provide some income, but it should be supplemented by private pensions as well as individual insurance, annuities, personal savings, and other investments.

Sacrifice in Individual Equity

Private insurance plans are designed to provide individual equity by treating individual policyowners fairly. In fact, state insurance laws prohibit insurance rates that are unfairly discriminatory. Each policyowner is placed in a group with other individuals who have similar loss-producing characteristics, and each member of a given group pays the same premium rate. A close relationship exists between this rate and the expected losses of the group.

In contrast, the OASDHI system stresses *social adequacy*. Two elements of the program ensure the social adequacy of the program:

1. Lower paid workers receive benefits that are a higher proportion of past earnings than do higher paid workers. The law also provides a "special" minimum benefit for workers who have worked under the program regularly over the years but at relatively low wage levels.

2. Benefits are provided for dependents and survivors of insured workers in order to reduce dependency. Thus, workers who have dependents get more protection in relation to their taxes than do workers who have no dependents.

Benefits Based on Earnings

Social Security benefits are a function of earnings—the higher a person's earnings, the greater the retirement, disability, or survivors benefits. However, the relationship between earnings and benefits is not based on individual equity; rather, lower paid workers receive *proportionately* larger benefits than higher paid workers. Benefits are subject to certain minimums and maximums. For example, in 1993, a worker who earned on average $3,800 a month before retirement might receive $1,213 per month of retirement income, while a worker who earned, on average, $1,125 per month before retirement might receive $592 in monthly retirement income. All insureds receive the same Medicare benefits. These benefits do not depend on the insured's earnings.

Contributory Funding

The OASDHI program (except Part B of Medicare) is financed by taxes levied on employers, employees, and the self-employed under the Federal Insurance Contributions Act (FICA). Employers and employees are subject to the same tax rate. Self-employed people must pay twice the employer (or employee) tax rate. The appropriate tax rate is applied to the wages paid by employers and received by employees and to the income earned by the self-employed.

Part B of Medicare is financed by monthly premiums paid by the insureds and contributions made by the federal government.

Pay-As-You-Go Funding

Social Security operates essentially on a **pay-as-you-go basis** under which current payments of benefits are met by current resources. During working years, employees, their employers, and covered self-employed persons pay

Social Security contributions through payroll taxes. This money is used largely to pay benefits to those currently receiving benefits and to cover administrative costs. When the earnings of present-day workers stop or are reduced because of retirement, death, or disability, benefits will be paid to them from the contributions of people who are still working. The pay-as-you-go method is a process of transferring income from one generation to another—sometimes referred to as **intergenerational transfer**.

The pay-as-you-go system may result in inequities since the benefits paid to each retired generation are financed by the current generation of workers, and the nation's birth rate has dropped in recent years while longevity has been increasing. This combination of fewer births and longer life means that the number of retired people will increase more rapidly than the number of active workers, and this may cause additional taxes to be required of the workers to cover the cost of benefits.

Benefits Prescribed by Law

The benefits under the OASDHI program are established, changed, and administered by the federal government.

Benefits Related to Presumed Need

An individual who meets the requirements for benefits in the OASDHI program is entitled to benefits as a matter of right—demonstration of need is not required. Thus, OASDHI is considered a *social insurance* program rather than an *assistance* or *welfare program* (which is based on level of income in relation to poverty level, such as Medicaid or Aid to Families with Dependent Children).

However, *presumed need is considered* in structuring these benefits. For example, under the Social Security earnings (or retirement) test a person who continues to be gainfully employed after beginning to receive Social Security retirement benefits may receive reduced benefits, or even no benefits at all, depending upon the amount of his or her earnings.

Levels of Eligibility

The right to receive benefits under the OASDHI program is based on three levels of eligibility:

* Fully insured
* Currently insured
* Disability insured

A worker's insured status is dependent upon the number of "quarters of coverage" earned by the worker. A **quarter of coverage** is defined as a dollar amount that a worker earns in covered employment during the year. This dollar amount is determined by a formula that varies from year to year but it is quite low. In 1993, one "quarter of coverage" equaled $590. Thus, in 1993, for every $590 a worker earned in covered employment, he or she received a quarter of coverage, subject to a maximum of four a year. For example, Sharon worked two-and-one-half months in 1993 and earned $1,800 during that time. She earned three quarters for 1993 ($1,800/$590 = 3.05, rounded down to three—the resulting number must always be rounded down).

Fully Insured

To be **fully insured**, a person must have a specified number of quarters of coverage. This number varies with the age of the worker. However, all workers are fully insured if they have forty or more quarters of coverage. If a worker has earned less than forty quarters of coverage, he or she is fully insured if he or she has earned at least six quarters of coverage and at least one quarter of coverage for each year after 1950 (or after the twenty-first birthday, if it occurs after 1950). All years up to but not including the year the worker attains age sixty-two, becomes disabled, or dies (whichever occurs first) are counted.

Currently Insured

A worker is **currently insured** if he or she has six quarters of coverage of the last thirteen quarters.

Disability Insured

To qualify as **disability insured**, a worker under age thirty-one at the time he or she is disabled must have quarters of coverage at least equal to the following:

- Six quarters of coverage (if under age twenty-four)
- One quarter of coverage for every two quarters since the worker turned twenty-one (for workers ages twenty-four to thirty)

A worker who is thirty-one or older must be fully insured and have at least twenty quarters of coverage of the last forty quarters, prior to disability. Workers younger than thirty-one may qualify with fewer quarters of coverage.

Eligibility for Medicare

Persons age sixty-five and over who are eligible for Social Security retirement or survivor benefits (described next) or railroad retirement benefits are automatically covered for Medicare Part A (Hospital Insurance, or HI). In addition, HI also covers other limited categories of persons, including certain disabled workers and persons with chronic renal disease.

A person is covered by Medicare even though he or she may still be working and have not actually retired. However, for employed persons and their spouses who are age sixty-five and over (working for employers with twenty or more employees), Medicare pays only after any employer-provided medical expense insurance pays its benefits, unless the worker elects otherwise. Thus, in this situation any employer-provided medical expense insurance is generally primary over Medicare.

Anyone eligible for HI is automatically covered by Medicare Part B (Supplementary Medical Insurance, or SMI). However, they may elect not to be so covered.[2]

Benefits

As mentioned earlier, the OASDHI program provides retirement, disability, survivors (death), and medical benefits.

Retirement (Old-Age) Benefits

The retirement program provides a monthly income for retired workers, their spouses, and some dependent children and grandchildren.

Worker A worker is entitled to full retirement benefits, if he or she is *fully insured*, at the full-benefit retirement age (or the Social Security normal retirement age), which is currently age sixty-five but which will increase to age sixty-seven by the year 2000.

- Workers can retire as early as age sixty-two. However workers who retire early receive a retirement benefit that is permanently reduced.
- Workers may also retire later than age sixty-five. If they do, their benefits are permanently increased.[3] However, they will begin to receive monthly retirement benefits upon turning sixty-five.

Spouse of Retired Worker The *spouse* of the retired worker eligible for retirement benefits is also entitled to spousal benefits if age sixty-five.

- The spouse of a retired worker can start benefits as early as age sixty-two, but the benefit is reduced.
- A spouse under sixty-two can receive benefits if the spouse is caring for an unmarried child who is younger than sixteen (or who is disabled before age twenty-two and not married).
- Increased benefits are available if benefits are started after age sixty-five.

The *divorced* spouse of a retired worker is entitled to retirement benefits if the divorce has been in effect for at least two years, the divorced spouse has not remarried, and the divorced spouse was married to the retired worker for at least ten years.

Dependent Children   Unmarried children who are younger than eighteen (or nineteen if full-time elementary or secondary school students) also are covered if the worker is eligible for retirement benefits. Children who are disabled before age twenty-two and who are not married are also covered.

Disability Benefits

The Social Security program provides disability benefits to covered workers who suffer a disability severe enough to keep them from engaging in *any* substantial and gainful activity for at least twelve months. A worker is entitled to disability benefits (monthly income) if he or she is *fully insured and disability insured*. If the worker is entitled to benefits, the spouse and dependent children described in the preceding section on retirement also are entitled to benefits.

Survivors (Death) Benefits

If a worker who is *fully insured* (or in some cases *currently insured*) dies, survivors benefits (monthly income) are payable to a spouse, unmarried children, and dependent parents.

- The spouse receives benefits if he or she is (1) sixty or older, (2) fifty or over and disabled, or (3) caring for an unmarried child who is under sixteen (or unmarried and disabled before age twenty-two).
- Children who are unmarried and under eighteen (or nineteen if full-time students in an elementary or secondary school) are covered.
- Dependent parents receive benefits if they are sixty-two or older.

A $255 lump-sum death benefit is also paid to the surviving spouse or dependents. If no surviving spouse or dependents exist, the lump-sum benefit is not paid.

If a worker is *currently insured*, survivors benefits are payable only to eligible children or a spouse taking care of unmarried children who are under sixteen (or unmarried and who were disabled before age twenty-two). The lump-sum death benefit also is payable.

Medicare—Part A (Hospital Insurance, or HI)

Hospital, psychiatric, posthospital skilled nursing home care, home health services, and hospice care benefits are payable under Medicare Part A.

Hospital   The first ninety days of hospital care for each "spell of illness" are covered. The patient pays a flat dollar deductible ($676 in 1993) for the first sixty days and then must make a flat dollar copayment ($169 per day in 1993) for each day from the sixty-first through the ninetieth day of hospitalization. Coverage for the first ninety days can be replenished after the patient has gone sixty consecutive days without being in a hospital or skilled nursing home, but a new deductible must be paid.

Sixty *lifetime days* (which, once used, cannot be replenished) can be used if a patient's hospitalization extends beyond ninety days for one period of illness. The patient has a copayment for each of these days.

Benefits cover only semiprivate rooms. HI covers neither the charges of physicians who work for the hospital nor the cost of private duty nurses.

HI deductibles and copayments (that is, cost-sharing provisions) are subject to automatic adjustments based on the trends of hospital costs. Thus, they normally change each year.

Psychiatric The benefit for psychiatric care is limited to a *lifetime maximum* of 190 days.

Posthospital Skilled Nursing Home Care Care is provided in a skilled nursing facility if (1) the patient has been hospitalized for at least three days and (2) care is started within thirty days of the patient's leaving a hospital. One hundred days of care are provided, but the patient has to pay a specified dollar copayment of the cost for each day after the twentieth day.

Home Health Services Home health-care visits are covered on an unlimited basis for part-time or intermittent care. In general, custodial care—that is, care not medically required—is not covered.

Hospice Care Hospice care can be selected by a patient who is terminally ill with a life expectancy of six months or less. The patient is entitled to two ninety-day periods of coverage. An additional thirty-day period is also available. A 5 percent coinsurance provision applies to inpatient care.

Medicare—Part B (Supplementary Medical Insurance, or SMI)

The coverage applies to physician and surgeon charges. It also applies to supplies and other medical services. "Supplies" include items used by physicians and surgeons when providing services. "Other medical services" include items such as X-rays, prosthetic devices, braces, and ambulance service. Coverage for unlimited home health-care visits on an intermittent basis is provided. Psychiatric benefits for treatment outside of hospital are limited to 62.5 percent of the first $500 of such expenses each year.

A $100 per person per year deductible applies to charges under Part B. The patient also pays 20 percent of the medical treatment costs. In addition, a patient may be responsible for items not covered by Medicare or for charges above the dollar amounts paid by Medicare. Medicare pays what it considers the reasonable charges for a medical expense under Part A or Part B. Any excess above the reasonable charges paid by Medicare must be absorbed by the patient.

As noted previously, purely custodial care is not considered a covered medical expense under Medicare. However, some custodial nursing home charges may be covered under Medicaid for those eligible for this welfare type of assistance.

Benefit Reductions

Retirement benefits and survivors benefits are reduced, based on the amount of "earnings" (wages from an employer and net earnings from self-employment) of a worker that exceeds a predetermined limit. A worker loses one dollar of benefits for each two or three dollars earned above the permissible limit. In 1993, a worker receiving retirement benefits lost $1 of his or her annual benefit for every $2 earned above the annual limit of $7,680 if between the ages of sixty-two and sixty-five and $1 for every $3 earned above $10,560 if between the ages of sixty-five and seventy. After age seventy, no reduction in benefits is made. For example, Donna began receiving her retirement benefit at age sixty-five, although she was still working. In 1993, when Donna was sixty-seven, she earned $13,002. Her Social Security retirement benefit for that year was reduced by $814 [($13,002 – $10,560) ÷ 3].

Benefit Reports

How can an individual determine the benefits he, she, or survivors can expect to receive upon retirement, disability, or death? In August 1988, the Social Security Administration announced a plan to make personalized reports—including estimates of benefits—available to all workers upon request. The form provides estimates of retirement benefits at sixty-five and seventy—and at an earlier age, if requested. A worksheet enables workers to estimate benefits based on expected future earnings. In addition, the form provides an estimate of disability and approximate survivors benefits currently available.

To obtain this personalized report, one should submit a Request for Earnings and Benefit Estimate Statement (Form SSA-7004). This form is available in local Social Security offices or by calling the toll-free number 1-800-772-1213. The Social Security Administration encourages workers to ask for a statement at least every three years.

Workers Compensation

Most employees do not consider workers compensation an employee benefit. It is, however, a part of the total package of benefits provided by an employer. In developing their personal risk management programs, employees should be aware of any workers compensation benefits they or their survivors might receive because of job-related injuries or death. However, workers compensation provides no benefits for nonoccupational injuries or diseases.

State workers compensation statutes represent the earliest widespread approach to providing some types of health coverage on a group basis. Although workers compensation benefits are paid to *employees*, workers compensation insurance actually protects *employers* against financial loss because of their liabilities under workers compensation statutes.

Covered Workers

Nearly all classes of employees must be provided access to workers compensation benefits under state or federal statutes. However, not all workers are covered under workers compensation laws. Certain workers, such as executive officers and sole proprietors, may elect to waive their workers compensation benefits. A few states allow employers who hire fewer than a stated number of employees to forgo workers compensation protection. Some states do not require benefits for farm or domestic employees or employees of nonprofit organizations. Finally, employees of common carriers operating in interstate commerce do not have to be included, but they do have their own liability system.

Benefits Available Under Workers Compensation

Workers compensation laws require that employers provide broad benefits for workers incurring job-related injuries or diseases. Benefits are available not only for a disabled employee, but also for survivors of an employee whose death is job related. Benefits are specified by state statutes, and the precise benefits vary from state to state.

Medical Coverage

The amount of medical expense coverage payable under workers compensation is generally unlimited as long as it is for necessary treatment.[4] The amount of payment for medical expenses has no impact on the other workers compensation benefits, described below, that may be available to an employee.

Disability

Four types of disability are recognized under state workers compensation laws:

- Temporary total disability
- Permanent total disability
- Temporary partial disability
- Permanent partial disability

The amount paid during a period of disability varies with the severity and duration of the disability. For example, for permanent total disability, a state may require that an employee be provided a disability benefit equal to 66 $^2/_3$ percent of his or her salary prior to disability.

States have established minimum and maximum payments that an employee can receive. These minimum amounts can be stated as a specific dollar figure or as a percentage of the *state average weekly wage*, which is the average weekly wage of employees in the same class and occupation as the injured worker in the state in which the workers compensation claim is filed.

Benefits are payable either for the term of the disability or for a maximum number of weeks. For example, in one state, permanent total disability payments are limited to 500 weeks, while another state's law requires benefits to be paid for the duration of the disability.

Most disability benefits under workers compensation are subject to waiting periods. The maximum waiting period used by any state is seven days. Normally, compensation is paid retroactive to the beginning of the disability period after a specified waiting period requirement has been satisfied. In addition, benefits are usually reduced by the amount received from Social Security.

Scheduled Injuries

In some cases, an employee loses—or loses the use of—an eye, an arm, a hand, an ear, or some other body part. When one of these losses occurs, an employee is paid a lump-sum benefit equal to disability income benefits times a specified number of weeks. For example, the loss of a hand may result in a lump sum equal to income benefits for 170 weeks. Thus, if a worker were to receive $150 a week for disability income, the lump-sum benefit for the loss of his or her hand would be $25,500 ($150 x 170).

Death Benefits

Death benefits are available under all workers compensation programs. These benefits include a burial allowance and payments to survivors. The amount of the burial allowance varies, but generally it does not exceed $3,500.

Survivors benefits are typically 66 $^2/_3$ percent of a deceased worker's wages.

Like disability payments, the maximum and minimum survivors benefits are stated as a fixed dollar amount or as a percentage of the state average weekly wage.

There is also a maximum benefit period. Although the period is usually stated in weeks, a state workers compensation law may provide that a widow receive benefits during her entire widowhood. Coverage for children generally continues until the children are over age eighteen or, if full-time students, some age such as twenty-two or twenty-five.

Rehabilitation

State workers compensation laws prescribe benefits to rehabilitate injured workers. The type of benefit varies significantly from state to state. Most state laws require that both a maintenance allowance and rehabilitation benefits be provided. An injured employee may lose benefits if he or she does not participate in a rehabilitation program.

Second Injury/Subsequent Injury Fund

An employee who is only partially disabled may still be able to work on a full-time basis. However, employers may not be willing to hire an individual who is partially disabled because another injury or the aggravation of an existing condition might result in permanent disability. To overcome this bias, states have established second injury funds, also known as subsequent injury funds. If another injury or the aggravation of preexisting injury or disease results in permanent or total disability, the employer is not required to pay benefits for the total disability. Instead, a **subsequent injury fund** or a **second injury fund** pays the difference between the benefits that would be payable because of the second illness or injury alone and the compound effect of all illnesses or injuries. The money for the operation of the second injury fund is provided through assessments levied on employers. It will be interesting to observe in the future the effect of the federal Americans with Disabilities Act passed in 1990. This law (and some comparable state laws) severely limits the legal rights of employers subject to the law to deny employment to job applicants because of existing physical disabilities.

Twenty-Four-Hour Coverage

The general concept of **twenty-four-hour coverage** is to integrate workers compensation and other employee benefits, such as medical coverage and disability income benefits, so that the benefits provided to injured or ill workers are at least partially consistent whether the injury or disease is job related or not. As a practical matter, such integration is difficult to achieve completely because workers compensation, which is statutory in nature and varies among the states, is quite different in its origins and structure from other employee benefits, which are generally voluntary and result from employer decisions or collective bargaining.

The term "twenty-four-hour coverage" can be used in several contexts. For example, sometimes it is used to mean coordinated claims management whereby a single insurer provides medical expense benefits to employees under separate workers compensation and group health policies or benefits. In other cases, it means an employer's providing supplementary coverage so that when a worker is entitled to receive certain workers compensation benefits (such as disability income), the injured or ill worker will receive at least as much as he or she would have received under the employer's regular disability income benefits program. Still another example of its use is to describe employer-provided disability income benefits in the employee benefit plan that cover both occupational and nonoccupational disabilities (that is, provide "twenty-four-hour coverage") but then deduct any disability income benefits payable under workers compensation from those otherwise payable under the employer-provided disability income plan. Group long-term disability (LTD) income insurance plans normally follow such a "twenty-four-hour coverage" approach.

Health-Care Cost Containment

One of the most pressing social and economic issues of our time has two facets: (1) how medical expense benefits should be provided to all the people and (2) how their skyrocketing costs can be contained. Another, related concern is how medical care should be financed. These are extremely difficult issues that, as of the time of this writing (April 1994), are being considered in the various proposals for health-care system reform now under debate.

Health-Care Funding

In discussing the health-care delivery system of the United States, it is helpful to consider the sources currently being used to fund personal health-care expenditures. Personal health-care expenditures include both private spending and public spending for direct health and medical services to individuals, such as expenditures for hospital care, professional services, drugs and medical sundries, and nursing home care. Thus, a wide variety of sources exist in the United States for the payment of personal medical expenses. The main sources for funding such expenditures are shown in Exhibit 2-1.

A wide variety of sources also exist in the United States for the payment of disability income benefits. This multiplicity of sources of payment presents substantial problems in the coordination of the benefits provided so that there is not overcompensation for the losses suffered. Just as in property-liability insurance lines, overinsurance is to be avoided because it tends to produce inflated and fraudulent claims, tends to result in inflation of costs, is wasteful of insurance resources, and is generally considered socially undesirable.

Exhibit 2-1
Sources of Payment of Personal Health-Care Expenditures in 1992 (in Billions)

Source of Payment	Amount of Payment*
Federal Government	258.9
Private Health Insurance	252.1
Direct Patient Payments	155.9
State and Local Governments	117.5
Other Private Funds	35.5
*Estimated	

Based on data from *Source Book of Health Insurance Data*, 1993, p. 79.

In the preceding discussions in this chapter, a number of provisions or approaches for coordinating or integrating these various types of benefits (for medical expense or disability income losses) were discussed. Some of them are as follows:

- Coordination of benefits (COB) provisions in group medical expense benefits plans (either insured or self-insured)

- Employer-provided medical expense plans, which are primary over Medicare for employees and their spouses age sixty-five and over when the employees are still actively employed

- Medicare, which is considered primary over other retiree health benefits (such as employer-provided retirement health benefits)

- Subrogation provisions in group health plans, which allow the plan to subrogate against auto and other liability recoveries

- Provisions integrating group long-term disability (LTD) plans with other group plans, other employer-provided disability benefits, Social Security disability benefits, workers compensation benefits, and other comparable plans

- The 80 percent provision coordinating workers compensation and Social Security disability benefits

- Consolidated Omnibus Budget Reconciliation Act of 1985 (COBRA) provisions regarding rights to continue employer-provided medical expense benefits

Despite all these efforts at coordination, however, overlap and gaps remain in benefits and coverage. The critical public policy issue of how the various existing systems for providing health-care benefits should be structured or integrated into a unified health-care system is hotly debated. For example, a critical issue that greatly affects the property-liability insurance industry is whether the medical benefits under workers compensation and automobile insurance should remain separate funding systems, or whether they should be integrated into some national health-care system.

Cost Containment Measures

Medical-care costs have continued to increase more rapidly than consumer prices in general. This disproportionate increase has led employers, insurers, government organizations, and individuals to seek methods for reducing the rising cost of medical care.

Cost containment measures may be characterized as cost transfer measures or cost reduction measures. **Cost transfer measures** shift health-care costs to a third party. For example, an employer can modify employee premium contributions, deductibles, or coinsurance percentages to shift a larger portion of costs to the employee. This action is cost containment *from the employer's perspective*, but not from the employee's viewpoint. **Cost reduction measures**, on the other hand, are those that actually reduce total costs for health care. For example, measures designed to reduce costly hospital stays, such as outpatient surgery, may reduce overall health-care costs.

The approaches described below illustrate some of the many cost containment measures that have been used. Some overlaps exist among these approaches, and more than one may be used in a given case.

Utilization Review

Utilization review involves an after-the-fact, or concurrent, review by a third party of the type and frequency of health-care services that have been provided. For example, an insurer might periodically review the hospital bills it pays for the employees of an employer. This is done to determine whether (1) excessive tests were authorized, (2) the right procedures were performed, (3) the right procedures were billed, and (4) bills were properly calculated.

Bills do not provide complete information, but they may indicate abuses. For example, review of a sample of billings from a particular hospital might indicate that hospital staff members take X-rays even when they are not necessary. The use of such tests could be challenged by the third-party reviewer.

Comparison of cost and utilization has been aided by the development of the concept of diagnosis-related groups, or DRGs. A DRG provides a standardized method for categorizing medical services. This makes it easier to compare the services provided by different health-care providers. The DRG concept is discussed later in this section.

Claims Audits

The purpose of a **claims audit** is to determine whether a health-care provider (for example, a hospital) has provided an accurate bill. Charging too much for a procedure, and charging for a procedure that was never performed, are examples of the errors that can be discovered. An audit can avoid payment of incorrect bills.

Preadmission Testing

Another cost containment measure is to perform tests on a patient *before* he or she enters a hospital—that is, **preadmission testing.** This serves two purposes. First, it can reduce the length of stay in a hospital. Second, it provides additional time for physicians to review the results of the tests. This can change the procedure to be used in treating a patient.

Second Opinions

Many health-care programs provide that proposed surgical procedures may be reviewed by at least two physicians. If the doctors disagree, a third opinion may be sought. Some plans even provide higher benefit levels if an insured gets a second opinion. The idea is that, by obtaining second opinions, surgical procedures that may be unnecessary or of little benefit can be avoided. On the other hand, some insurers have given up on this concept because it has not proven to be cost effective.

Outpatient Care and Alternative Facilities

Some programs are designed to provide higher benefit limits if procedures are performed on an outpatient basis (that is, if the patient does not remain in a hospital following treatment). For example, a surgical procedure might be covered completely if performed on an outpatient basis in a doctor's office or in a surgicenter, but, if it is not performed on an outpatient basis, only 70 percent of the cost may be covered. Usually, the savings that occur more than offset the increased costs that arise because a higher benefit level is being paid.

Other alternatives to remaining in a hospital for treatment include extended-care facilities and home health care. Providing coverage for using an extended-care facility or for services in the home can reduce costs. The assumption is that it is less expensive to use these alternatives than to pay for health care given in a hospital.

Copayments/Coinsurance

Many plans require the covered person to pay a portion of the medical costs (cost-sharing). The payment can require the covered person to pay either (1) a *flat amount*, such as a $250 deductible per year or $3 per prescription, or (2) a *percentage* of each dollar of covered medical costs.

Some plans, like comprehensive insurance plans, require that an insured pay a portion of the covered medical costs until a minimum, or threshold, amount is paid. For example, a comprehensive insurance plan might be designed so that the insured pays 20 percent of the covered medical costs until he or she has paid $2,000—after which 100 percent of subsequent covered medical costs are paid by the employer.

It is thought that adding such cost-sharing measures to a plan or increasing existing ones will reduce the cost for the employer and may discourage overutilization.

Diagnosis-Related Groups

Instead of paying hospital in-patient benefits on the basis of "reasonable charges," Medicare uses a system whereby hospital cases are classified into **diagnostic-related groups (DRGs)**. Reimbursement for a given treatment is determined in part by the applicable DRG. A medical-care provider is reimbursed the amount allotted by the government for a specific medical service, regardless of the amount the provider may charge. The intent is to force the health-care provider to provide services within the guidelines established by the government.

Employers and insurers may also use DRGs to control costs. Some use the DRGs established by the federal government. Others have devised their own systems.

Life-Style Modification ("Wellness" Programs)

Another method aimed at reducing health-care costs is **life-style modification (LSM)**, also known as **"wellness" programs**. The goal is to change the habits and activities of the insured individuals so that their morbidity declines.

A precursor to the LSM approach has existed for years—the antismoking movement. However, the focus now is on all aspects of an individual's life. The "wellness" approach considers the following areas:

- Diet
- Exercise
- Smoking
- Relaxation
- Prevention of substance abuse

Most of the other cost-containment methods that have been described focus on reducing costs when a medical-care procedure is required. The LSM focuses on loss prevention. Unfortunately, it is difficult to quantify the impact of LSM, especially in the short run.

Alternative Health-Care Systems

Some employers have turned to alternative health-care delivery systems—in particular, managed-care systems like HMOs and PPOs—to provide benefits to their employees. Since HMOs require only a fixed payment per employee per policy period, the risk of increasing medical costs may be partially absorbed by the health-care provider.

Providers of health-care services, insurance companies, and consumers have also sought alternative health-care delivery systems—that is, they too have attempted to develop a "managed" approach to health care. The need for managed health-care delivery and reimbursement systems has arisen because of the increasing cost of providing medical expense insurance benefits and the increasing demand for medical-care services.

Traditional group health insurance plans generally have concentrated on reimbursing either patients or selected health-care providers but not on actually providing or organizing health care. On the other hand, two alternative systems—health maintenance organizations (HMOs) and preferred provider organizations (PPOs)—do attempt to provide or arrange for health care as well as perform the financing function. Hence the term *managed care systems* may be used to refer to them. However, the term managed care is not precisely defined and may be used by some in other contexts of controlling health-care costs as well.

As explained in Chapter 1, HMOs and PPOs differ from traditional group health insurance in that they both finance and provide health-care services. A contractual agreement is usually established between a health-care purchaser, like an employer or insurer, and an HMO or health-care providers for a PPO. Under most of these agreements, the HMO or PPO providers agree to deliver health-care services for fees negotiated in advance. Hence, the purchaser is managing in varying degrees from whom health-care services are being purchased and at what prices.

An additional characteristic of these plans is the use of primary care physicians or gatekeepers (also as discussed in Chapter 1). Patients must contact or visit their primary care physicians before visiting another physician—usually a specialist. This requirement helps HMOs and PPOs to prevent overuse of expensive specialists by the plan members, and thus keeps down the costs of the entire plan.

Other Cost Considerations

The cost of health care continues to rise but, as of April 1994, at a decreasing rate. The cost is affected by many factors other than abuses and the general health of the population. Professional liability insurance premiums, new medical procedures, general inflationary trends, and an aging population with an extended life expectancy all have an impact on medical-care costs. While cost containment has been a concern of many health insurance programs, a particular emphasis has been placed on cost containment in recent years. It is also a central element in the various health-care reform proposals.

Summary

This chapter continued the analysis of health benefits, emphasizing group coverages, individual policy underwriting, social health coverages, and health-care cost containment. In this context, it discussed workers compensation benefits, standard group health insurance, Social Security and Medicare, the importance of reducing health-care costs, and self-funding and integrated health-care systems, among other subjects.

Group health insurance provides coverage primarily for medical expenses that are not work-related. Group health insurance is typically selected by employers for employees and by other group sponsors for group members. The benefits available and the amount of premium contributed by the employer vary. Group health insurance may include disability income coverage as well as dental-care benefits. The sponsor's decisions regarding group coverages are influenced by many factors, including cost and members' needs.

Group health insurance is not the only means by which a group sponsor, especially an employer, may provide such benefits. Alternative funding arrangements include fully self-funding to partially self-funding and hiring an administrator.

Three other means of treating sickness and injury exposures—individual health insurance, OASDHI, and workers compensation—are also examined. OASDHI provides retirement, disability, survivors, and medical-care benefits for workers and their families. Included in the discussion of individual health insurance are individual underwriting and rating factors and the terms of renewability (continuance) of coverage.

Workers compensation pays benefits to most classes of employees and their families for job-related injuries or diseases. In doing so, it protects employers against financial loss because of liability under workers compensation statutes. The benefits available under workers compensation include medical coverage, disability income payments, payment for scheduled injuries, death benefits, and rehabilitation benefits.

An important part of the chapter concentrates on the issue of health-care costs. Nine measures are suggested for containing costs: utilization review, claims audits, preadmission testing, second opinions, outpatient care and alternative facilities, copayments/coinsurance, diagnosis-related groups, life-style modification, and alternative health-care systems.

Chapter Notes

1. Texas Insurance Code, Art. 3, 51-6, § 2.
2. The law permits those, relatively few, persons who are age sixty-five or older and who are not otherwise eligible for Medicare to enroll voluntarily. However, such enrollees must pay the full monthly cost of their coverage. Such voluntary enrollees may enroll in SMI alone or in SMI and HI together.
3. The benefits may increase for two reasons: (1) for each month beyond normal retirement age a delayed retirement credit is earned, and (2) the earnings upon which benefits are based may be higher in the years worked beyond age sixty-five.
4. Although a state law sets forth guidelines for unlimited medical expenses for most injuries and diseases, there may be some exceptions for one or more diseases. For example, limited medical coverage may be provided for silicosis or asbestosis.

Chapter 3

Planning for Death

One of the facts of life is that death is inevitable. Although death is a certainty and cannot be avoided, the timing of a person's death is uncertain. As a result, many people try to prolong their lives as much as possible. In managing the death exposure, people use loss control—such as exercising daily, eating healthful foods, and receiving periodic physical examinations. People also manage the death exposure by active retention—such as prearranging and prepaying for burial services and accumulating personal wealth to provide for their dependents. However, the most common technique for managing the risk of death is life insurance.

The purchase of life insurance is a major consideration for many people. It should not be an impetuous purchase. People should consider their need for life insurance and develop a plan to purchase the types and amount of life insurance that best meet their needs.

Chapters 3 and 4 focus on the issues involved in the purchase of life insurance. Chapter 3 describes how to analyze the life insurance needs of individuals and families and discusses the most common provisions of life insurance policies. Then, Chapter 4 describes the available life insurance products and their uses.

The Exposure to Death

The exposure to death differs from the exposures to property loss, liability, and illness or injury in two important ways:

1. The exposure to death can involve long periods of time.
2. The exposure to death does not result in partial losses.

Duration of Life

Most property and liability insurance and health insurance contracts are written for relatively short time periods. However, life insurance contracts can remain in effect for the insured's lifetime and often are carried for many years. For example, a policy purchased on a young insured and kept in force at retirement might pay benefits to the insured for many years during retirement and then still pay significant death benefits to beneficiaries after the insured's death. Life insurance contracts can easily be effective for seventy or more years.

The duration of life insurance contracts is partly due to the nature of the death exposure, which requires a long-term approach to insurance. With the use of mortality tables, life insurance actuaries have been able to predict with a high degree of accuracy the **mortality rates** (the probabilities of death at specific ages) of large groups of people. Life insurance policies are not cancelable by the insurer and are, in fact, intended to be continuable at the option of the policyowner for the appropriate policy period, which can be for life. Moreover, premium rates and certain rating factors (such as minimum interest rates) might be guaranteed for the life of the policy.

On the other hand, with regard to property-liability insurance, it is difficult to predict confidently how the claims experience of a group will change over time, and the insurability of any given exposure can change rapidly. Therefore, property-liability contracts generally contain provisions giving the insurer the right to cancel upon proper notice to the insured, subject to applicable statutes. Likewise, property-liability insurers often reserve the right to increase premium rates upon renewal or to refuse renewal.

No Partial Losses

Frequent partial losses are typically the case in property insurance, and they may be dealt with by deductibles and coinsurance requirements. However, since there can be no such thing as a "partial death" in life insurance, deductibles and coinsurance requirements are not used in life insurance policies.

Life Insurance Considerations

Because the loss exposure treated with life insurance differs from the loss exposures treated by property and liability insurance and health insurance, the contracts for these different types of insurance also differ. The ways in which they differ can be divided into three categories: (1) the nature of the insurance contract, (2) the factors that affect the cost of the insurance, and (3) contract standardization. These topics are discussed below.

Life Insurance Versus Property and Liability Insurance

Certain features of life insurance policies set these contracts apart from property and liability insurance and health insurance policies. These features are discussed below.

Valued Policy Versus Contract of Indemnity

A distinction is made between **contracts of indemnity**—(which are intended to replace sums actually lost because of a covered event) and **valued policies**—(which pay a preestablished sum if an insured event occurs). Life insurance contracts are valued policies, because the face amount of the policy is paid in the event of the insured's death. Few property insurance contracts are valued policies. Generally, valued policies are employed in property insurance when it is difficult or impossible to establish the monetary extent of a loss at the time of loss—such as when coverage is written on fine arts.

Because life insurance policy limits often are not based on an objective method for placing a value on an insured life and because life insurers are not concerned with *underindemnity* (when the insured receives less than the amount lost), coinsurance and replacement cost clauses are not used in life insurance contracts. Furthermore, because life insurers are not concerned with coordinating coverage when more than one policy covers a single life, problems such as determining how much other insurance policies should pay do not exist. As a consequence, typical property-liability insurance provisions such as subrogation, appraisal, and "other insurance" clauses are not found in life insurance contracts.

Since life insurance policies are valued policies without coinsurance, deductibles, and replacement cost considerations, submitting death claims usually requires only that the insurance company be furnished with legal proof of an insured's death. This process is often much less complex than that required when filing a property, liability, or health claim.

Evidence of Insurable Interest

To obtain insurance coverage, insureds or potential insureds must establish an **insurable interest**—an exposure to financial loss if the item or person being insured is harmed. An applicant for life insurance must show insurable interest when applying for the life insurance. Once the life insurance is in force and is maintained, the policy benefits will be paid (subject to other policy conditions)—regardless of whether the insurable interest still exists at the time of the insured's death. For example, a married couple purchases life insurance on each spouse. They later divorce. The husband maintains his policy on his former wife's life by making the required premium payments, although he will no longer suffer a financial loss when she dies. If she should die while the policy is in force, the death benefit will be paid to the beneficiary.

Property and liability policies, on the other hand, require proof of insurable interest at the time of the loss.

The Whole Contract

For property and liability policies, the whole insurance contract consists of the declarations page, the policy, and its endorsements. With respect to life insurance, however, the application is also included in the policy contract.

Factors That Impact the Cost

The main factors influencing the premium cost of individual life insurance policies are the *mortality* of the insured group, *interest* (or investment returns) earned on funds held to support the policy, and the *expenses* of the insurance company in writing and administering the policy. The relative importance of these cost factors in individual life insurance depends on the type of policy being considered and on the pricing strategies of the particular life insurer.

Mortality Charge

The **mortality charge** estimates the cost of the expected death experience for the insureds.

Using calculations beyond the scope of this text, life insurers use mortality rates and life expectancies to estimate mortality expenses for their insureds and, thus, develop the mortality charge for life insurance premiums. The mortality rates and life expectancies used by a particular life insurer for determining rates are typically based on the current experience of the lives insured by that insurer and might be recorded in a mortality table similar in form to the Commissioner's 1980 Standard Ordinary Mortality Table (C.S.O. 80) reproduced in Exhibit 3-1. The C.S.O. 80, however, is based on mortality rates and life expectancy data from insurance company experience for 1970 to 1975 and is used primarily for valuing life insurance company liabilities and determining minimum nonforfeiture values (discussed later in this chapter). Hence, it is often referred to as a statutory table.

The C.S.O. 80 provides the mortality rates and life expectancy for males and females at ages zero through 100. (For the statistics contained in the table, everyone is assumed to die by age 100.) For example, the table shows that at age forty, the male mortality rate is 3.02, which means that roughly three of every one-thousand forty-year-old males will die before their next birthday. At the same age, the life expectancy for a male is 34.05, which indicates that if a man survives his fortieth year, he is expected to live about thirty-four more years.

Exhibit 3-1 illustrates that females have lower death rates than males. For this reason, females usually pay less than males per $1,000 unit of life insurance. Life insurers usually have separate mortality tables for males and females.

Because cigarette smoking affects the mortality rates of both males and females, life insurers account for a person's smoking experience in life insurance premiums. Nonsmokers usually pay less than smokers, per unit of life insurance. Many life insurers maintain separate mortality tables for nonsmokers and smokers.

Interest

When life insurers receive life insurance premiums, most of the premiums are set aside in investments until the funds are needed to pay policy death benefits. Because most insureds live for many years, the life insurer may invest premium dollars for a long time and accumulate interest and other investment income over that period. Life insurers consider expected investment experience when calculating premiums. Profitable investment experience decreases the overall cost of life insurance to insureds.

Expense Charge

Life insurance companies have operating and administrative expenses. A portion of each premium, known as the **expense charge**, covers these expenses. The expense charge is calculated and paid per unit of life insurance. This means that insureds who purchase larger life insurance policies may pay more towards expenses. Yet, at some point, the additional cost per unit of life insurance is near zero. In recognition of this, life insurers might offer discounts—in effect, a bulk discount—to insureds that purchase large life insurance policies. For example, premium rates are often *banded*, meaning that insurers charge lower rates per $1,000 as coverage amounts increase from one band to another. Thus an insurer might establish four bands of policy limits: $25,000 to $49,999, $50,000 to $99,999, $100,000 to $249,999, and $250,000 plus. The highest rate will be charged for policies in the $25,000-to-$49,999 band, and the lowest rate will be charged to policies in the $250,000-plus band.

Group Insurance Considerations

For group life insurance, group underwriting and rating methods are used. Therefore, while mortality, expenses, and interest still apply, they have

Exhibit 3-1
Mortality Table

	Commissioners 1980 Standard Ordinary (1970-1975)								
	Male		Female			Male		Female	
Age	Deaths per 1,000	Expectation of Life (Years)	Deaths per 1,000	Expectation of Life (Years)	Age	Deaths per 1,000	Expectation of Life (Years)	Deaths per 1,000	Expectation of Life (Years)
0	4.18	70.83	2.89	75.83	46	4.92	28.76	3.80	33.00
1	1.07	70.13	.87	75.04	47	5.32	27.90	4.05	32.12
2	.99	69.20	.81	74.11	48	5.74	27.04	4.33	31.25
3	.98	68.27	.79	73.17	49	6.21	26.20	4.63	30.39
4	.95	67.34	.77	72.23	50	6.71	25.36	4.96	29.53
5	.90	66.40	.76	71.28	51	7.30	24.52	5.31	28.67
6	.86	65.46	.73	70.34	52	7.96	23.70	5.70	27.82
7	.80	64.52	.72	69.39	53	8.71	22.89	6.15	26.98
8	.76	63.57	.70	68.44	54	9.56	22.08	6.61	26.14
9	.74	62.62	.69	67.48	55	10.47	21.29	7.09	25.31
10	.73	61.66	.68	66.53	56	11.46	20.51	7.57	24.49
11	.77	60.71	.69	65.58	57	12.49	19.74	8.03	23.67
12	.85	59.75	.72	64.62	58	13.59	18.99	8.47	22.86
13	.99	58.80	.75	63.67	59	14.77	18.24	8.94	22.05
14	1.15	57.86	.80	62.71	60	16.08	17.51	9.47	21.25
15	1.33	56.93	.85	61.76	61	17.54	16.79	10.13	20.44
16	1.51	56.00	.90	60.82	62	19.19	16.08	10.96	19.65
17	1.67	55.09	.95	59.87	63	21.06	15.38	12.02	18.86
18	1.78	54.18	.98	58.93	64	23.14	14.70	13.25	18.08
19	1.86	53.27	1.02	57.98	65	25.42	14.04	14.59	17.32
20	1.90	52.37	1.05	57.04	66	27.85	13.39	16.00	16.57
21	1.91	51.47	1.07	56.10	67	30.44	12.76	17.43	15.83
22	1.89	50.57	1.09	55.16	68	33.19	12.14	18.84	15.10
23	1.86	49.66	1.11	54.22	69	36.17	11.54	20.36	14.38
24	1.82	48.75	1.14	53.28	70	39.51	10.96	22.11	13.67
25	1.77	47.84	1.16	52.34	71	43.30	10.39	24.23	12.97
26	1.73	46.93	1.19	51.40	72	47.65	9.84	26.87	12.28
27	1.71	46.01	1.22	50.46	73	52.64	9.30	30.11	11.60
28	1.70	45.09	1.26	49.52	74	58.19	8.79	33.93	10.95
29	1.71	44.16	1.30	48.59	75	64.19	8.31	38.24	10.32
30	1.73	43.24	1.35	47.65	76	70.53	7.84	42.97	9.71
31	1.78	42.31	1.40	46.71	77	77.12	7.40	48.04	9.12
32	1.83	41.38	1.45	45.78	78	83.90	6.97	53.45	8.55
33	1.91	40.46	1.50	44.84	79	91.05	6.57	59.35	8.01
34	2.00	39.54	1.58	43.91	80	98.84	6.18	65.99	7.48
35	2.11	38.61	1.65	42.98	81	107.48	5.80	73.60	6.98
36	2.24	37.69	1.76	42.05	82	117.25	5.44	82.40	6.49
37	2.40	36.78	1.89	41.12	83	128.26	5.09	92.53	6.03
38	2.58	35.87	2.04	40.20	84	140.25	4.77	103.81	5.59
39	2.79	34.96	2.22	39.28	85	152.95	4.46	116.10	5.18
40	3.02	34.05	2.42	38.36	86	166.09	4.18	129.29	4.80
41	3.29	33.16	2.64	37.46	87	179.55	3.91	143.32	4.43
42	3.56	32.26	2.87	36.55	88	193.27	3.66	158.18	4.09
43	3.87	31.38	3.09	35.66	89	207.29	3.41	173.94	3.77
44	4.19	30.50	3.32	34.77	90	221.77	3.18	190.75	3.45
45	4.55	29.62	3.56	33.88	91	236.98	2.94	208.87	3.15

Exhibit 3-1
Mortality Table (continued)

	Male		Female			Male		Female	
Age	Deaths per 1,000	Expec- tation of Life (Years)	Deaths per 1,000	Expec- tation of Life (Years)	Age	Deaths per 1,000	Expec- tation of Life (Years)	Deaths per 1,000	Expec- tation of Life (Years)
92	253.45	2.70	228.81	2.85	104				
93	272.11	2.44	251.51	2.55	105				
94	295.90	2.17	279.31	2.24	106				
95	329.96	1.87	317.32	1.91	107				
96	384.55	1.54	375.74	1.56	108				
97	480.20	1.20	474.97	1.21	109				
98	657.98	.84	655.85	.84	110				
99	1,000.00	.50	1,000.00	.50	111				
100					112				
101					113				
102					114				
103					115				

Note: Mortality rates contained in the 1980 Commissioners Standard Ordinary Table were obtained from experience of 1970-1975, but contain an added element designed to generate life insurance reserves of a conservative nature in keeping with the long-term guarantees inherent in life insurance contracts. Premiums for life insurance policies, on the other hand, are based on assumptions that include expected mortality experience.

Mortality rates for the 1983 Individual Annuity Tables are, again, conservative as related to the actual and projected experience upon which they are based.

Projected to 1983

different effects and are treated differently. For example, because individuals covered by group life insurance are not individually underwritten, mortality costs might be higher than for individual policies. On the other hand, expenses are usually lower for group insurance.

Other Considerations

The premium cost of individual life insurance may not be the final measure of what the policy's "cost" to the consumer will be. For example, some policies, known as **participating policies**, provide for policy dividends. Policy dividends are considered a refund of paid premiums and may be taken as cash or be used to reduce the next period's premium, among other options that are discussed later in the chapter. The payment of policy dividends reduces the insured's cost for the life insurance policy. Thus, the amount of dividends a life insurer pays on a particular policy will be an important determinant of the final cost of the policy to consumers. Similarly, some life contracts (as explained in Chapter 4), consider current mortality, interest, and expense experience of the life insurer when calculating policy values. Methods for analyzing the "true" cost of individual life insurance are discussed later in this chapter.

Contract Standardization

Life insurance policies are not standard as such. However, a substantial degree of policy similarity exists because state laws require the inclusion of some policy provisions and companies have similar practices.

State laws neither require any standard policy format nor prescribe the exact wording of policy provisions. However, they deal with (1) mandatory, (2) permissible, and (3) prohibited provisions. They permit wording different from that in the law if the change is beneficial to policyowners. If a mandatory provision is omitted from a policy, the courts interpret the policy as though it includes the mandatory provision. Similarly, the courts ignore any prohibited provision contained in a policy. The result is that life insurance policies differ somewhat from each other in general appearance and format, but they are very similar in terms of policy provisions.

Life Insurance Planning

Social insurance and group insurance participants have few, if any, decisions to make regarding the benefits received through these programs. Participation in a social insurance program such as OASDHI is usually not voluntary, and the type and amount of benefits provided are beyond the control of individual participants. A participant in a group life insurance plan also has limited flexibility, because the type and perhaps the amount of benefits are predetermined. However, many modern group life insurance plans allow participants some flexibility in choosing the amounts of coverage they will have on their lives.

Individual life insurance, however, requires an individual to make a number of decisions. A life insurance program should be based on a comprehensive plan that recognizes the existence of social insurance as well as employment benefits.

Analysis of Life Insurance Needs

The first step in life insurance planning is to analyze the life insurance needs of the individual. These needs may be classified into two categories:

1. Family needs
2. Business and estate planning needs

The remainder of this chapter concentrates on family needs. Business situations and estate planning often involve different and additional life insurance needs, which are discussed in Chapter 8.

The analysis of personal life insurance needs requires answers to two questions:

1. *How much* money would be needed for specific purposes by the family if a given individual were to die immediately? It is necessary to base the approach on the assumption that the person will die immediately because this is the only method of determining one's *current* life insurance needs. Because life insurance needs change over time, a life insurance program should be reevaluated periodically.

2. *When* would the money be needed? Some money will be needed immediately to settle the decedent's estate; other needs, such as children's college expenses, may not require cash until some time in the future.

Many steps are involved in the analysis of personal life insurance needs. One of the first steps involves setting personal goals with respect to financial needs.

Individuals and families, and people who give them planning advice, need to determine which goals apply and how to assign priorities to those goals. This generally requires extensive information gathering and is best accomplished with the use of a checklist. A portion of one such checklist is reproduced in Exhibit 3-2.

The following pages include descriptions of many items considered in the checklist, which commonly require cash after the death of an income earner. Whether an item is applicable to a specific individual depends on the goals or objectives of that individual. For example, some people want to provide an income to a nonworking surviving spouse after dependent children become self-sufficient; this amount would appear in 3-E in Exhibit 3-2. In other cases in which both spouses are actively working outside the home, such income might not be necessary or the required income amount might be reduced.

Complete financial information is required to ascertain the appropriate amounts needed for the various checklist items. For example, items 3-A and 3-B of Exhibit 3-2 ask for the amount of outstanding debts. It is important to know these amounts and whether they will become due immediately upon a person's death.

Estate Settlement Fund

The most immediate need for funds upon death is to pay death expenses and to liquidate outstanding financial obligations. This is accomplished by means of an "estate settlement fund," which is also called a "cleanup fund," an "executor fund," or a "probate fund."

Exhibit 3-2
Insurance Planning Checklist

Estate Data

1. Amount of life insurance coverage from policies in event of death:
   _____

2. Members of family:
   A. Husband: _____   Date of Birth: _____
   B. Wife: _____   Date of Birth: _____
   C. Children: _____ Date of Birth: _____
      _____
      _____
      _____
      _____

   D. Other Dependents
      Name: _____ Relation: _____
      _____   _____
      _____   _____
      _____   _____
      _____   _____

3. Income needs of family in event of a death:
   A. Cash to pay bills—medical, funeral, taxes, and so on:
      _____

   B. Cash to liquidate mortgages, chattels, and so on:
      _____

   C. Monthly income to family during school years:
      _____

   D. Funds for college or specialized training:
      $_____
      at:_____
   E. Monthly income to spouse after children are grown:
      _____

4. Income or endowment to others—in detail:
   _____

5. What do you estimate your gross estate to be?
   _____

6. Is it advisable to set up a corporate trust?
   _____

7. Do you have a will?_____
   Date written:_____
   Where is it?_____
8. Does your spouse have a will?_____
9. Have arrangements been made for minor children?_____
10. Where do you keep valuable papers (deeds, securities, etc.)
    _____

Exhibit 3-2
Insurance Planning Checklist (continued)

11. Where do you keep your life insurance policies?

12. Where do you keep your general insurance policies?

13. Are you eligible for Social Security death benefits?

14. What amount of group life insurance do you have?

15. What amount of individual life insurance do you have?

16. Do you have any death benefits under retirement plans?
    If so, how much?

17. What types of life insurance coverage do you have?

18. Who is your beneficiary under your life insurance policies?

19. Do your insurance policies contain some provision to handle common disaster?

20. What types of investments do you have?

21. What is the financial size of your spouse's estate?

22. Does your estate qualify for the marital deduction?

23. Do you live in a community property state?

The purpose of an **estate settlement fund** is to pay expenses such as last-illness costs in excess of medical insurance, burial expenses, outstanding financial obligations, expenses of estate administration, and taxes.

Most amounts required for the estate settlement fund can be estimated with reasonable accuracy at a given point in time. However, the expenses of a last illness depend largely on the nature and duration of the disability before death and the amount of health insurance available.

Furthermore, the amount estimated for the estate settlement fund can quickly become dated since the component expenses in this need change from year to year. Finally, the size of the estate settlement fund varies with the size of the estate, which itself might fluctuate.

Readjustment Period Income

Most families are unable or unwilling to pay insurance premiums sufficient to provide surviving dependents with as much income as they enjoyed while the breadwinner was alive. Consequently, a family's income (from all sources including life insurance) typically decreases after the breadwinner's death.

It is considered advisable that the reduction in standard of living not be forced upon the family immediately after the breadwinner dies, but rather that the income level be maintained at the previous level for a period of time called the **readjustment period**. If the reduction is to be slight, a relatively short time (perhaps one year) is considered sufficient for the readjustment period. If, on the other hand, a major decrease is required, the readjustment period should be longer (perhaps two years or more). For example, Amanda and Brett are a married couple and are considering the purchase of life insurance on each other's life. Brett works part time outside their home. Amanda works full time and contributes 80 percent of the family income. The family might need only six months to adjust to a loss of 20 percent of their income if Brett dies, while it might need two years to adjust if Amanda dies.

Dependency Period Income

Most breadwinners feel a responsibility to ensure that their children have sufficient resources to live comfortably until the children become self-sufficient. The amount of income received from insurance during the children's **dependency period** is a matter of personal choice. This period can be considered to terminate when a child reaches the age of eighteen. If the children are college-bound, the dependency period may be extended to their anticipated age at graduation. Children with physical or mental handicaps might be dependent for their full lifetime.

For purposes of simplicity, the dependency period is considered by some to extend from the present until the time when the *youngest* child reaches age eighteen. In the actual computation of needs, it is more accurate to compute the amount needed for each child. If, for example, the children are ages eight and sixteen, the dependency period is not ten years. Instead, it is ten years for one child and two years for the other.

In addition to dependency period income for children, other dependents such as aging parents might need to be considered. Breadwinners might wish to ensure that these dependents are able to live comfortably until they die. Thus, the length of the dependency period and the desired or required income needs should be estimated for each dependent.

Life Income for Surviving Spouse

Historically, husbands have felt a moral obligation to provide a lifetime income for their widows, since many wives devoted their energies to the role of homemaker and did not develop or maintain employment skills. The situation today is much different and more diverse since in the majority of households both spouses work outside the home. However, even today, a surviving spouse, whether male or female, might not be able to live on only his or her income and might need an additional amount of income. Hence, life income for the surviving spouse should be applied to fit each family's situation and objectives.

Social Security provides an amount of dependency period income and life income for the surviving spouse. However, the surviving spouse's dependency period benefits cease when the youngest child reaches age sixteen, unless the child is disabled, and the life income benefits do not begin until the surviving spouse reaches age sixty (fifty if disabled). The period between the end of dependency period benefits and the start of life income or retirement benefits is referred to as the **blackout period**. Benefits for this period can be included as part of the life income for surviving spouse considerations. As with the life income needs, the need for blackout period income will be different for each family's situation and should be applied to fit the circumstances.

Mortgage Redemption

It can be desirable to pay off any remaining balance on a home mortgage if the breadwinner dies, since the complete and free ownership of a home relieves the survivors of a major financial obligation and simplifies the family's budgetary planning. Furthermore, there is some personal satisfaction in knowing that the family will not be forced to move from the family residence.

Certain circumstances exist when it is advantageous *not* to redeem the mortgage. For example, if the mortgage interest rate is favorable compared to the current market rate of interest, it might be wiser to invest any available money in higher interest-bearing investments. Paying off the mortgage might work to the detriment of the survivor.

Life insurance policies specifying the mortgage holder (lender) as the beneficiary (referred to as "mortgage life" policies) do not give the surviving family members the option of leaving the mortgage in place and using the proceeds for alternative purposes. Preserving that option can require changing the beneficiary designation of life insurance polices. Such a change of beneficiary might not be permitted with some forms of credit life insurance available through lending institutions.

Education Funds

Dependency period income provides funds for the education of children through secondary school. If the dependency period is considered to terminate at age eighteen and a college education is planned, additional funds will be needed. The time at which such funds are necessary is easy to determine, but the amount needed is difficult to estimate. If children are not near college age, an estimate based on projected costs is available from the education industry.

Extra Expense Fund

It is sound practice to establish an emergency fund as part of a general financial plan, not just as a life insurance consideration. However, income during the readjustment and dependency periods is likely to be less than desired, and, as a result, a financial emergency during this period could disrupt financial plans. An additional amount of emergency funds, which might be referred to as an **extra expense fund**, can be desirable in the event of the death of a breadwinner.

The size of the extra expense fund is a matter of judgment. An emergency fund of $5,000 to $10,000 is considered reasonable for most families. Some experts express the size of the emergency fund in terms of three or six months' income. For example, suppose a family currently has an emergency fund of $4,000 (one breadwinner's monthly salary), which it considers satisfactory as long as both spouses are alive and working. However, the family anticipates that a $10,000 emergency fund (2.5 times the monthly salary) will be needed if a breadwinner dies. The family should include a $6,000 extra expense fund among its life insurance needs.

Exhibit 3-3 shows a time line that includes each of the needs discussed in this section. It summarizes the timing of each of the needs and illustrates how the entire financial needs package fits together.

Insurance on Other Income Producers

Some families have only one breadwinner, but, as noted earlier, in many families today both spouses are employed outside the home. Logically, both lives should be insured to the extent that the death of either represents an income loss to the family.

The life of a spouse who works only in the home might also need to be insured because the spouse's death would involve death costs and, in many cases, future expenses. For example, the death of such a spouse would create a need for an estate settlement fund, and additional future expenses can be incurred for a housekeeper, child care, and like services.

Exhibit 3-3
Financial Needs Time Line

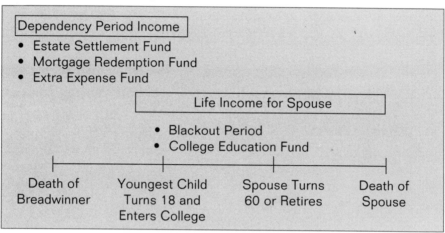

Arranging Life Insurance To Meet a Family's Needs

Purchasing life insurance to meet a single need without adequate consideration of other needs and resources may result in costly inefficiencies. Life insurance should be purchased as a method of solving interrelated financial problems, and this calls for a comprehensive plan that considers all important life insurance needs. The two basic methods for planning an individual life insurance program are programming and capital need analysis. Each method is discussed below.

Programming

The use of **programming** to plan an individual's or a family's life insurance needs involves three steps:

1. Determining the financial objectives of the individual or family
2. Establishing the extent to which existing resources meet the financial objectives
3. Estimating the additional amount of life insurance (if any) needed to meet the financial objectives

The programming process can be complex and generally requires the use of a computer program and the aid of a life insurance agent or a financial consultant. For these reasons, each of the steps is only briefly described below.

Determining Financial Objectives

First, the amount of money needed to meet each life insurance need, assuming the individual were to die immediately, must be determined. This assumption is necessary to determine the amount of life insurance needed *at the present time*.

A portion of this need can be determined easily, such as in the case of a mortgage redemption fund. However, most life insurance needs are difficult to measure because they cannot be estimated objectively. For example, the amount of income needed during the dependency period depends on the standard of living desired after the income earner dies and the rate of inflation during the period. Despite these problems, programming necessitates the estimation of the amount of money needed to meet each need, as well as the time at which income must begin and how long it should continue.

Evaluating Existing Resources

As a second step, the extent to which the family's needs are currently being met must be evaluated. Consideration should be given to Social Security benefits and any existing group or individual life insurance policies covering the breadwinner. The amount of lump-sum benefits and income benefits provided by these plans should be determined.

Determining Amount of Additional Insurance Needed

Upon completing the first two steps, the amounts needed and the amounts currently available can be compared to determine whether any additional insurance is needed to meet the family's needs. Such factors as interest rates, inflation, the length and timing of the benefit payments, and the amount of benefits are considered. The calculations can be complex and are beyond the scope of this text.

Advantages and Limitations

The main advantage of programming is that it provides a reasonably accurate method for matching needs with life insurance policies. Furthermore, the process can be adapted to recognize needs for disability and retirement purposes.

Detailed projections require the use of a computer. A computer is especially useful in exploring a variety of "what if" alternatives. Many different programming packages are available. Individuals and families, however, must keep in mind that the results from any package are only estimates.

Programming's objective is to determine a person's current life insurance needs; therefore, it must be assumed that the individual dies immediately. Thus, programming should be updated periodically as the individual's circumstances change.

Capital Need Analysis

A newer, relatively simple, and increasingly popular approach to life insurance planning is called **capital need analysis**. The assumption underlying capital need analysis is that all income needs will be met from investment earnings and that the estate will be kept intact (not liquidated) and available for the younger generation after the surviving spouse dies. This method indicates larger insurance needs than those derived from the programming approach, which is built on the assumption that all investments will be consumed during the lifetime of the surviving spouse. Both approaches require similar information to carry out the analysis.

Once the family has identified its future financial income and lump-sum needs, capital need analysis involves three steps:

1. Determining the current value of the estate
2. Estimating the amount of income-producing capital available to meet the financial objectives
3. Estimating the income position of the survivors

Determining the Current Value of the Estate

The first step for capital need analysis is to determine how much wealth the family has already accumulated. This entails constructing a personal balance sheet for the family. The balance sheet shows the current value of the estate and helps to evaluate how much wealth has to be accumulated to meet the family's financial needs.

The logic of capital need analysis is developed by means of an extended example. Assume that Wendy's personal balance sheet is as shown in Exhibit 3-4. In addition to the assets listed, Wendy receives $50,000 of life insurance as an employee benefit and she owns a $140,000 individual insurance policy on her life.

Determining the Amount of Income-Producing Capital

The second step in capital need analysis is to estimate the amount of capital available at Wendy's death to meet the income needs of her family. The calculation of Wendy's income-producing capital is shown in Exhibit 3-5. The amount of Wendy's assets and life insurance benefits (which will be paid to her family in the event of her death) is reduced by the following amounts:

1. Wendy's liabilities (line 2). Upon her death, her estate might be obligated to pay off all her bills and notes.
2. Taxes and costs of administration (line 3). These represent the costs of settling Wendy's estate.[1]
3. Wendy's family's lump-sum needs (lines 4 and 5). Wendy's survivors plan to pay off the mortgage at Wendy's death, and Wendy's eleven-year-old daughter plans to go to college.

Exhibit 3-4
Balance Sheet for Wendy*

	Assets	
Net equity in home		
Market value $200,000 Mortgage $120,000		$ 80,000
Personal property		40,000
Securities		66,500
Checking and savings accounts		3,500
Other assets		20,000
Total (Net of Mortgage)		$210,000
	Liabilities	
Current bills		$ 4,000
Notes		6,000
Total		$ 10,000

* Since the entire capital need analysis process involves estimates, it is not necessary to calculate to the penny. Consequently, all figures have been rounded to the nearest $500, and minor assets and liabilities have been ignored.

Exhibit 3-5
Capital Analysis for Wendy's Family

Line			
1A	Total assets (net of mortgage)	$210,000	
1B	Total life insurance benefits	190,000	
1C	Total funds available		$400,000
2	Liabilities	$ 10,000	
3	Taxes and costs of administration	13,000	
4	Payment of mortgage	120,000	
5	Cost of education	40,000	
6	Nonincome-producing property	120,000	
7	Total deductions		303,000
8	Capital available for income		$ 97,000

4. Nonincome producing property (line 6). Included are assets that do not produce any family income, such as equity in the home and personal property.

The total deductions from Wendy's assets are shown on line 7. The difference

Exhibit 3-6

Income Analysis for Wendy's Family

Line			
1	Present income		$60,000
2	Income objective (60 percent of line 1)		36,000
	Estimated income to be provided		
3	Capital available for income ($97,000 at 5 percent)	4,850	
4	Social Security and other government benefits	17,000	
5	Other income	0	
6	Total income provided now		$ 21,850
7	Income shortage		$ 14,150
8	Total new capital required		$282,000

between line 1C and line 7, shown on line 8, indicates the amount of income producing capital available to the family if Wendy dies.

Income Analysis

The third step in capital need analysis is to examine the income position of the family. Exhibit 3-6 presents an income analysis for Wendy's family.

Line 1 of Exhibit 3-6 lists the total, before-tax, annual family income. Line 2 shows the proportion of that income needed by the family should Wendy die. This percentage should be estimated based on specific details regarding the family budget. Wendy's family requires only 60 percent of the current income level. This indicates that 40 percent of the current income level is used to pay for such items as Wendy's living expenses, the mortgage, and Wendy's taxes.

The capital available for income (line 3) is taken from line 8 of Exhibit 3-5. Capital need analysis assumes that the capital will be invested and that the investment income earned will help to replace the income lost due to Wendy's death. The assumed interest rate should be conservative, probably no greater than 5 percent, since it represents the average rate that can be earned on safe investments over a long period of time. Furthermore, the excess earnings resulting from a higher rate will help offset the effects of inflation.

Social Security and other government sources of income are depicted on line 4 of Exhibit 3-6. The amount to be inserted can be calculated precisely, but a common practice is to use tables that show benefits.

Exhibit 3-6 shows that $21,850 is available annually from all sources (line 6), which is $14,150 less than desired. This shortfall can be eliminated by purchasing $283,000 of additional insurance. This figure was derived by dividing the income shortage by the assumed interest rate, in this case 5 percent ($14,150/0.05 = $283,000).

Advantages and Limitations

Capital need analysis is simpler and, consequently, easier to understand than the programming concept. Moreover, this approach deals with inflation more easily than does programming. The assumption that capital will be preserved rather than liquidated is an indirect method of offsetting the impact of inflation. However, this can be unrealistic and, in some cases, unaffordable. The estimated life insurance needed may be too expensive for the individual or family to purchase.

Computerized Planning

A wide variety of computer software is available for doing various aspects of financial planning. Some programs do life insurance programming, and some do capital need analysis. Also, a wide range exists in the complexity of these software packages and in what they will do. Many software packages deal only with a single function, such as calculating present values or preparing financial statements. The more sophisticated financial planning software handles nearly all aspects of comprehensive financial planning. The comprehensive packages are more complex and require much more knowledge to operate. More information also has to be provided before the software programs can be used to carry out any analysis.

The most sophisticated financial planning software allows the user to control the program approaches so that either capital need analysis or programming can be accomplished. Carrying out desired evaluations in some software packages requires that the user become extremely familiar with the internal logic of the program in order to use it correctly. Some of the more sophisticated packages require an hour or more for an experienced user to input case data and another half-hour to process that information and generate a plan evaluation. The final output from some financial planning software is voluminous and can be more detailed than some advisers or their clients want or need.

Criteria for Selecting the Appropriate Type of Policy

Once it is determined how much life insurance is needed for death protection for family needs or estate or business planning purposes, another important planning issue is deciding upon the appropriate type or types of policies to own (as described in Chapter 4). Often several types of policies will be used. It is common for persons to have a number of individual and group life insurance policies in their portfolios as time passes and their needs increase or change. A number of criteria or factors that enter into this decision are discussed in this section.

Period of Protection and Payments

Life insurance policies are generally designed to provide either permanent or temporary protection against the financial consequences associated with the death of an insured. **Permanent protection** implies that the policy will be valid throughout the insured's life, while **temporary protection** means that life insurance coverage will be available for only a limited period of time. Permanent policies (such as whole life or universal life) develop internal values referred to as *cash values*. Temporary policies might (as in an endowment), or might not (as in a term policy) develop cash values. The nature of the insured's financial needs often indicates the appropriate period of protection. Some examples follow.

The estate settlement need is lifelong. In fact, the general tendency of this need is to become greater as a person ages. The need for an extra expense fund can also be permanent. In both cases, adequate permanent protection is indicated.

An education fund is a temporary need. Even if a person plans to have additional children in the future, the need for educational funds will not exist when those children are past college age. Needs for readjustment income and income for the dependency period are also temporary. The same is true for a mortgage fund. For these needs, a form of life insurance that provides temporary protection might be recommended.

Premium Flexibility

Premium flexibility refers to the amount of variation allowed in the premium payment amount and the time schedule for premium payments. Many forms of life insurance contracts have fixed premium schedules. A specific premium amount must be paid on a fixed time schedule. If the premium is not paid on time or in the correct amount, the life insurance policy might **lapse** (the coverage will no longer be available because the contract will be terminated). However, some contracts do have optional provisions that will cover past due premiums and keep the coverage in force as long as an adequate cash value remains within the policy to cover premiums when due.

Permanent policies with a so-called "vanishing premium" structure (referred to as vanishing premium policies) have fixed premiums. These contracts are participating policies. The dividends (and, usually, part of the accumulated cash value) are used to pay all premiums beyond the *vanish point* (when it appears that premiums are no longer being paid). Dividends are not guaranteed by the insurance company, and it is possible that the actual dividends paid over time on a particular policy by a life insurance company might be more or less than anticipated. If the dividends fall short of the anticipated amount, it is possible that the policyowner would have to make additional premium payments beyond the point at which premiums are expected to vanish.

If a person needs premium flexibility, the life insurance policies offering the greatest premium flexibility are universal life policies and variable universal life policies. They permit policyowners to increase, decrease, accelerate, or defer premium payments within a very wide set of limitations. This feature can accommodate persons with erratic or unpredictable cash flows.

Death Benefit Flexibility

Another area of flexibility to be considered in selecting among types of individual life insurance policies is the ability of the policyowner to increase or decrease the amount of **death protection** (face amount of life insurance) to meet changing needs. Since life insurance is a "valued policy" (not one of indemnity), the face amount will be paid at death; therefore, this face amount might need to be adjusted as needs for death protection change.

A person's or family's needs for death protection normally do change over a life cycle. Young married persons with children usually need large amounts of death benefits for family protection purposes during the child-rearing period. For those in middle age, paying for education expenses, often a beginning concern for retirement planning, and possibly the need to care for aged parents can become major concerns. As the person or couple get older, retirement planning, estate planning, and the need for protection for the surviving spouse become of major significance. Depending on the person's estate liquidity and conservation needs and family needs, the amount of death protection needed as the person grows older might or might not decrease. In fact, many financially successful people find that their needs for life insurance protection actually increase as they grow older, even after their children are grown.

These changes in needs make death benefit flexibility a desirable characteristic of a life insurance policy. Although all individual life insurance policies have some degree of flexibility in this regard, some are, or can be, more flexible than others. The types of life insurance products are discussed in Chapter 4, where the reader can see the various ways in which death benefit flexibility is provided in the different types of contracts.

Savings and Investment Features

Life insurance products differ markedly in the extent and way in which they provide savings and investment features for the policyowners. They also differ in regard to where the investment risk lies—with the insurance company in noninterest-sensitive products or with the policyowner in the case of interest-sensitive life products. The characteristics of the different types of policies in this area are explored in greater detail in Chapter 4.

As is explained more fully in Chapter 4, so-called *cash-value* life insurance contracts (most contracts other than pure term insurance) will develop a cash value in the contract. This cash value is part of the life insurance policy. It arises because more premiums are paid during the early years of the policy than are necessary to meet death claims (for all similar policies written by the life insurer) and the expenses of the insurer in writing the insurance.

Life insurers guarantee that a minimum rate of interest will be paid on the cash value, although the life insurer can actually provide a higher interest rate. The year-to-year growth of the cash value is not currently subject to federal income taxation. This remains so as long as the cash value stays within the life insurance policy; however, if a policy is sold or surrendered for cash, the policyowner must pay taxes on the difference between the net premiums (total premiums less expense charges) paid and the amount of money received for the policy's cash value. The tax-deferred buildup of cash value within a life insurance policy is viewed as an attractive saving and investment opportunity.

If a person views life insurance cash values as an attractive method of saving and investment, he or she should consider permanent insurance. For example, some people view permanent insurance as a means to save additional retirement funds. Even temporary needs such as college expenses can be met with permanent insurance in these cases. Some people, however, believe life insurance cash value contracts are inadequate savings and investment devices. These individuals are inclined toward insurance that does not build up cash values. Unfortunately, in many cases a person's attitudes toward life insurance cash values are based on incomplete or inaccurate analysis.

The evaluation of life insurance cash values as a savings vehicle often surfaces as the "buy term and invest the difference" argument. The proponents of this concept argue that a person's financial welfare would be improved if he or she bought term insurance instead of cash value life insurance and invested the premium difference in some manner. Since, according to this view, a policy that builds up cash value is composed of increasing savings (the cash value) and decreasing protection, essentially the same or better benefits could be achieved by a term insurance policy with a decreasing death benefit and a separate savings or investment program.

However, many people argue that cash value life insurance has a number of attractive investment features, including certain tax advantages. In fact, *investment-oriented* life insurance products were developed in part to help diffuse the "buy term and invest the difference" argument. The issue of "buy term and invest the difference" versus cash value life insurance remains a hotly contested issue in financial planning.

The True Cost of Life Insurance

As mentioned earlier, the premiums paid by a policyowner for life insurance may not reflect the entire cost of the life insurance. Individuals and families should be aware of the different factors that influence the "true" cost of life insurance.

Need for Such Analysis

An important consideration in the purchase of life insurance is the cost of the policy. Determining the true cost is important not only in selecting the appropriate type of policy but also in comparing the costs of specific contracts. Unfortunately, analyzing the true cost of life insurance is complicated because of the effects of cash values and, for participating policies, dividends. For example, suppose a person can purchase a policy that has an annual premium of $1,200 from Insurer A and the same type of policy with an annual premium of $1,000 from Insurer B. Despite the higher premium, the true cost of Insurer A's policy might be lower than Insurer B's if A's cash values, dividends, or both, are higher. The method of analyzing life insurance cost is important, and different methods can yield different results.

Methods for Analyzing the True Cost

Over the years, a number of methods have been used or suggested to analyze the "true" cost of life insurance. They vary considerably in their complexity, and some are used more widely than others. The main methods are described in the following section.

Traditional Net Cost Method

Until recent years, life insurance costs were analyzed by the net cost method. This approach is simple and is easily understood by policyowners. It is also misleading in most cases. Briefly stated, the **net cost method** simply adds the total premiums to be paid over a specified period (usually twenty years) and subtracts the twentieth-year cash value and estimated dividends during the period. The difference is called the **net cost**.

Usually, the net cost is then divided by the number of years used for the calculation, and the result is the net cost per year. The net cost method calculates the cost as shown in the first section of Exhibit 3-7.

The net cost of the policy is shown to be negative! With these figures it is easy to argue that the policy has no cost and, indeed, "makes a profit." This result is not unusual with the net cost method. That is, it often produces a negative cost—or in some cases, a very low positive cost.

The fallacy in the traditional net cost method is that it ignores the time value of money. Money spent for insurance premiums has an opportunity cost that can be measured by the earnings that could be realized with an alternative use of the funds. Dollars spent for insurance premiums could be deposited in a savings account and accumulated at interest. Dollars tied up in dividends could be similarly used. The net cost method ignores these alternative interest costs, and, as a result, it understates the true cost of life insurance and its use is not recommended.

Interest-Adjusted Method

The **interest-adjusted method** is similar to the net cost method except that it recognizes the time value of money. Both premiums and dividends are compounded at a specified rate of interest to reflect the fact that these funds could have earned interest if they had not been allocated to life insurance. The interest rate normally used is 5 percent, because most state statutes requiring interest-adjusted indexes specify 5 percent.

Using the same policy that was previously introduced, the interest-adjusted method can be seen in the second section of Exhibit 3-7.

These figures recognize the opportunity cost concept. Referring to the above figures, a person could pay an annual premium of $600 or, alternatively, deposit the same amount each year into a savings account. If the savings account paid an after-tax return of 5 percent, it would accumulate to $20,831 in twenty years. Judged by the alternative value, the total value of the life insurance contract should be $20,831 after twenty years. One must recognize the value of the dividends and cash values, however. Subtracting both of these values leaves a difference of $5,552. This amount, therefore, must be the cost of the insurance protection because it is the amount by which the accumulated values (in the form of dividends and cash values) fall short of the amount that could be accumulated in a savings account.

The $5,552, however, is the cost over the twenty-year period. To decide how much the policy costs per year, we cannot simply divide the $5,552 by twenty. This would ignore the time value of money. Instead, we need an answer to the

Exhibit 3-7
Analyzing the True Cost of Life Insurance

This analysis compares four methods of measuring the true cost of a life insurance policy that has the following characteristics:	
Face amount	$25,000.00
Annual premium	600.00
Annual dividend	165.00
Projected dividends for 20 years	3,300.00
Cash value after 20th year	9,550.00

1. Traditional net cost method:

Total premiums for 20 years	$12,000.00
Less dividends for 20 years	3,300.00
Net premiums for 20 years	8,700.00
Less cash value at end of 20 years	9,550.00
Net cost	(850.00)
Net cost per year ($850/20)	(42.50)

2. Interest adjusted method:

Amount to which $1 deposited annually will increase in 20 years at 5% compound interest:	$ 34.72
Total premiums for 20 years accumulated at 5% ($600 x 34.72)	20,831.00
Less dividends for 20 years accumulated at 5% ($165 x 34.72)	5,729.00
Net premiums for 20 years	15,102.00
Less cash value at end of 20 years	9,550.00
Interest adjusted insurance cost	5,552.00
Interest adjusted cost per year ($5,552/34.72)	159.91

3. Interest adjusted surrender index:

Interest adjusted cost per year divided by thousands of coverage ($159.91/25)	6.40

4. Interest adjusted cost (payment) index:

Amount to which $1 deposited annually will increase in 20 years at 5% compound interest	$ 34.72
Total premiums for 20 years ($600 x 34.72)	20,831.00
Less dividends for 20 years ($165 x 34.72)	5,729.00
Net premiums for 20 years	15,102.00
Interest adjusted cost per year ($15,102/34.72)	434.98
Interest adjusted cost index ($434.98/25)	17.40

question, "How much would a person need to deposit each year to accumulate $5,552 in twenty years at 5 percent?" The answer is $159.91, because compound interest tables show that $159.91 deposited each year for twenty years at 5 percent would grow to $5,552. We can conclude that the true cost for the above policy, as measured by the interest-adjusted method, is $159.91 per year.

Interest-Adjusted Surrender Index

The **interest-adjusted surrender index** shown in the third section of Exhibit 3-7 is merely a conversion of the interest-adjusted cost per year to an interest-adjusted cost per thousand dollars of coverage. In other words, $159.91 is divided by 25 (representing the $25,000 face amount) to yield an interest-adjusted index of 6.40 as shown at the bottom of Exhibit 3-7. The surrender cost index is useful only as a comparative measurement with indexes calculated in the same way for other policies of a similar type. Lower index numbers indicate lower costs for coverage. Purchasers should seek policies from financially strong life insurance companies that have low interest-adjusted index numbers.

Interest-Adjusted Cost (Payment) Index

Many sales illustrations present four different interest-adjusted index numbers. In addition to a ten-year and a twenty-year surrender index, they often present ten-year and twenty-year cost indexes or payment indexes. These are two different names for the same index number. **Cost indexes** are calculated in the same way as the surrender indexes, with one major exception. Cost indexes do not take the cash value into account. The total premiums for twenty years are accumulated at 5 percent, which is $20,831, the same as in the previous example. Subtracted are the accumulated dividends for twenty years at 5 percent interest, which is again $5,729. After the subtraction, a net premium for 20 years of $15,102 is shown, which is converted to an interest-adjusted cost per year of $434.98. The final cost index is a cost index per thousand of 17.399—it costs $17.40 for each $1,000 of death benefit. Cost indexes are always higher than surrender indexes for policies that have a cash value. Term policies, because they have no cash value, will have identical values for a cost index and a surrender index. In fact, for policies that have no cash value and pay no dividends, the cost index is identical to the level annual premium.

In comparing policies, those policies with lower cost indexes and lower surrender indexes are preferable to similar policies with higher index numbers. However, life insurance policy selection should never be based solely on interest-adjusted indexes or any other cost-based measure.

Many states require life insurers to provide buyers' guides to prospective insureds that show the cost of life insurance calculated with the interest-adjusted method. Many major insurance companies deliver buyers' guides with all their policies, even in the states that do not have such a requirement. Interest-adjusted methods have essentially replaced the traditional net cost method for measuring life insurance costs.

Equal Outlay Evaluation

Another approach to life insurance policy comparisons is the **equal outlay method** of evaluation. It is most easily applied to proposed purchases of flexible premium policies or to comparing a given flexible premium policy with a fixed premium policy. The concept is relatively simple. By having equal death benefit amounts and equal premium outlays in each period and assuming the same interest rate for both policies, policies are made as nearly equivalent as possible. Any differences between the policies show up in the differences of accumulated cash values at various intervals during the policy period. The policy with the highest cash value at the end of the periods most relevant to the purchaser would be deemed the better performing policy. Because the interest rate is specified and held equal for both policies, differences observed in the cash value are attributable to differences in mortality costs and insurer expenses.

One major shortcoming of this evaluation method is that it ignores actual and potential differences in the interest rates that will be applicable to the respective policies. Consideration of these interest rates can only be based on observations of past interest rates credited by the respective companies and on analysis of current investment performance of the companies.

Factors Other Than Cost

Although it is important to keep the cost of life insurance in perspective, three other factors should be considered when purchasing life insurance:

- An insurer's financial strength
- The policyholder service provided by the insurer
- The relative benefits of different life insurance policies

Insurer's Financial Strength

Selecting policies only on the basis of the lowest possible premium can lead purchasers into contracts with insurance companies that eventually become insolvent. For that reason, prospective purchasers need to be concerned not only with premium levels but also with the financial strength of the insurance company. This issue has become particularly critical in recent years because of the well-publicized insolvencies of a few sizable life insurance companies and the reported financial difficulties of a few others. It should be observed, however, that over many years life insurance companies generally have been among the most financially sound financial institutions. Historically, very few life insurers have failed. Nevertheless, the financial soundness of insurers and their financial ratings by independent outside insurance rating services are important factors for consumers to consider.

Helpful information on the strength and quality of an insurance company can be found in *Best's Insurance Reports,*[2] which the A. M. Best Company produces annually. They cover nearly all insurance companies and present financial statements, history, management, product information, and a financial rating for each rated company. A. M. Best specializes in rating insurance companies and is the oldest rating agency in this field. Two other widely followed financial or claims-paying rating services for insurance companies are Moody's and Standard & Poor's. Also, two other frequently mentioned rating services for insurers are Duff & Phelps and Weiss Research. Each of these services differs in at least some respects from the others, and their rating grades are not uniform. As a result, some life insurers advertise or otherwise advise their policyowners and potential customers of their financial ratings through several of these rating services.

Policyholder Service

Other important factors do not lend themselves to quantification, and there are no reference services that rate insurance companies on these factors, one of which is the level of service provided to policyowners. Top-level service enables companies to handle claims and change-of-coverage information promptly, accurately, and pleasantly. At the other end of the spectrum, a few insurance companies provide a minimum of service, requiring more effort by the policyowner to initiate and carry out policy-related transactions.

Policy Comparisons

Prospective policyowners are often presented with policy proposals that are not directly comparable. Close scrutiny of those proposals might disclose issues that should be raised. Many supplemental benefits can be included in or omitted from a policy proposal, including accidental death benefits, waiver of premium, guaranteed purchase options, and cost-of-living adjustment options. Policy proposals are not comparable unless they treat each one of these options in a similar manner and for similar amounts of benefits.

Policy comparisons should also be tempered with appropriate warnings about the nonguaranteed or discretionary elements of those proposals. Dividends are not guaranteed and could vary significantly from the levels illustrated in a proposal. Similarly, interest credited to the cash value on a universal life policy over and above the minimum guaranteed rate is often purely at the discretion of the insurance company and can vary significantly from the amount shown in the policy illustration. Similarly, mortality charges might be shown at the current level with no emphasis on the right of the insurance company to use a higher level of charges in the future. In addition, some policies have significant surrender charges.

Policy Provisions

Like most insurance contracts, individual life insurance policies contain a number of provisions. States require that some provisions be in life insurance policies. Other provisions can be included in policies if desired by the insurer and the insured. Some of the more important life insurance contract provisions are described below.

General Provisions

Most life insurance policies *must* have certain provisions. These provisions are discussed in the following paragraphs.

Incontestability

For the consumer, one of the most important provisions in a life insurance policy is the incontestable clause. A typical incontestable clause allows the insurer to question the validity of a life insurance contract only during the contestable period. The **contestable period** is generally the first one or two years from the policy's inception, depending on the contract, during which the contract's validity can be questioned by the insurer. During this period, a life insurance company might successfully deny a claim on the grounds of misrepresentation, fraud, or concealment—or for nonpayment of premium—by contesting the policy. Upon the insured's death or after the expiration of the contestable period, the contract can be declared invalid only for nonpayment of premium and cannot otherwise be contested by the life insurer.[3]

The incontestable clause ensures that the validity of the life insurance contract will not be challenged by the insurance company after the contestable period has expired. It benefits innocent policyowners and their beneficiaries because it protects them against the possibility of a legal challenge to the contract after the contestable period. Without the clause, a policyowner could not be certain a death claim would be paid. The company might deny the claim by showing that the policy was obtained by fraud, misrepresentation, concealment, or some other questionable means. The company might deny liability for the claim even though the policy was obtained many years earlier and the insured—the one best able to defend against the insurer's allegation—is dead.

The incontestable clause does not require an insurance company to pay every death claim that occurs after the contestable period. It simply prevents an insurance company from questioning the validity of a life insurance policy after the contestable period. In some cases a company might admit the existence of a valid contract but deny liability for a claim because of the terms of the contract. For example, the company would not be liable for a death caused by an excluded hazard such as that contained in a war exclusion.

Adjusting benefits for misstatement of age and sex is not contesting the validity of a life insurance policy. Therefore, the incontestable clause does not apply to the misstatement of age and sex.

Misstatement of Age and Sex Provision

Most state laws require that all life insurance policies include a "misstatement of age" clause. A typical provision states the following:

> If the age or sex of the Insured has been misstated, any amount payable under this policy shall be such as the premium paid would have purchased on the basis of the correct age and sex according to the Company's published rate at date of issue.

To illustrate, assume a woman purchased a $10,000 ordinary life policy at a time when her company's rates were as follows:

Age	Rate per Thousand
34	$24.25
35	$25.00
36	$26.00

If the insured's true age at the time the policy was issued were thirty-five, but the policy were rated on an incorrect age of thirty-four, the annual premium would be $242.50 when it should be $250.00. If the mistake is discovered when the insured dies years later, the corrected death proceeds would be $9,700, as calculated in the following:

$$\left(\frac{\$242.50}{\$250} \right) \times \$10,000$$

If the insured had incorrectly given her age as thirty-six, the amount payable might be $10,400. However, in the event that an insured's age is overstated, some life insurers refund the difference between the premiums paid and the premiums required for the same death benefit at the correct age with interest.

Thus, the insured in the example would receive $10 per year ($260 – $250) plus interest.

A misstatement of sex is also treated by adjusting the face amount of the policy (different premiums usually apply for males and females). Normally, such a "misstatement" is the result of a clerical error in completing the application or in physically preparing the contract. In essence, the age and sex provision is designed to adjust the benefits (and proceeds) to what they would have been for the premium paid based on the insured's correct age and sex.

Suicide Exclusion

If there were no suicide provision in a life insurance policy, the contract would probably be interpreted to cover suicide. This would create a possibility of adverse selection for an insurance company since a person planning to commit suicide might purchase a large amount of life insurance a short time before ending his or her life. Consequently, all companies include a suicide provision that excludes coverage for the suicide of the insured, while sane or insane, within two years from the date of the policy issue.

Several variations in suicide provisions exist. For example, some policies exclude suicide for only one year from the effective date of the policy. In addition, most policies generally require the insurer to refund the premiums paid, less any acquisition expenses and premiums due, to the beneficiary of the insured in the event the insured commits suicide within the exempted period. However, in Missouri, suicide (at any time) does not relieve an insurance company from paying the full amount of the policy unless the company can prove that the insured was contemplating suicide when the policy was purchased.

The basic rationale for the suicide provision is that few individuals contemplate suicide, purchase a policy, and then wait a year or two before taking their lives. For those who commit suicide years after the policy is purchased, the company can pay the benefits to innocent beneficiaries without needing to be overly concerned with the adverse selection problem. However when suicide is alleged to occur, the general rule of law is that death is presumed to be unintentional—the individual did not intend to die. Therefore, the burden of proving suicide lies with the insurer.

Ownership and Beneficiary

In most cases, a person applies for insurance on his or her own life and becomes the owner of the policy. This person is the **applicant** (the person who applies for the insurance policy), **insured** (the person on whose life the policy is based), and **owner** (the person who controls the policy). However, it is possible for one person to apply for insurance on the life of someone else with even a third person as the policyowner. It is also possible for a policyowner-insured to absolutely assign ownership of a policy to someone else.

In some circumstances, it is desirable to designate a policyowner who is not the insured. Examples of such circumstances follow:

- If the insured is a child, then a parent or guardian can be designated as the policyowner. (The child often automatically becomes the owner upon reaching a certain age.)

- Life insurance purchased for business purposes is often owned by some party other than the insured.

- Estate tax considerations might make it desirable to name someone other than the insured as policyowner.

The policyowner of a life insurance contract has the right to name a beneficiary or beneficiaries to receive the death proceeds in the event of the insured's death. This beneficiary designation is not the same as policy ownership just discussed. If someone other than the insured is the owner of a policy, that person also can be named as beneficiary, and, in fact, should be so named in most cases. However, in most cases, the insured is the policyowner and someone else is named as beneficiary of the death proceeds.

Beneficiaries generally are named revocably. A **revocable beneficiary** can be changed at any time by the policyowner. Sometimes beneficiaries are named irrevocably, and the designation cannot be changed without the permission of the **irrevocable beneficiary**.

A **primary beneficiary** is often named as the recipient of the death benefit in the event of the insured's death. A **contingent beneficiary** can also be listed to receive the death benefit if the primary beneficiary dies before the insured.

Change of Owner or Beneficiary

A change of policy ownership might be effected at any time during the insured's lifetime by the owner's giving written notice to the insurance company. Revocable beneficiary designations can also be changed by the policyowner by filing the proper notice with the insurance company.

Assignment

The policyowner has the right to **assign** (transfer ownership of) the policy to anyone else—even to an individual who lacks an insurable interest in the insured's life. Assignment can be achieved without receipt of financial consideration.

Assignment of a life insurance policy may take place without the consent of the insurance company, but the assignment is not binding on the company until written notice is received by the insurer.

Two basic types of assignment exist in life insurance—absolute and collateral. An **absolute assignment** transfers to the assignee all of the ownership rights and interests possessed by the **assignor** (the owner transferring all of his or her rights). If an assignor is sole owner of a contract (or if all owners join in the assignment), an absolute assignment makes the assignee the new owner of the policy. As the new owner, the assignee can exercise any and all ownership rights.

A **collateral assignment** transfers ownership interests (when the owner is also the insured) only to the extent necessary to provide adequate collateral for a loan. In the event of the owner-borrower's death, the assignee-lender would be entitled to receive the amount of the unpaid debt, with interest, and the remaining proceeds would be payable to the beneficiaries named to the policy. The assignee-lender is protected to the extent of the debt, and the lender's rights to any proceeds are extinguished when the debt is repaid.

Nonforfeiture Options

To protect the financial interest of policyowners who terminate their policies, all states have enacted nonforfeiture laws that require that, at any time after a life insurance policy has begun to develop a cash value, the insured can discontinue premium payments and receive a portion of the policy's cash value. These laws set forth recommended actuarial assumptions and methods of calculating *minimum* nonforfeiture values. The **nonforfeiture value** is the amount of cash value a policyowner receives when he or she voluntarily terminates his or her life insurance policy.

In most cases, a minimum nonforfeiture value is required by the second or third policy year. However, in some plans a value is required during the first policy year, while in others a nonforfeiture value might not be necessary until the fourth, fifth, or subsequent years. Since the nonforfeiture laws are concerned with minimum values, insurance companies have wide latitude in setting surrender values.

A policyowner who voluntarily terminates a life insurance policy can choose one of three methods of taking the nonforfeiture value: (1) cash, (2) paid-up insurance, or (3) extended term insurance.[4] The values of each of these options are included in a nonforfeiture value table in all cash value policies. An example of a nonforfeiture value table is shown in Exhibit 3-8.

Exhibit 3-8

Table of Cash, Loan, and Nonforfeiture Values for Whole-Life Insurance for a Female—Issue Age Thirty-Nine (per $1,000 of Face Amount)

End of Policy Year	Tabular Cash or Loan Value	Participating Paid-Up Insurance	Nonparticipating Extended Insurance	
			Years	Days
1	$ 0.00	0	0	0
2	0.00	0	0	0
3	15.00	47	2	293
4	31.00	92	5	45
5	48.00	138	7	13
6	66.00	183	8	227
7	83.00	222	9	277
8	102.00	263	10	303
9	121.00	302	11	241
10	140.00	337	12	103
11	160.00	372	12	293
12	180.00	405	13	63
13	200.00	435	12	153
14	221.00	465	13	226
15	243.00	495	13	281
16	265.00	522	13	303
17	287.00	548	13	297
18	310.00	573	13	283
19	334.00	598	13	263
20	357.00	619	13	209
Age 60	377.00	640	13	152
Age 65	471.00	723	13	104

Cash

One option available to the policyowner is to receive the nonforfeiture value of a life insurance contract in cash. This option is referred to as **cash surrender**, and the **cash surrender value** is the amount of the nonforfeiture value received by the policyowner. A delay clause in all life insurance policies gives companies the legal right to postpone the payment of the cash surrender value for a period of up to six months, but this is rarely done.

When a life insurance policy is surrendered for cash, a check is sent to the policyowner, and all future obligations of the insurer are terminated. For example, as shown in the table in Exhibit 3-8, a whole life policy issued to a female, age thirty-nine, will have a twentieth-year cash surrender value ("Tabular Cash or Loan Value," second column) of approximately $357 for each $1,000 of the face amount. The value of any policy indebtedness (policy loans plus accumulated interest) will be deducted from the cash surrender. If this woman had a $50,000 death benefit and no policy indebtedness, she would receive $17,850 ($50,000/1,000 x $357). However, she would no longer have life insurance coverage. Exhibit 3-9 illustrates the status of the contract upon cash surrender.

Exhibit 3-9
Impact of Cash Surrender of a Whole Life Policy in the Twentieth Year

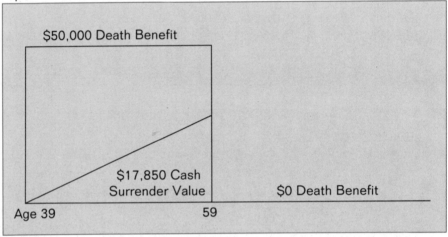

The cash option is usually the option selected by policyowners. However, it might not be the most appropriate option—unless the policyowner's need for funds exceeds the need for life insurance protection. If this is not the case, one of the other surrender options or a policy loan (discussed later in this chapter) normally should be used.[5] In actuality, however, surrender options other than the cash option are used as default options within the contract and are put into effect when a policyholder stops making premium payments but does not actively pursue a cash surrender.

Paid-Up Insurance

Under the paid-up insurance nonforfeiture option, the **net surrender value** (the cash value less any policy indebtedness) is applied as a net single premium to purchase **fully paid-up insurance** (permanent life insurance that does not require additional premium payments to remain in force).[6] The amount of the paid-up insurance is determined by the net surrender value, the insured's attained age, and the factors specified in the original contract. Since the amount of paid-up insurance is always less than the original face amount, this option is often called the *reduced paid-up option*. The paid-up policy contract is the same type as the original contract. Thus, if the paid-up policy option is chosen under a whole life policy, the paid-up policy is also a whole life policy. The amount of paid-up insurance per $1,000 of death benefit is listed in the nonforfeiture value table in Exhibit 3-10 for a policy issued to a female at age thirty-nine. If it is assumed that she decides to forfeit her current policy for a paid-up policy in the twentieth year, she will receive $619 of paid-up coverage for each $1,000 of coverage she has on the original policy. Using the $50,000 policy, this woman will receive a paid-up whole life policy with a death benefit of $30,950 ($50,000/1,000 x $619).

Exhibit 3-10 shows the effect of the nonforfeiture selection and indicates that the reduction in the amount of insurance as a result of exercising this option may be substantial. Note, however, that the cash value is not reduced by selection of the paid-up option. As a matter of fact, the cash value of a policy under this option will continue to increase but at a slower rate than it would have under the original policy.

Exhibit 3-10
Impact of Reduced Paid-Up Nonforfeiture Option of a Whole Life Policy

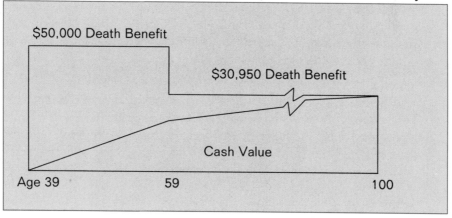

Normally, when a policy is converted to paid-up status, all supplementary contract benefits are eliminated including term riders, disability and accidental death riders, and so on. Dividends continue to be paid under participating policies.

This option is appropriate if the policyowner needs life insurance but cannot continue premium payments. This option provides greater flexibility than the other nonforfeiture options since the reduced paid-up policy contains a cash value. As a result, the paid-up policy can still serve as a source of funds in the event of a financial emergency or during retirement.

Extended Term Insurance

If the insured fails to choose a nonforfeiture option within (typically) sixty days, the policy automatically provides a selection. Usually, the automatic selection is the extended term option.

Just as the paid-up insurance option reduces the amount of insurance, the extended term option reduces the period of protection. Under this nonforfeiture option, the net surrender value of the policy is applied as a net single premium to purchase term insurance for as long a period as possible. The face amount of the term coverage is the same as the face amount of the original policy. If there is an outstanding policy loan, the insurer will reduce the face amount of the term coverage by that amount rather than shorten the period of coverage in order to protect the company from adverse selection. For example, assume that an unhealthy person owns a $50,000 policy with a $20,000 policy loan value. The extended term insurance will have a face amount of $30,000. If the face amount were not reduced, the policyowner could obtain $20,000 as a policy loan, and the beneficiary could receive $50,000 as a death benefit, for a total of $70,000.

As was the case with the reduced paid-up option, supplementary benefits are eliminated when this option is exercised. Furthermore, dividends are paid infrequently under this option because they are too small to justify the administrative expense of paying them.

The nonforfeiture value table in Exhibit 3-8 shows how long the extended term period is, depending on the length of time the contract has been in force. For example, after twenty years, the whole life policy issued to a female age thirty-nine would provide extended term insurance for thirteen years plus 209 days. Exhibit 3-11 illustrates this policy, assuming that this option is selected after twenty years, when the insured is age fifty-nine.

Exhibit 3-11
Whole Life Policy Extended Term Insurance Nonforfeiture Option

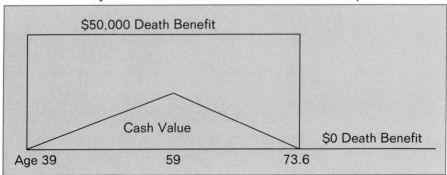

The essence of these nonforfeiture options is summarized below:

- The *extended term option* does not involve a reduction of death benefit but does have a definite expiration date. Although it is often used only as a default option, this might be the most appropriate selection if the insured is in poor health.[7]

- The *reduced paid-up option* provides an amount of coverage that is smaller than before. As mentioned, this option is not usually chosen but is effected as a default option. Nevertheless, this option might be the best choice if the insured is in good health and wishes to continue life insurance coverage without paying additional premiums.

- The *cash surrender option* results in complete discontinuance of insurance protection. The policyowner also relinquishes any contractual reinstatement privileges and can incur some income tax liability. Although this option is inappropriate if the policyowner wants to continue some protection, it is usually the option chosen by the policyowner.

Policy Loans

Life insurance policies that develop a cash value contain a policy loan provision. This provision provides a valuable benefit to policyowners since the policy's cash value can be borrowed at any time by sending a written request to the insurance company. As in the case of cash surrenders, the company *might* defer the granting of a loan for up to six months, but loans have seldom been postponed. However, a policy loan does not require a credit investigation.

The policyowner has maximum flexibility in repaying the policy loan. It can be repaid at any time, since there is no repayment schedule or due date. If a loan has not been repaid at the time of the insured's death, the amount of the loan, plus unpaid interest, is deducted from the death proceeds. If a loan is outstanding when the policy is surrendered for cash, then the loan, plus unpaid interest, is deducted from the cash surrender value.

The interest rate payable on policy loans has been the subject of much debate in recent years. In the past, most policies stipulated a rate of 5 or 6 percent, and the rate was embodied in the contractual guarantees of the policy and could not be changed. In many cases, this provided a valuable benefit to policyowners because the policy loan interest rate was lower than most other interest rates. Consequently, policyowners frequently found that policy loans provided the lowest possible cost for obtaining funds. This caused a problem for insurers, since the loan provision obligated the insurance company to provide funds to policyowners at a lower rate than the company could obtain from other investments. This is an example of adverse *financial* selection and has caused many insurance companies to favor changes in policy loan laws.

States have recognized this situation and have allowed the establishment of a more flexible interest rate system that allows the policy loan interest rate to better relate to prevailing rates at the time of the loan. Another approach being followed by states is to increase the policy loan rate. Still another approach that many companies have used with regard to participating policies is referred to as **direct recognition**. This means that the policy dividends are lower for policies with policy loans against them than for comparable policies without policy loans.

The important point for a policyowner is that, under any traditional approach, the policy loan interest rate, or method of determining the interest rate, or direct recognition provision must be specified in the policy and cannot be changed during the life of the contract. Changes might be attempted by offering to exchange the existing policy for a new policy with higher death benefits at the same premium and with higher policy loan interest charges or variable interest rates. However, the policyowner does not have to accept such an exchange offer from the company.

In recent years, policy loan interest rates have been lower than commercial rates. This market condition has not always been the case, and the situation might be reversed in the future. If so, a policyowner might still obtain a lower rate by using the policy as collateral for a loan from a bank or other lender. Of course, the interest rate is only one factor to consider. It can be quicker, more convenient, more private, and more flexible to obtain a policy loan from the insurance company than to borrow money from a commercial lender. In addition, participating policies continue to pay dividends on the entire cash value of the policy (including any amount outstanding due to the loan), thus the true cost of loans in these policies will be lower since the interest paid *is reduced by* the dividends paid.

Many policies contain an **automatic premium loan provision**, which acts as a special application of the policy loan provision. The automatic premium loan serves a purpose similar to nonforfeiture options: a policyowner can discontinue premium payments, and the policy will remain in force for a specified period of time. Automatic loans are made each time a grace period (discussed later in this chapter) is expiring, unless a premium has been paid or the cash value is inadequate to cover the premium. Subsequent automatic premium loans and accumulating interest may eventually exhaust the policy's cash value. Exhibit 3-12 illustrates the status of a policy using the automatic premium loan feature.

The automatic premium loan is most appropriate when the policyowner intends to resume the premium payments or when it is important to keep the supplementary benefits in force. If premiums are not resumed under the automatic premium loan feature, the amount of the death benefit will be less than it would have been under the extended term insurance nonforfeiture option since the accumulated indebtedness must be deducted from the proceeds. Furthermore, coverage will last longer if the extended term insurance option is used.

Exhibit 3-12
Impact of the Automatic Premium Loan

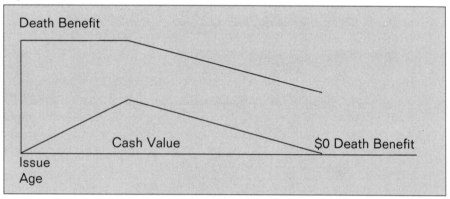

Today most insurance companies make the provision available. A life insurance applicant is usually asked whether the automatic loan provision is desired. Some insurers routinely include the provision but give policyowners the option of deleting it.

As a general rule, a policyowner should include the automatic premium loan provision. It provides a convenient method of handling premium payments that are missed inadvertently or premiums the policyowner is temporarily unable to meet. However, frequent reliance on the automatic loan provision is unwise since the policy will terminate if the remaining cash value is inadequate to pay the premium.[8]

When premium payments are made automatically by a policy loan, all benefits (such as dividends) and options (like waiver of premium) remain in effect just as though the premiums were paid directly by the policyowner. If a policyowner decides to resume premium payments after they have been paid automatically by loans, no evidence of insurability is required.

To protect the policyowner against an unintended serious reduction in the policy proceeds should death occur during the operation of the automatic premium loan option, some companies limit its use to two consecutive missed premiums if the mode of premium payment is other than monthly or to six consecutive missed premiums if monthly. Further exercise of this option might be arranged by application to the life insurance company at the premium due dates, but such payments are not automatic. However, some insurance companies do not limit the application of automatic premium loans.

Premiums

Premiums for a fixed-premium type of policy (such as a whole life policy) are payable in accordance with a premium schedule. Generally, such premiums are paid on an annual, semiannual, quarterly, or monthly basis. As the premium payment frequency is increased, the total annual premium is increased. For example, a $100 annual premium might be made in two $52 semiannual payments or four $27 quarterly premiums.

Premiums can also be paid through a **preauthorized** (or **automatic**) **check plan**, whereby the insurer is authorized to draw the premium payment directly from the owner's checking account. This is often done for monthly premiums. The insured's cost with a preauthorized check plan is less than that associated with a regular monthly premium, since collection expenses are lower and there is less likelihood of lapse.

On the other hand, the payment of premiums for the flexible premium type of policies (such as universal life policies) is largely at the discretion of the policyowner. The insurance company requires at least a minimum initial premium payment to start the coverage. Thereafter, the policyowner, within broad limits and subject to other policy provisions, can increase, decrease, discontinue, or resume premium payments at will. Insurers also set maximum amounts that can be paid into such contracts as premiums.

Grace Period

The laws of most states require insurers to include a **grace period** in their life insurance policies. This provision continues a policy in full force for thirty or thirty-one days after the premium due date, during which time the policyowner can pay the overdue premium without penalty. The purpose of the grace period is to avoid lapse of the policy due to a late premium payment.

The laws of most states allow an insurer to charge interest on overdue premiums, but few insurance companies do. They are more concerned with preventing a lapse than with losing a relatively insignificant amount of interest.

Reinstatement

When a policyowner stops making premium payments as needed to keep the policy in force, one of the following will take place:

1. The premiums will be paid by an automatic premium loan provision.
2. The policy will be surrendered for cash.
3. The policy will terminate without value (if premiums are discontinued and the cash value is less than the premium due or the policy is a term policy without cash value).
4. The policy will be placed on one of the other nonforfeiture options.[9]

The reinstatement provision allows a policyowner to revive a policy after it lapses. Under alternative 1 above, there is no need to reinstate the policy. A policyowner can simply repay the indebtedness and resume premium payments. The death proceeds then would be the same as they were before the policy loans were used.

Reinstatement generally is not allowed if the policy has been surrendered for its cash value (alternative 2 above). However, some insurance companies allow reinstatement by company practice—not policy provision—if the contract has been surrendered for cash.

The typical reinstatement provision allows that reinstatement if a policy has been terminated without value (alternative 3 above) or has been placed on one of the other nonforfeiture options (alternative 4 above). In some companies reinstatement is provided only if the policy has been placed on a nonforfeiture option.

The typical reinstatement provision requires that reinstatement be made within five years after default in payment of premium. The insurer usually requires:

1. *Evidence of insurability.* The insurance company has the right to require such proof in order to prevent adverse mortality selection since individuals in poor health are more likely to request reinstatement than those who believe that they are in good health. This problem is particularly relevant when a long time has elapsed after the premium default.
2. *Payment of all overdue premiums with interest.*
3. *Payment of any indebtedness outstanding* at the end of the grace period, with interest, plus any outstanding indebtedness incurred thereafter.

However, if the insurer receives the payments required under 2 and 3 above within thirty-one days after expiration of the grace period while the insured is still living, the insurer will usually waive evidence of insurability. Short-term lapses often occur when a policyowner unintentionally misses a premium payment. Recognizing this, many insurance companies are liberal when reinstatement is requested shortly after premium default and might require nothing more than a written statement from the insured indicating that he or she is in good health. The evidence of insurability required, if any, depends on the size of the policy.

A reinstatement provision is not mandatory in all states. However, almost all policies contain the clause. The most common variation among companies is that some allow reinstatement within three years of default, other companies permit reinstatement within five years, and some companies use even longer periods.

A policyowner might prefer to reinstate an old policy rather than purchase a new one for any of several reasons:

1. A new policy will require a higher premium since the insured is older than he or she was when the original policy was purchased.

2. A new policy might not develop a cash value for several years because of the expenses incurred in its issue.

3. A new contract can contain more restrictive provisions than those found in the original policy (the policy loan interest rate, for example, might be higher in the new contract).

4. The suicide and incontestable periods *might* have expired under the reinstated policy. In general, reinstatement of a policy does not reopen the suicide period, and a contestable period begins anew only with respect to the statements in the reinstatement application.

Settlement Options

Life insurance proceeds are payable in a single sum but, at the option of the policyowner or beneficiary, they can also be payable in the form of periodic income by using one of the "settlement options." The options are (1) interest only, (2) fixed period installments, (3) fixed amount installments, and (4) payments as a lifetime income.

Note the distinction between settlement options and nonforfeiture options. Basically, *settlement options* are alternative methods of receiving death proceeds once the insured is dead, while *nonforfeiture options* are exercised by living policyowners to receive value (other than death proceeds) from the policy. Many insurance companies, however, allow living policyowners to liquidate their cash values under one or more of the settlement options. Thus, the policy might specifically state that cash values can be taken under the settlement options. Even if the contract does not specifically grant this right, many companies will, upon request, pay cash values in this manner as a matter of company practice.

A settlement option may be selected by the policyowner prior to the death of the insured, leaving the beneficiary with no choice in the matter. Alternatively, the beneficiary may be given the right to make a wide range of decisions in the use of settlement options. Which method is more appropriate depends on the ability of the policyowner to foresee the needs of the beneficiary and the ability of the beneficiary to make intelligent decisions during a period of stress following the insured's death. Obviously, neither approach is always best.

The use of settlement options may be specified in the policy itself in connection with the beneficiary designation, or in a separate settlement agreement by endorsement to the contract. Once the periodic income payments of the settlement option begin and the life insurance policy itself is surrendered, the company issues a new contract (usually called a *supplementary contract* or *supplementary agreement*) that sets forth the provisions of the optional mode(s) of settlement.

Interest Option

Under the interest option, the company retains the proceeds of the policy and pays only interest to the primary beneficiary at periodic intervals. Usually, the company guarantees a minimum rate of interest, such as 3 percent, but the insurer actually pays a higher rate that is a function of the rate the company is currently earning. Interest payments to the beneficiary can be monthly, quarterly, semiannual, or annual.

Most companies will not accumulate interest. This option is an interim method of handling the proceeds and is usually followed either by a lump-sum payment or by one of the other settlement options. The interest option might seem to have limited appeal, but it provides great flexibility and is useful in a number of situations:

1. When the primary beneficiary is incapacitated in some way.
2. When the proceeds are not needed until sometime after the insured's death. For instance, funds needed for estate clearance purposes normally are not required for several months after the insured dies. There is no reason that interest should not be earned until the funds are needed.
3. When interest on the proceeds is large enough to provide an adequate income to the primary beneficiary. It is not uncommon to provide for interest income to a spouse (as primary beneficiary) and later pay the remaining proceeds to children (as secondary beneficiaries). The primary beneficiary may be granted liberal (or total) rights of withdrawal or the right to change to other settlement options.

4. When the proceeds are payable to a minor beneficiary. Many companies will accumulate the proceeds and interest until the minor reaches the age of legal capacity.

5. When there is a need to supplement a spouse's income during the blackout period and preserve the policy proceeds to the end of that period.

Assuming a 3 percent guaranteed minimum interest rate for this option, $100,000 of proceeds would provide an annual income of $3,000, a semiannual income of $1,500, a quarterly income of $750, or a monthly income of $250. Excess interest earnings could significantly increase this periodic income. For example, a company might be paying 8 percent with the excess paid annually regardless of the method of regular payments. This excess interest (of 5 percentage points in this example) raises the annual income from the guaranteed minimum of $3,000 to $8,000.

Fixed Period Option

The fixed period option is also known as the *installment certain, installment time,* or *period certain* option. With this option, the proceeds are liquidated over a specific period of time. The periodic payment is a function of the amount of proceeds, the rate of interest, the frequency of benefit payments, and the time period selected. The installment benefits are not contingent upon the death or survival of any person. A primary beneficiary might outlive the benefits, or, if the primary beneficiary dies before the benefits are exhausted, they will be paid to a secondary beneficiary or to the primary beneficiary's estate.

The typical policy provision specifies the monthly payment for each $1,000 of proceeds for different durations. For example, the schedule in Exhibit 3-13 provides that if the period selected is ten years, the monthly income would be $9.39 for each $1,000 of proceeds. Thus, if the policy provided for $150,000 in proceeds, the monthly income over a ten-year period would be $1,408.50 ($150,000/1,000 x $9.39). If the insured wishes to arrange for a guaranteed minimum monthly income of $1,000 for ten years, the proceeds of the policy would have to be $106,496 ($1,000/$9.39 x $1,000, rounded to the nearest dollar).

This option is convenient when it is possible to ascertain how long income will be needed. For example, if the insured's youngest child is eight years of age and income is desired until the child reaches age eighteen, benefits are needed for ten years. However, one disadvantage of this option is that it requires periodic evaluation and changes before death to adapt the period to changing needs. Moreover, partial withdrawals during the income payment period are normally not permitted.

Exhibit 3-13

Amount of Monthly Benefits Guaranteed Under Fixed Period Option

Period (years)	1	5	10	15	20	25
Monthly Payment (per $1,000 death benefit)	$84.28	$17.70	$9.39	$6.64	$5.27	$4.46

Fixed Amount Option

The *installment amount, installments of a fixed amount,* or *amount certain* options usually are simply called the fixed amount option. This option pays periodic payments of a predetermined amount to the beneficiary. The individual determines the amount of income needed which, in turn, determines the duration of the benefits. Suppose, for example, that a policyowner wants to provide $500 a month to the beneficiary. Given proceeds of $25,000 and 3 percent interest, $500 a month can be provided for four years and five months. Because the amount of each installment is "fixed" under this option, excess interest extends the benefit period.

If the fixed amount option is selected, the beneficiary might take the following actions:

1. *Obtain a limited or unlimited right of withdrawal.* Withdrawals decrease the benefit period, but it is unnecessary to recompute the benefit amount.
2. *Change the benefit amount.* For example, a beneficiary might decide to take $500 a month rather than the $400 a month originally intended by the policyowner. It is even possible to vary the monthly benefits, that is, to take various amounts as needed. In some cases a beneficiary can decline benefits during selected months.[10]
3. *Place any unpaid proceeds under another option.*

The amount of flexibility given to a beneficiary under the fixed amount option is subject to the policyowner's discretion.

Life Income Options

Several forms of life income options are available. These options provide income to the beneficiary for the remainder of his or her life. The amount of life income per month per $1,000 of death benefit is guaranteed when the contract is issued.

The monthly life income payment per $1,000 of proceeds is specified in a table in the policy and is determined by the sex of the beneficiary and by the age of the beneficiary at the time the income payments begin. Exhibit 3-14 provides an example of such a benefit table. For example, a female beneficiary, age sixty-five at the time she begins to receive life income benefits, will be paid $4.70 per month per $1,000 of death benefit. Thus, if the amount of proceeds is $75,000, she will receive $352.50 ($75,000/1,000 × 4.70) per month for the rest of her life.

Exhibit 3-14
Amount of Monthly Benefits Guaranteed Under Life Income Option

Age of Payee Male	Female	Amount (per $1,000)	Age of Payee Male	Female	Amount (per $1,000)
11*	16*	$2.70	50	55	$4.12
15	20	2.77	55	60	4.41
20	25	2.88	60	65	4.70
25	30	3.02	65	70	4.94
30	35	3.18	70	75	5.12
35	40	3.37	75	80	5.22
40	45	3.59	80	85	5.26
45	50	3.84	85+	90+	5.27

* And younger
\+ And older

Policyowner Decisions Concerning Settlement Options

Policyowners have considerable discretion in the amount of latitude they give beneficiaries to select one of the settlement options, withdraw part or all of the proceeds, or select a second beneficiary. The policyowner might permit the beneficiary to change from one settlement option to another or to request a lump-sum payment. This right can be limited to a specified period of time.

The policyowner can also specify whether the beneficiary has the right to withdraw any or all of the proceeds held by the insurance company. Some insurers limit the number of such withdrawals in one year. Moreover, most companies permit the withdrawal privilege only under certain options.

Advantages and Limitations of Settlement Options

The policyowner has control over the degree of flexibility the beneficiary has in selecting a settlement option. For example, it is possible to apply different settlement options to different portions of the proceeds. The beneficiary might be given no flexibility for a portion of the proceeds but can be given considerable flexibility in determining how the remainder will be used.

Settlement options represent valuable rights to beneficiaries or policyowners for several reasons. Funds so invested are not subject to market loss, and they earn interest that cannot fall below a certain minimum rate. Also, no financial institutions other than life insurance companies are able to offer a guaranteed, lifetime income.

However, certain disadvantages are associated with settlement options:

1. The interest rate applied to funds invested with insurance companies might not be attractive when compared to current yields on alternative investments.

2. Settlement options do not offer a hedge against inflation. Of course, this argument applies equally well to other fixed-dollar investments.

3. Settlement options can be inflexible if the beneficiary is given little freedom to invade the principal. However, this type of inflexibility might be good in that it ensures that the funds are used as the policyowner had desired rather than being dissipated by the beneficiary.

Designating a trust as the policy beneficiary is suggested by some as a solution to these three problems. The trust receives the lump-sum death benefit, and the trustee can exercise discretion within the terms of the trust. Trusts are allowed greater investment flexibility, which can help to increase investment yields and provide a better hedge against inflation. Furthermore, the trust can be designed to provide some flexibility to the surviving dependents to receive principal payments as needed. However, the trustee does not guarantee the principal being administered, as a life insurance company does under settlement options. Also, trustees often charge an annual fee for their services while there is no separate fee charged for settlement options.

Dividend Options

After prospective policyowners have decided to purchase insurance, they must then decide whether to purchase a participating or a nonparticipating policy. A *participating* (*par*) policy pays dividends to policyowners, while a *nonparticipating* (*nonpar*) policy does not. The term "par" stems from the fact that policyowners participate in the actual mortality, investment, and expense experience of the company. To the extent that the experience is more favorable than expected, dividends will increase and vice versa. Policyowners' dividends represent the return of part of the insurance premium and are not subject to federal income taxation.

Assuming that the decision is made to purchase a participating policy, the policyowner must then decide which dividend option to select. Nearly all policies issued by mutual life insurers are par, while stock companies issue both par and nonpar contracts.

As noted earlier in this chapter, life insurance premiums are mainly a function of three major factors: mortality, interest, and expenses. As experience proves more favorable than the assumptions used in the ratemaking process, the surplus of the company is increased and the directors of the company might distribute part of this surplus as policyowner dividends.

If an individual purchases a par policy, he or she can select one of the following methods of receiving dividends:

- Cash
- Premium reduction
- Accumulation at interest
- Paid-up additions
- Term insurance

In most cases, the choice is made when the application is completed, but it can be changed later. If no option is selected, one method will automatically be effective.

Cash

Policyowners have the opportunity to receive cash dividends. The cash option can be a reasonable choice when the policy is paid up (such as during retirement) or when the policyowner has a need for cash.

Reduced Premiums

If this option is selected, a policyowner remits only the *net premium* (the next premium less the actual dividend paid). Some companies stipulate in their policies that the company has no obligation to apply the dividend to the premium due unless the balance of the amount due is paid.

Accumulation at Interest

Under this option, dividends are accumulated by the company with interest compounded annually. The interest rate credited to the accumulated dividends is usually determined annually by the company, and is often in excess of the guaranteed minimum rate specified in the policy.

Most companies allow a policyowner to withdraw the accumulated dividends at any time. However, some life insurance companies allow withdrawals only on the policy anniversary. Once withdrawn by the policyowner, the amounts cannot be redeposited.

In most cases the accumulated dividends are distributed when the policy is surrendered, when the insured dies, or upon retirement of the insured. This has the effect of increasing the amount available to the policyowner or beneficiaries.

Interest earnings on accumulated dividends are taxable income in the year credited. This might make this option undesirable for some policyowners.

Paid-Up Additions

If this option is selected, dividends are used each year to purchase amounts of single-premium, paid-up insurance. The amount of insurance is the amount the dividend will purchase at *net rates* (some or all of the expense factor is not included in the premium) at the insured's attained age. These additions mature at the same time as the basic policy. Generally, this option is not available on term policies.

The paid-up additions increase the basic death benefit and add to the cash value of the basic policy. A policyowner can surrender the paid-up insurance for its cash value without disturbing the basic policy.

One advantage of this option is that the additions are relatively inexpensive since they are purchased at net rates. Moreover, they are purchased without evidence of insurability. Unlike the accumulation at interest option, this option does not create a current income tax liability, and the cash values of the paid-up additions might not be substantially less than the cash that could be provided through dividend accumulations. Evidence of insurability might be required if a policyowner wants to change to this option after the policy is issued.

Purchase Term Insurance; Fifth Dividend Option

Some companies will apply the current dividend to purchase as much term insurance as possible. A more popular form of this option, usually called the *"fifth dividend option,"* does not necessarily purchase the maximum amount of term insurance. Instead, the dividend is used first to purchase one-year term insurance in the amount of the cash value of the policy, and any remaining dividend value is applied to one of the other noncash dividend options, usually the accumulated at interest option. Later, when the premium for the term insurance is higher than the amount of the dividend, the accumulated dividends are used to increase the amount of term insurance to the cash value. With this approach a policyowner purchases one-year term insurance equal to the cash value for a long period of time, and this increases the death benefit for a temporary period as needed. The option terminates when the dividends are inadequate to purchase term insurance equal to the cash value. From then on, the dividends are applied under one of the other options.

Supplementary Benefits

Most life insurance policies provide a basic level of protection against the financial consequences associated with the death of an insured. Additional forms of coverages, commonly referred to as **riders**, are available to life insurance policyowners and can be added to the basic life insurance contracts to customize the policies to better meet the needs of insureds and provide the life insurers with more marketable products. Some of the more common riders are discussed below.

Waiver of Premium

The waiver of premium benefit is the option most commonly added to or included in a life insurance policy. The benefit is automatically included in many contracts. The premium required for this benefit is usually no more than 1 to 3 percent of the premium for the death benefit.

Under this benefit, the insurance company agrees to waive the payment of any premium falling due while the policyowner or insured is disabled as defined in the waiver of premium provision. The provisions, values, and benefits of the policy will be the same as if the premium payments had actually been made to the insurer (instead of being waived).

The insured peril is *total* disability, so the benefit really is a form of health insurance protection. Because total disability is more difficult to determine than death, all life insurance policies with this benefit contain a careful definition of total disability.

Many insurance companies waive premiums during an initial period of time (usually two-to-five years) so long as the policyowner cannot perform the major obligations of *his or her own* occupation. After the stipulated period, the definition becomes more strict, requiring that the insured be unable to perform the duties of *any* occupation. This usually is interpreted to mean any occupation for which the insured is fitted by reason of education, training, and experience. Some insurers use only the strict definition for the entire period of disability.

Before premiums are waived, the disability must exist for a period of time known as a *waiting period*. Most insurance companies use a six-month waiting period, but many companies require a shorter period such as four months. The policyowner is responsible for paying any premiums due during the waiting period.

The waiver of premium benefit covers disabilities resulting from both accidental injury and sickness. Virtually all provisions exclude self-inflicted injuries and disabilities resulting from war. Some companies also add other exclusions such as injuries or diseases resulting from private air travel or travel in foreign countries.

To be eligible for the benefit, the policyowner must have incurred a disability prior to a stipulated age. Most contracts stipulate age seventy or lower. The premium for the benefit is discontinued after the policyowner reaches the stipulated age (except for those policies that include this feature as an indivisible part of their coverage).

The age cutoff specifies the age before which the disability must occur if the premiums are to be waived. It does not operate to terminate benefits. If a disability occurs before the stipulated age, all future premiums are waived. Life policies might provide that the premiums will be waived until the insured reaches age sixty-five, and, at that time, the policyowner will be granted a paid-up policy. Other life contracts provide that the policy will mature as an endowment at age sixty-five. In still other policies, the waiver of premium benefit simply continues until the end of the premium payment period.

Accidental Death Benefits

This supplementary benefit or rider, popularly known as *double indemnity*, is added to many life insurance policies. Some insurance companies automatically include this benefit in the policy and do not make a separate charge. The benefit typically provides an additional death benefit when death results from accidental bodily injury or accidental means.

In most cases, the amount of the accidental death benefit is equal to the face amount of the basic policy—in other words, it doubles the amount payable for *accidental* death, hence the name "double indemnity." A $100,000 policy, for example, will pay $200,000 to the beneficiary if the death of the insured meets the requirements of the clause. In some policies, the amount of the accidental death benefit is some other multiple of the face amount, such as twice the face amount of the policy (which might be called "triple indemnity"—the basic policy benefit plus twice the face amount equals a "triple" benefit).

The typical accidental death benefit provision stipulates that the death of the insured must occur within ninety days of the injury. This addresses the problem of establishing whether the accidental injury was the proximate cause of death. The ninety-day requirement is becoming a problem, as medical technology is better able to prolong life. Therefore, companies are increasingly specifying a longer period, such as 120 or 180 days. At least one state prohibits the use of a time limitation in the accidental death definition.

The accidental death benefit generally terminates on the next policy anniversary after the insured reaches some specified age (for example, sixty, sixty-five, or seventy), but some policies provide lifetime accidental death benefits. Any extra premium for the benefit terminates with the coverage. This rider has no effect on cash values.

There is considerable variation in the exclusions that apply to the accidental death benefit. Some policies contain many exclusions; others contain few exclusions. The most common exclusions are the following:

1. Suicide and self-inflicted injuries
2. Inhalation of gas or fumes
3. Injuries occurring during commission of a felony
4. Aviation (except as a fare-paying passenger)
5. War
6. Illness or disease

The accidental death benefit is added to many policies, probably because the cost is low and many individuals believe that their death is unlikely while they are young, unless they die accidentally. The cost varies, but at age thirty-five it costs approximately $.60 per $1,000 of coverage. At this rate, an individual can add the rider to a $150,000 policy for only $90 per year.

The desirability of the accidental death benefit is questionable. Critics point out that the rider is detrimental if the benefit absorbs premium dollars that should be used to buy a larger policy. Furthermore, this coverage gives many policyowners an inaccurate perception of the amount of life insurance protection they have. For example, it is not uncommon for a person who owns a $50,000 policy with an accidental death benefit to believe that he or she has a "$100,000 policy."

Despite these weaknesses, some argue that the accidental death benefit does provide a form of limited protection. Because of its low cost, it is unlikely that it diverts substantial premium dollars from the purchase of more life insurance.

However, because it is impossible to confidently predict that an individual's death will be accidental, the accidental death benefit should not be included for life insurance planning purposes. If a life insurance need exists, the need is present for both accidental and nonaccidental deaths.

Guaranteed Purchase Option

This option has a variety of names but is often called the *guaranteed purchase option* (GPO), *guaranteed insurability option* (GIO), or *option to purchase additional insurance*. It is added to many policies, particularly those issued to younger insureds. Since it provides a means of purchasing life insurance at specified times in the future without evidence of insurability, this option must normally be purchased prior to a certain age, often forty.

The type and amount of insurance that may be purchased under this option are limited, usually to a form of whole life insurance with the face amount of the original policy or some specified maximum portion of the face. Often a minimum amount applies to the exercise of each option. The option dates are usually set at uniform intervals based on the insured's attained age. A common approach is to allow purchases every three or five years, but some companies use other time intervals.

In some cases the GPO rider permits acceleration of option dates upon the occurrence of certain events such as marriage or the birth or adoption of a child. A policyowner usually has thirty or sixty days before or after the option date to exercise the purchase privilege. An unexercised option cannot be used after the purchase period expires, but future options are unaffected by failure to exercise an option.

GPOs take different approaches as to what happens to the policyowner's rights for additional purchases when premiums on the base policy are being waived because of disability. One approach allows the policyowner to purchase a new insurance policy at each option date, and the premiums for the newly acquired policies are waived as well as those for the original contract. The policyowner is permitted no choice in selecting the type of policy that may be purchased in order to minimize adverse selection. A second approach permits the disabled insured to exercise this GPO, but the new premiums are not waived.

The guaranteed purchase option provides a reasonable method of protecting the future insurability of the insured. Its cost varies from about $.50 per $1,000 to approximately $2 per $1,000, depending upon the insured's age.

Long-Term Care (LTC) Riders

Some life insurance companies offer long-term care (LTC) riders to individual life insurance contracts for an additional premium. These riders provide long-term care benefits for skilled or intermediate nursing home care, custodial care, and home health care. As in the case of other LTC coverages, the modern tendency is for daily, weekly, or monthly benefits to be paid when the insured person is unable to perform a certain number (such as two or three) of a list of activities of daily living (ADLs), such as eating, bathing, dressing, general mobility, toileting, and taking medication. Some LTC riders on life contracts are called *dependent riders*, under which the death and cash value benefits of the life policy are reduced by LTC benefits paid. Other LTC riders are referred to as *independent riders* because their benefits may be paid without reducing the underlying life policy's benefits. The benefits of LTC riders on life policies are often based on percentages of the face amount of the underlying life policy subject to some limitations. As of this writing, LTC riders on life insurance policies are still in their early stages of development and their tax status is uncertain.

Accelerated Death Benefits

A somewhat different approach to final care issues is that of some life insurance companies that offer policies or riders on policies that provide for the discounted value or a portion of such value (such as 50 percent) of the policy death benefit to be paid to the policyowner in the event of certain contingencies. An example of such a contingency might be the onset of a *terminal illness* (generally an illness expected to result in the insured's death within one year), the insured's contracting a dread disease, or the insured's taking up permanent residence in a nursing home.

Such accelerated death benefits reduce the cash value and death benefits of the underlying life policy. An initial premium might be charged for this benefit. However, sometimes it can be provided for existing policies by insurance company practice.

Summary

This chapter dealt with the exposure to death, life insurance planning, and specific contractual provisions found in life insurance policies.

The most appropriate policy depends on the life insurance plan of the consumer. This chapter focused on life insurance planning based on an individual's or family's needs.

The first step in developing a plan is to identify one's needs by asking, how much money would the family need if the "breadwinner" died, and when would the money be needed? Once these needs, such as an estate settlement fund, life income for the surviving spouse, and education funds, are identified, a corresponding life insurance plan can be developed through programming or capital need analysis.

The next step is to analyze the true costs of the policy or policies under consideration. The most common methods of analysis are the interest-adjusted method and the interest-adjusted cost (payment) index.

Finally, it is important to consider factors in the selection of an insurance company and policy other than cost. In this area, the financial strength of the insurer obviously is vital.

The final part of the chapter covered various important life insurance policy provisions. These included general provisions such as the incontestable clause and nonforfeiture options, as well as supplementary benefits such as the waiver of premium benefit and the guaranteed purchase option. Most general provisions must be included in life insurance policies. However, life insurers and policyowners decide whether supplementary benefits will be added to the contract.

Chapter Notes

1. The amount of taxes and administrative costs can be taken from tables that show average amounts for estates of various sizes.

2. Published by A. M. Best Company, Somerville, N.J.

3. At least three situations that have been adjudicated hold that if the policy never legally existed, it could never become incontestable. These are cases in which the applicant purchased the policy with the intent to murder the insured (not a valid contract as it is against public policy); cases in which a healthy person impersonated the person to be insured to the medical examiner (the "person to be insured" was not the *life* insured, hence there was no contract on that life); and cases where the applicant was other than the insured and lacked an insurable interest at the formation of the contract.

4. In many cases, a living policyowner can also use one of the settlement options as a method of receiving the nonforfeiture value.

5. It is often preferable to borrow the loan value rather than surrender the policy for its cash value. The loan value is essentially the same as the cash surrender value, with the only difference in some companies being the deduction of an interest charge in advance. If the contract is surrendered for its cash value, many life insurance companies, by contract provision, will not permit reinstatement. If the loan value is borrowed, restoration of the full benefits of the contract is automatic upon repayment of the loan (and applicable interest) *without* the necessity for a reinstatement application and evidence of insurability. Moreover, if surrendered for cash, there would not be any death benefit; while if a loan is made, the death benefit would be the face of the policy less the indebtedness. Further, policy loans from most life insurance policies are not viewed as potentially taxable distributions for federal income tax purposes. However, the surrender of a life insurance policy for its cash value can produce gross ordinary income for federal income tax purposes as described previously. Of course, the policyowner must pay generally nondeductible interest on a policy loan.

6. In a few companies, policy indebtedness is not deducted (in order to purchase a larger amount of paid-up insurance), but the policy loans are continued under the new policy. This is not the usual approach, however.

7. Many life insurance companies delete the extended term insurance nonforfeiture option from policies issued to substandard insureds.

8. As with all policy loans or other indebtedness, should death occur before the loan is repaid, the amount of the loan plus any unpaid interest is deducted from the

proceeds at death. The automatic premium loan option reduces these proceeds rather dramatically if it is allowed to operate for several years. See the discussion on nonforfeiture options earlier in this chapter.

9. It is necessary to distinguish among these alternatives because there is considerable disagreement about the meaning of the word "lapse." Some experts maintain that a policy lapses only if it terminates without value (alternative 3 above). Others maintain that lapse occurs whether alternative 1, 2, or 4 takes place.

10. For example, many life insurance companies make available, upon policyowner request, an educational settlement option. This could, for example, provide $100 monthly for four years plus an additional $1,000 payable during each September and January of those years.

Chapter 4

Life Insurance Products and Their Uses

Life insurance is used by many individuals to provide protection against the financial consequences of their deaths to their families. Surviving dependents have various types of lump sum and income needs, as identified in Chapter 3. One form of life insurance often is not enough to meet the different family needs and situations. Therefore, several alternative life insurance products are available.

Some life insurance policies provide a basic level of protection and might accumulate cash value that some individuals use for saving. Other life insurance policies are designed not only to provide protection but also to actively offer investment features. Both the categories of life insurance products and their more common uses are discussed in this chapter.

Life Insurance Products

Life insurance products have undergone considerable transformation in recent years with the emergence of so-called "interest-sensitive" or investment-oriented individual life insurance policies.

At one time, there were essentially three "traditional" basic types of individual life insurance policies: term insurance, whole life insurance, and endowment life insurance. Other kinds of policies written by life insurance companies were combinations of these basic types.

For many years, the traditional policies were the only forms of life insurance sold in the United States. Now they share the market with newer, more investment-oriented life insurance products. The newer types of individual life insurance policies being sold include variable life (VL), universal life (UL), variable universal life (VUL), and interest sensitive or current assumption whole life policies. These policies have one or more characteristics that are quite different from those of the "traditional" products, such as flexible premiums, unbundled benefits, investment decisions and risks placed more on the policyowner, and greater emphasis on the investment aspects of life insurance. The tax aspects of life insurance have also received considerable attention in recent years. Further, insurers can now use various combinations of cash value life insurance and term insurance in one policy to meet the insured's needs and ability to pay.

Term Insurance

Term insurance provides financial protection for a limited period of time only. If the insured dies during that period, the face amount of the policy is paid to the beneficiary. If the insured survives the policy period, either the policy expires and the obligations of the insurance company terminate or the policyowner may renew the policy for an additional period or periods, depending on the provisions of the term contract.

Basic Characteristics

Term insurance is the simplest form of life insurance coverage and the type that most closely resembles property and liability insurance. If a building is insured against loss by fire and does not suffer any damage during the policy period, the obligation of the insurer ceases. The premium is fully earned by the insurance company—although the insured has received no financial indemnity from the insurer, the policyowner received value by having insurance protection during the policy period. The same is true concerning term life insurance. The insurance company is liable for the policy's face amount only if the insured dies during the policy period. If the insured survives the policy period, he or she nevertheless received value by having been protected.

Period of Protection

Most term policies provide protection for a specified duration (usually one, five, ten, fifteen, or twenty years) or to some specified age (such as sixty-five or seventy). Consequently, term insurance is often referred to as "temporary" protection.

Period of Premium Payments

Premiums for term policies typically are level during the policy period. For example, an individual who purchases a five-year term insurance policy would pay the same premium each year for five years. Annual premiums vary depending on the length of the contract, since the policies with longer durations include protection at older ages when mortality rates are higher. Generally speaking, for any given age, the premium for term insurance is lower than the premium for any other plan of insurance purchased at that age. A popular form of term insurance now is yearly renewable term (YRT) or annually renewable term (ART), in which the premium increases with each year of continued coverage.

Premium and Death Benefit Flexibility

Term insurance can be a very flexible type of contract. Younger persons with large needs for death protection often start out with substantial amounts of term insurance at a lower premium and then, as they grow older, (1) continue to renew some or all of the term protection at constantly increasing premiums, (2) convert some or all of the term coverage to cash value type policies, or (3) perhaps discontinue some of the term coverage or acquire more coverage. This section examines some of the areas of possible flexibility in term policies that can aid the policyowner in his or her insurance and financial planning.

Renewability   A **renewability provision** gives the insured the option to renew the contract without proof of insurability. Without this option, an unhealthy insured could be without insurance after the policy has expired and would be unable to purchase new coverage. In effect, this provision permits continuation of the coverage at the option of the policyowner, rather than at the option of the insurance company.

Every time a term policy is renewed, the premium increases to reflect the current age of the insured. The original contract might or might not stipulate a guaranteed scale of renewal rates. Exhibit 4-1 illustrates how premiums increase for a person who continues to exercise the renewal option on a five-year term policy. Increases in the premium are slight at the younger ages, but, as a person grows older, premiums increase more rapidly to reflect the higher mortality rates at advanced ages.

The renewal privilege is obviously a valuable option for those insureds who become uninsurable, but it is also beneficial to insureds who remain insurable. It is normally more convenient for a policyowner to renew an existing term policy than to purchase a new one. Giving written notice or remitting the renewal premium with the insurer's renewal notice to the insurance company is generally all that is required to exercise the renewal option.

Exhibit 4-1
Annual Premiums for a Five-Year Renewable Term Policy

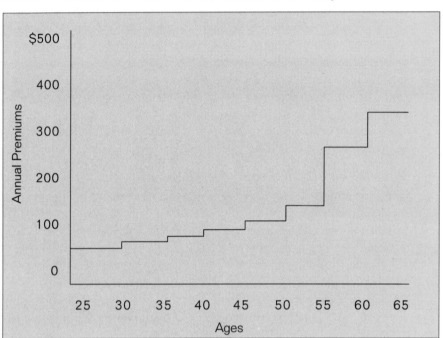

Another advantage of renewal for insurable policyowners is that the suicide and incontestable periods do not start again at each renewal as they would in a newly purchased contract. These are two significant reasons that policyowners may prefer to renew a policy under which some time has already elapsed rather than start over with a new policy.

Insurance companies, however, face a problem with renewable policies. Insureds who believe they are in good health become increasingly reluctant to pay the higher premiums required upon renewal, and some allow their coverages to expire. At the same time, insureds who believe they are in poor health generally renew their policies. As a result, the insurer experiences **adverse mortality selection** because the mortality experience of those remaining in the plan tends to become less favorable than for the original group of insureds. Term insurance premiums account for this tendency. Life insurers also place limitations on the policyowner's right to renew the contract. For example, a ten-year renewable term policy issued at age thirty-five might be renewable twice—at ages forty-five and fifty-five—or the contract might stipulate a maximum age beyond which the contract cannot be renewed, such as age seventy-five.

Convertibility   A **convertible term policy** allows a policyowner to exchange the term policy or part of the term policy for another form of insurance (other than term) without providing evidence of insurability. The conversion feature is a more effective method of protecting insurability than the renewability provision since it gives the policyowner access to an insurance plan that can be continued indefinitely. A policyowner can obtain permanent insurance through conversion, but with the renewal option the policyowner can extend the term coverage for only a specified period.

A policyowner is not required to wait until the end of the policy period to exercise the conversion privilege. In fact, many convertible term policies stipulate that the option can be exercised only a certain amount of time before the expiration of the coverage. For example, a five-year policy may be convertible only during the first four policy years, or a fifteen-year plan may be convertible only during the first twelve policy years. Restrictions of this type are supposed to minimize adverse mortality selection. The effectiveness of these restrictions, however, is questionable, and many insurance companies use conversion provisions that permit conversion at any time during the policy period.

In most term policies a policyowner might use either the attained age method or the original age method of conversion. However, some term policies are automatically converted.

The **attained age method** of conversion is the simpler and more common of these two methods. With this approach, the premium rate and policy form of the new contract are the same as those being used by the insurance company on the conversion date. This is similar to terminating the old policy and purchasing a new one, with the following important differences:

1. Evidence of insurability is not required.
2. The new policy will be incontestable.
3. The suicide exclusion will not apply to the new policy.
4. The policyowner might benefit from a conversion credit.

If a conversion credit is available (not all insurance companies follow this practice), it is usually based on the policy reserve and is available to the policyowner only as a credit toward conversion; it cannot be taken in cash.

Some insurance companies use policy provisions that allow conversion only on the attained age basis. Many of these companies, however, permit original age conversion when it is requested, as a matter of company practice rather than a contractual right.

With the **original age method** of conversion, the new policy premium is the same as would have been paid if the policyowner had purchased the new policy in the first place. The advantage to the policyowner is that future premiums will be lower than they would be with an attained age conversion. Depending on the terms of the conversion privilege, the policyowner can receive the same policy form as provided by the company at the insured's original age, or the new policy might be exactly the same as those currently being issued (at the insured's attained age).

An original age conversion necessitates an adjustment to place the insurance company in the same financial position that would have resulted had the policyowner initially purchased the new (higher premium) policy. The insured is, therefore, required to make a lump-sum payment to the insurer. The original term contract stipulates how the lump-sum payment must be computed. Usually, it equals the difference in reserves or cash values between the two policies, or the difference in premiums, with interest.

Original age conversion can be attractive to policyowners because of the lower premium and the belief that the lump-sum payment to the insurance company is invested and credited with retroactive interest. Actually, there is no substantial financial advantage to the policyowner with original age conversion. The financial adjustment simply places both parties in the financial position that would have resulted if the new policy had been purchased initially.

The primary factors to be considered when choosing between an original age and an attained age conversion are the insured's health and his or her preference for spreading the insurance cost. A healthy person who has the financial resources to pay the required adjustment and who prefers lower future premiums might logically choose an original age conversion. Otherwise, the preferable choice would be an attained age conversion. For example, an insurable person with a health impairment that might result ultimately in his or her becoming uninsurable should purchase additional insurance with the funds that otherwise would be used to adjust for the original age conversion. If the person is uninsurable, it makes little sense to make the lump-sum payment to the insurance company for original age conversion, because the death benefits would be no greater than they would be by converting with the attained age approach.

Some life insurers issue nonrenewable term policies that are *automatically converted* at some specified date. The policyowner can choose to convert before the automatic date, but, if no such decision is made, the policy automatically converts to a predetermined form.

Reentry Term   A variation of term insurance that provides some premium flexibility is called **reentry term** (or **revertible term**). The premium at each renewal period depends on evidence of insurability. As long as the insured periodically continues to demonstrate good health, the premiums for reentry term insurance remain relatively low. However, if the insured fails to periodically reestablish his or her insurability with the insurance company, the term rates under reentry term tend to increase substantially.

Decreasing Term The face amount of insurance in a term policy is not necessarily the same throughout the policy period. Many term policies have a level face amount, but decreasing term insurance (either as a rider to a basic policy or as a separate contract) is also common. The face amount of a decreasing term policy (or rider) declines yearly or monthly according to a stipulated schedule. Mortgage life insurance and car payment life insurance are examples of decreasing term policies. Only the amount of the outstanding loan would be payable to the lender at the borrower's/insured's death.

The premium usually remains level but in some cases is not payable for the full policy period. For example, a twenty-year decreasing term policy might require premium payments for only the first seventeen years. Premiums are calculated in this manner to avoid paying a relatively large premium for a small amount of protection in the last years of the policy.

Due to the possibility of adverse mortality selection, the conversion feature in a decreasing term policy never allows a policyowner to convert, without evidence of insurability, for the original amount of the decreasing term coverage. Instead, conversion of the amount of insurance that is effective at the time of the conversion is permitted. In some policies, the insured can convert only a certain percentage, such as 75 percent, of the amount of insurance in force.

Increasing Term Another form of term insurance that provides limited death benefit flexibility is increasing term insurance. The face amount of increasing term insurance rises during the policy period. Life insurers seldom issue an increasing term policy as a separate contract. This type of protection is issued as a rider to other types of policies.

Cost for Protection

Since term insurance by its nature is "pure" insurance protection, having no or little cash value, it normally involves a low initial premium outlay by the policyowner. Also, as far as cost alone is concerned, it is easier to compare term contracts than whole life or other cash-value type contracts because future cash values and dividend accumulations are not significant considerations. Term insurance costs are quite competitive and can vary considerably for comparable ages and policies among insurers.

However, term policies can have *rate structures* (premium rates for each age) that are guaranteed, or they can have indeterminate premiums. When a **guaranteed rate structure** is used, the term premium rates for each age are set when the policy is issued, and they cannot be increased in the future. Under **indeterminate premium** policies, on the other hand, there is an initial rate structure when the policy is issued, but these initial rates for each age can be increased or decreased by the insurance company in the future according to the company's actuarial experience. However, there is normally a maximum guaranteed level of rates beyond which the insurer cannot increase its rates under indeterminate premium policies. Thus, if an insurer's term mortality experience deteriorates, the insurer can raise rates up to the maximum under indeterminate premium policies, but cannot do so under guaranteed premium policies. On the other hand, the initial term rates for comparable policies are usually lower for indeterminate premium policies than for guaranteed premium policies.

Uses of Term Insurance

Term insurance is a popular form of life insurance. It can be used for the reasons discussed below.

Meeting Substantial Insurance Needs With Limited Resources

A person who needs a large amount of life insurance but can afford only relatively small premiums should consider purchasing term insurance. For example, consider a married couple who has a young child and one of the partners is completing his or her education. In the face of a limited budget, a person who needs a large amount of protection should purchase term insurance so that amount of the insurance protection will most closely approximate the amount of coverage needed.

Securing Outstanding Loans

Many lenders, where permitted by state law, require a term insurance policy as a prerequisite for a loan. If insurance is required, the lender will insist that the policy's proceeds be made payable to the lender. Even in states where life insurance cannot be required to protect a loan, a life insurance policy can still be used for this purpose. Term insurance might make the transaction acceptable to the lender, who is then willing to lend funds that would otherwise not be available.

Term insurance is normally appropriate to secure a loan because of its low premium and because the policy period can be made to coincide with the duration of the loan. If the loan is repaid in installments, a decreasing term policy might be appropriate to reflect the decreasing obligation of the borrower.

Protecting Insurability

The need for guaranteed access to life insurance can be met by purchasing term insurance that is renewable and convertible. Other methods of meeting this need are available, but term insurance involves the lowest premium outlay.

Providing Dependency Period Income

Term insurance on the life of the wage earner(s) is often used to meet the need for income during the limited dependency period. For example, suppose a family has children aged fifteen, twelve, and six. The father or mother might purchase a fifteen-year decreasing term policy (to expire when the youngest child will be twenty-one). Another approach would be to purchase a twenty- or twenty-five-year decreasing term policy at the birth of each child. Also, some life insurance policies, recognizing the importance of the need for dependency period income, include term protection as an integral part of the contract.

Limitations of Term Insurance

Although term insurance is useful for a variety of reasons, it does have limitations. These are discussed in the following paragraphs.

Lack of Cash or Loan Values

Term insurance rarely contains any cash or loan value. Therefore, it cannot provide funds to the policyowner (except indirectly by enhancing credit) either while the policy is in force or at its expiration. This can lead some to complain that they pay premiums over a long period of time and "receive nothing in return." A policyowner does receive value for term insurance premiums through protection obtained.

Limited Period of Protection

A person's life insurance needs change frequently. It is sometimes difficult to predict exactly what kind of protection will be required for a specific need. As a result, an individual might purchase term insurance and find that his or her need for life insurance protection extends beyond the duration of the policy. In an effort to prevent this, many advisers recommend renewable and convertible term whenever term insurance is used. Even with renewable and convertible term, or with long-term policies, coverage will normally expire at some specified age.

Increasing Premium

One of the main attractions of term insurance is its low premium. The shorter the policy period, the lower the annual premium. For example, the premium is lower for a ten-year term policy than for a twenty-year term policy, and even lower for a five-year or one-year policy. However, the premium will increase each time the policy is renewed.

At the insured's younger ages, the increase in the premium upon renewal is slight. With each renewal, however, the premium increases, and at the older ages the increase in the premium becomes substantial. Some policyowners are likely to regard the increased premium as prohibitive at some point and to let their protection expire. It is important that the insurance adviser inform each policyowner that because the premium increases after each term, it will become very expensive at the older ages.

Whole Life Insurance

Whole life insurance is designed to provide death protection for all of a person's life, at a level premium, and thus a cash value develops within the life insurance policy. For these reasons, whole life insurance is commonly called *permanent life insurance* or *cash value life insurance*. In the early 1990s, the bulk of the cash value life insurance sold in the United States was whole life insurance.

Basic Characteristics

Whole life insurance is "traditional" cash value life insurance. This means it has the following characteristics:

- The policy is generally sold at a fixed, level premium.
- The policy develops a minimum cash value that increases within the policy according to a set schedule.
- The cash value is guaranteed by the insurance company.
- The policy is intended to provide at least a minimum level of death benefits for the whole of life.
- The policy can be participating or nonparticipating.

Period of Protection

Whole life insurance is designed so that coverage can be continued throughout all of life at a level premium that can be paid either for the insured's whole lifetime or for a limited time period. A policyowner, of course, can surrender, borrow against, or otherwise reduce coverage under a whole life policy at his or her discretion, and so the coverage might not, in fact, be for the whole of the insured's lifetime. However, death protection is available as long as the policyowner keeps the coverage in force.

Period of Premium Payments

Two major types of whole life insurance are *straight life* policies and *limited payment* policies. Single premium whole life has gained enough attention to merit separate discussion later in this chapter.

Straight Life **Straight life** (or **ordinary life**) policies provide permanent protection, and their premiums and policy values are based on the assumption that premiums will be paid periodically until the insured dies or reaches age 100. Because the mortality tables used by most insurance companies for life insurance purposes assume that all insureds die before reaching age 100, in the rare cases in which a person lives to celebrate a 100th birthday, the insurance company pays the face amount to the policyowner.

Limited Payment **Limited payment life insurance** provides permanent protection, but its premiums are only paid for a limited number of years. Terminology is again sometimes confusing: some limited payment policies are described by the number of years premiums will be paid—for example, a twenty-payment life policy requires twenty annual premiums. Others are described by the age to which premiums are payable—for example, a life-paid-up-at-sixty-five policy requires annual premium payments until the insured turns sixty-five. Of course, the longer the premium paying period, the more closely the contract resembles the straight life approach.

A limited payment policy generates cash values faster than a straight life contract. If both a straight life policy and a limited payment contract provide the same death benefit, the limited payment policy requires the same benefit to be purchased by fewer premiums. It follows that each premium for the limited payment policy must be higher than those paid for a straight life policy. Higher premiums, of course, imply that the initial cash value buildup in the level premium system will be greater, and as a result, cash values will be greater in the limited payment contract. Exhibit 4-2 illustrates the differences in cash values.

Premium Flexibility

Whole life insurance policies are **fixed premium** contracts. This means that a definite, usually level, gross premium per $1,000 of insurance is determined at the time the policy is issued.

Of course, if the policy is *participating*, the premium payments might be reduced (or even paid) by the policy dividends declared by the insurer on the policy. Policy dividends can become quite large, particularly for policies that have been in force for a long period of time. Naturally, however, these policy dividends are not guaranteed by the insurance company.

Exhibit 4-2

Illustration of the Difference in Cash Value Between a Limited Payment Policy and a Straight Life Policy

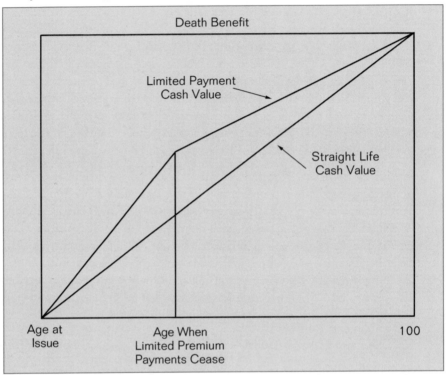

One recent and popular approach for attaining premium flexibility under participating fixed-premium whole life policies is to use the policy dividends, and perhaps the cash values of surrendered, previously existing paid-up additions, to pay the current premiums for the policy as they come due. When the policy values (current dividends and paid-up additions) reach the point at which this is possible (after the policy has been in force for a number of years), the policy premiums, when paid in this way, are said to "vanish." Hence, this approach is known as **vanishing premiums**, which is a misnomer, because the premiums do not actually "vanish" or go away in any fashion. Rather, they are being paid by the current year's policy dividend. In the event that the dividend is not sufficient to pay the whole premium, the premiums are paid by the cash value from the surrender of just enough previously purchased paid-up additions to make up the difference between the premium and the year's policy dividend. (Of course, this reduces the total amount of the death benefit from what would otherwise be the case.)

It must be carefully noted that this vanishing premium concept is not the same as having *a paid-up life insurance policy*. When a life insurance policy is paid up, the insurer *guarantees* that no further premium payments are required to keep the policy in force until the insured's death. Both participating and nonparticipating policies can be or become paid up, but only participating policies can have vanishing premiums.

Death Benefit Flexibility

Traditional, fixed-premium whole life insurance is not primarily designed to provide death benefit flexibility. However, various kinds of term riders and guaranteed insurability options can be added to whole life policies for an additional premium.

The death benefit under whole life policies can be affected in a number of ways. In the case of participating whole life insurance, the policyowner in effect can increase the amount of the death benefit by electing to use policy dividends to purchase paid-up additions or to buy additional one-year term insurance usually equal to the policy's cash value. Hence, the choice of dividend options under participating policies can provide some death benefit flexibility. Also, taking a policy loan in effect reduces the death benefit by the amount of the outstanding loan. Further, use of the reduced paid-up or extended term nonforfeiture options can provide some death benefit flexibility. Finally, a portion (or all) of a whole life policy can be surrendered for cash, thereby reducing the death benefit by the amount surrendered.

Cost for Protection

The true "cost" of whole life insurance is very difficult to determine and is a controversial issue. It is part of the debate over whether it is better to purchase cash value life insurance or to purchase term insurance for pure protection and then invest the "difference" in other investment media outside the life insurance policy. Various approaches for determining the "cost" of whole life insurance were explained in Chapter 3. In general, because of the level premium plan, whole life insurance premiums are larger than term life premiums at younger ages and less than term life premiums at older ages.

The Level Premium Technique

A **level premium insurance plan** is designed so that annual premiums will not increase during the premium-paying period. The premium-paying period might or might not be as long as the period during which protection is provided. Although simple in concept, the level premium technique provides a sound basis for fixed-premium whole life insurance protection over a long period.

Because of the nature of mortality rates, life insurance costs have a natural tendency to increase with age. However, with policies that provide protection over a long period, it is possible to structure annual premium payments so that they do not increase. This occurs because premiums can be calculated so that they are more than adequate to pay death claims in the early policy years, when the insured is younger. These "more-than-adequate" premiums (excess premiums) create a cash buildup that can help pay for the higher mortality costs among older insureds for whom actual collected premiums are "less-than-adequate." In other words, a level premium can be substituted for a premium that has a strong natural tendency to increase.

Exhibit 4-3 is an illustration of the level premium technique for a whole life policy issued at age thirty-five, which provides protection for thirty years. The straight line in Exhibit 4-3 represents the net annual level premium that is the mathematical equivalent of a series of annually increasing premiums. The net level premium is not simply the average of each of the annual yearly renewable term premiums. Rather, it is calculated to recognize the following factors:

1. *Mortality losses.* Some insureds will not survive to pay all of the premiums—the yearly renewable term premium is adjusted upward each year to reflect that fact.
2. *Interest earnings.* The amount accumulated from the excess of the net level premium over the yearly renewable term premium during the early years of the policy is invested, and interest is earned on the invested funds. This reduces the premiums otherwise required.

In actual practice, a life insurance company would charge something more than the net level premium in order to cover its operating expenses, to contribute to the surplus of the organization, and to allow for the discrepancies inherent in its rating assumptions.

Although the level premium in the early years is more than is needed to pay for *current* mortality costs, the same level premium is inadequate to pay for mortality costs that will be incurred at a later date. In effect, the level premium system is a method of keeping the annual premium within reasonable bounds for policyowners when protection is provided over a long period of time. A roughly comparable technique is typically used with auto loans and home mortgages: loan payments are kept level even though the remaining balance due on the loan continues to decline.

Cash Values

The funds collected during the early policy years, over and above the amounts currently needed to cover mortality costs, are accounted for by accumulation

Exhibit 4-3
The Level Premium Technique

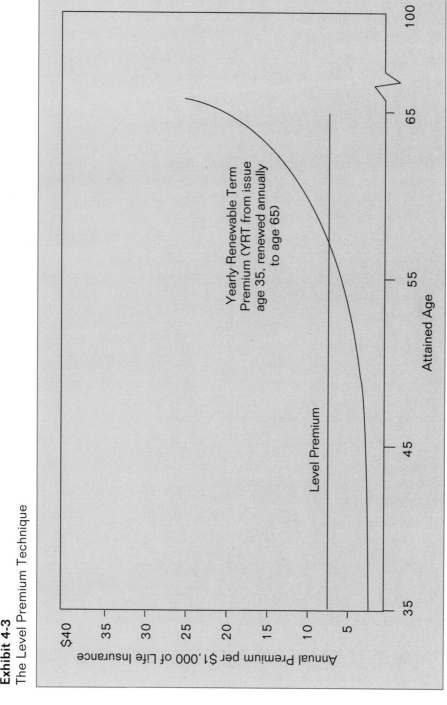

of values within the policy. The cash value element in a whole life policy is a direct result of the leveling of premiums. Policies without level premiums can also have policy cash values, as long as premiums in the early years are more than sufficient to pay expected claims.[1]

Since the cash value builds up within a policy using the level premium technique, while the face amount of a policy remains level, a portion of any death claim would be paid from the cash value. Therefore, the amount of pure protection provided by the life insurer (referred to as the *net amount at risk* for the life insurer) necessarily decreases as the cash value increases. As a result, many people view whole life insurance as a combination of decreasing amounts of insurance (pure protection) and increasing amounts of savings. However, others have argued that a level premium policy is not a combination of protection and savings. They argue that the elements are inextricably intertwined and should not be thought of as separate.

Whether or not a life insurance policy is actually composed of protection and savings elements is not important for our purposes. However, people might refer to policy values as the *cash value*, the *reserve*, the *nonforfeiture value*, or the *policy loan value*. When these terms are used interchangeably, distortion results.

Policy Reserves

The primary purpose of the policy reserve is to ensure that adequate funds will be available to the insurer when needed. A reserve is neither an asset nor a fund. A policy reserve is a *liability* of the insurance company. The reserve protects the insurer's policyowners because the insurance company is required to have assets exceeding the total of all its policy obligations. More accurately, the **policy reserve** can be defined by the following formula:

$$\text{Policy reserve} = \text{Present value of future benefits} - \text{Present value of future net premiums}$$

By definition, the policy reserve must accumulate to the total face amount of the insurer's policies at the maturity of these life insurance contracts.

With the use of a mortality table, the expected number of deaths that will occur each year can be predicted. And with a specified rate of interest, the present value of future death claims can be determined. This is an estimate of the amount of money needed, at present, that along with interest will pay the death claims that will occur in the future.

The second element in the reserve formula is an estimate of the amount of future net premiums that will be collected, but discounted to their present value. Only *net* premiums are considered, because it is assumed that the expense factor in the premium will *not* be available to pay death claims.

The reserve formula clarifies that the primary function of the policy reserve is to ensure that adequate funds are available when claims come due. For example, if an insurance company expects future claims to have a present value of $10 million, but the present value of future net premiums is only $9 million, the company's potential obligation for death claims is greater than the potential net premium income. In this situation the insurance company would be required to show a reserve for $1 million. By maintaining assets in an amount greater than the reserve, the insurance company preserves the financial strength necessary to meet its long-term obligations.

Nonforfeiture Values

Nonforfeiture values are a by-product of the level premium payment plan. Policyowners have a right to most or all of the value built up in their life insurance policies due to the level premium payments. Upon terminating their coverage after paying level premiums over a period of time, policyowners always receive a guaranteed value (in one form or another). Insurers are generally required to establish nonforfeiture values whenever premiums have been paid for at least three years.

Policy Loan Values

Another policy value that arises from the level premium technique is the policy loan value. The loan value of a contract is based on its cash value.

A policy loan is also an insurance company asset. The company can invest its funds (from the cash value) in bonds, real estate, or some other asset, or it can provide them to a policyowner by means of a policy loan. In a policy loan, the company has a perfectly secure investment (which will be either repaid by the policyowner or deducted from the death proceeds) and an interest-earning asset.

Uses of Whole Life Insurance

Because whole life insurance provides permanent protection, it can be used to meet life insurance needs that are likely to continue throughout one's life. For example, funds must be available to pay for last illness and funeral expenses, regardless of the age at which death occurs. Whole life insurance is also used to meet many estate planning needs, which are discussed in Chapter 8. On these bases, it can be argued that almost everyone should have some whole life insurance.

Many individuals believe that whole life insurance offers a desirable combination of protection and savings. In a sense, whole life insurance enables a person to guarantee that an estate of a certain size will be created. The insured can allow the protection to continue until death, at which time the face amount is paid to the beneficiary. Or, if the insured lives long enough, the cash value will accumulate for use later in life.

Whole life insurance offers some degree of flexibility. Most of the flexibility is derived from the nonforfeiture options, from the availability of policy loans, and from the use of dividends in the case of participating policies. In addition, an exchange feature of whole life insurance can have advantages for a policyowner. Most insurance companies include a provision in their policies that allows a policyowner to exchange a contract, without evidence of insurability, for any other form of coverage requiring a higher premium rate.

From a tax standpoint, the growth of the cash value inside whole life insurance is not currently subject to federal (or state) income taxation. This "tax-deferred" inside buildup of cash values of life insurance policies for tax purposes is an important advantage of any form of cash value life insurance.

Limitations of Whole Life Insurance

When compared with term insurance, whole life insurance does not provide as much protection per premium dollar as does term insurance. Thus, for insureds who need substantial death protection but who have limited current financial ability to pay insurance premiums, substantial amounts of term insurance might be the answer at least for the present.

Another argument against traditional whole life insurance is that the policyowner does not have discretion or flexibility with regard to premium payments. The policyowner must pay the fixed amount specified by the life insurer when the insurer schedules the payments. However, proponents of whole life insurance counter that a fixed premium provides policyowners with the encouragement or discipline to make the necessary premium payments. They argue that a flexible premium structure might lull policyowners into a false sense of security with regard to premium payments, particularly if interest earnings on the cash value fall short of expectations and more premiums are required to make up the difference.

Whole life insurance will normally develop a cash value and thus, in effect, will become a savings and investment vehicle for the policyowner. An argument against traditional whole life insurance is that the policyowner does not have investment choices or flexibility with regard to the cash value. The policyowner must abide by the investment choices of the life insurer. This brings up the fundamental issue of whether an individual wants to have at least part of his or her savings and investment dollars in the cash values of a permanent (cash value) life insurance policy or policies, or whether he or she prefers to purchase term insurance to provide pure death protection and then invest his or her savings and investment dollars elsewhere.

This controversial issue lies at the heart of the evaluation of whole life insurance as well as the evaluations of the other kinds of cash value life insurance covered in this chapter. It has been hotly debated for a great many years and will doubtlessly continue to be so debated for many more. Nevertheless, it is a strategic decision issue regarding life insurance that consumers must make. Perhaps a diversified approach (some cash value life insurance and some term with other investments) is a satisfactory compromise for consumers, depending on their needs and resources. However, proponents of traditional whole life insurance emphasize the insurance company's guarantees of the dollar value of and a minimum rate of return on the cash value, so the investment risks are mainly taken by the life insurance company rather than the policyowner. In addition, whole life policies do not charge explicit expense fees for changes in investments as is usually done for mutual funds and other investments and for other life insurance policies (discussed later in the chapter).

Variable Life Insurance

Fixed premium variable life insurance policies were introduced in the United States in 1976, but flexible premium designs were not permitted in the United States until 1984. Discussion here deals only with fixed premium variable life. Flexible premium designs will be discussed later under "Variable Universal Life."

Fixed premium variable life insurance resembles traditional whole life policies. Level premiums are fixed, and cash values are developed from which policy loans are available. The main difference between variable life and whole life policies is that variable life insurance shifts the investment risks and returns to the policyowner.

Several investment portfolios are generally available, and the policyowner has the option of choosing those in which the cash value of the policy will be invested. The policyowner receives additional coverage, in the form of increased death benefits, if investment performance of the selected funds is favorable. The policyowner also assumes the downside risk and receives reduced coverage, subject to the minimum death benefit guarantee, if investment performance is unfavorable.

Variable life currently has a relatively small share of the life insurance market. In 1991 only about 1.2 percent of the amount of new individual life insurance purchases in the United States were of variable life insurance.

Basic Characteristics

Variable life insurance can briefly be described as a type of life insurance having the following characteristics:

- The policyowner generally has the ability to select the investments behind the contract from among those offered under the policy by the insurance company.

- Policy benefits relate to the value of the investments behind the contract at the time the benefit is paid.

- The death benefit (ignoring policy loans) is never less than the initial death benefit payable under the policy but can be more if investment experience is favorable.

The idea behind variable life is that the additional amounts of coverage resulting from favorable investment returns should keep pace with inflation over the long run. However, subject to the minimum death benefit, the policyowner bears the investment risk.

Variable Death Benefit

The mechanism of a variable life insurance policy is relatively simple. The policy provides a cash value type of coverage with level premium payments.

The fixed premium is based on some assumptions regarding the rate of return that will be earned by the funds in which the policy's cash value is invested. The target investment rate of return is referred to as an **assumed interest rate (AIR)**.

The actual investment return, of course, will probably differ from the AIR. If the actual return on investment, referred to as the **actual net investment rate (ANIR)**, is less than the AIR, the policy will have an inadequate premium level. If the actual investment returns exceed the assumed returns, the premium will be more than adequate.

Any excess of the ANIR over the AIR (referred to as **excess investment results**) finances additional death benefits. The additional insurance may be provided either as a single premium addition or as a level premium addition.

- A **single premium addition** provides an additional amount of paid-up insurance.

- A **level premium addition** increases the death benefit of the policy as long as the favorable investment performance continues to support the premiums for this additional coverage.

A level premium addition immediately increases the death benefit more than a single premium addition based on the same excess investment results. However, level premium additions result in more volatile death benefits since coverage will decrease more rapidly when the ANIR is less than the AIR.

When additional coverage has been provided through single premium additions, investment shortfalls must be balanced by surrendering part of the paid-up coverage and releasing a corresponding amount of cash value. If the policy has had level premium additions, the cash value must be reduced to supplement the deficient investment return. Funds will not be available to cover the level premium of the additional coverage. Without excess investment returns in subsequent years, the additional coverage will lapse.

Minimum Death Benefit Guarantees

Variable life policies have a **minimum death benefit guarantee**, which provides that the death benefit will never be less than the death benefit that originally existed when the policy was issued. The death benefit is permitted to decrease, but only if there have been prior years in which favorable investment performance led to increases in the death benefit.

Investment Allocation

The cash value of a variable life policy can be invested in investment accounts managed by the life insurance company or some other investment manager. Generally, the life insurance company gives policyowners a choice of three or more investment portfolios. At minimum, the policyowner can usually choose between a stock fund, a bond fund, and a money market fund. Some insurers offer a wider range of choices.

Policyowners can choose to put all investments into a single fund, or they can apportion the investments among the available funds. Generally, insurers will not permit policyowners to allocate less than 10 percent of the assets to any one fund. Policyowners are also permitted to change the allocation of investments up to four or five times a year without paying a separate fee for the exchange.

Transfer of Risk

With variable life insurance, the insurance company assumes the risk that mortality and expense experience will be greater than expected. However, there are no minimum interest rate guarantees or minimum cash value guarantees in variable life insurance policies. The policyowner assumes the risk that investment income will be less than expected.

SEC Requirements

The Securities and Exchange Commission (SEC) considers a variable life insurance contract to be a security similar to a mutual fund. Consequently, variable life can be sold only by persons licensed as registered representatives of licensed securities dealers. The sale must always be accompanied by a prospectus whose format and content are specified by the SEC. The prospectus spells out in detail all aspects of the contract and applicable expenses such as premium taxes, investment management fees (which can vary depending on the investments the policyowner selects), mortality and expense charges, and other administrative fees. The SEC also specifies that the investments backing variable life insurance contracts must be segregated from the general portfolio of the life insurance company.

Uses of Variable Life Insurance

People who are interested in taking an active role in investment decision making may have an interest in variable life insurance. Policyowners purchasing variable life contracts should be familiar and comfortable with common stocks, which fluctuate widely in value. The lack of interest rate guarantees and cash value guarantees make variable life inappropriate for people desiring known and predictable future cash value levels.

Variable life insurance might be most attractive to potential buyers when common stocks have been increasing steadily in value over an extended period. Conversely, the variable life concept falls out of favor after stock prices experience significant decreases in value.

The investments backing variable life policies might be more *aggressive* (that is, higher risk) than those backing traditional whole life contracts. Insurers are prohibited from investing more than 10 percent of their general assets in common stocks. Most of an insurer's general account portfolio is invested in mortgages and bonds. In contrast, a high proportion of variable life policy investments might be directed by policyowners to separate accounts invested in common stocks and other relatively volatile issues.

Variable life insurance is viewed by some as a hedge against long-term inflation. Cash values and death benefits are directly linked to investment performance. Favorable investment returns cause these values to increase and, therefore, these additional amounts of values should keep pace with inflation over the long term.

Limitations of Variable Life Insurance

The limitations of variable life insurance are generally the reverse of its advantages. The disadvantages generally arise from shifting the investment decision making, and hence investment risks, under the policies largely from the insurance company to the policyowner.

In a traditional whole life policy, the cash value at any time is determined by a schedule established when the policy is issued and by the cash values of any dividend additions in the case of participating policies. The cash value of a variable policy is directly tied to the value of the related investment funds. The cash value of those funds fluctuates with the prices of the stocks, bonds, or other investments, in which the funds are invested. If the policyowner selects funds that go down in value, the policy's cash value (and perhaps death benefit) decreases correspondingly.

Although poor investment performance will not decrease the death benefit below the original amount purchased when the policy was issued, previously available additional amounts of death protection can be lost if the actual investment performance under the policy does not match the assumed performance. Such a reduction might occur at just the wrong time for the insured's beneficiaries.

Common stocks, and hence stock-based insurance products, might not necessarily be a good "hedge against inflation" at all times. Common stocks do not necessarily increase in value during inflationary periods. The economy sometimes encounters short-term periods of inflation during which the prices of stock stay constant or even decrease.

Consumers should be careful to evaluate the investment management and other expense charges and fees under variable life policies. Unlike whole life policies, variable policies generally have significant surrender charges when a policy is terminated.

Universal Life Insurance

Universal life insurance is a relative "innovation" in life insurance, although it is no longer a new product. Even though it has not had a long history compared with traditional whole life products, it represents a significant proportion (about 21 percent in 1992[2]) of the amount of new individual (ordinary) life insurance purchases in the United States.

Basic Characteristics

Universal life insurance (or **flexible premium life insurance**) is a policy under which the following can occur:

- The policyowner can change the death benefit from time to time (with satisfactory evidence of insurability for increases).
- The policyowner can vary the amount and timing of premium payments without prior notice or negotiation.

- Premiums are credited to a policy account from which mortality and expense charges are deducted and to which interest is credited at rates that may change from time to time.

- The policyowner can make partial withdrawals of cash value

Part of the mortality risk and part of the investment risk is transferred to the policyowner. However, the *insurer* decides how policy assets will be invested, guarantees a minimum rate of return on policy accumulations, calculates existing policy cash values, and usually determines what current interest rates will be credited to the policy. The insurer discloses the internal allocation between mortality, expenses, and interest (often referred to as "unbundling" the contract).

Death Benefit Flexibility

Universal life policies include the option of either a level death benefit or an increasing death benefit configuration. The level death benefit design is often referred to by the interchangeable terms "Type A," "Type 1," "Option A," and "Option 1." Likewise, the increasing benefit design is referred to as "Type B," "Type 2," "Option B," or "Option 2." There is no inherent advantage of one design over the other. A preference might be based on insurance needs—specifically, whether the policyowner needs level benefits or death benefits that increase to reflect inflationary trends. With universal life, policyowners are also permitted to change from one type of death benefit to the other by negotiating the change with the insurance company.

Level Death Benefit   The **level death benefit** design is similar to a whole life policy. The death benefit is comprised of two elements—(1) pure protection and (2) savings. In equation form,

Death benefit = Increasing cash value + Decreasing pure protection

The increasing cash value (savings) reduces the amount of pure protection, thereby reducing the insurer's mortality risk and the proportion of the death benefit to which the mortality charge is applied.

For example, consider the universal life policy represented in Exhibit 4-4. Coverage begins at age thirty-five with a $100,000 level death benefit. By age fifty, the policyowner plans to pay enough premium to build the cash value to $30,000. The amount of protection to which the mortality charge will apply is $70,000 ($100,000 – $30,000). At age eighty, the cash value is expected to be $75,000. At that time the policyowner will pay the mortality charge for $25,000 of protection. Note, however, that the policy is required to maintain at least a minimum "corridor" where the death benefit exceeds the cash value

Exhibit 4-4
Level Death Benefit Illustration

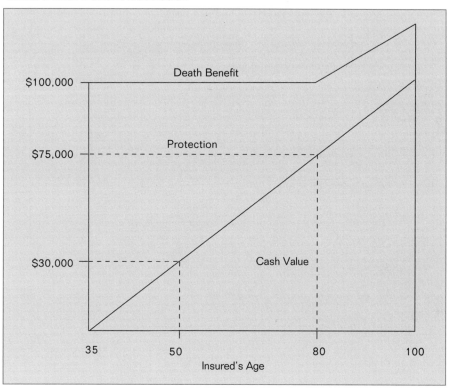

by at least a minimum level to qualify as a life insurance contract (and retain its tax advantages).

Increasing Death Benefit   The **increasing death benefit** design pays a death benefit equal to the cash value of the policy plus a stipulated amount of pure protection (the face amount at policy inception). In equation form,

Death benefit = Increasing cash value + Level pure protection

For example, if a policy with the increasing death benefit design begins with a $100,000 death benefit, it will pay $100,000 *plus the amount in the cash value account* (less any policy loans or indebtedness against the policy). The increasing death benefit option provides a higher death benefit, but it also requires an appropriately increased mortality charge as the insured ages.

Consider the universal life policy depicted in Exhibit 4-5. The policy begins at age thirty-five with a $100,000 death benefit. By age fifty, the policyowner plans to have $10,000 in cash value. At age fifty, therefore, the death benefit

Exhibit 4-5
Increasing Death Benefit Illustration

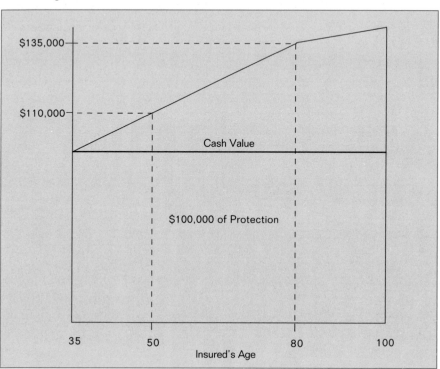

is $110,000 ($100,000 + $10,000) and the policyowner pays a mortality charge for $100,000 of protection. When the policyowner is age eighty, the cash value is expected to be $35,000. At that time, the death benefit will be $135,000 and the policyowner will still pay a mortality charge for $100,000 of protection.

Flexibility   The flexibility of the universal life policy allows policyowners to switch from one type of death benefit to the other by negotiating such a change with the insurance company. The policyowner can also negotiate increases or decreases in the death benefit itself. Increases in the amount of pure protection require evidence of insurability.

The flexibility of changing both the *amount* and *type* of coverage allows the policyowner to change the policy based on changes in his or her economic circumstances or family situation. Adjustments can be made without purchasing separate contracts to supplement or replace a basic policy.

Premium Flexibility

Universal life introduces premium flexibility unheard of in traditional whole life contracts. Universal life policies require a stipulated minimum premium payment during only the first year of coverage. After the first year, the premium on a universal life policy is payable at the discretion of the policyowner. A target level premium amount might be suggested to keep the policy in force or to accumulate a desired cash value at some future time. However, the policyowner can skip premiums, delay payments, pay extra premiums, or pay whatever premium amounts he or she wants. Limitations (minimums and maximums) apply to the premium payments, but wide latitude is possible within those limits.

Upper Limit One upper limit on premiums is established by the Internal Revenue Code.[3] The limitation prevents the policyowner from accumulating too high a cash value relative to the death benefit. Exceeding this statutory limitation results in the policy's classification as a *modified endowment contract* (MEC). This would subject to income taxes any cash value increases withdrawn from the policy as partial withdrawals (discussed later in this chapter) or loans, or at policy termination. Universal life policies contain a provision permitting the insurer to refuse additional premium payments whenever the upper limits are reached.

Lower Limit The lower limit on premium payments is merely the minimum premium required to keep the policy in force. If the policy has a cash value adequate to cover the next two monthly mortality charges, no premium payment is mandatory. Whenever the cash value gets so low that it will not cover the mortality charges, the minimum premium payments necessary to keep the policy in force are those amounts that will cover both mortality charges and any explicit expense charges. When the policyowner pays only the minimum premiums, the cash value will be inadequate to offset increases in the mortality charges (as the insured ages), and higher future premium payments will be required.

Number of Premium Payments It is possible for a policyowner to pay a first-year premium high enough to carry the policy in force for a relatively long period without additional premium payments. In fact, a universal life policy can be purchased with a single premium payment. However, this does not guarantee the future adequacy of the single premium under the universal life policy. In other words, if the insurer's long-term experience under the universal life policy does not match assumptions, it is possible that additional premium payments or a reduction in the death benefit will be required to keep the policy in force.

Allocation of Premiums Many variations exist in the ways universal life contracts allocate premiums among expenses, protection, and cash values.

Every premium payment (less a deduction for expenses, if applicable) goes into the cash value of the policy, where it is added to any existing cash value already accumulated from prior payments. Interest is credited to the cash value, usually monthly, and a deduction is made from the cash value account, usually each month, for the mortality charge covering the amount at risk. If adequate premium payments are made, the sum of:

1. Net premiums going to the cash value, plus
2. Interest earnings on the cash value

will exceed the mortality deductions, and the cash value will increase as the policy remains in force. The cash value will decrease only if the combination of premiums and cash value investment earnings is insufficient to meet the mortality charges and expense charges.

Expenses can be allocated by one of two general methods:

- *Fixed percentage of premiums to expenses.* Some insurance companies' universal life policies allocate a fixed percentage (such as 5 or 7 percent) of every premium payment to cover insurance company expenses. The remainder of any such premium goes directly to the cash value of the policy.
- *No explicit expense loading on premiums.* Some insurance companies credit the entire premium payment to the cash value of the policy and do not explicitly impose an expense loading on premiums. Instead, they utilize part of the investment income to cover expenses and credit the remaining portion to the cash value. Insurers using this approach do not disclose how much is being allocated to expenses.

Furthermore, some insurers will *back load* some expenses. They require that a declining deferred sales charge be paid if the policy is surrendered during a certain period after the policy inception (usually ten to fifteen years). The sales charge is largest in the first year and decreases to nothing by the end of the last year of the specified period.

Partial Withdrawals

Universal life insurance policies make cash available to policyowners in the same ways as traditional life insurance contracts—through policy loans and cash surrender of the policy. In addition, universal life insurance policies introduce another means for policyowners to access the cash value: universal life policies allow *partial* withdrawals of the policy cash value.

With **partial withdrawals,** the policyowner is permitted to determine the amount of the withdrawal as long as it is not so large that the remaining cash value balance drops below a specified minimum, such as $250 or $500. Most insurers impose a transaction fee, such as $25, on each partial withdrawal.

Unlike a policy loan, a partial withdrawal merely reduces the cash value account in the policy. The policyowner is under no obligation to repay the insurance company or to pay interest on the funds withdrawn. Funds withdrawn in this manner can be restored through additional premium payments.

- For a level death benefit policy, a partial withdrawal usually has no effect on the amount of death benefit payable. However, partial withdrawals might increase the amount of protection purchased, which in turn increases the mortality charge.

- For increasing death benefit policies, partial withdrawals merely reduce— by the same amount—both the cash value and the death benefit payable.

Partial withdrawals in excess of premiums paid are normally taxable income to the policyowner. For that reason, most insurance companies suggest that partial withdrawals be limited to the aggregate amount of premiums paid on the policy.

Interest Rates on Cash Value

The interest rate being credited to the cash value is heavily emphasized for universal life insurance. A universal life policy contains a guaranteed rate of interest. Insurance companies use different guaranteed rates, but the rates tend to range between 3.5 and 4.5 percent and cannot exceed the limit set forth in the reserve and nonforfeiture statutes of the appropriate state. However, the interest rate actually applicable to the cash value is usually greater than the guaranteed (minimum) rate specified in the policy. Under most contracts the amount by which the interest credited to the cash value exceeds the guaranteed rate is at the discretion of the insurance company.

Some universal life contracts use an external index (for example, the current rate on one-year Treasury bills) for specifying the interest rate to be credited to cash values. However, the chosen indexes have not always performed well, and some insurance companies using an index have found it necessary to supplement the index rate on a discretionary basis.

It is relatively easy to obtain information on both the interest rate credited currently and the rate the insurance company has credited in recent years on its universal life policies. This information can be obtained from the insurer directly, and comparative information is published monthly by the Life Insurance Marketing and Research Association (LIMRA) and annually in *Best's Review* and the *Flitcraft Compend*.

Mortality Charges

The **mortality charge** is the amount currently charged for pure protection under a universal life policy. The **amount at risk** is the difference between the death benefit under the policy and the cash value of the policy. It is "at risk" because it will be paid only at death and the insurer is uncertain when it will need to be paid to beneficiaries. The mortality charge is based on a *mortality rate* that is applied to each thousand dollars "at risk." Although universal life policies contain a guaranteed maximum mortality rate, the mortality rate actually charged is often lower.

Universal life insurance policies contain a schedule of *guaranteed maximum mortality rates*. The schedule contains monthly mortality rates per thousand dollars of pure protection for each attained age under the contract. These mortality rates are similar to those used for annual renewable term insurance. Thus, as a person gets older, these rates can be quite significant.

The *actual mortality rate* used in each monthly mortality charge is often less than the guaranteed maximum and is at the discretion of the insurance company. Competitive forces and low mortality claims experience can help keep the actual mortality charge below the guaranteed maximum. It is not unusual for the mortality rate actually charged to be as low as 50 percent of the guaranteed maximum.

The mortality rate actually charged is applied to the amount currently at risk under the policy:

- In a level death benefit design, as the cash value increases, the amount at risk decreases; however, the mortality rate itself increases as the insured ages. Thus, the mortality charge generally decreases, but might increase at older ages.

- With an increasing death benefit design, the amount at risk remains constant, and the mortality rate is applied to the same amount at risk each period. Since the mortality rate increases as the insured ages, the mortality charge increases as the insured ages.

Many insurance companies have increased their mortality charges above the rates that were used in point-of-sale policy illustrations. The mortality rates used in policy illustrations are not guaranteed and can differ significantly from the rates actually applied as the policy continues in force. Thus, the policyowner bears a risk of mortality rate increases under universal life policies.

It is important to consider mortality rates currently being charged. High mortality rates can more than negate the benefit of a higher interest rate being paid on the cash value. The current mortality charge shown in policy illustrations can be used to derive the actual mortality rate currently being charged. The calculation described here can be used to compare currently illustrated mortality charges made by different insurance companies.

The calculation is relatively simple: the dollar mortality charge reflected in any given month is divided by the amount at risk in thousands of dollars, as shown in the following formula:

$$\frac{\text{Monthly mortality charge}}{\text{Amount at risk/\$1,000}} = \text{Mortality rate}$$

For example, suppose a $20 monthly mortality charge is made on a policy with $100,000 "at risk." The monthly mortality rate is $0.20 per thousand, determined as follows:

$$\frac{\$20.00}{\$100,000/\$1,000} = \$0.20$$

Under an increasing death benefit design, the amount at risk remains constant, so the same amount would always be divided into the mortality charge amount shown for each year of the illustration.

For a level death benefit design, however, the amount at risk decreases as the cash value increases. Consider a $100,000 policy with a $40,000 cash value in a month in which the illustration shows an $18 charge for mortality. Since this is a level death benefit policy, the amount at risk is $100,000 – $40,000, or $60,000. The mortality rate is calculated as follows:

$$\frac{\$18.00}{\$60,000/\$1,000} = \$0.30$$

In this case, the mortality rate is determined to be $0.30 per thousand per month.

Expense Charges

The expense charges applicable to universal life policies vary widely among insurance companies. Nearly every policy design introduced before 1982 contained explicit charges for insurance company operating expenses and commissions. As mentioned earlier some insurers still have explicit charges, referred to as *front-end loads*, applicable to every premium dollar collected from the policyowner. However, many universal life policies introduced after 1982 do not have front-end loading expenses. Instead, they rely on part of the investment income to cover these expenses. They credit to the cash value a lower rate of interest than they earn on their portfolio. In concert with moving away from front-end expense loadings, insurance companies have increased the *surrender fees*, or *back-end loads*, charged for making full withdrawals or exchanges of the cash value.

Surrender Fees   The purpose of surrender fees or back-end loads is twofold:

- They discourage policyowners from using universal life insurance policies as short-term investment vehicles.
- They allow insurers to recover their front-end expenses when the policies are surrendered or exchanged relatively soon after issuance.

The surrender fee is highest during the first policy year and decreases gradually with policy duration, usually vanishing for policies that have been in force more than ten or fifteen years. Some insurers use surrender charges that remain constant for five or ten years and then gradually decrease over the next five years.

Surrender fees are limited by statute but can be quite significant. For example, a full 8 percent surrender charge could be levied against the cash value of a single premium universal life policy. Policies with high surrender charges tend to have lower front-end expenses or none at all. Conversely, policies with very low surrender charges tend to have front-end charges.

Some life insurance companies have introduced the idea of **new money-based surrender charges**. They apply the regular surrender fee structure to each year's premium payments ("new money") as if that payment were associated with a new policy. Under this design, some of the cash value will be subject to a surrender charge under any policy that has continuous premium payments.

Transaction Fees   Nearly every universal life policy has a transaction fee, such as $25 per transaction, applicable to partial withdrawals of cash value other than as policy loans.

Actual Expense Charges   As with mortality charges, it is important to consider current expense charges. High explicit expense charges can more than negate the benefit of higher interest rates being paid on the cash value. A calculation similar to that described for mortality rates can be used. For example, if the dollar expense charge is given in the monthly statement, the current expense rate can be calculated as follows:

$$\frac{\text{Expense charge}}{\text{Amount at risk}/\$1,000} = \text{Expense rate}$$

Suppose a policy has $70,000 at risk and the expense charge is $14. The expense rate is $0.20, as calculated below:

$$\frac{\$14.00}{\$70,000/\$1,000} = \$0.20$$

Annual Policy Report

Each year that the universal life policy is in force, the insurance company must provide to the policyowner a ledger sheet detailing and summarizing the previous year's transactions for that policy. This annual policy report can be compared with the original illustration to determine whether there have been changes in the mortality rates applied or variations in the interest rate credited.

Uses of Universal Life Insurance

In terms of providing for basic life insurance needs, this form of cash value life insurance has much the same uses as does fixed-premium whole life insurance. Of course, as emphasized throughout the preceding discussion, universal life is more flexible in premium payment structure, death benefits, and the availability of partial withdrawals than is traditional whole life.

Universal life has been referred to as an **unbundled contract,** which means that its cash value, in effect, is separated from its death benefit and that the life insurance cost elements—interest, mortality, and expenses—are separately stated in the policy and illustrations for all to see and evaluate. Since interest is such an important cost element and helps to build policy values inside a life insurance contract, the unbundled characteristic of universal life as a practical matter has tended to result in universal life being sold in the marketplace as an investment-oriented insurance product. Sales illustrations tend to emphasize the growth in cash values under various interest rate (and mortality cost) scenarios.

Limitations of Universal Life Insurance

The limitations of universal life insurance, as far as consumers are concerned, tend to center around concerns about the flexibility in premium payments and the possibility of the public's misunderstanding the nature of these contracts. Some view the flexibility of universal life insurance as a disadvantage because of the loss of the discipline of making fixed premium payments and of possible confusion on the part of policyowners as to what financial commitments are required to keep their universal life policies in force, particularly during periods of declining interest rates or possibly rising mortality charges.

Variable Universal Life Insurance

Variable universal life insurance is one of the newer innovations in life insurance products. It was introduced in 1984, and sales of this product have been modest. As of 1991, about 3.9 percent of the amount of new individual life insurance purchases in the United States were of variable universal life insurance.

Basic Characteristics

Variable universal life insurance combines many flexibility features of universal life insurance with the investment flexibility of variable life insurance. The product is also known as universal variable life, universal life II, flexible premium variable life, and flexible premium variable universal life.

The features that variable universal life insurance has in common with universal life include the following:

- True premium flexibility after the first policy year, since the policyowner decides if, when, and how much to pay in premiums. Premiums can be skipped or extra premiums paid, so long as the limiting conditions are met.
- The choice of either of the standard universal life death benefit configurations—level death benefits or increasing death benefits.
- The ability to make policy loans and partial withdrawals of the cash value.

As with variable life insurance in general, variable universal life insurance contains the following features:

- The policyowner assumes all investment risk, with no interest rate guarantee or minimum cash value guarantee on the variable portion of the policy.
- The policyowner is permitted to allocate the investments supporting the life insurance policy among a limited number of available separate accounts.
- The policyowner is permitted to reallocate these investments up to four or five times a year without any transaction charge.

Because the policyowner assumes the investment risk and variable life is considered a security for regulatory purposes, variable universal life insurance is subject to SEC regulation, and a prospectus is required. Variable universal life can be sold only by persons who are licensed both as life insurance agents and as securities dealers.

Death Benefit Type

Policyowners can purchase variable universal life with either level or increasing death benefits. Under either design, favorable investment performance directly enhances the cash value in the contract. However, the ways in which death benefits are affected differ.

Level Death Benefit Design   Under the level death benefit design, the death benefit payable does not increase—regardless of investment performance. Instead, favorable investment performance results in increases in the policy's cash value, which in turn reduces the amount at risk and, consequently, the applicable mortality charge usually decreases but may increase at older ages.

Increasing Death Benefit Design   With the increasing death benefit design, the death benefit always increases by the same amount that the cash value increases. Unlike a fixed premium variable life contract, there is no separate purchase of additional coverage from favorable investment results under a variable universal life policy.

Expenses

The expenses applicable to variable universal life policies include front-end expenses applicable to premium payments and back-end loadings in the form of surrender charges and transaction fees.

Front-End Charges   Front-end loading includes the costs of managing policy investments and commission fees for stock and bond transactions made within the investment fund. The loading can be a flat percentage or a two-tiered percentage. Under *a two-tiered percentage*, the front-end loading might involve, for example, (1) 15 percent of monthly premium payments under $100 plus (2) 5 percent of premiums in excess of $100.

Some insurance companies also have a *flat processing fee* per premium payment.

Back-End Charges   Back-end expenses take several forms:

- *Surrender charges* might be applied whenever a policy is surrendered or exchanged for its cash value. Surrender charges can apply up to fifteen years after policy issuance. The surrender charge is highest in the first policy year and decreases gradually over the next ten or fifteen years. In some policies, it remains level for as long as eleven years before decreasing.
- Insurance companies might also apply some sort of *transaction fee* to any partial withdrawals of cash value.

Uses and Limitations of Variable Universal Life Insurance

Variable universal life policies are appropriate for policyowners desiring both (1) the flexibility of universal life and (2) the ability to direct the investments supporting the life insurance policy, in conjunction with assuming the investment risk

The limitations of this product parallel those of variable life and universal life combined. Stock market prices and other investment conditions can influence the sales volume of variable universal life. No minimum rate of interest is guaranteed. Variable universal life is not appropriate for individuals who will be uncomfortable with fluctuations in cash value because of investment price changes. Furthermore, some policyowners might not want the available flexibility.

Interest Sensitive or Current Assumption Whole Life Insurance

Some life insurance companies have chosen to avoid the costs of developing and supporting a universal life product. Instead, they have introduced less complex enhancements to their traditional whole life policies. These enhanced policies often are referred to as either *interest sensitive whole life* or *current assumption whole life* policies. Interest sensitive or current assumption whole life policies are designed to emphasize a more investment-oriented approach to coverage than had been followed in the past.

Basic Characteristics

The basic foundation of **interest sensitive whole life** or **current assumption whole life** is a traditional whole life policy, which is modified in two ways:

- First, the highest interest assumptions and lowest mortality rates that the insurance company actuarial staff deems acceptable are used when determining the premium level.
- Second, accumulation funds, indeterminate premiums, and surrender charges are incorporated.

Accumulation Fund

The **accumulation fund** of an interest sensitive or current assumption whole life policy is its cash value determined by using the current experience of the life insurance company. Hence the term "interest sensitive" is applied to it. Two approaches can be used to determine accumulation funds:

- One approach utilizes regular, scheduled cash values in the policy and a *separate accumulation fund* for excess interest credited to the policy. The aggregate cash value with this approach is the sum of the scheduled cash value plus the balance in the accumulation fund.
- The other approach uses a *single accumulation fund*, reflecting the aggregate cash value, without distinguishing between the base cash value and excess interest earnings components.

The net result is essentially the same under either approach. The insurance company can ensure that the cash value will equal or exceed a specified minimum amount at the end of each policy year. Since these policies do not permit partial withdrawals or excess premium contributions, the accumulation funds are not subject to unpredictable variation because of acts of the policyowner.

Indeterminate Premiums

Interest sensitive or current assumption whole life policies involve a **maximum premium guarantee,** which stipulates the *maximum* periodic premium charge. The actual current premium charge will be lower than the guaranteed premium amount whenever experience under the group of policies is favorable enough to warrant a premium reduction. (This is the equivalent of paying a policyowner dividend but allowing it to be applied only to reduce premiums.) The amount of premium reduction is often substantial.

Some life insurance companies are willing to guarantee the level of premium reduction for the first two or three years of the policy. After an initial guarantee period, premium reductions are made purely at the discretion of the insurance company.

These policies are fixed premium contracts and require premium payments when due. The policyowner does not have the option to skip or reduce premium payments. Failure to pay a premium will result in a lapsed policy unless the policyowner has agreed to automatic premium loans.

Surrender Charges

Interest sensitive or current assumption whole life policies tend to be aggressively priced, providing limited profits for insurers in the short run. Surrender charges are an incentive for policyowners to keep coverage in force long enough for the insurance company to recover its acquisition costs.

Surrender charges tend to be highest in the first policy year and gradually decrease over a period of ten or fifteen years. Some insurance companies maintain level surrender charges for a specified number of years before the charge starts decreasing. In most cases, the surrender charge will decrease to zero in the policy year that the insurance company expects the policy to generate its first profit for the insurer.

Evaluation of Interest Sensitive or Current Assumption Whole Life Insurance

Interest sensitive or current assumption whole life insurance recognizes the current actuarial experience of the insurance company in a policy that calls for at least an indeterminate premium on a fixed periodic basis. The insurer guarantees that this premium will not be above a maximum amount, and it normally would be lower than this maximum, based on the actual experience of the insurance company. Thus, the policy occupies something of a middle ground between traditional fixed-premium whole life and flexible premium universal life with some of the advantages and limitations of both. It is, however, among the group of newer, investment-oriented life insurance policies because of the current application of the life insurer's current interest (and mortality) assumptions to the policy's cash value.

Other Life Insurance Policies

The life insurance policies discussed in the first part of this chapter are the most popular forms of life insurance. However, other types of life insurance are available, and they are discussed below.

Joint Survivorship Life (Second-To-Die) Insurance

Traditionally, life insurance policies have paid their death benefit at the death of *one* insured person. In the case of **joint survivorship life insurance** (also called *joint life, joint last survivor life, survivorship life*, and *second-to-die* policies), the life policy normally covers *two* lives as the insureds in a single policy, and the death proceeds are payable to the beneficiary at the death of the second insured.

The two lives insured are usually those of a husband and wife. These policies have become particularly popular in recent years as a way to pay the federal estate tax due in larger estates and as a way to conserve the size of larger estates for the children and perhaps grandchildren after the death of the survivor of a husband and wife. These topics are further discussed in Chapter 8.

Joint life policies might also have other uses, such as making up for the loss of family wealth when charitable trusts have been used to pass property to a charity after the death of the second spouse or in certain business or other estate planning situations. It should be noted, however, that joint life policies are not appropriate when the life insurance is intended to meet family income needs (including needs of a surviving spouse) after the death of the first spouse.

Joint survivorship policies can be written in a number of ways. They can be traditional fixed-premium whole life policies (either participating or nonparticipating), interest-sensitive or current assumption whole life, universal life, or some combination of permanent and term life insurance. Policies can be tailored to fit the needs and current ability of the policyowners to pay.

The premiums for joint survivorship life insurance are normally considerably less than the premiums for comparable individual policies on a single life of the same age, sex, and amount of life insurance. This occurs because two lives are insured and the proceeds are not payable until the second death. However, the mix of permanent life insurance and term life insurance in a joint life plan can significantly affect policy comparisons. Care should always be taken that the policies being compared are comparable and are being analyzed under the same general assumptions.

Single Premium Whole Life Insurance

As the name implies, **single premium whole life insurance (SPWL)** has a single lump-sum premium, due at the time of policy issue. The policy provides a specified death benefit, and the beginning cash value is usually equal to the single premium amount.

In the past, many people purchased single premium whole life insurance primarily for its investment and tax shelter aspects. The tax treatment of single premium and other policies with short premium-paying designs was significantly changed and made less favorable by changes in the federal tax law enacted in 1988. The changes were intended to discourage the use of these policies for short-term investment objectives by, in effect, subjecting policy loans and partial withdrawals (to the extent of any investment earnings in the policy) to immediate federal (and usually state) income taxation. Also, funds distributed from the policy before the insured's age of fifty-nine and a half are not only taxed as ordinary income but also incur a 10 percent penalty tax. The new tax law preserves the former, more favorable tax treatment for policies entered into before June 21, 1988. However, these "grandfathered" policies can lose these former tax advantages if the policy undergoes a material change (basically an increase of both death benefits and premiums).

The policies (including SPWL policies) subject to these more restrictive 1988 tax law changes are called *modified endowment contracts (MECs)*. However, the internal cash value gains of MEC policies still are not subject to income taxation unless policy funds are distributed to the policyowner prior to the insured's death. Also, death benefit payments under MEC policies are still generally exempt from federal income taxation, just like nonMEC and grandfathered MEC policies. On the other hand, the Internal Revenue Code has, for many years, explicitly prohibited any tax deduction for interest payable on loans from or to carry single premium policies.

Single premium whole life policies have been available for many years and many are in effect. However, as a result of the tax law changes described above, SPWL policies are much less popular today than they were prior to 1988.

Endowment Insurance

An **endowment life insurance policy** provides life insurance protection for a limited period of time and pays the full face amount at the end of the specified period if the insured is still living. In other words, the insurance company pays if the insured dies during the policy period, *and* it pays if the insured survives to the end of the policy period. For this reason, endowments are relatively expensive.

Endowments can be purchased for various durations—such as ten or twenty years, or can cover an insured to a certain age—such as endowments at age sixty or sixty-five.

Endowments are usually temporary cash value policies. However, they can be designed and sold as fairly permanent policies. For example, a straight life policy might be regarded as an endowment at age 100. In fact, some life insurance companies issue an "endowment at age ninety." A policy of this type, for all practical purposes, is a straight life policy—although the premiums are slightly higher and the nonforfeiture values grow a little faster than in a typical straight life policy. In general, policies of this type are issued to make a contract appear unique or to provide a competitive advantage.

Traditionally, endowments were used to provide for retirement. Currently endowments are not as widely used because they have been replaced by retirement plans (which are discussed in Chapters 6 and 7) and other forms of life insurance.

Adjustable Life Insurance

Adjustable life insurance can briefly be described as a type of life insurance that allows the policyowner to perform several tasks:

- *Raise or lower the face amount of the policy.* To increase the death benefit, the insured must furnish evidence of insurability and pay higher future premiums. In the event the death benefit is lowered, future premiums will decrease.

- *Lengthen or shorten the protection period.* The policyowner chooses the desired protection period at policy inception as either temporary or permanent. As needs change, the policyowner can request a change in the policy period and, if the request is accepted by the insurer, premiums will be changed to reflect the shorter or longer policy period.

- *Increase or decrease the premium.* As the face amount and protection period change, premiums are adjusted to reflect the changes. However, when the protection period and the face amount are set, premiums are paid in fixed amounts according to fixed payment schedules.

Adjustable life insurance policies attracted widespread attention when they were introduced because of their flexibility to the policyowner while the insurance company continued to bear the investment, mortality, and expense risks. However, they quickly lost their popularity following the introduction of universal life insurance policies, which contained even more flexible features.

Industrial Life Insurance

Industrial life insurance was developed at the beginning of the twentieth century and was sold primarily to factory workers, hence the derivation of its name. Today, "industrial life" is used synonymously with "debit life," and, when combined with whole life insurance paid for with a monthly premium, it has come to be known as **home service life insurance**. Some of the distinguishing characteristics of this type of life insurance are as follows:

- *The average policy in force has a face amount of less than $1,000.* However, this is changing, since the average size of new policies slightly exceeds $1,000.

- *Historically, premiums were collected in person by the agent at the insured's residence or place of employment on a weekly basis.* However, with increasing collection costs, insurers have moved toward biweekly and monthly premium collections. Insurance companies also tend to reduce the premium rates of policyowners who mail or deliver premiums to a regional or district office.

- In the absence of a surviving or locatable beneficiary, *the insurance company can pay the policy proceeds to anyone equitably entitled to such payment* (for example, the individual who pays for the insured's funeral).

- *Death benefits are almost always paid in a lump sum,* since the small amounts involved do not warrant the use of settlement options.

Industrial or home service life insurance was once an important element in the life insurance market. However, today it has largely been displaced by group life insurance and represents a relatively small and diminishing share of that market.

Group Life Insurance

Group insurance provides coverage to a number of individuals under one master contract issued to a sponsoring organization. The insured members are not parties to the contract and do not receive individual policies. Instead, they receive certificates of insurance as evidence of their protection.

Eligible Groups

Initially, group insurance was issued only to employer-employee groups, but now group insurance is issued to many types of groups. Many states restrict the types of groups that are eligible for group insurance, but there is considerable variation in these restrictions. In general, however, the different types of eligible groups can be classified into the four basic categories discussed below.

Employers

Employer groups can be individual employers or can be multi-employer arrangements. *Individual employers* represent the largest category covered by group insurance. An employer might be covered as a sole proprietorship, partnership, or corporation. Employee eligibility for coverage is determined by state law and company underwriting standards. Generally, persons can be covered if they are directors of a corporation, partners, sole proprietors, retired, employees of a subsidiary or affiliated firm, or independent contractors. Most states also permit dependents of employees to be covered in a group life plan.

Multi-employer arrangements make it possible to provide group insurance coverage for employees of different organizations generally within the same industry. This includes negotiated trusteeships that arise from collective bargaining (as, for example, when members of the same union work for several employers), voluntary trade associations (for example, groups made up of employers in the same industry), and multi-employer trusts (METs) that have been designed for small employers. Under an MET, the group contract is issued to the trust, and the employer becomes a subscriber to the trust for purposes of obtaining coverage for employees.

Unions

A master contract can be issued directly to a union to cover union members.

Debtors of a Common Creditor

Credit life insurance—issued through a commercial bank, finance company, credit union, appliance dealer, or other lender—is a form of group term life insurance. Credit life is designed specifically to cover only the amount of the outstanding balance. The master contract is issued to the creditor. In the event of the debtor's death, the insurance proceeds are paid to the creditor and the debt is extinguished. Credit life insurance allows the beneficiary no flexibility and is not necessarily the most cost effective way to buy decreasing term insurance. It is designed primarily to protect the lender.

Miscellaneous Groups

Most states permit many other types of groups to participate in a group insurance arrangement. These include, but are not limited to, members of professional or veterans associations, alumni groups, religious groups, and even hobbyist organizations. However, insurance companies often require that the group exist for some purpose other than to purchase insurance (with the exception of the multi-employer arrangements described above).

Group Selection

Group insurance is generally provided without a medical examination or other evidence of insurability. A person in poor health who is unable to purchase individual life insurance might obtain group life insurance coverage if he or she is a member of an eligible group. Obviously, this is advantageous to those in poor health.

Mortality experience is slightly higher in group life insurance than with individually selected coverage because group underwriters are not concerned with the specific health, morals, habits, or heredity of individuals within the group. Instead, the characteristics of the group as a whole—such as turnover rates, industry, stability of the group members, and average age—are underwritten. For example, it is desirable to add young, healthy individuals to the group periodically to replace older members who leave the group. Otherwise, the average mortality of the group will increase and the cost of insurance may become prohibitive, leading to plan termination. If a group is acceptable, then generally all members of the group are eligible for coverage; otherwise the entire group is rejected, regardless of how healthy any given member of the group is. However, smaller groups might have individuals specifically underwritten and, thus, the group contract might include specific limitations for certain individuals.

Eligible Employees or Members

Generally, group insurance protects all regular, full-time employees (or members) of an organization; however, this is not a statutory requirement. According to state laws and most insurer underwriting rules, an employer can establish standards to cover only certain classes of employees—but the standards cannot exclude individuals on the basis of age, sex, race, or religion. Some employers also cover part-time employees under their group life plans. In general, methods of excluding classes of employees must be based on conditions of employment.

Probationary Period Requirement

Many plans have a probationary period requirement. The **probationary period** is a period of time, usually from one to three months after the employee joins a company, during which he or she receives no coverage. The purpose of a probationary period is to exclude temporary workers and those who are terminally ill when they are hired. Probationary period requirements vary according to whether the plan is noncontributory or contributory:

- In plans financed solely by employers without any contributions from employees (**noncontributory plans**), coverage automatically becomes effective on the date on which an employee completes the probationary period. Insurers typically require 100 percent participation of all eligible employees to minimize the chance of insuring an unusual proportion of unhealthy lives. In addition, some states' laws also require the plan to include all eligible employees if the group is of a certain size (such as more than ten eligible employees).

- In plans that require contributions from employees (**contributory plans**), individual employees are not covered after completing the probationary period unless they elect coverage during the probationary period and agree to the necessary payroll deductions. Insurers usually require that a certain percent (generally about 75 percent) of eligible employees participate to guard against adverse selection.

Actively at Work Requirement

Most plans also require, before coverage commences, that employees must be actively at work on the first day after the probationary period expires. This rule applies to those employed at the inception of a plan, to new employees, and to all those employed at times when benefits are increased. This requirement minimizes the risk of insuring those who are too ill to work and helps reduce adverse selection.

Benefits

The amount of group life insurance that can be sold on one life is often subject to restrictions. The amount of life insurance might be determined automatically, usually through a formula or schedule, to minimize adverse selection for the insurer. Otherwise, those in poor health are likely to choose large amounts of insurance, which would adversely affect the mortality experience of the insurance company.

However, in some plans (known as *flexible benefits* or *cafeteria compensation* plans), employees can choose from among a number of kinds and amounts of employee benefits and thus tailor-make to a certain degree their own benefit plans. Group life insurance is often a part of the flexible benefits, and employees often can choose the amounts of group term life insurance they want for themselves and also, perhaps, for their dependents. This violates to some degree the group underwriting principle just stated. However, in cafeteria plans, employees usually must show individual evidence of insurability when they select group life insurance over certain amounts to help avoid adverse selection.

Ideally, the benefit formula should recognize the items in the following list:

1. The life insurance needs of individual employees
2. The employees' ability to pay (if the plan is contributory)
3. The overall cost of the plan
4. The need for administrative simplicity

Under any type of schedule, the amount of life insurance is adjusted as employees move from one employment classification to another.[4]

One common type of benefit formula uses an employee's *earnings* to determine the amount of coverage for which he or she qualifies. This approach is illustrated as follows:

Monthly Earnings	Amount of Insurance
Less than $1,000	$20,000
$1,000-$1,500	25,000
$1,501-$2,000	30,000
$2,501-$3,000	35,000
More than $3,000	40,000

Although there are many formulas or schedules for relating the amount of insurance to earnings, popular practice is to provide life insurance equal to some multiple of the employee's annual earnings, often one, two, or three rounded off to the nearest $500 or $1,000.

Another type of benefit formula relates the amount of life insurance to the employee's *position* as in the following example:

Position	Amount of Insurance
Officers	$45,000
Department heads	39,000
Supervisors	33,000
Salespersons	25,000
All other employees	20,000

One of the problems with a position schedule is that it is sometimes difficult to classify each employee by position.

Flat amount plans provide the same amount of insurance to all employees. These plans are commonly used when the group life benefit is tied to the group health plan. For example, a health insurance company might require a small group to purchase at least a minimum life benefit for all eligible employees as a condition to it providing health coverage.

Regardless of the type of benefit formula or schedule, many insurance companies stipulate a minimum and maximum amount of insurance that can be issued on any life. Some companies impose a minimum such as $1,000, $5,000, or $7,500, depending on group size, to spread expenses over a larger volume of insurance. The maximum amount of group life insurance that will be issued on one life is subject to the insurer's underwriting practices.

Aside from cafeteria plans mentioned previously, employers often offer supplemental group life insurance plans under which employees can obtain additional group life insurance coverage, typically on an employee-pay-all basis. It is common for these plans to let employees select the amount of coverage, within limits. For example, a plan might allow employees to purchase an amount of coverage equal to one, two, or even three times their own salary. To minimize adverse selection, supplemental group life insurance plans require that a large percentage of eligible employees participate. In addition, amounts of coverage in excess of a specified limit may be subject to evidence of insurability.

Types of Coverage

Group life insurance is available in certain "traditional" plans, such as (1) yearly renewable term insurance, (2) group paid-up insurance, and sometimes (3) group whole life insurance. In addition, some newer forms, such as group universal life insurance plans (GULP) and group survivor benefit insurance sometimes are provided as a supplement.

Traditional Group Plans

Almost all group life insurance today on employer-employee groups is *yearly renewable term* insurance. This coverage, of course, is pure protection and does not develop a cash value. If a covered employee dies, a death benefit is payable, but no benefits are payable if an employee lives beyond the period of protection. Yearly renewable term protection expires at the end of each policy year but is automatically renewed. The premium charged the employer usually changes annually to reflect the experience of the group being insured.

The popularity of the yearly renewable term plan is due to three factors:

1. The premiums are lower for term insurance than for other plans.
2. It is simple to administer.
3. There are clear income tax advantages.

The Internal Revenue Code[5] allows employees to exclude from their gross wages amounts paid by the employer on their behalf to purchase group term life insurance. This favorable tax treatment, however, is limited: The cost of the first $50,000 of coverage is not included in the employee's gross income. If the employer does provide more than $50,000 in coverage (under one or more plans), the employee is required to include the "cost" of the insurance in excess of $50,000 (less any employee contributions to the entire amount of coverage) in his or her gross wages. The "cost" used for tax purposes is derived from a table prepared by the IRS and commonly referred to as the "Uniform Premium Table I," or simply "Table I." Table I and a related example are shown in Exhibit 4-6.

Although almost no traditional *group paid-up insurance* is currently being sold, some coverage remains in force. This approach uses a combination of (1) annually increasing single-premium permanent whole life insurance with cash values and (2) decreasing one-year renewable term insurance.

Employee contributions are applied solely to purchase units of fully paid-up whole life insurance, while employer contributions go only to purchase term insurance.

Paid-up whole life insurance provides a specified benefit whenever the insured dies (or at age 100 if the insured survives) and requires only a single premium. The amount of fully paid-up insurance that each employee's contribution purchases is determined by the size of his or her contribution and the employee's attained age. The total amount of paid-up insurance covering that employee's life increases as each premium is paid. Term insurance is purchased by employer contributions in an amount necessary to make up the difference between the total amount of insurance called for by the benefit schedule and the accumulated amount of paid-up insurance.

Group ordinary products are level premium cash value forms of life insurance under which the premium is allocated to the pure protection portion and the cash value portion of the coverage. Generally, the employer pays for the pure protection portion of the coverage, and the employee pays for the cash value portion. This kind of plan was once quite popular because it was designed to provide cash value life insurance on a group basis to employees that could be continued during their retirement on a level premium basis. However, the income tax rules applying to such insurance benefits are complex and difficult. As a result, group ordinary is not widely used today.

Exhibit 4-6
Uniform Premium Table I and Example

Uniform Premium Table I

Age	Cost per Month per $1,000 of Coverage
29 and under	$.08
30-34	.09
35-39	.11
40-44	.17
45-49	.29
50-54	.48
55-59	.75
60-64	1.17
65-69	2.10
70 and above	3.76

Example

Anita, aged 48, is insured in the amount of $120,000 with group term insurance and contributes $0.12 per month for each $1,000 of coverage. The amount to be included in gross wages for federal tax purposes would be:

Amount of Insurance Provided	$120,000.00
Minus Section 79 Exclusion	50,000.00
Remainder Subject to Taxation	$ 70,000.00
Table I Cost (per $1,000 of coverage)	$ .29
Monthly Cost ($.29 x 70)	20.30
Annual Cost ($20.30 x 12)	243.60
Minus Employee's Annual Contribution (.12 x 70 x 12 months)	100.80
Amount Reportable as Gross Wages	$ 142.80

Group Universal Life Plans (GULP)

Although the dominant group life insurance benefit is still yearly renewable term, some employers are now offering their employees group universal life coverage as a supplementary employee-pay-all group coverage.

In group universal life offerings, the employer provides essentially payroll deduction administration services. One hundred percent of the premium payment is deducted from the after-tax salary and wages of the employees. The employees are permitted to select the level of coverage and perhaps the type of death benefit within limits.

The same premium flexibility found in individual universal life policies is applicable to GULP, but changing the level of premium payments is a little more cumbersome because the payroll deduction amount must be altered. Insurance companies hope the payroll deduction mechanism will lead to predictable level premium contributions.

There is often no individual underwriting under these plans. The GULP coverage is voluntary with the employees; however, insurance companies are often willing to write this coverage on a *guaranteed issue basis* (meaning that all eligible employees who apply for coverage will be accepted within certain amounts of insurance limitations).

Group Survivor Income Benefit Insurance (SIBI)

As the name implies, this benefit provides, not a cash sum, but a stream of monthly income payments to survivors of the insured employee. Benefits under a survivor income benefit plan are payable only to qualified survivors. For example, a surviving spouse is eligible for benefits, but usually only if living with the insured employee at the time of death. Some plans stipulate that the spouse must have been married for a certain period of time—such as one or two years. Dependent children are also eligible for benefits in most plans.

The duration of monthly benefits varies from plan to plan. Some provide spouse's benefits for only a short period—such as five years, while others provide lifetime benefits. Other plans provide spouse's benefits until the spouse reaches age sixty-five or becomes eligible for Social Security benefits. Almost all plans discontinue benefits if a spouse remarries, but some continue benefits for a period after remarriage—typically one or two years. Benefits for a dependent child are terminated when the child reaches a certain age such as eighteen or twenty-one, or they might extend up to age twenty-three as long as the dependent child is a full-time student.

Duration of Coverage

Normally, an employee's group life coverage is not affected by temporary absences from work for reasons such as vacation, strike, accident, sickness, or even a leave of absence. Protection is continued if premium payments are continued. In deciding whether premium payments will be continued for those temporarily unemployed, an employer must use a system that prevents individual selection. For example, a company might have a policy of continuing to pay premiums for employees who are expected to return to work within some specified period, such as three months.

Termination of Employment

If an employee's service is terminated, the group life coverage will continue automatically for thirty-one days. In many cases, this will be adequate since it will be only a short time before the individual starts another job and acquires new coverage.

Conversion Provision

An important feature of most group life plans is the **conversion provision**, which allows an employee to obtain an individual policy if employment is terminated or if the master contract is discontinued. The conversion clause permits an employee, within thirty-one days after severing employment, to obtain an individual life insurance policy without providing evidence of insurability.

The conversion provision in group life insurance generally allows an employee to purchase any form of life insurance customarily issued by the insurer, except term insurance. A few insurers make term insurance available, and some states require that employees be allowed to purchase term life insurance for a limited duration, such as one year, after which they can convert to a form of cash value insurance.

The mortality experience on converted group insurance is extremely unfavorable, and premiums tend to be high. Generally, only otherwise uninsurable employees are like to convert.

Advantages of Group Life Insurance

Group life insurance offers several advantages to insureds. These are discussed below.

Low Cost to Insureds

Group life insurance might cost less for covered employees than individual insurance for the following reasons:

- The employer often pays or contributes to the premium.
- Insurer expenses are relatively low because agents' commissions are reduced and many administrative expenses are assumed by employers.
- Flat rates for group life insurance generally make it a special bargain for older group members. (However, younger group members might be able to purchase individual coverage at a rate lower than the group's flat rate.)

Convenience

For the following reasons, one of the attractions of group life insurance is convenience:

- Payroll deduction is an easy method of paying premiums.
- Few decisions by group members are necessary. When enrolling in a group plan, an employee does not have to be concerned with the choice of an insurance company. Also, deciding on the amount of life insurance to purchase is simplified because benefits will be determined automatically, under the terms of the plan.
- Group underwriting generally does not involve proof of insurability (which, for example, might require a physical examination).

Tax Advantage

An employer's contributions are not gross income to an employee unless the amount of group life insurance exceeds $50,000, provided the plan is not discriminatory as defined by IRS rules.

Problems or Limitations of Group Life Insurance

Although group life insurance is beneficial to insureds in some ways, it also can present some problems. These are discussed below.

Benefit Amounts

Depending on company underwriting practices and the benefit schedule, an individual might be able to obtain only a small amount of protection under a group life insurance plan. Also, a benefit schedule might provide relatively smaller amounts of coverage to young employees (who are often paid less, but who generally need more protection than do older workers).

Termination of Employment

As mentioned earlier, group life coverage is continued for thirty-one days beyond termination of employment. Although this extension might be adequate for many people, others can be unemployed for a long time. Furthermore, a new employer might have no group insurance, or the amount of insurance might be substantially less than the previous amount of protection. In addition, the employee might have developed health problems that make him or her ineligible for new coverage. Of course, an employee who is terminating might convert his or her group term life insurance, particularly if he or she is in poor health.

Post-Retirement Coverage

One serious limitation of some group life insurance plans is the lack of post-retirement coverage. Group life plans generally provide only term insurance coverage that builds up no cash values that could extend coverage beyond retirement.

Providing insurance protection after retirement can involve problems. For one thing, unless pension payments are being made, a convenient method of collecting premiums from retired employees is not available. More importantly, the cost of term insurance at advanced ages rises rapidly.

However, despite these problems, many group life plans now provide at least limited coverage for retired employees. The benefit amount might be reduced immediately upon retirement to a flat, small amount or to a percentage such as 25 to 33 percent of the amount of insurance in force at retirement. In some plans, the benefit amount is reduced each year until a certain amount (or percentage of prior benefits) is reached. Often, the employer pays the full cost of benefits during retirement.

Lack of Professional Service

Group insurance is sold on a mass production basis, and employees might not receive expert advice. The insurer and the employer must provide a summary plan description that describes the plan benefits and provisions. If an employee needs answers to nonroutine questions, the employer, the insurance agent, or the insurance company might provide some assistance. However, a group life plan cannot be tailored in amount or in design to meet the specific needs of individual employees. Most people need individual life insurance coverage—in addition to group life insurance—to address their financial planning needs. Consequently, most people with group life insurance have a need (whether or not it is met) to seek the advice of a competent insurance or financial planning professional.

Individual Life Insurance

This section presents some of the advantages and limitations of the individual approach to buying life insurance, particularly as they compare with group insurance. The types of individual life insurance policies and their contract provisions have already been described in this and the previous chapter.

Advantages of Individual Life Insurance

Individually purchased life insurance policies are not employment or group related, so the policyowner can *control* his or her own insurance coverage. The insurance is not subject to changes in the employer's plan or to loss of coverage in the event of changes in employers or termination of employment. Correspondingly, the policyowner can continue full individual coverage into retirement if he or she wishes.

Many more choices as to the types and terms of individual life insurance contracts are available to the policyowner. In group insurance, the choice is made by the employer or group and is generally group term life insurance up to some multiple or multiples of an employee's wages or salary. In individual insurance, the types of contracts purchased can range from yearly renewable term insurance (YRT) to investment-oriented contracts. Also, within the very broad financial underwriting rules of life insurance companies, policyowners can decide what amounts of life insurance they need and can afford to buy.

Further, for some insured employees the cost of individual life insurance might be less than for group term life insurance. In particular, younger group members in good health might find individual life insurance less expensive than group coverage. Executives might also find individual life insurance less expensive after considering the impact of income tax provisions on imputed income from employer-paid premiums for group term life benefits over $50,000.

A final advantage is that individual life insurance can be sold by a life insurance agent who should render *professional service to the policyowner.*

Problems or Limitations of Individual Life Insurance

The problems or limitations of individual life insurance, as compared with group life, are almost the reverse of the advantages of group life insurance noted previously.

For most employees the cost of individual life insurance is probably greater than that of comparable group insurance because of the lower administrative costs for group coverage and the employer's contribution to the cost.

Specific action must be taken by purchasers of individual life insurance. Therefore, its purchase is less convenient than receiving group coverage from one's employer.

Fewer tax advantages exist for individual life insurance than for group term life insurance. The premium for individual coverage is paid with after-tax dollars by the purchaser, while the first $50,000 of employer-provided group term life insurance is available to employees without any current imputed income to employees for federal income tax purposes as a result of the group coverage.

Finally, individual life insurance generally is *individually underwritten* by the insurance company. In group term life insurance, by contrast, the group itself is underwritten but the individuals in the group generally are not. Thus, individuals who have health problems might not be able to secure individual life insurance or might be able to secure it only on a rated or other substandard basis, but if they were active members of an otherwise acceptable employer group, they could probably secure regular group term life insurance without individual underwriting on the same basis as the other employees.

Summary

This chapter first discussed the basic types of individual life insurance that are summarized in Exhibit 4-7. Then it focused on some uses of life insurance, including group life insurance, key employee life insurance, and split dollar plans.

Term life insurance provides financial protection for a limited period of time. If the insured dies during that period, the face amount of the policy is paid to the beneficiary. If the insured survives the policy period, the policy expires and the obligations of the insurance company terminate. The advantages of term life are that it helps those with limited resources meet substantial insurance needs, can be used to secure outstanding loans, protects insurability, and provides dependency period income. It is limited in the sense that it provides no cash value, offers protection for only a limited period, and increases in cost whenever it is renewed.

Whole life insurance is often called "permanent." Three types of whole life insurance exist—straight life, limited payment, and single premium whole life policies. The premium for whole life insurance is based on the level premium technique, which keeps the premium at the same level throughout the premium paying period. The leveling of premiums results in the accumulation of cash values within the policy.

The life insurance products described in this chapter also include newer, more investment-oriented policies. These policies are discussed in terms of the

Exhibit 4-7
Life Insurance Comparison Chart

	Term	Whole Life	Variable Life	Universal Life	Variable Universal Life	Interest Sensitive Current Assumption
Death Benefits	Level or decreasing	Fixed level	Guaranteed min. level plus increases from investments	Either level or increasing (amount + cash value)	Guaranteed prem. level or min. + cash value	Fixed level
Cash Value	None	Scheduled and guaranteed	Depends on investment performance	Guaranteed min. interest rate + excess interest	Depends on investment performance	Scheduled and guaranteed + accumulation fund from excess interest
Premium	Increase at each renewal	Level for period selected	Fixed level	Flexible premium required 1st yr. target (suggested) level premium	Flexible premium required 1st yr. target (suggested) level premium	May vary based on experience Guaranteed max. level
Policy Loans	No	Yes	Yes	Yes Loans affect interest rate credited to cash value	Yes	Yes
Partial Withdrawals of Cash Value	No	No	No	Yes	Yes	Yes
Surrender Charges	No	No	No	Yes	Yes	Yes

flexibility they offer the policyowner, the risks they present, and the returns they may generate.

The degree of flexibility and the levels of risk and return differ with each of the life insurance products that were described in this chapter. Variable life insurance, which transfers the investment risk to the policyowner, gives the policyowner some ability to select the investment behind the contract, adjusts policy benefits to reflect the value of the investments behind the contract when the benefit is paid, and guarantees a minimum death benefit. In universal life insurance, the policyowner can change the death benefit and vary the amount and timing of premium payments without notice or negotiation. In addition, premiums are credited to a policy account from which mortality charges are deducted and to which interest is credited. The mortality and investment risks are partly transferred to the policyowner. Variable universal life combines features of variable and universal life. Other kinds of individual policies covered in this chapter include interest sensitive or current assumption whole life, joint survivorship life, and single premium whole life.

Group life insurance provides coverage to a number of individuals under one master contract issued to a sponsoring organization. Groups eligible for this type of coverage include employer groups. Group life insurance for employer-employee groups is usually written as yearly renewable term insurance.

Chapter Notes

1. Technically, a leveling of premiums and a temporary difference between premiums and mortality costs occur even in term policies of short duration at younger ages. However, the cash accumulation is slight—both because the policy period is short and because the mortality curve is not increasing rapidly. For practical purposes, the cash value is insignificant, and most term policies have no cash value.

2. *1993 Life Insurance Fact Book Update* (Washington, DC: American Council of Life Insurance, 1993), p. 6.

3. Section 7702, which is the general definition of what is a life insurance contract for purposes of the income tax law.

4. Many plans provide that the amount of insurance on an employee will not be adjusted downward.

5. Under Section 79 of the IRC.

Chapter 5

Investment Planning

From a risk management perspective, individuals and families use investments to actively retain certain loss exposures. For example, a family might withdraw funds from a savings account to pay for a new bicycle when an old one is damaged beyond repair or to pay for the repair of a refrigerator that is not working correctly.

In fact, investments complement insurance in many well-planned risk management programs. The person who has set aside an adequate emergency fund often has the resources to purchase property or health insurance with higher deductibles, retain certain otherwise insurable exposures (such as the auto physical damage exposure on an older car), or purchase smaller amounts of life insurance.

This chapter begins by examining the personal uses of investments. That section is followed by a discussion of the general nature of investment risks and returns, as well as other factors influencing investment decisions. The remainder of the chapter examines specific characteristics of various types of savings and investment vehicles.

Uses of Investment by Individuals

People accumulate capital and make investments for many different reasons. One major reason for capital accumulation is to build a retirement fund. People also accumulate funds to meet college expenses, to purchase a house or car, or to provide a general measure of security. Investments can also provide emergency funds to handle unexpected financial needs.

Supplement Retirement Funding

Accumulating capital for retirement is an important objective for many people, particularly as they reach middle age. They want investment income and capital to supplement their anticipated retirement benefits from sources such as Social Security and employer-provided retirement plans. A properly structured investment portfolio might also help mitigate the effects of inflation during retirement years.

Increase Wealth

People also create an investment fund to accumulate capital. Investment funds can be used for the following reasons:

- To achieve a better standard of living in the future
- To purchase a house
- To supplement employment earnings
- To achieve greater financial security in the event of uncertainties of life, such as unemployment
- To retire earlier than an otherwise contemplated normal retirement age
- To create a sizable estate to pass on to children or grandchildren
- To meet educational expenses

Build Emergency Fund

As mentioned in Chapter 3, financial planners recommend that individuals and families establish and maintain emergency funds equal to two to four months' income, depending on such factors as the stability of their sources of income and their usual financial obligations. Individuals and families often experience financial setbacks that can be more easily overcome with the use of an emergency fund than without such a fund. Savings and investments are useful for establishing an emergency fund.

For example, suppose a family's home sustains $5,000 in uninsured flood damage following a torrential rainstorm. If the family has set aside an emergency fund of $10,000 in a savings account, cleanup can begin immediately and the damaged furniture and fixtures can be replaced in little time. The family will not have to obtain a loan, use a credit card for the losses, or cash in a life insurance policy.

The same holds true if one of a family's wage earners loses his or her job through layoff or termination. Having an adequate cash reserve will enable the family to pay bills without having to cash in insurance or investments designed to meet other family goals, such as protection or retirement planning.

Investment Risk and Return

The major goal of investment planning is to maximize *investment return* consistent with an acceptable level of *investment risk.* These concepts are discussed in the following section.

Investment Return

People make investments to realize investment return. **Investment return** can be derived from (1) increases in the value of the **principal** (the original investment) and (2) income earned by the investment (for example, interest, dividends, and rent). The **total return** from an investment is the sum of (1) and (2).

Capital Appreciation

Capital appreciation, often referred to as **capital gains**, occurs when an asset is, or could be, sold at a price higher than its purchase price. Virtually all investments provide the opportunity for capital gains. Exhibit 5-1 illustrates an investment providing capital appreciation at the rate of 5 percent per year, but no investment income. Over the ten-year period depicted, the investment grows from a value of $1,000 to over $1,600 in value.

Exhibit 5-1
Investment With Capital Appreciation

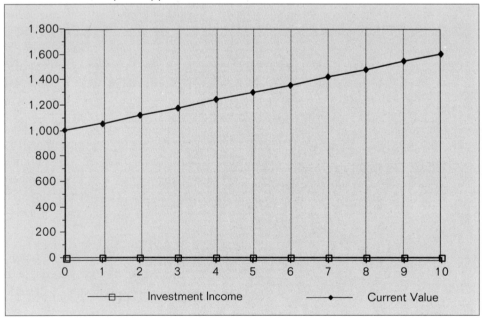

Income

Investment income is income paid to the owner of the investment and is normally received in the form of periodic interest, dividends, or rental payments. Investment income may be taken as cash, or it may be **reinvested** (that is, used to make additional investments). Certificates of deposit, most bonds, some common stocks, and some mutual funds are investment vehicles emphasizing income. Exhibit 5-2 illustrates an investment paying interest at a rate of 5 percent per year, but with no capital appreciation. The investment simply provides $50 per year of investment income.

Exhibit 5-2
Investment With Current Income

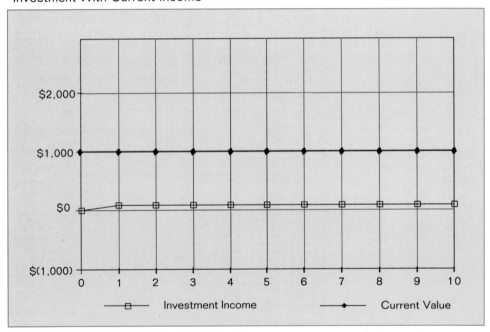

Investors often seek a balance between capital appreciation and income. Some investors might put together balanced portfolios by making some investments that emphasize capital appreciation and others that emphasize income. Other investors might invest in certain stocks or mutual funds that provide both capital appreciation and income.

The foregoing statements might have suggested that all investments are designed to increase in value—or at least to preserve the value of the principal. Some investments are designed to *decrease* in value while providing a high level of current income. For example, Exhibit 5-3 illustrates an annuity that pays the investor $129.50 per year for ten years. Each of these annual payments is partly interest income (at a 5 percent annual rate) and partly a return of the original $1,000 investment. At the end of ten years, the entire investment has been liquidated.

Exhibit 5-3
Liquidation of Capital

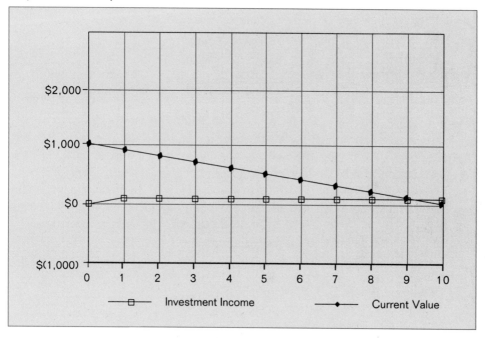

In some cases, investments may be designed to increase in value but do not. When an such an investment decreases—rather than increases—in value to an amount less than the principal, a **capital loss** has occurred.

Measuring Rate of Return

When investment return is expressed as a percent of the *principal*, the percent represents the investment's **rate of return**, or **yield**. Thus, if the rate of return is 20 percent, the investor has earned an investment return equal to 20 percent of the *original investment amount*. For example, Drew earned 20 percent on an investment of $400. This means he received $80 ($400 **x** .20) of investment return.

To measure an investment's rate of return, the total return is divided by the original amount invested. For example, Sally invested $100 in stock. A year later she sold the stock for $120. During the course of the year, she received

$10 as dividend income. Her rate of return for this investment is 30 percent, as calculated in Exhibit 5-4.

Exhibit 5-4
Sally's Rate of Return

Original investment	$100			
Capital appreciation	$120	– $100	=	$20
Investment income				$10
Total return				$30
Rate of return	$30	/ $100	=	30 percent

If an investment is made for a period of years, the rate of return is usually expressed on an annual basis—the **average annual rate of return**. An easy method for *estimating* the average annual rate of return is to divide the investments' total rate of return by the number of years the investment is held. For example, Doug invested $400 in a stock. He sold the stock two years later for $425. During the first year he received $5 in dividend income, and during the second year he received $7.50 in dividends. His average annual rate of return is 4.69 percent, as calculated in Exhibit 5-5.

Exhibit 5-5
Doug's Average Annual Rate of Return

Original investment	$400		
Years held	2		
Capital appreciation		$425 – 400 =	$25.00
Investment income			
Year 1			5.00
Year 2			7.50
Total return			$37.50
Rate of return		$37.50 / $400	= 9.38 percent
Average annual rate of return		9.38 / 2	= 4.69 percent

Investment Risk

Investments *intentionally* involve speculative risk. **Speculative risk** involves three possible outcomes: (1) gain, (2) no gain or loss, or (3) loss. Most investments are expected to produce positive investment returns, but the possibility of breaking even or suffering an investment loss also exists.

The **investment risk** associated with a particular investment is a measure of the *possible variation* of its total return. The level of investment risk that can be satisfactorily tolerated depends on factors such as the investor's investment goals and life cycle stage. For example, the need for financial security of a couple about to retire might lead them to seek a relatively low level of investment risk (that is, an investment with a relatively stable expected total return) as compared with a young single person with no dependents who might seek an investment with a high level of investment risk (that is, an investment with potentially high volatility of its investment return).

The Trade-Off Between Risk and Return

All investments offer investment return and have investment risk. However, an investment's expected amount of return is affected by its risk. The general relationship between investment risk and investment return is as follows: *As the amount of investment risk increases, the size of the potential investment return (either positive or negative) also increases.* So, the more risk an investor is willing to take, the greater his or her expected return.

Exhibit 5-6 compares the results of two hypothetical $1,000 investments, one invested at "lower risk" and the other at "higher risk." At the end of ten years, the higher risk investment is worth approximately $2,200, while the lower risk investment is worth approximately $1,350. At many points shown in the exhibit, the high-risk investment outperformed the low-risk investment. However, at the end of years 1 and 4, the low-risk investment actually showed better results, and at the end of years 2, 5, and 9, the performance of both investments was essentially identical.

As Exhibit 5-6 points out, *in the long run*, an investor should normally receive greater overall positive returns from a higher risk investment. On the other hand, a lower risk investment normally shows a slow and steady growth pattern, coupled with much greater security. Which type of investment is more desirable depends on the investor's personal characteristics and objectives.

Exhibit 5-6 merely represents results that might have occurred with one higher risk and one lower risk investment. Results with any other two investments could be different.

Investment risks can affect the value of the principal, the level of investment income, or both. Exhibit 5-7 illustrates an investment that provides a steady flow of investment income. The investment pays interest at the rate of 10 percent per year, but the value of the principal is subject to considerable variation.

Exhibit 5-6
Comparing Risks and Returns

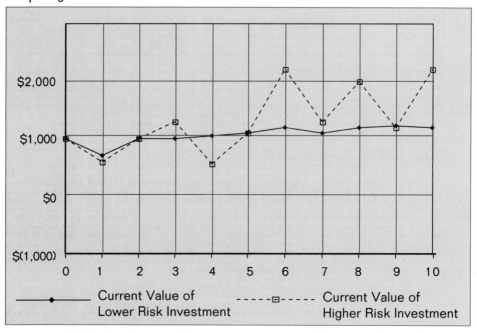

Exhibit 5-7
Volatile Principal, Stable Income

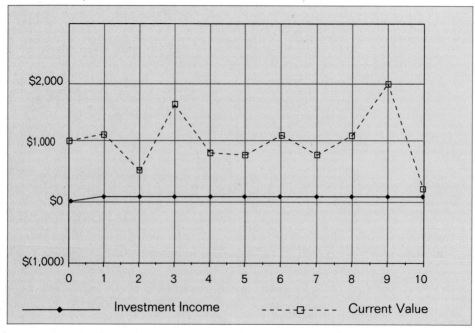

In contrast, Exhibit 5-8 illustrates an investment with complete stability of principal, but subject to variations in investment income. And Exhibit 5-9 illustrates an investment subject to wide variations in both principal and current income.[1]

Exhibit 5-8
Volatile Income, Stable Principal

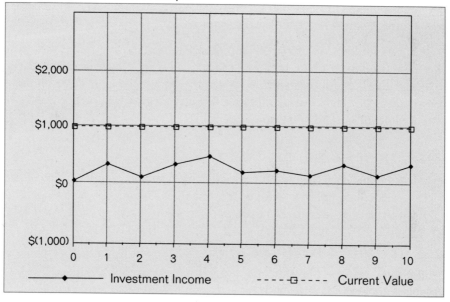

Exhibit 5-9
Volatile Income, Volatile Principal

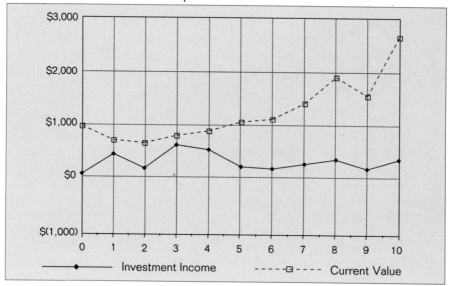

Factors Affecting Investment Decisions

It is relatively easy to evaluate past performance as done in connection with Exhibits 5-6 through 5-9. It is much more difficult to predict future investment performance. Investment planning requires an understanding of the many factors affecting investment risks and returns.

For example, investment risks include the purchasing power risk, financial risk, interest rate risk, and market risk. Leverage can be used to increase risk, and diversification can be used to reduce risk. Other factors—such as marketability, liquidity, divisibility, tax considerations, and use value—are also important in many investment decisions.

Investment Versus Savings

Savings produce the funds necessary for investment. Thus, savings occur when a person's or entity's income (or revenues) is greater than expenses. The investment process then translates those savings into productive investments.

Risk to Principal and Income

Risk to principal and income arises from a variety of sources. Five of these sources—purchasing power risk, financial risk, business risk, interest rate risk, and market risk—are discussed below.

Purchasing Power Risk

Cash might appear to be one of the most risk-free ways of saving money. Although cash produces no investment income, the dollar value of cash remains absolutely constant. However, the problem with any savings device that merely preserves principal is that the *purchasing power* of the dollar tends to decrease.

Purchasing power risk is uncertainty regarding the future value of investment principal and income caused by changes in the overall price level. In short, purchasing power risk is the effect of inflation on investment returns. If consumer prices increase 5 percent during the coming year, $1,050 in cash a year from now will have the same purchasing power as $1,000 currently does. And, if consumer prices continue to increase, the purchasing power of the $1,000 will continue to decrease.

The **Consumer Price Index (CPI)** can be used to measure the effect of inflation on a consumer's purchasing power. The annual U.S. Consumer Price

Index and its percent change from the previous year for ten years is shown in Exhibit 5-10.

Exhibit 5-10
U.S. Consumer Price Index (Basis: 1980 = 100)

Year	CPI	Percent Change from Previous Year
1983	99.6	3.2
1984	103.9	4.3
1985	107.6	3.6
1986	109.6	1.9
1987	113.6	3.6
1988	118.3	4.1
1989	124.0	4.8
1990	130.7	5.4
1991	136.2	4.2
1992	140.3	3.0
1993	144.5	3.0

A current dollar amount of money can be converted to the value in any past year by using the following formula:

$$\frac{\text{Past year's CPI}}{\text{Current year's CPI}} \times \text{Current dollar amount} = \text{Value of current dollar amount in past year's dollars}$$

The following example shows how this formula can be used. Suppose Jerry placed $1,000 in his mattress in 1983 and removed it in 1993. How much purchasing power has he lost? In other words, what is this $1,000 worth in 1983 dollars? Applying the above formula to this example would result in the following equations:

$$\frac{\text{1983 CPI}}{\text{1993 CPI}} \times \$1,000 = \text{Value in 1983 dollars}$$

or

$$\frac{99.6}{144.5} \times \$1,000 = \$689.27$$

When Jerry removed his money from his mattress in 1993, it had as much purchasing power as $689.27 had in 1983. Jerry had $1,000 cash in 1983, and he also had $1,000 cash in 1993. However, the $1,000 he held in 1993 had much less purchasing power than the $1,000 he started with.

Conversely, Jerry needs $1,450.80 in 1993 dollars to have the same purchasing power as he had with $1,000 in 1983. This figure is derived by using the conversion formula but solving for the current dollar amount. Thus,

$$\text{Current dollar amount} = \frac{\text{Value of current dollar amount}}{\text{in past year's dollars}} \times \frac{\text{Current year's CPI}}{\text{Past year's CPI}}$$

If Jerry had $1,000 in 1983, the amount needed in 1993 to purchase the same value of goods is

$$\$1,000 \times \frac{\text{1993 CPI}}{\text{1983 CPI}} = \$1,000 \times \frac{144.5}{99.6} = \$1,450.80$$

Unless investment returns equal or exceed the rate of inflation, the investor loses purchasing power. This point is illustrated in Exhibit 5-11. The bottom line in Exhibit 5-11 shows the amount that would be accumulated in an investment increasing in value at a compound annual after-tax rate of 3 percent. The top line shows the amount of money necessary to maintain the purchasing power of $1,000 in 1983. Although having an investment that earns 3 percent annual after-tax interest is clearly better than keeping money in a mattress, an after-tax investment return of 3 percent would not have kept pace with consumer prices during this particular ten-year period. Stated differently, the investor who earned a 3 percent investment return, after taxes, during these ten years ended up with more dollars but less purchasing power.

The discussion here might seem to imply that inflation is inevitable. Price levels do not *always* increase, but the historical evidence is that they *almost always* do. The Consumer Price Index has declined in only one year since 1950. In the past seventy-five years, only during the Great Depression (1930-1933) did prices decrease in three or more consecutive years.

To avoid a loss of purchasing power, an investment must increase in value at a rate that at least offsets the effect of inflation and taxes. One important characteristic of many investments is that their returns tend to vary as general price levels vary. These investments are considered to provide some measure of prevention (a **hedge**) against purchasing power risk.

Financial Risk

Financial risk is uncertainty regarding the future investment returns of a given asset because of the amount of debt carried by the organization on which the

Exhibit 5-11

Purchasing Power Risk

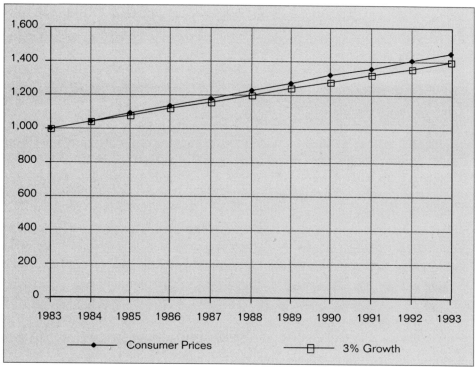

investment is based. For example, the value of stocks or bonds will decline if the corporation that issued the stock or bond experiences financial difficulty and cannot make required payments on outstanding debt. Likewise, the value might increase substantially if the organization does well and has no trouble meeting its debt obligations. Financial risk affects most investments to some degree.

Business Risk

Business risk is investment risk associated with the overall health of the organization on which the investment is based. Many factors can cause an organization's health to deteriorate. Some of the more important sources of financial risk are high operating expenses; changes in demand for the firm's product or service; uninsured liability and property losses; and changes in the economic, political, and social environments. Likewise, many factors can contribute to an organization's success, such as effective and efficient management, productive employees, and public need for the products and services supplied by the organization. Business risk affects most investments to some degree, depending on the overall stability of the organization issuing the security.

Interest Rate Risk

Interest rate risk is the uncertainty regarding the future value of an investment because of changes in the general level of interest rates. Although changes in interest rates affect the value of all investments to some extent, interest rate risk is closely associated with fixed income securities such as bonds. (Further discussion of investment rate risk is provided in the section on bonds.)

Market Risk

Market risk is defined as uncertainty concerning the future value of an investment because of potential changes in the market for investments of that type. The value of a common stock, for example, can fluctuate because of market conditions. Consider October 1987, when the stock market reached unprecedented high levels followed by a precipitous decline. A corporation might have been in excellent financial health, showing no signs of financial or business risk—yet, because of stock market forces, the market price of its common stock might suddenly have dropped.

Market risk also applies to investments other than securities. The market price of a house, for example, is affected by the general price level of houses in its geographic area. If houses in a neighborhood begin to sell for lower prices, the market value of a similar house in the same neighborhood will also decrease, although the house has not physically changed.

Leverage

Leverage occurs when a person borrows money to invest. When an investor borrows money with a fixed cost of borrowing (the interest expense) and the rate of return on the investment is greater than this fixed cost, the investor's profits are magnified. Leverage can be used to increase investment risk—and increased investment risk is accompanied by potentially greater returns. The following example illustrates the effect of leverage.

Suppose Woody has $5,000 to invest. The "no leverage" line of Exhibit 5-12 shows Woody's results if the investment produces income of 0 percent, 5 percent, 10 percent, 15 percent, 20 percent, 25 percent, or 30 percent of the original $5,000 investment. If the investment produces no income, Woody will have no investment return. However, if the investment produces income at the rate of 20 percent, Woody's investment return will be $1,000.

Suppose Woody predicts that this investment will produce a rate of return better than 10 percent, so he borrows another $5,000 from a bank at 10 percent interest and adds it to his own $5,000, resulting in a total investment

Exhibit 5-12
Effect of Leverage

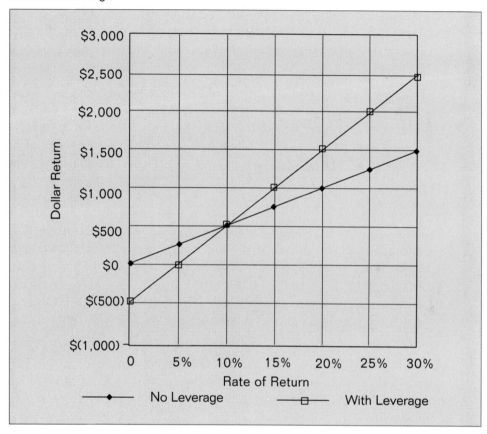

of $10,000. Woody will have to pay the bank $500 interest per year on this loan, but he expects to make enough money on the investment to cover the loan and leave a profit. The "leverage" line in Exhibit 5-12 shows the possible results of this leveraged investment over a one-year period.

- If the $10,000 investment produces a 20 percent rate of return, Woody will receive $2,000 in investment income, pay the bank $500 in interest, and have a $1,500 investment return left over. Woody's investment rate of return is 30 percent ($1,500 investment return/$5,000 principal) rather than the 20 percent he would have earned on an unleveraged investment.

- If the investment produces a 10 percent rate of return, Woody will receive $1,000, pay the bank $500 in interest on the loan, and have a $500 net investment return. Woody's investment rate of return is 10 percent ($500/ $5,000). In this situation, Woody's net results are the same whether or not he used leverage because the rate of return on his investment equals the rate of interest on his loan.

- However, if the investment produces no income, Woody still pays the bank $500 interest. The net effect to Woody will be a $500 loss. Woody's investment rate of return is a negative 10 percent. If Woody had not leveraged his investment, he would have earned a 0 percent rate of return.

Leverage increases the possible variation of the investment return and magnifies investment risk. Investors hope to increase their investment returns by using leverage. However, financial leverage can also magnify losses.

Liquidity and Marketability

Although liquidity and marketability are not entirely synonymous, the terms are closely related.

- **Liquidity** is the ability to rapidly convert an investment to cash *with a minimal loss of principal*. A passbook savings account, for example, can be liquidated easily; an apartment building generally cannot.
- **Marketability** is the ability to sell an investment, at any given time, *at a price not far below that for which it could currently be purchased*. Common stock that is regularly traded on the stock market is usually highly marketable.

An example might help to stress the difference in meaning of these two terms. Suppose Dana purchases 100 shares of common stock for $30 per share. When he needs to sell them, the market price per share is $38. He sells his shares for $38 per share.

- The stock is liquid because he is immediately able to sell the shares without sustaining a loss of principal. In fact, he sells at a price greater than the original purchase price.
- The stock is marketable because he is able to sell the shares immediately for $38 per share—the market price per share.

Cash is completely liquid and marketable. As applied to noncash investments, liquidity and marketability are not absolute, but relative, terms. Thus, a given investment is not necessarily "liquid" or "marketable," but it can be more readily liquidated or marketed than another investment. An investment that can be promptly and easily converted to cash at a fairly stable price has a high degree of liquidity and marketability, such as Dana's stock. An investment that cannot be promptly and easily converted to cash at a fairly stable price, such as some pieces of real estate, has a low degree of liquidity and marketability.

As a general rule, investments that are not easy to liquidate or are not very marketable command a lower market price than they otherwise would. This compensates for the liquidity and marketability risks by allowing the expected return to be higher for such investments.

Most people hold at least a portion of their investment portfolio in highly marketable, liquid investments such as a bank account. An emergency fund, for example, might need to be tapped on short notice regardless of current market conditions. On the other hand, a person who has the following might have minimal need for marketable, liquid assets:

1. A secure source of income (low unemployment risk)
2. A comfortable margin between income and expenses (providing a cushion to absorb minor unforeseen expenses)
3. An excellent health insurance program (reducing the need for emergency medical care expenses or income loss due to disability)
4. Easy access to credit (to get cash for an emergency)

To the extent that these criteria are not met, a strong case can be made for holding at least some investments with high marketability and liquidity.

Diversification

Diversification is the technique of reducing one's overall investment risk by investing in several investments with differing investment risks. Diversification attempts to achieve a "spread of risk." In everyday terms, diversification means not putting all your eggs in the same basket.

Effective diversification relies on a portfolio comprising investments with returns not highly correlated with one another. For example, an investor might make some investments with relatively high financial risk. Other investments might include some bonds and stocks with low financial risk. Certain investments might emphasize capital appreciation while others emphasize income. Some might be liquid and highly marketable, while others might not.

Systematic Versus Unsystematic Risk

Understanding the distinction between *systematic risk* and *unsystematic risk* is essential to the investor who hopes to achieve effective diversification.

- **Systematic risk** arises from factors that simultaneously affect the prices of all securities. For example, interest rate risk is a systematic risk.
- **Unsystematic** (or **specific**) **risk** arises from factors that are unique to a

particular investment. For stock in a particular corporation, these factors include financial risk and business risk.

Diversification can reduce the specific risks associated with an investment portfolio. For example, a portfolio of stocks and bonds in a variety of industries is less dramatically affected by specific risks than is a portfolio invested entirely in the petroleum industry. Furthermore, stock is generally less affected than bonds by changing interest rates; thus, the overall interest rate risk is reduced.

Benefits of Diversification

An effectively diversified portfolio enables the investor to achieve a spread of risk by balancing the results of several kinds of investments. The practical implications of effective diversification are significant, even for relatively small investors. The concept of diversification applies to all forms of investments—not just stocks and bonds. For example, a person who owns a home, has cash value life insurance, maintains a savings account, owns several stocks, and invests in a mutual fund might have a substantial degree of effective diversification.

On the other hand, a person who invests in several high-yield bonds from one company, some investment-grade bonds from a second company, and some preferred stock of a third company might not be effectively diversified. Although he or she has invested in three different kinds of investments, from three different companies, this portfolio is not very well diversified because the investment risks of all the securities are similar. For example, all are significantly affected by changing interest rates. The returns on all of the investments are likely to follow the same general pattern.

Divisibility

People who have only a small amount of money to invest are unable to take advantage of investments that require a large initial outlay. For example, a large apartment complex might be an excellent investment, but an individual investor might be unable to meet the down payment. In some cases, however, a large investment can be divided into smaller portions in which more investors can participate. This is referred to as **divisibility**. Continuing the above example, while it is usually impossible to purchase only one unit in an apartment building, a single unit in a condominium complex can be purchased for rental to others as an investment.

Common stock is divisible because it can be purchased in a wide variety of amounts. An investor can buy one, ten, one hundred, a thousand, or more shares of stock, depending on his or her financial resources.

An investment that can be purchased in manageable units can also be resold in units that another buyer can manage. Thus, a close relationship exists between divisibility and marketability. Generally, an investment that can be easily divided is more readily marketable.

Tax Considerations

Considerable variation exists among the tax treatments accorded to different kinds of investments. Since investors seek to maximize *after-tax* investment returns, tax considerations can have a significant influence on investors' decisions. For example, despite their lower yields, tax-exempt municipal bonds are attractive to many investors.

Some types of financial instruments have the advantage of postponing income taxation. Series EE bonds, discussed later in this chapter, are a good example of investments offering this advantage.

A **tax shelter** is an investment that provides some tax savings. For example, investment in real estate provides the investor the ability to deduct mainte-nance expenses and most depreciation from the investment income, thus reducing the amount subject to income tax. Tax shelters have understandably been popular, but their advantages have been reduced in recent years by several major changes in the tax laws.

Use Value

Many investments have additional value because they can be used by the investor in ways other than their use as investments. A major investment for most families is the residence they own or are purchasing. The house might be selected, in part, because it is considered a good investment. Most families, however, consider it even more important to select a house that provides a comfortable place to live and is consistent with the family's lifestyle.

Some people choose to invest in collectibles such as art or antiques. In addition to capital appreciation, the investor usually receives some benefit from being able to admire the items or show them to others.

Types of Savings and Investment Vehicles

A wide variety of savings and investment vehicles is available to individual investors. Several types of these vehicles are discussed in this section.

Savings Accounts

Savings accounts of various types are offered by commercial banks, savings and loan associations, savings banks, credit unions, and other financial institutions.

A saver should not select a certain type of financial institution solely on the assumption that the highest returns can be obtained from that type of organization. A person considering a savings account should examine the factors relevant to the selection of any savings or investment vehicle—return, risks, liquidity, and so on.

General Nature of Savings Accounts

In general, savings accounts are considered safe investment vehicles. Many people prefer savings accounts to other forms of investment because of this safeness combined with their ease of use and liquidity. The investment considerations of savings accounts are described below.

Deposit Insurance

The preponderance of deposits in commercial and savings banks and savings and loans are insured through the Federal Deposit Insurance Corporation (FDIC). In addition, many credit union accounts are insured by the National Credit Union Administration (NCUA).

The FDIC and NCUA provide essentially the same protection. Each depositor is protected against loss of savings (and any interest earned) up to a maximum of $100,000. The $100,000 limit applies to all account balances in the same name in a single institution. In practice, a person who needs more than $100,000 in protection can open additional accounts in other institutions, open an account under the name of a spouse, open a joint account with a spouse, and open accounts with other parties (such as a trustee).

Not all financial institutions are insured. About 98 percent of all commercial banks have insurance, but some mutual savings banks, savings and loan associations, and credit unions are not insured. It could be argued that insurance is not necessary to protect savers, because virtually all financial institutions are subject to extensive regulation. However, losses and failures among financial institutions do occur, and depositors can lose money.

Investment Risk

The most serious risk for savings accounts is the purchasing power risk. Although financial institutions can raise interest rates during an inflationary period, savings account rates of return have tended not to keep pace with inflation.

Virtually no financial risk or business risk exists for savings account depositors. Most financial institutions provide federal insurance, which minimizes the financial risk for most depositors. Furthermore, if accounts are split, as necessary, to obtain adequate protection, financial risk is reduced for depositors of more than $100,000.

Interest rate risk generally does not apply to the principal in a savings account because changes in interest rates cannot affect the principal that has been saved. Changes in overall interest rates, however, affect the savings account interest that will be paid in the future. When overall interest rates decline, financial institutions have a legal right to decrease the rates of interest paid on their own savings accounts unless a fixed interest rate has been guaranteed for a certain period of time.

Investment Return

Because savings accounts have only minimal financial business, market, and interest rate risks, the investment return for the saver is relatively low. In some cases, higher interest rates can be obtained if the investor is willing to agree to leave his or her savings in a bank account for several years.

Liquidity

Savings accounts are highly liquid investments. Savings can be withdrawn at any time from many accounts. Savings accounts may be combined with checking accounts at some banks and, thus, checks can be written on the accounts. Automatic teller machines provide access to some accounts twenty-four hours a day, seven days a week.

Certain savings accounts (referred to as **time deposits**) cannot be liquidated before a specified date, such as six months from their inception. Other time deposits can be liquidated only with an interest penalty. For example, some time deposits do not allow the investor to withdraw his or her savings, except at the end of each quarter, without forfeiting accrued interest.

Diversification

In a well-diversified investment portfolio, insured savings accounts can provide a secure, liquid, but relatively low-yielding, investment medium. Savings accounts thus can be one component of a diversified portfolio. Assuming that the accounts are fully insured, it probably is not necessary for an investor to diversify by having several savings accounts in different financial institutions.

Divisibility

Savings accounts generally are easily divisible since deposits can be made in almost any amount. However, certificates of deposit (CDs), described later in this section, might have certain minimum amount purchase requirements.

Taxes

The interest payments on savings accounts, whether paid out to the account holder or accumulated in the account, are taxable as ordinary income to the account holder(s) in the year credited to him or her (them) for federal and state income tax purposes. Thus, such accounts do not have the tax-deferred inside buildup feature that is such an important tax advantage for cash value life insurance.

Types of Savings Accounts

Several different types of accounts or funds could be considered under this heading. Regular savings accounts, money market accounts, and certificates of deposit are discussed below.

Regular Savings Accounts

Regular savings accounts generally are immediately withdrawable by the owner or owners with no interest penalty for early withdrawal. They pay interest fixed by the bank or other financial institution and have no fixed term or maturity date. They can also be insured through the FDIC. Thus, such accounts are highly secure, very liquid, and also convenient for the depositor. However, their investment income tends to be lower than that for other comparably liquid investments.

Money Market Accounts

Banks and other eligible financial institutions offer federally insured **money market accounts** that are highly liquid and pay interest rates determined by the rates of return of the securities constituting the accounts. These money market vehicles are accounts in the bank or other eligible financial institution and hence can be insured up to $100,000 per eligible account by the FDIC.

Money market mutual funds are not bank accounts but are a type of mutual fund. (Mutual funds are described later in this chapter.) Like money market accounts, money market mutual funds are highly secure, liquid investments that are commonly used by investors for the liquid portion of their investment portfolios. However, these funds are not subject to FDIC coverage. Money market mutual funds have generally provided higher investment yields than bank money market accounts.

Certificates of Deposit

Certificates of deposit (CDs) issued by banks are a special type of savings account. CDs are time deposits that mature in six months, one year, or longer. Many banks require a minimum deposit of $250, $500, or more. The primary advantage of CDs is the relatively high rate of interest they earn. However, compared with other savings accounts and money market accounts, CDs are less liquid and a substantial amount of interest can be forfeited by the saver who makes an early withdrawal, before the CD matures.

Bonds

Bonds are generally promises by a corporation or government entity (the **issuer**) to periodically pay interest at a stated rate and to pay the bond principal (face amount) at a specified maturity date. In some cases the stated rate is periodically adjusted according to some market rate.

Bonds are debt instruments. The principal is really a loan by the purchasers of bonds (bondholders) to the bond issuer. The bond interest, on the other hand, is a payment by the bond issuer to the bondholders for the use of the borrowed funds.

Bonds are initially sold by the issuers to the purchasers, either directly or through investment management companies. Once bonds have been initially sold and until they mature, bonds might be bought and sold among investors in the bond market. However, some bonds are held by the initial purchaser to their maturity.

Common Terms

The following are some common terms used with regard to bonds.

Bond Indenture

A bond is a debt instrument under which a government or corporation borrows money for a long term. The written agreement containing the terms and conditions of the lending arrangement is known as the **bond indenture**.

Par Value

The **par value** of a bond is the face amount or the amount that the issuer will pay at maturity. A bond can be sold at a price below its par value—sold at a **discount**—or it can be sold at a price above its par value—sold at a **premium**.

Maturity

The **maturity date** of a bond is the date at which the principal or par value becomes payable to the bondholder. For example, a bond that is issued in 1995 with a maturity of twenty years from its date of issue will mature in 2015.

Coupon Payment

The **coupon** is the dollar amount of the annual interest payment stated on the face of a bond. The **coupon rate** is the dollar amount of annual interest stated as a percentage of the par value of the bond. For example, a corporate bond might be issued with a twenty-year maturity date, a $1,000 par value, and a 7 percent coupon rate. This means that the corporation issuing this bond will pay $70 per year to the bondholder for twenty years.

Zero coupon bonds do not pay periodic interest income. Zero coupon bonds are issued at a large discount from par; for example, a twenty-five-year zero coupon bond may be issued at $200 with a par value of $1,000. The difference between the issue or purchase price and the par value is the interest earned on a zero coupon bond. Thus, the bond issued at $200 and held to maturity will receive $800 in interest income ($1,000 – $200).

Default
In some cases, the bond issuer might not be able to meet its obligation to make the required interest payments or the principal payment at maturity. In these situations, the bond issuer is in **default**.

Callable
Many bonds are **callable**. This means that the bond issuer can redeem the bond at a stated amount, referred to as the **call price**, before the bond's stated maturity date. This is often an undesirable feature from the investor's point of view; generally issuers call a bond because they can currently refinance at a lower rate of interest. The bondholder might then find it necessary to reinvest the bond proceeds at a lower interest rate.

One possible consolation to the investor in the case when an issuer calls a bond is the possibility of a **call premium**—an amount by which the call price must exceed the par value. The call premium often approximates one year's interest on the bond. For example, a bond with a $1,000 par value and a 10 percent coupon rate might have a call price of $1,100—the $100 above par represents the bond's call premium.

The General Nature of Bonds
The following discussion of bonds focuses on the general factors common to most bonds. Characteristics unique to a particular type of bond are discussed in the section describing that bond.

Investment Return
Bonds provide investment return in the form of income and capital appreciation. As noted above, many bonds make coupon payments to the bondholder over the life of the bond. These interest payments provide investment income to the bondholder.

In addition to the interest income, bonds offer the possibility of capital gains (and losses). An investor can often buy a bond in the market and later sell it, prior to maturity, at a higher—or lower—price. Furthermore, if a bond is purchased at discount and held to maturity, a capital gain is earned (except in those cases in which the difference between purchase price and par value is considered interest, as with a zero coupon bond).

The investment return provided by bonds can be estimated in a variety of ways, most of which are beyond the scope of this text. However, a simple and widely used measure is the current yield.

Current yield is equal to the *annual* coupon payment divided by the current market price of the bond. Thus, if a bond has an annual coupon payment of $70 and is selling on the market at $1,010, its current yield is 6.9 percent ($70/ $1,010).

Investment Risk

Interest rate risk is significant for bond investors because investment returns are strongly influenced by changes in general interest rates. At any given time, the coupon rate available on other bonds of comparable quality can be higher or lower than the coupon rate on the bond held by an investor. The market price of the bond fluctuates to reflect changes in the market interest rate. If general market interest rates increase, the bond's market price decreases. Conversely, if interest rates decrease, the market price of the bond increases.

Since bonds represent fixed income investments, purchasing power risk is another major concern. The income from a bond must represent a rate significantly greater than the inflation rate to offset the purchasing power risk.

The financial risk and business risk for high-quality (**investment grade**) bonds in general has been relatively low. For specific bonds, the financial risk and business risk can be *estimated* by bond ratings. Several investment services, such as Standard & Poor's and Moody's, provide reasonably reliable, objective ratings for the bonds of most large companies and for many municipalities. For example, bonds with AAA or AA ratings have a small chance of default and are usually considered investment grade bonds of the highest quality. Medium grade bonds are often rated A or BBB. Bonds with ratings lower than BBB are usually considered below investment grade and might be referred to as **junk bonds**. So, the lower the rating, the more financial risk associated with a particular bond.

Market risk might be of lesser concern to bond investors than financial risk and interest rate risk. Bond prices are principally determined by interest rates and by the financial stability of the issuing corporation. Thus, the bond market is generally not as volatile as the market for other investments, such as stock.

Liquidity and Marketability

The ability of a bondholder to readily sell his or her bonds before maturity depends on the nature of the bond. Established markets exist for many bonds issued by corporations and governments. However, bonds of smaller issuers or issues of small numbers of bonds might not be as easily marketable.

The market prices of bonds that are bought and sold prior to their maturity will fluctuate with interest rates, market conditions, and perhaps the current financial standing of the issuer. These price fluctuations can be considerable and can greatly affect the liquidity of bonds.

Diversification

Bond investors can diversify their bond portfolios in a variety of ways. First, diversification can be made by broad types of issuers; that is, diversification among corporate bonds, U.S. government bonds, and the bonds of local and state governments (*municipal bonds*). Next, diversification can be made by bond quality, with perhaps a percentage of a bond portfolio in high-yield junk bonds and the remainder in investment grade bonds. Third, a portfolio can be diversified among issuers of the same type. For example, a portfolio of corporate bonds might include bonds issued by companies in different industries or from different geographic regions. Finally, bonds can be diversified according to maturity, with a portfolio consisting of some short-term bonds (which mature in less than one year), some intermediate-term bonds (which mature in one to ten years), and some long-term bonds (which mature after ten years). Thus, not all the bonds will be maturing at once.

Bonds can also be a part of a broad diversification strategy by types of investments. Thus, an investor can allocate part of his or her total portfolio to bonds—part to common stocks, part to life insurance cash values, part to real estate, and part to money market accounts.

Divisibility

Corporate bonds normally have a $1,000 face amount and, therefore, must normally be purchased in at least this amount. Municipal bonds generally have face amounts of $1,000, and U.S. government bonds can have face values of $10,000 or more. However, in the bond market itself, bonds are often sold in customary units (called "round lots"). For example, municipal bonds are often bought and sold in the market in $5,000 face amount lots although the bond face amounts are each $1,000.

Taxes

The federal and state income tax treatment of the interest from bonds varies by the issuer of and the nature of the bonds involved. The income tax treatment of particular bonds is mentioned in the discussion of each type of bond.

Types of Bonds

A wide variety of bonds is available to investors. U.S. government securities, corporate bonds, and municipal bonds are discussed below.

U.S. Government Securities

Securities issued by the United States government include savings bonds, Treasury bills, Treasury bonds and notes, and agency securities. The interest earned on U.S. government securities is subject to federal income tax. However, it might not be taxable by state and local governments.

Savings Bonds Different series of savings bonds have been issued, but Series EE and HH are the issues currently available to individual investors. Like most other U.S. Treasury bonds, both series of savings bonds are not callable. The U.S. government cannot force the investor to submit the bonds for redemption.

Savings bonds virtually have no financial risk or business risk, because they are backed by the full faith and credit of the U.S. government. Savings bonds have no practical interest rate risk. They guarantee a minimum rate of interest. The actual interest earned is based on the interest paid on long-term Treasury securities and is adjusted at six-month intervals. Savings bonds have no market risk because they can only be redeemed by the federal government. Savings bonds enjoy almost perfect liquidity because they can be redeemed at any time after six months from the issue date. Savings bonds can be purchased in amounts small enough to be within the reach of virtually all investors. For example, some savings bonds can be purchased for as little as $25.

Series EE bonds are purchased at a discount. Investment return is provided through appreciation in the value of the bond, rather than through periodic payments of bond interest. However, when an EE bond is redeemed, the difference between its original cost and the redemption value is considered *interest.* Series EE bonds can be redeemed at most banks and many other financial institutions (after they have been outstanding six months or longer).

Federal income taxes on the EE bond interest can be deferred, at the owner's option, until the bonds are redeemed, are disposed of, or reach maturity—whichever occurs first. In addition, EE bond interest might be exempted from income taxes if the bonds are cashed in to pay for educational funding, subject to certain conditions and restrictions. Taxation can be postponed even longer by exchanging Series EE bonds for Series HH bonds.

Unlike Series EE bonds, Series HH bonds are sold at face value, and interest, the bonds' only form of investment return, is paid semiannually. The bonds must be held for six months. The bonds are redeemed at face value.[2]

Treasury Bills   Treasury bills (T-bills) are short-term debt instruments issued by the federal government. Most T-bills are issued for periods of either three months or six months, although the maturity can be as long as one year. These investments are purchased at a discount and do not make periodic interest payments. However, the difference between the purchase price and the face value, at which they are redeemed, is considered interest. The return on T-bills fluctuates with conditions in the short-term money market. Since 1970, yields have been as low as 2.5 percent and as high as nearly 15 percent.

T-bills offer the lowest return of any marketable security because they involve little risk. Financial risk and business risk do not exist with them because the U.S. government guarantees redemption of Treasury securities. Because of their short-term nature, T-bills have essentially no purchasing power risk or interest rate risk. However, an investor might find it difficult to reinvest T-bill proceeds at a comparable rate of interest. Divisibility is not a feature of T-bills, since the minimum denomination is $10,000.

Treasury Notes and Bonds   Treasury notes are debt instruments issued by the federal government that have maturities ranging from one to ten years; **Treasury bonds** are similar, but they have maturities beyond ten years. Often investment returns on Treasury bonds are higher than the yields on Treasury notes, which, in turn, are higher than those on T-bills—in other words, the longer the maturity, the higher the yield. On occasion, however, market conditions create an exception to this general rule, as in early 1980, when longer duration notes and bonds yielded under 13 percent, while T-bills yielded up to 16.5 percent.

Investment risks, other than financial risk and business risk (which are virtually absent), are minimal on shorter-term issues. However, as the duration of Treasury notes and bonds increases, the purchasing power risk and the interest rate risk become more significant.

Agency Securities   Several U.S. government agencies, including the Federal National Mortgage Association (FNMA), the Government National Mortgage Association (GNMA), and the Federal Home Loan Banks, among others, issue debt instruments. These generally carry slightly more investment risk than Treasury securities because they are not fully backed by the federal government. Therefore, the investment return on these bonds tends to be higher than that on Treasury securities.

Corporate Bonds

A **corporate bond** is a bond issued by a corporation. The issuing corporation assumes the legal obligations to make coupon payments—usually semiannually—and to redeem the bond for its full face value at maturity. The interest payments and any capital appreciation are generally taxable at federal, state, and local levels.

The investment risk associated with corporate bonds is affected by market risk. Bonds are bought and sold among investors, and as such their market value is affected by market activities. Although corporate bonds have more investment risk than U.S. government bonds, the investment risk associated with specific corporate bonds varies by company and by bond type.

Bondholders are creditors of the corporation. As such, they are legally entitled to receive bond interest before dividends are paid to common and preferred stockholders. Moreover, if the corporation fails, reorganizes, or is liquidated, bondholders have a prior claim to the corporation's assets, ahead of the claims of stockholders. For these reasons, corporate bonds generally have less financial risk than stocks. However, because a corporate bond's performance is dependent on the corporation's performance, financial risk exists.

Each corporation has its own financial risk, and each can have different market risk depending on the market's perception of the corporation. In addition certain types of bonds have more risk than others.

Many bonds are known by the type of collateral backing they issue as security. The risk of the bond is based on the marketability and liquidity of the collateral:

- *Mortgage bonds* are backed by the issuing company's real property—land, buildings, or both. If the company defaults on an interest payment or fails to redeem the bonds at maturity, the bond trustee can safeguard bondholders' rights by foreclosing the mortgage.

- *Collateral trust bonds* are secured by specific securities, usually the bonds or common stocks of other corporations.

- *Equipment trust bonds*, also known as *equipment trust certificates*, are backed by business personal property—usually heavy equipment. These bonds are popular with railroads and other transportation companies; "rolling stock" (freight cars, locomotives, buses, airplanes, and so forth) is used as collateral.

Debentures are bonds that have no specific assets as collateral. These bonds are generally more risky than secured bonds offered by the same company because debentures are backed only by the general credit rating of the issuing company.

- *Debentures* provide the investor with the right to receive income and assets after the rights of holders of collateralized or other senior bonds have been satisfied.
- *Subordinated debentures* provide a right to receive income and assets only after the rights of debenture bondholders have been satisfied.
- *Income bonds* have the lowest priority. These are debt instruments, but the borrowing company has a legal obligation to pay interest *only* if the company has earnings from which the interest can be paid.

In the past, the type of security behind a bond was considered extremely important. Today, much more emphasis is placed on the earning power behind the borrowing company. It is common for the debentures of a financially strong company to have a higher quality rating than the first mortgage bonds of a weaker organization.

Sometimes it is convenient to characterize bonds according to their repayment method:

- *Sinking fund bonds* require a corporation to periodically set aside a specific sum for the purpose of retiring the securities. In some cases, the company places an amount in escrow every year to retire the whole bond issue at the maturity date. In other cases, bonds are either bought in the market or selected at random to be redeemed each year, and the sinking fund payment is used to pay the bondholders.
- *Serial bonds* are bonds scheduled to mature each year. Investors know when the issuing corporation will redeem each bond. For example, a company may borrow $20 million through a bond issue that consists of $1 million in bonds maturing in one year and another $1 million maturing each subsequent year for the next nineteen years.

Some corporate bonds are convertible. **Convertible bonds** give the bondholder the option of exchanging the bonds for another type of security of the issuing corporation—usually common stock. The bond indenture specifies the terms of the conversion and the ratio at which each bond can be converted, and it safeguards for the rights of bondholders.

As an example of how such a conversion feature works, assume that a bond with a $1,000 face amount could be converted "at 50." This conversion price ($50) divided into the face amount ($1,000) indicates that the bond could be exchanged for twenty shares of common stock (because $1,000/$50 = 20). A convertible bond offers investors the secure income of a bond but provides the opportunity for appreciation if the stock price rises.

Municipal Bonds

Municipal bonds are issued by state and local governments or governmental agencies. They fall into three categories:

- *Full faith and credit bonds,* also called *general obligation bonds,* are unconditionally backed by the total taxing power of the issuer. These bonds usually bear the lowest investment risk of municipal bonds. However, because municipalities do not have the financial backing that the federal government does, some investment risk exists.

- *Revenue bonds* are backed by specific revenues—usually only those obtained from the assets constructed with the bond proceeds. For example, a state government may issue revenue bonds to finance the construction of a toll bridge. Interest is paid to investors from the toll receipts. Thus, the risk associated with the underlying asset affects the risk of the bond. Generally revenue bonds are more risky than general obligation bonds.

- *Assessment bonds* finance improvements such as streets, sidewalks, and sewers. The issuing agency pays the interest from its user assessments. The investment risk of assessment bonds is associated with the financial strength of the issuing agency.

The most distinctive feature of municipal bonds is their tax-exempt status. Although some exceptions exist, interest income received from a municipal bond is generally exempt from federal income taxes. Most states also provide a state tax exemption for interest received from their own bonds and from bonds issued by local governmental units within the state.

To make a decision regarding investment in municipal bonds, the return on municipal bonds must often be compared with returns available on taxable bonds. The returns on taxable and nontaxable bonds can be compared by using the following formula:

Taxable yield x (1 – Tax rate) = Equivalent tax-exempt yield

An example illustrates the use of this formula. Suppose an investor in the 30 percent marginal income tax bracket (including both federal and states taxes) can buy a taxable corporate bond that pays 8 percent or a nontaxable municipal bond paying 6 percent, and assume that the bonds are of equal quality. The equivalent tax-exempt rate of return with regard to the corporate bond as calculated by the formula is 5.6 percent (8% x (1 – 30%). Since the corporate bond produces an after-tax return of 5.6 percent while the municipal bond pays a 6 percent return after taxes; in this case the municipal bond provides a greater after-tax investment return.

Municipal bonds are most attractive to people in higher tax brackets. Conversely, municipal bonds are relatively less attractive to investors with low marginal tax rates. High income investors bid up the price of municipal bonds, sometimes to the point at which the return to lower income investors is not attractive—even when the tax advantage is taken into account.

Stocks

Corporations raise capital by selling shares of stock to investors. Two categories of stock are available to a corporation for this purpose: common stock and preferred stock. The amount or value of preferred stock that has been issued is small relative to the amount or value of common stock that has been issued.

Common Stock

By purchasing common stock, investors become owners of a corporation. Thus, a **share** of common stock represents a piece of the corporation, and the owner of a share receives certain rights and privileges.

Common stockholders normally have the right to vote on important corporate matters. Generally, each share of common stock entitles the shareholder to one vote. As a practical matter, most stockholders of large corporations vote their stock by way of a **proxy**, which legally designates another person (often a corporate officer) to vote their shares for them according to their instructions. In some cases, however, a corporation can have nonvoting common stock shares that limit or eliminate the shareholders' voting rights.

Common stockholders have the legal right to receive a pro rata share of the residual value of the corporation if it is liquidated. As a practical matter, however, a bankrupt organization might not have any residual value for common stockholders after the claims of bondholders and other creditors are satisfied.

Investment Return

An important right of common stockholders is the right to receive an equal dividend per share *if dividends are declared*. **Dividends** represent the common stockholders' share in company profits as owners and provide investment income to the common stockholders as investors. Some common stockholders believe they have a legal right to dividends, but they do not. They are entitled only to those dividends declared by the company's board of directors.

The company's board of directors decides whether and when to declare a dividend. If a company has an established track record of paying regular dividends that have increased over time, that company is likely to continue paying regular dividends in the future with somewhat predictable increases. However, under normal circumstances, it is virtually impossible to force the board to declare a dividend.

In addition to dividend income, an investor can benefit from capital appreciation when common stock is sold for more than its purchase price. Conversely, the investor might also sell stock at a loss.

The *price* of a share of common stock is easy to determine if an active market for the shares exists. For example, an investor can look up the stock in a newspaper or call an investment counselor. However, determining the *value* of the stock is much more difficult. **Stock valuation** is essentially the process of estimating "true" intrinsic worth of the stock.

If price and value were always the same, "overpriced" or "underpriced" stocks would not exist—but they do. An investor who believes a stock has an underlying value of $20 per share but a current market price of $12 per share has discovered a "bargain." However, stock prices tend to move toward their true values. If a stock is, indeed, bargain priced, other investors are likely to discover the discrepancy and bid up the price of the stock.

Common stock valuation is a complex matter, largely beyond the scope of this text. However, a simple and popular stock valuation technique uses the **price/ earnings (P/E) ratio**. The P/E ratio is the market price of a share of common stock divided by the corporation's earnings per share. The P/E ratio measures how much an investor will pay (per share) for a dollar of earnings. The usual P/E ratio for a stock can be multiplied by the current earnings per share of the issuing company to estimate the stock's value. For example, suppose the usual P/E ratio for a stock is eight and the issuing company's current earnings per share is $2. The estimated value of the stock is $16. The estimate is compared to the current market price of the stock to determine whether it is correctly valued by the market and whether the investor should purchase it. Suppose the stock is currently selling at $20. Because the estimated value is $16, the stock seems to be overpriced. However, if the stock is currently selling at $10, it might be a bargain.

It is important to remember that this method only provides an *estimate* of the stock's value. The P/E ratio changes over time. Furthermore, an investor might disagree with the results. However, it can provide a starting point for investigation.

Investment rate of return for common stock can be measured by dividing the total investment return by the stock's purchase price. Thus, if a stock has provided $3 in dividends and gained $7 in value since its purchase at $50, its investment rate of return is 20 percent ($3 + $7/$50). Investment returns of common stocks are largely unpredictable. Historically, investors who have owned a diversified group of stocks and have held them for long enough periods have generally received a rate of return higher than that obtainable from investments carrying less investment risk. However, superior long-term performance by common stock is not guaranteed, and periods can exist during which common stocks do not perform well.

Investment Risk

For many years, common stock has been regarded as an effective hedge against inflation. The general theory is that common stock prices tend to rise as consumer prices rise, offsetting the effect of economic inflation for the investor and minimizing purchasing power risk.

Common stock prices have tended to rise faster than consumer prices over extended periods of time. However, on a year-by-year basis, investment in common stock does not always provide an effective hedge against inflation. Exhibit 5-13 compares growth in consumer prices with growth in common stock prices from 1981 to 1992. An investor who purchased some typical shares of common stock in 1981, expecting a hedge against inflation, would have suffered a loss of purchasing power during the first years. On the other hand, if the stocks were held until 1991, the result would have been a substantial gain in purchasing power.

Exhibit 5-13
Comparing Stock Prices With the Consumer Price Index

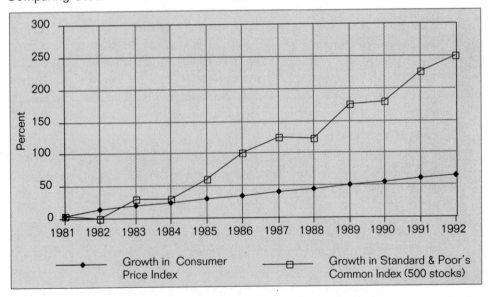

Results could be different for other time periods, and future results might be different from those experienced in the past. Common stocks do tend to increase in value over the long run, but they are by no means a perfect hedge against inflation in the short-term.

Because common stock prices are affected by investors' expectations about the future, the stock market is subject to extreme fluctuations, and, as such, is susceptible to significant market risk. Some type of "mass psychology" appears to produce overreactions in the market—in both directions. Bad news can depress the market more than the news itself would seem to justify. Likewise, the market can make a major advance on the basis of a little good news.

When the stock market undergoes a major shift, most stocks are pulled in the same direction. Indeed, the reason for distinguishing market risk from financial risk is to indicate that security prices can be adversely affected when the market turns downward, even if a company is enjoying profitable years. However, substantial financial risk and business risk are associated with many common stocks. Unless a company is large, established, and growing at a reasonable rate, financial risk and business risk might be important factors affecting investment decisions.

Some well-established companies have an excellent record of paying regular, stable stockholder dividends. Their common stocks might be regarded as "income" securities. For these stocks, the interest rate risk assumes importance. As with corporate bonds, an increase in general interest rates is likely to reduce the market price of the stock, and vice versa. However, if the corporation's normal dividends continue to increase, less interest rate risk is associated with the stock.

Liquidity and Marketability

Common stock that is regularly traded on organized exchanges is normally highly marketable. It might not, however, be highly liquid, depending on market conditions. Common stock of closely held corporations is often neither highly marketable nor highly liquid. (Closely held corporations are corporations whose stock is owned by a small group of investors; the investors often work for and manage the company.)

Diversification

Investments in common stock can be diversified in several ways. They can be diversified by general types of stocks, such as the following:

- *Growth stock*—the stock of a company that is growing at a faster rate than the general economy

- *Cyclical stock*—the stock of a company whose earnings move with the economic cycle
- *Defensive stock*—the stock of a company whose earnings move counter to the economic cycle
- *Income stock*—the stock of a company with an established record of dividend payments

Common stock can also be diversified by industry and by geographical area. Furthermore, common stock can be purchased over time.

To achieve diversification when investing in common stock, investors must be able to purchase at least several other types of common stock. For some individual investors, this can be difficult because of the prices of the various shares and the transaction costs involved when purchasing common stock shares.

Divisibility

Common stock can be purchased in relatively small quantities, such as one share, ten shares, or fifty shares. However, common stock is typically sold in round lots of 100 shares. Transaction costs tend to increase proportionately when smaller numbers and odd lots (less than 100 shares) of shares or smaller dollar amounts of stock are purchased.

Taxes

The dividend payments from common stock are considered ordinary income for federal income tax purposes. Capital gains or losses from the sale or exchange of common stock shares are subject to the rules of capital gains taxation. In general, capital gains on common stock are subject to the investor's marginal federal income tax rate, up to a maximum of 28 percent.

Preferred Stock

Preferred stock is a hybrid security. In some ways it resembles common stock, but in other ways it resembles a bond.

Preferred stock shares the following characteristics with common stock:

- Preferred stock represents an ownership interest in a corporation. However, most companies restrict the voting rights of preferred stockholders. As a rule, preferred stockholders cannot vote unless dividends have been missed.
- If the corporation is liquidated, claims of creditors—including bondholders—must be satisfied before payments can be made to preferred stock-

holders, but the claims of preferred stockholders come before those of common stockholders.

- Preferred dividends are paid only after being declared by a company's board of directors.

- Preferred dividends and capital gains from the sale of preferred stock shares represent taxable income to stockholders.

- Preferred stock that is regularly traded on organized exchanges has high marketability, but its liquidity depends upon market conditions.

- Diversification when investing in preferred stock is possible, although it is subject to the same constraints as mentioned for common stock.

- Preferred stock can be purchased in relatively small amounts.

Preferred stock shares the following characteristics with bonds:

- Dividends on preferred stock are usually stated as a percentage of par value and are fixed. For example, a 6 percent preferred stock with a par value of $100 would pay a dividend of $6 per year. However, bond interest must be paid, whereas a corporation's board of directors can legally elect to pass preferred stock dividend payments. But, most preferred stock is **cumulative**, which means that both dividends that have been missed and current dividends must be paid before the corporation is allowed to pay dividends to common stockholders.

- Like bonds, preferred stock might be callable by the issuing corporation; the call provisions are similar to those of bonds. For example, a call premium may be required.

- Sinking funds can be associated with preferred stock.

- Some preferred stock is convertible into common stock.

In general, the holders of preferred stock are in a less secure position than bondholders. Compared to preferred stock, bonds provide prior claims both to corporate earnings and to company assets upon liquidation. Obviously, in a company that issues both bonds and preferred stocks, the preferred stockholders assume greater risk.

Considering these factors, it would be logical to assume that investors would prefer the more secure position of bonds, bidding up bond prices higher than preferred stock prices, or that interest rates on bonds would be lower than the rates on preferred stock. While this is a logical line of reasoning, it does not hold true in practice. As a general rule, interest on a company's bonds provides a greater income than its dividends on preferred stock.

This apparent anomaly is the result of federal income tax law. To avoid double taxation, the Internal Revenue Service allows many corporations to exclude from their taxable income at least 70 percent of all dividend income received from other corporations. This tax advantage is not available to individual investors. Thus, preferred stock is more attractive to corporate investors than to individuals. As a result, corporations tend to bid up the prices of preferred stock to the point at which the after-tax yield to individual investors is less than the yield generally available from investment grade corporate bonds.

The purchasing power risk for preferred stock is substantial. Dividend income from preferred stock will not increase over a long period even if inflation persists, and an investor's real income can be eroded by price level increases.

Furthermore, because preferred stock generally provides a fixed dividend income, the interest rate risk is substantial for most preferred stock. Because of the effect of interest rates, the market price of preferred stock can be unstable, and an investor might sustain losses if interest rates increase after the stock is purchased.

The rating services that evaluate bond quality also rate preferred stock. These ratings, in effect, provide a good estimate of the financial risk associated with a preferred stock issue. As with bonds, the ratings vary from AAA to speculative.

Mutual Funds

Mutual funds are large investment portfolios comprised of many different securities—either stock, bonds, or both, in addition to other investments. Mutual funds are organized as investment companies in which investors can purchase shares. Thus, mutual funds provide investors with an indirect means of owning stock, bonds, and other investments.

Mutual funds address several problems otherwise faced by many people who would like to invest in stocks and bonds:

- *Management expertise.* The individual investor might lack the expertise needed to select appropriate investments and to monitor an investment portfolio. Mutual fund investment portfolios are managed by experienced account managers (either individual investment advisors or independent management companies) whose job it is to select sound investments and monitor their performance.

- *Effective diversification.* Even if investments are properly managed, an individual investor might be able to purchase securities from only a few corporations, making it difficult to achieve effective diversification. Mutual funds, by their very nature, invest in a large number of different securities. When an investor purchases a share of a mutual fund, he or she purchases a piece of each security in the mutual fund's investment portfolio; thus, diversification is immediately achieved.

- *Less expense.* The inadequate divisibility of investments can make it impossible for an investor with limited funds to invest in an otherwise desirable investment. Mutual fund shares are often less expensive than the prices of the individual securities in which the funds are invested. With a relatively small amount of money, an investor can purchase a piece of a stock or bond that he or she would otherwise have been unable to purchase due to its high cost.

- *More marketability and liquidity.* Both marketability and liquidity are limited for investments not regularly traded on the open market. Many mutual fund shares are actively traded on the open market, even if their investment portfolios contain illiquid and less marketable securities.

The most popular type of mutual fund is the **open-end fund**. In this type of fund, new mutual fund shares are continuously offered for sale, and the mutual fund itself will redeem any outstanding shares based on the current net asset value per share. The **net asset value (NAV)** per share is the mutual fund's net worth (assets less liabilities) divided by the number of mutual fund shares outstanding. For example, if a mutual fund has a net worth of $2,500,000 and one million shares are outstanding, the mutual fund's NAV is $2.50 ($2,500,000/1,000,000). The market price per share of an open-ended mutual fund varies directly with the value of the mutual fund's investment portfolio.

Closed-end funds also exist. A closed-end fund generally sells a fixed number of shares in the mutual fund itself. The shares are not redeemable by the mutual fund but can be sold to outside parties. Shares of closed-end mutual funds are actively traded in the securities markets, and the price of these shares is determined by market forces. As a result, shares in closed-end mutual funds might sell at a price that is higher or lower than the net asset value of the company.

Mutual Fund Objectives

Different mutual funds have different investment objectives, and investors should choose mutual funds having objectives consistent with their own. Classifications of funds by their investment objectives include the following:

- *Corporate bond funds*—invest in corporate bonds. Investors usually seek high current income, but the NAV of the shares fluctuates with changes in interest rates. Bond funds generally invest in *either* investment grade bonds *or* junk bonds.

- *Municipal bond funds*—invest in tax-exempt municipal bonds. Fund investors receive tax advantages.

- *Growth stock funds*—seek long-term capital growth by investing in growth stocks. Little investment income is received, but capital appreciation might be above average.

- *Aggressive growth funds*—seek maximum capital growth. These funds often invest in speculative securities, and capital appreciation can be rapid.

- *Income funds*—seek a high level of dividend income from investments in bonds, preferred stocks, and common stocks. The securities are generally safe and provide a large amount of investment income.

- *Growth and income funds*—emphasize both capital appreciation and current dividends. These funds strive for long-term growth without much fluctuation in share prices. They are usually comprised of stocks of large, well-established companies—often called "blue chip" stocks.

- *Balanced funds*—invest in bonds and stocks, like a growth and income fund, but selecting investments that emphasize safety rather than current performance. Generally, no more than 60 percent of the fund value is invested in any one type of investment.

- *International funds*—invest primarily in securities of companies domiciled outside the U.S. These funds offer an added degree of diversification.

- *Money market funds*—emphasize short-term investments such as Treasury bills, commercial paper, and other short-term debt instruments. Many money-market mutual funds provide the investor with drafts that can be used much like bank checks. Generally, the drafts can be written only for amounts exceeding some minimum, such as $500. When the payee presents the draft for payment, the amount of the draft is deducted from the investor's account.

- *Metals funds*—concentrate their holdings in precious or strategic metal securities or in stocks of companies dealing with the mining of these metals. In general, these funds face the investment risks associated with individual investment in precious metals, as discussed later.

- *Specialized* or *sector funds*—concentrate in one or two fields or industries. The success of these funds rises and falls with the fortunes of the particular sectors in which they are invested.

Many investment management companies that manage several mutual funds (that is, have a *family* of mutual funds) give investors the right to switch money from one of their funds to another with little or no charge. Since different funds usually have different investment objectives, this exchange privilege can be convenient. For example, consider the investor who has owned a growth fund and would like to change to an income fund. Without the exchange privilege, the investor would have to sell the shares in the growth fund and then possibly pay sales commissions to another investment company to buy shares in its income fund. With the exchange privilege, the transaction can be handled by a single telephone call. However, every exchange might have tax implications.

General Nature of Mutual Funds

Although mutual funds have varied portfolio policies and objectives, they share several characteristics. These factors are discussed below.

Investment Return

Mutual funds can provide investment income in the form of dividends and capital gains. Dividends, if paid, are similar to dividends on stock—an investor earns a stated amount per share. The investor can take the dividends as cash or, for open-end funds, can reinvest them in the mutual fund. In fact, **automatic dividend reinvestment** is commonly available in open-end funds. If an investor chooses this option, all dividends provided by the fund are automatically reinvested in additional shares of the fund.

Capital gains from open-end mutual funds arise from the securities within the mutual funds' investment portfolios. Because mutual funds invest in many different securities, they receive dividend and interest payments from their investments and can experience capital gains as their portfolios increase in value or securities are sold by the funds. The NAV of open-end funds grows with the capital gains experienced by and the investment income received by the mutual fund's portfolio. Thus, the market value of the mutual fund's shares increases, and the investors experience capital gains.

Capital gains from closed-end funds can arise in a similar fashion. However, they can also result from trading the fund's shares. Recall that closed-end fund shares are actively bought and sold in the market at prices that can differ from the net asset value. Thus, an investor in a closed-end fund might obtain capital gains through increases in the value of the investment portfolio held by the fund or by trading the fund's shares in the market.

SEC regulations stipulate that mutual fund advertising of yields must provide historical information based on yield or total return. Furthermore, comparisons of a fund's total return must be made to total returns earned on investments with comparable investment objectives to the fund.

- The **yield** of a mutual fund expresses the rate of income the fund earns on its investments as a percentage of the fund's share price. Net income per share is calculated by totaling the interest and dividend income earned on the fund's portfolio for a thirty-day period, subtracting fund expenses, and dividing by the number of fund shares. This net income per share is divided by the fund's share price at the end of the thirty-day period and then converted to an annual figure.

- The yearly **total return** is the mutual fund's overall change in value for the year and is measured by the following formula: dividends and capital gains from the sale of securities and changes in the value of remaining securities less investment costs.

Investment Risk

Because of the wide variety of mutual funds, it is difficult to generalize about the *types* of investment risks investors face. The types and degrees of investment risk depend on the objectives of the mutual fund involved and on the types of securities in the investment company's portfolio. A fund consisting almost entirely of investment grade bonds, for example, would be subject to the investment risks affecting such bonds; a fund specializing in common stock would be subject to the investment risks affecting such stock; and so forth. Thus, mutual funds might be subject to *one or more* of (1) purchasing power risk, (2) market risk, (3) financial risk, and (4) interest rate risk, depending on the underlying securities in the fund.

Liquidity and Marketability

Open-ended mutual funds are normally highly marketable because the fund stands ready to buy back the shares at their NAV (or sometimes at their NAV less a small redemption fee or load or both). Closed-end funds generally are highly marketable because their shares are actively traded on securities exchanges. The liquidity of mutual funds depends on the investment portfolio of the fund being considered. For example, money market mutual funds are intended to be completely liquid; short-term investment grade bond mutual funds are quite liquid; and long-term bond mutual funds and common stock mutual funds are much less liquid.

Diversification

As mentioned above, mutual funds provide immediate diversification to the investor. Each share of a mutual fund represents a piece of every security in its investment portfolio. Thus, by owning a few shares of a mutual fund, an investor can indirectly own a piece of a hundred different securities.

One of the prime advantages of mutual funds is their use of diversification to minimize the effects of financial risk. Financial risk often is a major problem if an investor owns only a small number of common stock shares. However, if an investor owns a larger number of securities, financial risk is reduced through diversification.

Divisibility

Undoubtedly, a second major attraction for mutual fund investors is the ability to purchase shares in almost any amount. Most mutual funds allow investors to purchase portions of shares. For example, an investor may wish to invest $1,000 in a mutual fund whose shares are selling at $30. Ignoring any transaction costs, the investor may purchase 33 1/3 shares of the mutual fund. Thus, mutual funds permit investors to gradually establish an investment program.

Taxes

Mutual funds are taxed under the Internal Revenue Code as regulated investment companies. As such, they and their shareholders are taxed on the investment returns from the securities held by the fund essentially on a pass-through basis. That is, the mutual fund pays out its investment income to its shareholders as dividends. The shareholders report these dividends (to the extent required by the tax law) on their own tax returns, depending on the tax classification of the dividends.

For these tax classifications, three kinds of mutual fund dividends exist:

1. **Ordinary income dividends** from the fund's net investment income, such as taxable dividends and interest. They are taxed currently as either interest or dividend income of the shareholder.

2. **Tax-exempt interest dividends** from the fund's tax-exempt investment income, such as municipal bond interest payments. They are normally tax-free to the shareholder.

3. **Capital gains dividends** from capital gains to the fund. They are taxed as capital gains to the shareholder.

Mutual fund dividends that are reinvested in additional fund shares are treated for tax purposes as being constructively received by the shareholders and taxed currently to the shareholders, depending on the type of dividends, as just explained.

Capital gains generated by the sale, exchange, or redemption of an investor's mutual fund shares are taxable under the regular rules of capital gains taxation, as are capital gains from other investments the person might have received.

Management Services

A major feature of mutual funds is professional management. Once investors select the mutual fund or funds in which to invest, they can choose to turn over their investment problems to the mutual fund's investment experts. However, these management services are not free. Investors pay some type of management or administrative fee or fees for services.

Load funds charge a sales commission to an investor when shares are purchased or sold. **Front-end load funds** charge commissions when shares are purchased. **Back-end load funds** charge commissions when shares are sold. The sales load for most load funds is determined by a sliding scale of rates, such as those shown in Exhibit 5-14. Considerable variation exists, and these figures are illustrative only. Still, two features are noteworthy:

1. Since the load is highest for small purchases, most individual investors pay the maximum rate.

2. The percent figure shown might be misleading because sales charges are stated as a percentage of the offering price. Suppose an investor makes a $1,000 investment and the quoted sales charge is 6 percent, or $60. After deducting the sales charge, $940 is invested ($1,000 – $60 = $940). If the sales charge is expressed as a percentage of the amount actually invested—which might seem more appropriate—the sales charge is actually 6.4 percent ($60/$940 = 6.4%).

Exhibit 5-14
Sliding Scale of Rates

Amount Purchased	Sales Charge
Less than $20,000	8.25%
$20,000-29,999.99	7.00
$30,000-39,999.99	6.00
$40,000-49,999.99	4.25
$50,000 or more	3.50

Alternatives to load funds include low-load funds and no-load funds. **Low-load funds** with sales charges of about 2 to 4 percent—half the charge for load funds—have become popular in recent years. **No-load funds** sell directly to investors and therefore incur no sales commission. However, some no-load funds (as well as some load funds) allow the recovery of marketing expenses as an *annual* charge, called **12(b)-1 fees**, against the net assets of the fund. These funds might be referred to as **hidden-load funds** and the charges sometimes are as high as 1.5 percent of the investment value.

As noted previously, both load (including low-load) and no-load funds charge investors for operating expenses on an annual basis. This charge might be related to the performance of the fund. If performance is good, the investment adviser earns a higher percentage. The advisory fee is also frequently related to the size of the fund—the percentage charges become smaller as the fund becomes larger. It is difficult to generalize, but a typical fee is usually about 1 percent per year.

Systematic Withdrawal

A systematic withdrawal or liquidation can be arranged to liquidate a mutual fund investment over time. Under this arrangement, the mutual fund makes periodic payments of a specified amount to the investor. Payments are made first from dividend income, if any; if dividends are inadequate, a sufficient number of shares is automatically redeemed. While a withdrawal plan might be convenient, most investors cannot confidently predict how long the payments will be continued.

Mutual Fund Insurance

A small number of mutual funds offer the option of buying insurance that protects investors against losses in their accounts. The insurance plan guarantees that investors will receive at least the amount they paid for their shares. However, policy periods last from ten to fifteen years, and the investment must be held for the entire policy period before compensation for loss will be made. In effect, this type of insurance is designed to eliminate the financial risk and business risk of such an investment. Practically, diversification within the fund should have effectively reduced the risks. Further diversification can be achieved by investing in several different funds.

Life Insurance Benefits

Some mutual funds provide life insurance benefits. Life insurance can be tied to the amount of shares purchased to date; other mutual funds offer sufficient life insurance to complete an investment program if the investor dies.

Speculative Investments

Speculative investments are characterized by higher investment risk than most of the investments discussed thus far. Warrants, options, commodities, and financial futures are among the speculative investments that are traded in security markets.

Warrants

A **warrant** gives the owner the right to *buy* from a *corporation* a specific number of shares of a security (usually common stock) at a stated price (the **exercise price**) during a certain period of time. Note that a warrant owner is not obligated to buy the shares; the owner *can* purchase the shares if he or she desires. No transaction fee applies when the warrant is exercised.

For example, the ABC Corporation might sell warrants that allow the warrant owners to buy one share of ABC common stock per warrant from ABC at a price of $80. An ABC Corporation warrant owner *might* exercise his or her right at any time but is most likely to exercise the right if the price of the underlying ABC stock equals or exceeds $80 per share.

Warrants can be traded among investors in securities markets just like stock. However, warrants always sell at a price lower—usually much lower—than the price of the underlying security.

Warrants are *inherently leveraged*. The percentage price changes in warrants will be greater than the market price changes in common stock. This results primarily from the fact that the exercise price does not change.

Suppose ABC Corporation warrants will not expire for another five years and are selling for $2 each when the underlying stock is selling at $40 per share. If the stock price moves upward, say to $50, investors will see a greater likelihood that the stock price will exceed the exercise price of $80, and they will bid up the price of the warrants. The warrants might increase to $4, for example. In this example, the stock appreciates from $40 to $50, or an increase of 25 percent. The value of the warrant, however, increases 100 percent—from $2 to $4.

Warrants can contain other features. The number of shares of underlying stock is stated as more or less than one share of common stock. Some warrants have an exercise price that changes over time. Some warrants allow investors to use either cash or debt of the company to buy the underlying stock.

Warrants offer the possibility of sizable financial rewards and, of course, the possibility of substantial losses. Investment returns are realized through capital gains or losses. The investment risks associated with warrants are the same as those that apply to common stock. In fact, the investment risks inherent in a specific warrant are derived from the risks related to the common stock of the same corporation. However, the potential *size* of returns and risks associated with warrants is magnified.

Options

An **option** is an agreement between two parties giving the owner or *holder* of the option the right to *buy* or *sell* an investment at a stipulated exercise price within a certain period of time. The standard option contract is for 100 shares of a common stock, which is referred to as the *underlying security*.

As with warrants, the option holder is not obligated to buy or sell the underlying security. However, the seller or *writer* of the option may be obligated to complete the transaction if the option holder chooses to exercise his or her option.

Most options are for three, six, or nine months. All listed options expire at 11:59 P.M. Eastern time on the Saturday following the third Friday of the month of expiration. Although trading stops at 3:00 P.M. on the previous business day, the options can be exercised until 5:30 P.M.

As indicated in the definition, two basic types of options exist: options to buy a set amount of the underlying security (**call options**) and options to sell a set amount of the underlying security (**put options**).

Investors typically purchase *call options* because they believe the price of the underlying stock will increase before the option expires. If the price of the underlying security rises above the exercise price, investors might exercise the options because they can purchase the underlying securities at a bargain price.

A person who thinks the price of a stock will decline might buy a *put option*. If the price of the underlying security decreases to below the exercise price, the investor might exercise his or her option to sell the security at the exercise price, and thus earn a profit.

Inherent leverage is the enticing feature of options. For example, if a stock moved from $32 to $40, a person owning that stock would experience a return of 25 percent. In the same situation, the value of a call option with the same stock as the underlying security could go from $2 to $10—a gain of 400 percent. Of course, this leverage can also magnify losses in a declining stock market.

Buying a put or call option entails substantial risk. A large majority of options expire without being exercised. Of course, in these cases the loss is limited to the premium paid (and transaction costs).

Unlike the writer of a warrant, the writer of an option is another investor, not an issuing company. The writer of an option provides the contract. The writer's inducement is the premium that can be obtained. While buying puts or calls is quite speculative, a strategy of writing call options on stock one owns is generally considered conservative.

- If the writer owns the stock, the call option is *covered*. The writer receives premium income and knows that the option will not be exercised if the stock price falls. However, the writer sacrifices potential gains. If the stock appreciates beyond the exercise price, the holder might exercise the option, and the writer will be required to deliver the stock at the exercise price.

- If the writer does not own the stock, this is an *uncovered* position, and the call option is a *naked option*. The risk in this situation is different. If the option is exercised, the stock must immediately be obtained for delivery at whatever price the market requires. The writer might sustain a large loss.

Commodities

Goods traditionally offered on the **commodity** market include grains, livestock, fibers, foods, and metals. Commodities are usually produced, shipped, and stored in large quantities. They are fairly uniform in size and substance; can be precisely measured, weighed, and counted; and are likely to be supplied seasonally. Prices generally fluctuate according to supply and demand. They are widely marketable, needed by many different kinds of consumers, and produced by many different producers. Commodities are generally regarded as highly speculative investments.

The commodity purchaser buys a definite quantity of the commodity—for example, 5,000 bushels of wheat. Most commodities investors buy **commodities futures**—contracts either to make or to accept a delivery of a specified commodity on a given future date. When that date is reached, the investor must either deliver the commodity or pay cash to receive it. Because commodity prices fluctuate widely, commodity futures involve high investment risk and offer potentially high returns. These risks and returns are usually magnified through the use of leverage.

Financial Futures

In recent years, several exchanges have developed contracts for financial futures that are modeled after commodities futures. In these contracts one investor agrees to buy and another investor agrees to sell financial instruments at a specified price and date. Futures contracts exist for Treasury bills, stock portfolios, gold, and foreign currencies.

Cash Value Life Insurance as an Investment

The concept of cash value life insurance as a form of protection against the death of the insured has already been presented in Chapters 3 and 4. This discussion considers cash value life insurance in the context of investment planning.

Liquidity and Marketability

The ability to quickly convert investments or savings into cash with little or no loss of principal is an important consideration. Life insurance cash values are almost perfectly liquid and marketable. Normally, cash can be obtained from a policy in a matter of hours or a few days.

Only one factor detracts from the otherwise perfect liquidity of life insurance cash values. As a result of the Great Depression, life insurance companies include a **delay clause** in the policy. This provision gives the company the right to postpone the payment of the cash value for a period of up to six months. In actual practice, however, very few companies have exercised the delay provision. To do so would tend to encourage a "run" on cash values, and therefore, companies have a strong incentive to ignore the clause and pay cash values promptly.

Diversification

Diversification is an important characteristic of cash value life insurance as an investment. By purchasing a cash value life insurance policy as an investment, a policyowner obtains a high degree of diversification.

The life insurance industry uses several methods to diversify its investments. For example, life insurance companies place their funds into many types of industries. An adverse experience in one particular industry will have only minor effects upon the entire investment portfolio.

Diversification is also achieved by spreading investments over a wide territory. This restricts losses that might occur if one region of the country suffered an economic recession. Excluding investments in Canada, only a small proportion of life insurance company funds are allocated to foreign securities.

In addition, diversification of investments over time is used by life insurers. Securities are purchased so that the maturity dates will vary. If maturities were not spread over time, insurance companies might be forced to obtain a large amount of funds at a time when investment conditions are unfavorable. Diversity by date of maturity increases the regularity of life insurers' income. Thus, life insurers are seldom forced to liquidate investments to meet obligations because the proceeds from maturing investments cover their needs. This regularity enables insurance companies to take full advantage of the most favorable security prices.

A final method of diversification is by number of investments. If a policyowner has $10,000 of cash value in a life insurance policy and the company has 500 different investments, the policyowner has, in effect, $20 invested in each of the investments. Therefore, the sheer number of investments acts to minimize overall risk.

Divisibility

Since cash value life insurance can be purchased in small or large amounts (assuming the person seeking to be insured is insurable) cash value life insurance is divisible as an investment medium.

Taxes

The taxation of cash value life insurance has been briefly discussed in Chapters 3 and 4. Several tax aspects of cash value life insurance are favorable for life insurance as an investment:

- Life insurance cash values earn investment returns on a tax-deferred basis. The policyowner is not taxed on the investment growth unless it is withdrawn from the policy.

- Policy loans from a cash value life insurance policy are generally not considered distributions from the policy for income tax purposes (unless it is a modified endowment contract).

- Life insurance proceeds paid by reason of the insured's death are generally income-tax-free to the policy beneficiary.

Use Value

Cash value life insurance serves the dual function of providing insurance protection for the policyowner's family or other death protection needs and providing a tax-advantageous way of accumulating capital. It thus provides both a use value and an investment medium for the policyowner.

Investment Return

Comparing the rate of return from a cash value life insurance policy with that from other sources is exceedingly complex. Although generalizations about the rate of return in a cash value life insurance policy are common, they are often misleading.

To estimate the rate of return for a policyowner, the following major facts or assumptions are needed:

1. The premium required for a cash value policy
2. The cost of term insurance in an amount equal, each year, to the amount of protection needed

3. The period of time over which the comparison will be made

4. The amount of the cash value in the policy at the end of the given period of time

5. The amount of life insurance policy dividends that will be paid each year (if any)

6. The income-tax bracket of the individual (each year)

With this information, a person can determine whether buying term and investing the difference would be better for investment purposes than purchasing a cash value policy. The objective is to determine the interest rate necessary to make the separate investment fund (accumulated from the difference between the premiums on the term and cash value policies) equal to the cash surrender value of the cash value life insurance policy at the end of a specified period.

The interpretation of any published rates of return for cash value life insurance policies must be made with caution. The rates of return can vary greatly, depending upon (1) the age of issue, (2) the number of years projected, (3) the premiums, dividends, and cash values of the whole life, universal life, or endowment policy, (4) the term insurance rates assumed, (5) the type of policy, and (6) the tax bracket of the policyowner.

Investment Risk

Traditional cash value life insurance is essentially a fixed-dollar investment and hence is unfavorably affected by inflation. With regard to variable life insurance, the impact of the purchasing power risk depends on the investment choices the policyowner makes with regard to the policy's cash value and his or her premium payments.

Historically, no type of private financial institution or business organization has equaled the solvency record of the life insurance industry. Three major reasons account for this remarkable record:

1. *Volume of assets.* The volume of assets in many companies is tremendous, by almost any standard, and therefore life insurers strive to obtain competent investment personnel.

2. *Safe investments.* Life insurance companies are required to place their funds in rather conservative, safe investments by life insurance regulations. Exhibit 5-15 shows the volume of assets held by life insurance companies in each of the major types of investments. Notice that the preponderance of investments is in corporate bonds, government securities, and mortgages, with a relatively small portion in more speculative investments. Of

course, the relative proportions of the investments change over time. At the end of World War II, U.S. government bonds accounted for almost half of the life insurance industry assets, but in recent years a smaller percentage of investments are in government bonds.

3. *Diversification.* As noted previously, the life insurance industry uses several methods of diversification that effectively reduce the financial risk associated with cash value life insurance as an investment.

Exhibit 5-15
Distribution of Assets of U.S. Life Insurance Companies, 1992
(000,000 omitted)

Type of Asset	Amount	Percentage of Total
Government Securities	$ 320,109	19.2
Corporate Bonds	670,206	40.3
Stock	192,403	11.5
Mortgages	246,702	14.8
Real Estate	50,595	3.1
Policy Loans	72,058	4.3
Miscellaneous	112,458	6.8
Total	$1,664,531	100.0%

Adapted from *Life Insurance Fact Book Update* (Washington, DC: American Council on Life Insurance, 1993), p. 46.

Traditional life insurance cash values are guaranteed by the insurance company and hence generally are not subject to interest rate risk. The extent to which variable life insurance policy cash values are subject to interest rate risk depends on the type or types of separate investment accounts into which the policyowner elects to have his or her cash values placed. Traditional life insurance cash values are not subject to market risk, but variable policy cash values might depend on how they are allocated among the variable policy's separate accounts by the policyowner.

Other Considerations

In addition to the previous investment characteristics identified for cash value life insurance, it is a convenient investment for many individuals. It also provides a semicompulsory investment plan.

Convenience

The time, effort, and ability required to manage an investment or savings program should not be underestimated. A life insurance policyowner has virtually no managerial problems with the investment or savings program. These are turned over to the professional staff of the insurer.

Semicompulsory Nature

Perhaps the most important consideration for a person considering the "buy term and invest the difference" approach is the question of whether the "difference" will actually be invested regularly over a long period of time. Most individuals find it extremely difficult to continue a savings program over a long time. It is easy for a savings program to be interrupted or discontinued when unexpected financial needs arise.

A savings program through life insurance is much easier to continue than most other savings plans because of its semicompulsory nature. A policyowner is under no contractual obligation to continue a life insurance policy, but in many cases, he or she is reluctant to let the protection terminate. Consequently, he or she continues to pay the premium, and the savings in the form of cash values continue to grow.

Nonfinancial Investments

Many investments do not involve the purchase of financial instruments such as stocks and bonds. Many people choose to invest in nonfinancial investments that involve the purchase of, among other things, real estate, precious metals, and art and antiques. While the investor's interest in such items might be purely financial, these items are generally of value for reasons beyond finances—such as the ability to use real estate and the ability to view and appreciate art.

Real Estate

An individual can invest in real estate by becoming an owner or a creditor of real estate. For many families, the home they occupy is their most substantial real estate investment. However, emphasis in this discussion is on investments in real estate other than a person's primary residence.

Investing in Real Estate as an Owner

Owners of investment real estate usually earn investment income through rent from tenants of the owned property. Owners can also experience capital appreciation as the value of the real estate increases.

Investment risk associated with owning real estate varies with the property owned, due to market risk. The real estate market's perceptions of the value of the property significantly influence its value. If the property is in an unattractive location, for example, its market value generally falls.

Purchasing power risk can be significant, depending on the economy. Most real estate increases in value as the economy continues to grow. However, in recessionary periods, some property values plummet.

Owning real estate as an investment can also be characterized by the following:

- *Low liquidity and low marketability*. It is not always easy to find a buyer willing to pay a fair price for a piece of property. However, the investment return on real estate can compensate for the lack of liquidity and marketability.
- *Lack of diversification*. Individual investors typically cannot afford to purchase many different pieces of real estate.
- *Low divisibility*. A real estate investment property is often expensive and cannot be purchased by a single investor or purchased in smaller pieces.
- *Complex tax issues*. The taxation of real estate transactions is complex and generally beyond the scope of this text. Investors interested in real estate for investment purposes should seek advice from experts in the field of real estate.

Real estate ownership can take several forms. *Individual ownership* or *regular partnerships* offer the simplest and most direct type of investment. These approaches normally involve one or a small number of investors who acquire the property and often manage it themselves. Advantages of these ownership forms include quick management decisions and total control among the owners. The primary disadvantages are limited capital, limited management ability, limited diversification, and unlimited personal liability.

Limited partnerships are a mechanism for combining the financial resources of a larger number of individuals. *Joint ventures* and *real estate syndicates* are similar arrangements. A person can participate in a limited partnership, joint venture, or syndicate in units with minimum amounts as low as $1,000. The partnership syndicate owns the property, and the general partner (also referred to as the promoter or sponsor) manages the real estate investment. Not only does such participation provide opportunities for small investors to invest in real estate; it also allows an individual to diversify real estate investments by participating in more than one syndicate. Another advantage is that most limited partnerships provide expert management, thus freeing individual investors from real estate management problems. Furthermore, the limited partners have limited liability for any partnership debts.

Real estate limited partnerships, however, are not free of problems. A potential investor must have some understanding of the real estate investments to be undertaken. It is most important to evaluate the sponsor of the partnership. This individual or firm must have a good record of achievement, a high credit rating, an impeccable record of honesty, and administrative and managerial ability. Another factor that should be analyzed carefully is the legal agreement between investors and the sponsor or promoter. A well-designed agreement will be specific about possible assessments of participants, compensation of the sponsor, possible conflicts of interest, broker's fees, and the allocation of profits and expenses.

Individuals can also invest in real estate through *real estate investment trusts* (REITs). REITs operate much like mutual funds but with investments placed in real estate rather than in financial instruments.

Investing in Real Estate as a Creditor

A real estate investor can become a creditor by purchasing mortgages rather than actually owning real estate. For individual investors, the most common method of becoming a real estate creditor involves second mortgages (or, third or fourth mortgages).

The second mortgage on a piece of real estate is subordinate to the primary or first mortgage on the property. A second mortgage is generally involved when a buyer does not have enough cash for a down payment when purchasing a home or when a homeowner needs to finance home improvements. A second mortgage usually runs for five or ten years at an interest rate higher than the rate on the first mortgage.

In some cases, the person who accepts a second mortgage is more interested in receiving cash. He or she therefore sells the second mortgage to an investor whose investment return is the principal and interest payments made by the mortgagee over the term of the mortgage. Although the market for second mortgages is not well-developed, most localities have firms or individuals who periodically purchase second mortgages. Often, real estate brokers are helpful in establishing and maintaining such a market.

Investment risk for individual investors in purchasing second mortgages can be significant. The income is generally fixed, and thus purchasing power risk can be great. Interest rates in the market might increase above the rate earned on the mortgage, so interest rate risk can also be significant. Furthermore, the mortgage is subordinate to a first mortgage in making a claim against the assets.

Precious Metals

Gold, silver, and platinum are among the precious metals used for investment purposes. However, since different precious metals share investment characteristics, this discussion concentrates on gold.

Gold has intrigued investors for centuries, but it was not until 1975 that gold bullion became a legal investment in the United States. An investor can invest in gold through six investment vehicles:

1. Gold bullion
2. Gold coins
3. Gold futures
4. Investment companies that specialize in gold or the stocks of gold mining companies
5. Common stock of gold mining companies
6. Gold certificates issued against vault holdings

The price of gold is determined by supply and demand factors in a worldwide market. Historically, the world price of gold has shown wide swings, indicating that investors have had opportunities for large profits and that they have suffered large losses. For example, during early 1980, the price of gold skyrocketed to over $800 per ounce when speculators entered the market. Three months later, the price was just over $500 per ounce. Clearly, gold is a speculative investment.

Gold reputedly provides an effective hedge against poor business conditions and unstable economic conditions. World unrest, economic uncertainty, and unexpected inflation are the primary causes of rises in the price of gold.

The possible disadvantages of gold bullion and coins as investments include the following:

*   They generate no current income.
*   They require maintenance expenses such as insurance premiums and fees for safekeeping. Indeed, gold is highly attractive to thieves and therefore subject to loss by theft.
*   Commissions and sales taxes are involved in gold transactions.
*   Fraudulent gold bars are not common, but investors should be on guard and consider gold investments only through highly reputable bullion dealers.

Art and Antiques

Objects of art and antiques are often owned for personal reasons as well as for their investment value. Assets in these categories usually generate no invest-

Exhibit 5-16
Sotheby's Art Index

Index Sectors	July 1992	One Month Ago	One Year Ago	Two Years Ago	Five Years Ago	Ten Years Ago
Old Master Paintings	811	728	728	612	349	199
19th Century European Paintings	643	625	653	679	303	183
Impressionist & Post-Impressionist Art	913	913	1,113	1,728	661	255
Modern Paintings (1900-1950)	1,037	1,018	1,200	1,774	666	245
Contemporary Art (1945 on)*	1,121	1,181	1,165	1,686	597	285
American Paintings (1800-pre-WW II)	1,179	1,142	1,105	1,371	789	459
Continental Ceramics	864	796	696	555	320	266
Chinese Ceramics	925	1,003	1,003	1,010	550	460
English Silver	440	439	459	453	349	197
Continental Silver	428	428	436	395	201	134
American Furniture	527	516	513	510	452	213
French and Continental Furniture	648	648	564	500	319	234
English Furniture	906	924	926	917	594	271
Aggregate Index	797	788	841	1,067	475	252

Basis 1975 = 100($)

*Contemporary art was added to the Art Index in September 1987. The aggregate index excludes this category prior to that date.

Sotheby's Art Index reflects subjective analyses and opinions of Sotheby's art experts, based on auction sales and other information deemed relevant. Nothing in Sotheby's Art Index is intended or should be relied upon as investment advice or as a prediction or guarantee of future performance or otherwise.

ment income and often require maintenance expenses and insurance coverage. Investment return is essentially limited to capital appreciation. In addition, liquidity and marketability can present major problems for investors. Loss control measures and appropriate property insurance are advisable because these assets are clearly exposed to property risks such as theft, fire, and breakage.

Experts warn investors against investment in art and antiques. Market risk can be substantial. Prices for both art and antiques have shown a decline during recessions. Liquidity and marketability can be low. Of course, buyers usually can be found, but the markets for art and antiques are not nearly so developed and efficient as markets for many other investments. Furthermore, these markets are influenced by fads that favorably and unfavorably affect the prices of art and antiques. Placing a value on works of art is exceedingly difficult and largely subjective. Even for recognized masterpieces, expert valuations often differ considerably.

Despite valuation problems, indexes showing changes in prices of paintings are available. One of the most respected indexes, Sotheby's Art Index, is published periodically in *Barron's*. *Sotheby's tracks price trends; its index does not predict prices nor indicate value of pieces of art.* As was shown in Exhibit 5-16, performance among the different art categories varies significantly.

The investor in art and antiques should have a high degree of expertise. An investor who is not knowledgeable about this type of investment is at a significant disadvantage and should seek other investment opportunities.

Summary

When planning to invest, an individual should consider his or her investment goals and the risks and returns associated with each investment. This chapter has described investment risks, investment returns, and other factors affecting investment decisions. It also has described the characteristics of a variety of savings and investment vehicles.

Investments intentionally involve speculative risk. Most investments are expected to increase in value, although they will not necessarily do so. In making an investment, the investor weighs the potential investment return against the investment risks. In the long run, higher risk investments generally provide the highest potential return. However, it is entirely possible that a lower risk investment will produce better results, especially in the short run.

Capital appreciation and income are two kinds of investment return. Investment return is affected by four sources of investment risk—purchasing power risk, financial risk, interest rate risk, and market risk. Other factors should also be considered when making an investment decision: leverage; liquidity and marketability; diversification; and divisibility. The tax status of an investment is important to investors interested in minimizing their tax liability and maximizing after-tax returns. Finally, many individuals seek investments not only for their monetary value, but also because they provide living space (a house) or aesthetic pleasure (fine arts).

Investment vehicles include savings accounts, securities issued by the U.S. government (savings bonds, Treasury bills, and Treasury bonds and notes), corporate bonds, municipal bonds, common stocks, preferred stocks, mutual funds, warrants and options, commodities, life insurance, real estate, precious metals, and arts and antiques. This chapter has described the characteristics of each of these types of investments. Exhibit 5-17 provides a continuum that summarizes the investment risk—investment return of these investments.

Exhibit 5-17
Risk-Return Continuum for Selected Investments

Investment Risk		Investment Return
Low	Cash	Low
	Savings Accounts	
	Cash Value Life Insurance	
	Savings Bonds	
	T-Bills	
	T-Bonds and T-Notes	
	Municipal Bonds	
	Bond Mutual Funds	
	Corporate Bonds	
	Preferred Stock	
	Balanced Mutual Funds	
	Stock Mutual Funds	
	Common Stock	
	Junk Bonds	
	Warrants	
	Options	
	Commodities	
High	Financial Futures	High
	Real Estate	
	Gold	
	Art and Antiques	

No single investment is right for all investors or for all investment purposes. Most desirable is a diversified investment portfolio, including a variety of investments, that provides the desired forms of investment return at an acceptable degree of investment risk.

Chapter Notes

1. The careful reader may have noticed that Exhibits 5-7, 5-8, and especially 5-9, depict investments with a greater potential return than those shown in Exhibits 5-2 and 5-3. This illustrates the general relationship between risk and return discussed earlier—that investments with greater volatility offer potentially higher returns. Later sections of this chapter examine the extent to which various investment instruments provide stability of principal and/or income.

2. For more information on either Series EE or Series HH bonds, write to the U.S. Savings Bonds Marketing Office at Suite 800, 800 "K" St. N.W., Washington, DC, 20226. It is recommended that this request for information be made by postcard.

Chapter 6

Planning for Retirement: Annuities and Pensions

Most workers look forward to the time when they can retire and terminate active employment. However, retirement is also accompanied by the termination of actively earned income, and the loss of this income flow can cause severe financial problems for many individuals and families. One problem of retirement is that the retiree might outlive his or her financial resources. This chapter analyzes the retirement exposure and discusses annuities and pension plans as ways to address the exposure.

Surviving to Retirement Age

Analysis of the retirement exposure starts by examining the probability of surviving to retirement. An easy method of estimating the chances of survival is simply to note the number of persons living at various ages. Exhibit 6-1 provides the information needed to estimate the chances of survival.

For a male forty years of age, the probability of living to age sixty-five is calculated by dividing the number of men alive at age sixty-five—6,910,600—by the number of men alive at age forty—9,357,600. Thus, a forty-year-old man has a 73.9 percent chance of surviving to age sixty-five. For males at age sixty, the probability of living to age sixty-five is approximately 87.7 percent (6,910,600 ÷ 7,880,700).

A female, age forty, has around an 83.3 percent chance of living to age sixty-five. Once she reaches age sixty, her probability of surviving to age sixty-five is approximately 93.4 percent.

A person's chance of surviving to retirement age increases with age. In other words, a person who reaches age forty has a better chance of living to retirement age than does a person only twenty years old. This is a natural result of the fact that a younger person has many years of exposure to death before reaching retirement age, while an older person has already survived some of those years.

Exhibit 6-1
Number Living

Age	Male	Female
0	10,000,000	10,000,000
5	9,918,300	9,938,700
10	9,877,700	9,902,700
15	9,832,800	9,866,300
20	9,751,300	9,819,300
25	9,657,500	9,764,700
30	9,571,300	9,703,400
35	9,478,800	9,630,600
40	9,357,600	9,535,000
45	9,178,300	9,391,600
50	8,910,900	9,187,900
55	8,508,500	8,900,600
60	7,880,700	8,499,600
65	6,910,600	7,941,300

Adapted from the 1980 CSO Mortality Table

Retirement Planning

For Americans, the chance of survival until retirement is very high. Therefore, retirement planning has become an important part of the overall financial planning process. Two key questions in retirement planning are as follows:

1. How long might a person live past retirement?
2. How can that individual prevent outliving his or her financial resources?

Life Expectancy

Life expectancy is the number of years a person is expected to live beyond reaching a certain age. The life expectancy at retirement age provides an answer to question 1 above.

Exhibit 6-2 contains life expectancies for certain ages. The table can be used to estimate how long a person is expected to live beyond retirement. For example, a woman who retires at age seventy is expected to live an additional 13.67 years, while a man who retires at age sixty is expected to survive for another 17.51 years.

Exhibit 6-2
Life Expectancies

Age	Male	Female
0	70.83	75.83
5	66.40	71.28
10	61.66	66.53
15	56.93	61.76
20	52.37	57.04
25	47.84	52.34
30	43.24	47.65
35	38.61	42.98
40	34.05	38.36
45	29.62	33.88
50	25.36	29.53
55	21.29	25.31
60	17.51	21.25
65	14.04	17.32
70	10.96	13.67
75	8.31	10.32
80	6.18	7.48
85	4.46	5.18
90	3.18	3.45
95	1.87	1.91

Adapted from the 1980 CSO Mortality Table

Analysis of Financial Needs

To prevent outliving their financial resources, and to answer question 2 above, people should estimate what their financial needs will be during retirement. This is difficult, even for a person who has just reached retirement age. For younger people, the problem is even greater. Most families have a hard time estimating financial needs even a year or two into the future. Nevertheless, if individuals and families are to plan for retirement in an intelligent manner, they must estimate their financial needs far into the future.

To estimate financial needs for retirement, an individual must consider his or her desired standard of living upon retiring. This standard can serve as the goal of retirement planning. If individuals consider how well off they want to be upon retiring, they can then determine how much wealth they need to attain their desired standard of living. Included for consideration are the following items that will influence individuals' financial needs during retirement:

- Support for any dependents, such as a disabled child
- Debts to be repaid, such as a mortgage or college tuition
- Lifestyle, such as travel, housing, and hobbies

Once people have determined where they want to be financially during retirement, they must consider how to achieve their financial goals. This process involves the following steps:

- Estimating future benefits from Social Security and pension plans
- Estimating expected investment results
- Determining the additional amount needed to achieve financial retirement goals
- Considering the effects of inflation on the cost of living

In recent years, financial advisers have increasingly used computer software programs to estimate the financial resources a person needs for retirement. These programs range from the extremely simple to the amazingly complex and sophisticated. Detailed analysis of these programs is beyond the scope of this text.

Accumulating Funds

Because income taxation is fundamentally important to retirement income planning, the following four basic ways to accumulate funds for retirement are categorized according to their income tax aspects:

1. *Taxable investments.* No tax advantages are associated with this approach. Earned income is taxed the year it is earned, and only after-tax earned income is available for investment. Investment earnings are taxed in the year they are earned. An example of a taxable investment is a certificate of deposit (discussed in Chapter 5).

2. *Tax-deferred investments.* These investments accumulate from year to year without current taxation. Taxes on capital gains and investment income

are not due until the funds are distributed, and only the *gain* (the increase in value over the original amount invested or income tax basis) is taxable. The investor might be in a lower tax bracket after retirement, when the funds are taken, than during his or her years of employment. However, such is not necessarily the case, because tax laws change each year. An annuity (discussed later in this chapter) exemplifies the tax-deferred approach.

3. *Tax-deductible and tax-deferred investments.* A tax deduction (or its equivalent) is provided when the investment is made; in effect, the investment is made with before-tax income. These investments also accumulate from year to year without taxation. Taxes, however, are paid on *all* funds withdrawn—not just on the gain—at the time they are taken. A pension plan (discussed later in this chapter) is a good example of this approach.

4. *Tax-free investments.* These investments are made with after-tax income; in other words, no tax deduction is taken when the investment is made. Subsequent investment income is received tax-free. Municipal bonds (discussed in Chapter 5) are in this category.

Exhibit 6-3 shows how funds accumulate under each of the above approaches. The exhibit assumes that 7.5 percent can be earned on investments (5.5 percent on tax-free investments), and a marginal combined tax bracket (federal and state) of 30 percent. (Note that interest rates, investment returns, and tax rates can change rapidly in the real world. Therefore, the reader will recognize that the figures used here and elsewhere in this chapter might differ from those existing at any given time. However, the principles illustrated remain the same.) The exhibit makes these two points:

- With a *taxable* investment, $1 of earnings each year will be reduced annually by taxes and will grow to $1.95 in twenty years.
- With an investment that is both *tax-deductible and tax-deferred*, $1 of earnings will grow to $2.97 in twenty years.

Clearly, tax advantages are important considerations in accumulating assets.

Retirement Planning Example

The concepts described above are illustrated by the following example. Sam, now fifty-five years old, is contemplating retirement at age sixty-five. He believes he can earn 7.5 percent (before taxes) on his investments (and 5.5 percent on tax-free investments), and he now has $100,000 invested. In addition, Sam is covered by Social Security and participates in an employer-sponsored retirement plan. Sam and his wife, Beth, estimate that they will need a total of $33,000 per year (after taxes, at current price levels) from all

Exhibit 6-3

The Importance of Tax Advantages

	Taxable Investment[1]	Tax- Deferred Investment[2]	Tax- Deductible & Deferred Investment[2]	Tax- Free Investment
Pre-Tax $ Available	$1.00	$1.00	$1.00	$1.00
Less Taxes[3]	0.30	0.30	0.00	0.30
Net Amount Available for Investment	$0.70	$0.70	$1.00	$0.70
Pre-Tax Interest Rate	7.5%	7.5%	7.5%	5.5%
After-Tax Interest Rate	5.25%	7.5%	7.5%	5.5%
In Five Years				
Investment Value	$0.90	$1.00	$1.44	$0.91
Less Taxes[3]	0.00	0.09	0.43	0.00
Net Amount After Taxes	$0.90	$0.91	$1.01	$0.91
In Ten Years				
Investment Value	$1.17	$1.44	$2.06	$1.20
Less Taxes[3]	0.00	0.22	0.62	0.00
Net Amount After Taxes	$1.17	$1.22	$1.44	$1.20
In Fifteen Years				
Investment Value	$1.51	$2.07	$2.96	$1.56
Less Taxes[3]	0.00	0.41	0.89	0.00
Net Amount After Taxes	$1.51	$1.66	$2.07	$1.56
In Twenty Years				
Investment Value	$1.95	$2.97	$4.25	$2.04
Less Taxes[3]	0.00	0.68	1.28	0.00
Net Amount After Taxes	$1.95	$2.29	$2.97	$2.04

1. No taxes are paid when the investment is liquidated, because the investment is made with after-tax dollars and the interest income is included in the investor's taxable income each year.
2. For illustrative purposes, the net amount after taxes is calculated at each interval although taxes would only be deducted in the year the investment was actually liquidated.
3. All tax computations assume a combined tax rate of 30 percent.

sources to provide a comfortable retirement income. However, Sam believes that inflation will average about 4 percent per year, and he definitely wants his annual retirement income to keep pace with inflation. Sam and Beth expect to survive for at least twenty years of retirement.

Exhibit 6-4 shows that Sam will need $48,848 annual income after taxes in the year of his retirement, and he will need $107,032 at age eighty-five. As shown in Exhibit 6-5, Sam will receive $27,500 per year from his pension plan, and his Social Security benefits are expected to increase from $11,812 at age sixty-five to $21,334 at age eighty-five. Exhibit 6-6 combines the results of Exhibits 6-4 and 6-5, indicating that Sam needs a net amount—after Social Security and the company retirement plan—that grows from $9,536 to $58,198.

Exhibit 6-4
Inflation's Impact on Sam's Annual Retirement Needs

Age	Amount Needed Today	Inflation Rate	Need With Inflation
55	$33,000	4.0%	—
65	33,000	4.0%	48,848
70	33,000	4.0%	59,431
75	33,000	4.0%	72,307
80	33,000	4.0%	87,973
85	33,000	4.0%	107,032

Exhibit 6-5
Sam's Retirement Plan Benefits (After Tax)

Age	Social Security	Pension Plan	Total Retirement Benefits
55	—	—	—
65	$11,812	$27,500	$39,312
70	13,693	27,500	41,193
75	15,874	27,500	43,374
80	18,403	27,500	45,903
85	21,334	27,500	48,834

Exhibit 6-6
Additional Amount Needed by Sam

Age	(1) Need With Inflation	(2) Total Retirement Benefits	(1) – (2) Net Amount Needed
55	—	—	—
65	$ 48,848	$39,312	$ 9,536
70	59,431	41,193	18,238
75	72,307	43,374	28,933
80	87,973	45,903	42,070
85	107,032	48,834	58,198

Exhibit 6-7 summarizes the four basic methods of accumulating assets for Sam's retirement. In each case, it is assumed that Sam will deposit $100,000 into a fund and make annual contributions to the fund until he retires. The following conclusions can be drawn from Exhibit 6-7.

- With a *taxable* investment, he must invest $12,878 each year to meet his goal. This requires $18,398 of before-tax earnings each year. This is clearly the least preferable approach for this purpose.

- The *tax-free* approach is also not very attractive, because it requires $16,693 of earnings.

- The tax-deductible and tax-deferred investment requires an annual investment of $11,410, and is the most attractive of the four investment opportunities.

Exhibit 6-7
Sam's Capital Needs Under the Four Methods for Accumulating Wealth

	Taxable	Tax-Deferred	Tax-Deductible & Tax-Deferred	Tax-Free
Capital Needed To Meet Retirement Needs	$330,691	$351,506	$367,522	$321,264
Investment Required Each Year for the Additional 10 Work Years	$ 12,878	$ 10,278	$ 11,410	$11,685
Required Earnings	$ 18,398	$ 14,683	$ 11,410	$16,693
(Minus Taxes at 30%)	5,520	4,405	0	5,008

Retirement Planning Principles

The above information underscores several important retirement planning principles:

1. The amount of money a person needs for retirement depends on the method that will be used to accumulate funds. Notice in Exhibit 6-7 that Sam needs $351,506 if a tax-deferred investment is used, but $321,264 if a tax-free investment is used.

2. The method of accumulation determines how benefits will be taxed when funds are distributed during retirement. This also affects the amount that must be accumulated to provide the desired amount of after-tax retirement income.

3. On the basis of tax planning, the *tax-deductible and tax-deferred* approach is the best method of accumulating funds for retirement—even after considering the taxes that must be paid during retirement. Furthermore, the advantage of this approach is substantial. The major problem, as shown in subsequent pages, is that a person is limited in the amount he or she can put into a tax-favored retirement plan. Also, a person might need the funds to meet living expenses before retirement, if economic circumstances change.

4. On the basis of tax planning, the least favorable method is an ordinary *taxable* investment. Nevertheless, this method is widely used because it offers liquidity. Further, as explained later, money cannot be withdrawn from tax-advantaged retirement plans and tax-deferred investments before a certain age without income tax penalties.

Major Problems in Retirement Planning

Many people are not financially prepared for retirement. Why do so many people fail to provide for adequate retirement income? Many reasons exist. Some of these reasons are discussed below.

Inadequate Planning

Many people plan rather poorly, if at all, for retirement. Many people underestimate the magnitude of the problem. People tend not to become concerned about retirement until middle age or later—often too late to accumulate sufficient assets to provide a meaningful retirement income. Young people have the advantage of having a long time to accumulate assets; however, they often have low incomes and high expenses. Furthermore, retirement is too far into the future for many young people to give it a high priority.

Exhibit 6-8 stresses the importance of planning for retirement at an early age. The exhibit shows the monthly dollar investment needed for a tax-deductible and tax-deferred vehicle to accumulate a $100,000 retirement fund at age sixty-five starting at age twenty-five, thirty-five, forty-five, and fifty-five and earning 5 percent, 7.5 percent, and 10 percent. For example, John begins at age thirty-five to plan for retirement at age sixty-five by investing in a tax-deductible and tax-deferred vehicle earning 7.5 percent annually. He should invest $74.21 monthly to accumulate $100,000 by age sixty-five. If he waits until age fifty-five to begin his retirement planning with an investment in a similar vehicle, he would need to invest $562.02 each month to accumulate $100,000 by age sixty-five.

Exhibit 6-8
Monthly Dollar Investment[1]

Beginning Age	Annual Return		
	5 percent	7.5 percent	10 percent
25	$ 65.52	$ 33.07	$ 15.81
35	120.15	74.21	44.24
45	243.28	180.59	131.69
55	643.97	562.02	488.17

1. Investment in a tax-deductible and tax-deferred vehicle to accumulate $100,000 at age sixty-five.

Limited Employment Opportunities After Retirement

Some people undoubtedly anticipate some type of employment after retirement. Still, the possible problems they face are formidable: poor health, reduced physical capacity, out-of-date skills, and low earnings.

Longer Retirement Period

In the United States, people are working for shorter periods of time and retiring for longer periods than they used to. The primary reasons for shorter working lives are early retirement and longer periods of formal education before employment is started. The main reasons for longer retirement periods are the increase in life expectancy and, again, early retirement. When people have less time to prepare for retirement and longer retirement periods, the financial problem increases dramatically.

Inflation

Rising prices are a problem for retired people living on fixed incomes. Spiraling costs of medical care have been especially onerous. Medicare and postretirement medical coverage provided by some employers offer some relief from these rising medical care costs, but many retirees do not find them adequate to cover their medical care costs during retirement.

Employee Retirement Income Security Act of 1974

One of the major pieces of federal legislation that affects retirement planning is the Employee Retirement Income Security Act of 1974 (ERISA). ERISA establishes guidelines and requirements that affect the legal, tax, investment, and accounting aspects of employer-provided retirement plans and retirement plans established by the self-employed, as well as of other employee benefit plans offered by employers.

Among other requirements, ERISA specifies rules for the following:

1. Eligibility in most retirement plans
2. Access to contributions made to retirement plans
3. Methods for funding retirement plan obligations
4. Minimum funding requirements

Each of these areas is discussed later in this chapter and in Chapter 7.

An important part of ERISA was the establishment of an alternative retirement planning vehicle—individual retirement accounts (IRAs). IRAs are discussed in greater detail in Chapter 7.

Vehicles for Accumulating Retirement Funds

A variety of retirement planning vehicles are available to help individuals accumulate funds for retirement. Individual annuities and pension plans are discussed in this chapter. Additional retirement programs are discussed in Chapter 7.

Individual Annuities

Annuities are tax-deferred savings vehicles that can be used to provide an income source at some point in the future. They can be purchased individually or on a group basis from life insurance companies. This discussion is concerned only with individual annuities. In the past, individual annuities were not a particularly important method of providing retirement income. However, individual annuities have become popular in recent years. In addition, annuities might serve as the funding instrument for a retirement plan sponsored by an employer.

The Nature of Annuities

Insurance requires a large number of individuals to contribute to a fund so that claims can be paid when losses occur. Both life insurance and annuities involve premium payments by a large number of individuals. However, different events trigger claims payments:

- In life insurance, the insurer pays—or begins to pay—when the insured *dies*.
- With annuities, however, the insurer begins to pay when the insured person (**annuitant**) *survives* past a specified date (or, more precisely, beyond a series of specified dates). Under a pure annuity, benefit payments stop when the annuitant dies.

Life insurance and annuities also serve different purposes:

- Life insurance is designed primarily to *accumulate* a sum of money that provides an estate for the use of *survivors*.
- Annuities are often designed primarily to first accumulate a sum of money for the annuitant and to then *liquidate* that sum for the use of the *annuitant*.

The Annuity Principle

The **annuity principle** involves a systematic liquidation of a principal sum. This systematic liquidation of principal has two significant effects:

1. The annuity income can be guaranteed for life.
2. The annual benefit is a combination of principal, interest, and survival benefits and should therefore be larger than the amount that could be provided by interest income alone.

Survival benefits arise from the process in which life insurance companies group annuitants and pool their premiums into a fund from which insurers pay monthly benefits to annuitants. Some people in a plan might die soon after purchasing the annuity; others, however, might live much longer than their life expectancy. Those who live longer benefit at the expense of those who die early. This is the essence of sharing losses through the insurance technique. Those who die give up their principal (unless, as allowed by some types of annuities, a beneficiary is designated to receive the remaining principal). The principal given up by the deceased annuitants helps to finance the benefits of those who survive.

Annuity Rates

Exhibit 6-9 shows the single premium that would be charged for annuities available from one life insurer. (A single premium annuity, as the name implies, requires only one premium payment.) The column on the left indicates the age at which the annuity is purchased. The other columns indicate separately, for males and females, the age at which annuity payments begin. The period between the age of the purchase and the age at which the benefit begins is known as the **accumulation period,** since interest earnings can be "accumulated" on the deposited premiums during that period. The period during which benefits are paid is referred to as the **liquidation period.** A thirty-year-old man must pay a single premium of $1,128 to purchase an annuity that would provide $100 per month for life beginning when the man reaches age sixty-five. This annuity would have a thirty-five-year accumulation period (from age thirty to age sixty-five).

Exhibit 6-9
Illustrative Annuity Single Premiums

Age of Purchase	Male Benefit starts:		Female Benefit starts:	
	Age 65	Age 70	Age 65	Age 70
30	$ 1,128	$ 701	$ 1,253	$ 782
40	2,219	1,378	2,465	1,539
50	4,365	2,712	4,849	3,027
60	8,586	5,334	9,538	5,955
65	12,042	7,481	13,378	8,353

To provide a $100.00 per month benefit for life, straight life annuity.

Analysis of the rates in the table reveals several important facts:

1. Annuity premiums are much lower at younger ages since the accumulation period is longer.

2. Starting the payout period at a higher age significantly reduces the premium cost. This reflects both a longer accumulation period and a shorter payout period (because of the shorter life expectancy at a higher age).

3. Individual (nonemployment-related) annuity premiums are higher for females. This reflects their longer life expectancy.

Rates for *individual*, nonemployment-related annuities are typically sex based—females are charged more than males of the same age to purchase equal annuity benefits. However, pension plans (described later) and other annuity and retirement plans furnished as part of the employment relationship now provide annuity options based on unisex rates. This is required by Title VII of the Civil Rights Act of 1964.[1]

Taxation of Annuities

With regard to the federal income taxation of annuities, two broad categories of annuities can be considered: (1) qualified annuities and other generally employment-based plans that have special tax features, and (2) nonqualified annuities that are sold to the general public by life insurance companies as retirement products unrelated to the purchasers' employment or any employee benefit plan. In connection with the *federal income taxation of nonqualified individual annuities*, the general tax rules of the Internal Revenue Code concerning annuities and distributions from annuities apply. First, the premium or premiums paid for the contract by the annuity owner are not deductible for income tax purposes and hence are paid with after-tax dollars. However, since taxes have, in effect, already been paid on these net premiums, the annuity owner (or the beneficiary under the annuity contract in the event of the annuitant's death) is entitled to recoup the premium amounts invested in the contract income tax free when benefits (distributions) are taken from the annuity.

Second, during the accumulation period of a deferred annuity, the interest or investment earnings on the cash value of the contract increase (or possibly decrease) without current federal income taxation. This is often referred to as the *tax-deferred buildup of annuity cash values*, as long as those cash values remain within an annuity contract. This is an example of *tax-deferred saving for retirement* and is one of the main advantages of individual annuities over many other kinds of investment media. However, the income taxes on the inside buildup in annuity policies must eventually be paid, either when the annuitant begins to receive distributions from the policy or when the beneficiary under the annuity receives the annuity cash value as a death benefit in the event of the annuitant's death.[2]

The taxation of distributions from annuities can be complex. When distributions are taken as a *periodic income* (that is, as a life income or in substantially equal installments for more than one year), they are taxed under the general annuity rules of the Internal Revenue Code, which are designed to subject only the portion of the distribution that is investment income to income taxation.[3]

When an individual nonqualified annuity contract is entirely surrendered for cash, the difference between the cash surrender value received and the investment in the contract is taxed as ordinary income to the annuity owner in the year of surrender. For example, suppose that Angelena purchased an annuity policy twenty years ago and paid premiums for the policy averaging $2,000 per year (or $40,000 in total net premiums paid). She now is age sixty and is planning to retire soon. The cash surrender value of her annuity is $120,000. If Angelena surrenders her annuity entirely for cash this year (at age sixty), she will have a gross income for federal income tax purposes this year of $80,000 ($120,000 cash value less her after-tax investment in the contract of $40,000).

When there are partial withdrawals or distributions (that is, partial distributions that do not meet the definition cited above for periodic payments), they are viewed for tax purposes as first coming from the potentially taxable investment earnings in the policy and are taxed as ordinary income until such investment earnings are exhausted. Then, any further withdrawals are viewed as a tax-free return of the annuity owner's after-tax investment in the policy. Thus, continuing the previous example, if instead of completely surrendering her annuity policy, Angelena had decided to take a $20,000 partial (that is, nonperiodic) withdrawal from the contract (say, to help with her grandchild's college expenses), this partial distribution would be considered for tax purposes to come first from the $80,000 of untaxed investment earnings within the policy; hence, the entire $20,000 partial distribution would be taxed to Angelena as ordinary income in the year of the distribution.

Further, policy loans from nonqualified annuities are considered for income tax purposes to be distributions from the contract and thus are taxable the same as for partial distributions.

Finally, for nonqualified annuity policies issued after January 18, 1985, any taxable amount received or withdrawn *before* age fifty-nine and one-half will generally be subject to a 10 percent excise tax on premature distributions subject to certain exceptions. This 10 percent tax applies in addition to the regular income tax that is payable.

However, certain exceptions to the 10 percent penalty tax exist. These exceptions include the following:

- Distributions in the event of the annuity owner's death or disability

- Payments made in substantially equal periodic installments for the lifetime or over a period at least equal to the life expectancy of the annuitant, or for the joint lifetimes or life expectancies of the annuitant and his or her beneficiary
- Purchases of an immediate annuity (described later)

Classifications of Annuities

Annuities can be categorized according to the following criteria:

1. Time when benefits begin
2. Method of paying premiums
3. Annuity forms
4. Number of lives covered
5. Type of investment funds or benefit units (fixed or variable)

Time When Benefits Begin

Annuities can be (1) immediate or (2) deferred.

Immediate Annuities   An **immediate annuity** has no accumulation period. When a person buys an immediate annuity, benefit payments usually start one payment interval after the purchase. For example, if a person buys an immediate annuity that pays monthly benefits, the first benefit will be paid one month after the annuity is purchased.

An immediate annuity must be purchased with a single premium. An insurer will not start to pay benefits until an annuity is fully paid for.

Deferred Annuities   **Deferred annuities** have an accumulation period. In other words, a period of time longer than one payment interval exists between the start of premium payments and the start of benefit payments. The accumulation period usually lasts a number of years. For example, a person could purchase an annuity at age fifty, but the benefit payments might not begin until age seventy.

Deferred annuities are often purchased with flexible premiums over a number of years but can be purchased with a single premium. Thus, the fifty-year-old referred to above could pay annual premiums for fifteen or twenty years (or more or less) or could pay only one premium at age fifty.

With most insurance companies and contracts, considerable flexibility exists in selecting the date at which benefit payments commence. Thus, if a person elects early or postponed retirement, benefits can be made to coincide with the time at which funds are needed. The annuitant can make the choice at any time. But once the liquidation period begins, the decision cannot be reversed.

Under any of the deferred annuities, money accumulates more rapidly than in comparable taxable investments because *investment earnings are not taxable to the annuity owner as long as the funds remain with the insurer.* The advantage of tax deferral can be an important consideration—especially for annuity owners in high marginal income tax brackets. However, when funds are withdrawn, the owner is taxed on any amounts that are not considered a return of principal. In addition, a tax penalty can apply in certain circumstances—the most common of which arises when annuity withdrawals are made prior to age fifty-nine and one-half.

Method of Paying Premiums

Annuities can be purchased with (1) fixed periodic premiums, (2) flexible premiums, or (3) a single premium.

Fixed Premium Retirement Annuities **Fixed premium annuities** are purchased over time—usually with premiums paid in either annual or monthly installments. The generic name for an installment premium annuity is simply **"retirement annuity."** However, insurers use a variety of names for their products.

Prior to maturity, the plan is nothing more than a method of accumulating money with an insurance company. If the annuitant wishes to discontinue premium payments, he or she can withdraw the cash value (which equals the premiums plus interest minus an expense charge) or elect a paid-up annuity (which requires no additional premium payments yet remains in force) for a smaller amount. If the entire cash value is taken, the contract is terminated. If the annuitant dies before the annuity matures, the insurance company will pay the larger of (1) the cash value (less any outstanding policy loans) or (2) the total premiums paid on the contract (less any outstanding policy loans).

Flexible Premium Deferred Annuities In recent years, **flexible premium deferred annuities (FPDAs)** have become the predominate approach to writing annuity contracts. The newer FPDAs have no predetermined premium amount or required payment frequency. Before the start of the liquidation period, an FPDA is simply, in effect, a type of savings account. Contributions generally can be made as frequently or infrequently as the owner desires. Most insurance companies do not even require a payment each year. However, if a payment is made, a minimum amount (such as $50) is usually required.

Single Premium Annuities Annuities can also be purchased with a single premium. As indicated earlier, immediate annuities are necessarily single premium annuities. However, a single premium can also be used to purchase a deferred annuity.

Annuity Forms

If an annuitant dies during the *accumulation* period, his or her beneficiaries receive the greater of (1) the accumulated cash value (less any outstanding policy loans), or (2) the total premiums paid (less any outstanding policy loans). However, the amount, if any, that an annuitant's beneficiaries receive if the annuitant dies during the *liquidation* period depends on the annuity form.

Pure (Straight Life) Annuity In a **pure annuity**, usually called a **straight life annuity**, all obligations of the insurance company cease when the annuitant dies—none of the premium or cash value is refunded. Because a straight life annuity provides no refunds, it produces the largest periodic benefit payments for each dollar of the purchase price. Thus, it might be preferred when there are no heirs to receive a refund and the annuitant is in good health—and, perhaps, when maximum benefit payments are crucial.

Many people dislike the possibility of losing all, or a large portion, of their investment if death should occur near the beginning of the liquidation phase. The would-be beneficiaries in such a case are likely to feel "cheated" in the absence of some refund. If a guaranteed minimum amount of benefits is desired, several types of contracts are available.

Life Annuity Period Certain One common type of guaranteed minimum payout provision is found in a **life annuity period certain** contract. This plan promises benefits for the life of the annuitant or a guaranteed period, whichever is longer. A common *period certain* or *guaranteed period* is ten years, but other lengths of time are available.

To illustrate a life annuity with ten years certain, consider a man whose benefits under such a contract started at age sixty-five. If the annuitant dies at age sixty-eight, benefits will be continued, payable to the annuitant's beneficiary, for seven years (the remainder of the ten-year period). On the other hand, if the annuitant lives past age seventy-five, benefits under the annuity will be paid until his death, and upon his death, all obligations of the insurance company cease.

Refund Annuities A **refund annuity** pays beneficiaries the difference (if greater than zero) between the purchase price and the total benefit payments received by the annuitant prior to death. The refund benefits can be continued as periodic income payments until the full purchase price has been received by the beneficiaries (an **installment refund annuity**) or the refund can be paid in cash in one lump sum to the beneficiaries (a **cash refund annuity**).

A cash refund annuity is more costly to the insurance company than an installment refund annuity because the company cannot benefit from interest earnings if the refund is paid immediately in cash. If benefits are continued in installments, the insurance company has use of the money until the proceeds are exhausted.

Selecting Among Annuity Forms   Selecting an appropriate annuity form is important because it has a significant impact on the cost of an annuity. Exhibit 6-10 shows this clearly. The longer the period of guaranteed payments, the lower the benefit payment of the annuitant. This reflects the increased costs the insurer experiences in guaranteeing income during a period when the annuitant may not be alive.

For example, suppose a sixty-year-old man has accumulated an annuity with a $100,000 cash value. If he chooses an annuity with no refund, he will receive a monthly benefit of $889 ($8.89 per $1,000 of annuity cash value, which for this man is $8.89 x 100). But, if he chooses an annuity with a ten-year period certain, he will receive only $858 per month. The $31 difference reflects the insurer's cost of guaranteeing at least ten years of benefit payments.

Notice that Exhibit 6-10 indicates that the cost of the guarantee feature accelerates with the age at which annuity payments begin. For example, if a fifty-five-year-old chooses a ten-year-certain annuity instead of an annuity with no refund, the monthly benefits are reduced by approximately 2.25 percent. However, if a sixty-five-year-old makes the same choice, the monthly benefit is reduced by almost 6 percent. This results from the higher probability of death and the resulting greater chance that the guarantee feature will come into play at the older ages. At the advanced ages, the guarantee feature is also likely to provide greater benefits.

Exhibit 6-10
Amount of Monthly Income per $1,000 Provided Under Different Kinds of Annuities (on Male Lives)

Age[1]	Straight Life	5 Year Certain	10 Year Certain	20 Year Certain	Installment Refund
55	$ 8.39	$ 8.33	$8.20	$7.86	$8.19
60	8.89	8.79	8.58	8.03	8.59
65	9.65	9.47	9.08	8.19	9.16
70	10.77	10.41	9.68	8.32	9.93

1. When annuity payments commence.

An individual can select the most appropriate annuity form only by evaluating (1) the cost of the various annuities, (2) his or her physical and financial condition, and (3) the desirability of leaving money to others. For example, a person in good health with no heirs and a strong need to receive maximum benefits might choose a straight life annuity. If, on the other hand, the provision of benefits to heirs is important, some type of guarantee feature might be appropriate.

Two notes of caution should be recognized in selecting an annuity or an annuity payout form. First, a person who has a strong desire to leave funds to dependents and is therefore inclined toward an annuity with a strong guarantee feature, should *carefully consider life insurance protection*. Many insurance companies allow an annuitant to convert an annuity into a life insurance policy. The annuitant must provide evidence of insurability at the time of the conversion, but the terms and rates of the life insurance policy will be those included in the policy when the annuity was originally purchased.

A second caution is that *an annuity might be a poor purchase for a person in ill health*. While physical examinations might be required for life insurance, they are never required for annuities. The greatest benefit from an annuity goes to a person who lives a long time. The person who benefits least from an annuity is the one who dies soon after buying it. It might be wise, therefore, for a prospective annuitant to have a complete physical examination before buying an annuity.

Number of Lives Covered

Annuities can be based on one or more lives. The cost of and the benefits provided by annuities based on a single life are determined by the characteristics of the annuitant, such as his or her age, health, and life expectancy. Annuities based on more than one life consider these factors for more than one annuitant. Two common annuities that cover more than one life are (1) joint life annuities and (2) joint-and-last-survivor annuities.

Joint Life Annuities   Joint life annuities covering two persons provide an income as long as *both* annuitants are alive. Benefit payments stop when either annuitant dies. Such a plan is appropriate only when two people have an income from another source that is adequate for one person, but not for both. The market for joint annuities is very limited, and these contracts are not popular.

Joint-and-Last-Survivor Annuities   With a joint-and-last-survivor annuity, the insurer agrees to pay an income as long as *either* of two annuitants is alive. Overall, the insurance company assumes the obligation of paying benefits for longer periods of time than under single life annuities. Therefore, joint-and-last-survivor annuities are more expensive than other annuities.

Still, the contract is appealing to many couples who need an income as long as either is alive.

The cost of joint-and-last-survivor annuities can be kept reasonably low by two features. First, most joint-and-last-survivor annuities do not include any guarantee feature. This feature is usually not needed because benefit payments will continue for the surviving annuitant. Second, many joint-and-last-survivor annuities reduce the payments when one of the annuitants dies. For example, a popular plan is known as the **joint-and-two-thirds annuity**. With this contract, benefits are reduced by one-third when the first annuitant dies. The surviving annuitant continues to receive two-thirds of the previous benefit for life. The cost can be decreased even further (and larger joint benefits can be provided) if the survivor receives only one-half of the joint benefit.

Joint-and-last-survivor forms are frequently available as life insurance settlement options. They are also used widely in pension plans. In fact, a *joint-and-one-half-survivor* annuity is the minimum payout option allowed by law for a married person in a qualified pension plan unless the participant elects a different option in writing and this election is consented to in writing and in the proper way by the participant's spouse.

Benefit Units—Fixed Versus Variable

Most annuities provide fixed dollar benefits. For example, a person may buy an annuity with a monthly benefit of $1,000 per month. If prices rise, and therefore the purchasing power of the benefit decreases, there can be a serious erosion of value.

The **variable annuity** was developed as an attempt to protect the purchasing power of annuitants. The basic mechanism for achieving this goal is to provide benefits that are expressed in units rather than in dollars. In a variable annuity, when an annuitant enters the liquidation period, he or she is guaranteed to receive the value of a stipulated number of units. The value of the units may change, but the number of units does not. If the value of the units increases because of increases in the value of the underlying investments, the dollar benefits increase—perhaps enough to offset inflation or even to increase purchasing power.

Variable Annuities

Variable annuities, as described above, were developed to provide a hedge against rising prices for annuitants. The operation of variable annuities differs from the operation of nonvariable annuities during both the accumulation period and the benefit payment period.

The Accumulation Period

Some differences exist among the variable annuities issued by different insurers. However, variable annuities often include the following common features during the accumulation period:

1. *Accumulation units.* Variable annuity premiums are used to purchase units of coverage. The number of units purchased with each premium depends on the value of a unit. The value of the units depends on an annuity's underlying investments, which are generally large portfolios of stocks and bonds. Like the person who invests in a mutual fund, a variable annuity owner achieves the practical result of sharing in a large portfolio of common stocks. Often, a variable annuity plan will own thirty, forty, or more individual common stocks. Adverse performance of a few stocks, therefore, is likely to be offset by the superior performance of other stocks. A variable annuity owner does not *legally* own the individual securities in the plan. Legal ownership is held by the plan itself.

   As a result of the investment feature, the value of the accumulation fund and the annuity changes in two ways. First, the premiums are used to purchase additional accumulation units. Second, the value of the accumulation units varies with the value of the underlying investments.

2. *Allocation among portfolios.* In a variable annuity, the premiums paid by policyholders can be invested in common stocks. Most of the present variable annuity programs allow investors to place their funds into one or more different, diversified portfolios or "buckets." Exhibit 6-11 shows the choices for one major insurance company. Usually, funds can be reallocated among portfolios by the investor periodically (such as once per month) with no charges. More frequent transfers might involve a small fee. In addition, insurance companies usually charge investment management fees of different annual percentages for the different accounts. For example, the annual fee associated with a money market account might be 0.5 percent of assets in the fund, while the annual fee for a growth stock portfolio might be 0.75 percent to 1 percent of assets.

3. *Guaranteed death benefit.* Some insurance companies guarantee that the beneficiary will receive the current value of the account or the original purchase price, less withdrawals, whichever is greater.

4. *Surrender charges.* In addition to possible penalties imposed by the IRS, many insurance companies impose surrender charges. For example, withdrawal charges might be 7 to 10 percent the first year, declining to 0 percent in the tenth or later years.

Exhibit 6-11
Investment Choices

Money Market	Fixed Income	Government Securities
Capital Market—Cash	Capital Market—Debt	Capital Market—Debt
Goal—To provide current income while protecting principal from market fluctuations.	Goal—To seek current income by investing in a diversified portfolio of high-quality (AA+) corporate and government bonds of an intermediate maturity. These bonds can provide a higher degree of income at moderate to low risk.	Goal—To provide a high current return at no credit risk by investing in obligations issued, guaranteed, or insured by the U.S. Government or its agencies.
High Yield	Convertible Securities	Foreign Securities
Capital Market—Debt	Capital Market—Debt/Equity	Capital Market—Debt/Equity
Goal—To offer the opportunity for both high current income and capital appreciation. This portfolio will invest primarily in lower-quality, high-yielding, income-producing corporate bonds at a higher level of risk.	Goal—To provide high current income and long-term capital appreciation by investing in convertible bonds and preferred stocks.	Goal—To offer capital appreciation by investing primarily in equities issued by growth-oriented foreign companies. This portfolio may also invest in foreign debt instruments.
Growth	Aggressive Growth	Guaranteed Account
Capital Market—Equity	Capital Market—Equity	
Goal—To supply long-term capital appreciation by investing primarily in classic growth-oriented stocks with above-average growth prospects and moderate risk.	Goal—To provide high, long-term capital appreciation by taking an extra degree of risk. The portfolio will emphasize aggressive growth stocks issued by emerging growth-oriented companies.	Goal—Part of the General Account of the life insurance company, this portfolio guarantees a fixed return for one contract year and guarantees principal against loss.

continued on next page

Conservative Multi-Asset Portfolio	Aggressive Multi-Asset Portfolio
Capital Market—Cash, Debt & Equity	Capital Market—Cash, Debt & Equity
Goal—To allocate assets among the more conservative segments of the major asset categories as dictated by current market conditions and the expected investment environment. The portfolio offers long-term total return while minimizing risk.	Goal—To achieve high, long-term total return by allocating assets among the more aggressive major asset categories. This fund provides a higher level of investment risk for the potential of superior growth.

The Benefit Payment Period

Upon reaching the benefit payment period, the annuitant generally has two options under a variable annuity:

1. To receive a benefit payment that is *fixed* throughout the payment period

2. To receive a benefit payment that *can vary* throughout payment period

If the annuitant chooses the fixed payment option, the accumulation fund is set at the then current total dollar value of the number of units accumulated. For example, if the annuitant has purchased 500 units during the accumulation period and at the start of the benefit payment period each unit is worth $50, the accumulation fund value is $25,000. Given the fund's value, the annuitant's life expectancy, and the annuity form selected (among other things), a fixed amount of periodic income can be determined. The dollar amount of the periodic income will remain constant.

If the annuitant chooses the variable benefit payment options, the accumulation fund units are converted to benefit payment units. A unit value is determined for the benefit payment unit each period that considers the value of the underlying investments, the annuitant's life expectancy, and the annuity form selected (among other things). The benefit payment is calculated each period by multiplying the number of benefit payment units by the current unit value and, therefore, varies with the unit value. In this manner, the annuitant's purchasing power is expected to be maintained throughout the benefit payment period.

Advantages and Disadvantages of Variable Annuities

Variable annuities provide a unique combination of features. A variable annuity offers the opportunity for diversified investment in the annuitant's choice of investment vehicles, while allowing annuitants to receive income for the rest of their lives, if a life annuity form is elected. These are major advantages—especially since they are combined in a single instrument. However, the impact of inflation, expense charges, and taxes should be considered.

Variable annuities are touted as a means of providing retirement income that keeps pace with the cost of living. However, stock market returns might not always correlate with consumer prices. Sometimes stock prices do not keep pace with inflation, but at other times they perform much better than the rate of inflation. It is impossible to know whether variable annuity benefits will maintain an individual's purchasing power in the future, but various studies have shown that common stock values have more than done so in the past over the long term. However, it is clear that variable annuities should be viewed as a *long-range* method of dealing with retirement income needs. They should not be judged on the basis of results over a period of only a few years.

Tax considerations are another reason that variable annuities should be considered as long-range investments. As explained previously in this chapter, the owner of an individual variable annuity incurs no federal income tax liability during the accumulation period for increases in the value of accumulation funds. However, after the annuitant retires, variable annuity benefits are taxed in essentially the same manner as conventional annuities. Basically, the intent of the tax law is to tax the *appreciation* (the investment gain) but not the portion of the annuity benefit representing return of the after-tax investment in the contract.

Pension Plans

A **pension plan** is a program designed primarily to provide employees with retirement income. It is basically the application of the group technique to the retirement exposure. The group technique allows administrative economies and produces several other advantages for both employers and employees, as discussed in previous chapters.

From an employer's point of view, a pension plan can accomplish several purposes:

1. Enable a company to attract and retain employees (because many of them expect pension benefits)

2. Allow a company to meet union demands

3. Encourage greater employee productivity

4. Provide a humane method to retire aging, less efficient workers

From an employee's point of view, a pension plan can be a convenient, efficient, tax-advantageous method of accumulating funds for liquidation during retirement.

Qualified Versus Nonqualified Plans

A **qualified retirement plan** meets the requirements established by the Internal Revenue Service for favorable tax treatment. A **nonqualified retirement plan** does not meet those requirements. The major tax advantages of qualified plans are as follows:

1. Contributions to the plan by the employer (within limits) are tax deductible by the employer as a business expense.

2. Employees are not considered to have taxable income from employer contributions on their behalf or from the investment earnings in the plan for federal income tax purposes until they receive benefit payments.

3. Distributions from the plan can receive certain limited favorable income tax treatment.

Nonqualified plans do not have the same tax advantages as qualified retirement plans, but they have greater flexibility and few regulations. The individual annuities discussed in the preceding section of this chapter are individual nonqualified plans. As a practical matter, employers often choose qualified plans because of the tax advantages.

Basic Types of Plans

Two basic types of pension plans exist: defined contribution plans and defined benefit plans. In the past, defined benefit plans have been more common than defined contribution plans, primarily because employees and unions have historically favored these plans. However, with the passage of the Employment Retirement Income Security Act (ERISA) in 1974, defined contribution plans in general have grown in relative importance. Both defined contribution plans and defined benefit plans are discussed below.

Defined Contribution Plans

In a **defined contribution plan**, the contribution rate is defined and is almost always a percentage of the participating employee's earnings. For example, an employer might contribute an amount equal to 10 percent of an employee's earnings to the plan.

A defined contribution formula generally produces a wide variation in benefits among employees. Those who participate in the plan for long periods tend to generate large benefit amounts, while employees who enter the plan at an advanced age might not have enough time to accumulate adequate pension benefits. In addition, investment results vary.

In any defined contribution pension plan, the amount that can be added to an individual's account in any one year is limited. The maximum "annual addition" cannot exceed 25 percent of compensation or $30,000, whichever is lower.[4] The **annual addition** is defined as the sum of three factors:

1. Employer contributions
2. Reallocated forfeitures
3. Employee contributions to the plan (not including "rollover" contributions, which are discussed in Chapter 7).

Forfeitures occur when a participant terminates employment, is not "fully vested" (discussed in more detail later in this chapter) in his or her account, and, thus, must leave at least part of the contributions made by the employer on his or her behalf in the employer's pension plan. If an employee is "fully vested," he or she is entitled to the total value of his or her retirement account upon preretirement termination. However, a terminating participant who is, for example, 60 percent vested would take only 60 percent of the account value, and the nonvested portion (40 percent) would become a forfeiture.

Forfeitures in a defined contribution plan can be used to reduce the employer's next annual contribution or can be reallocated among the accounts of remaining participants.

The most common criticism of defined contribution plans is that actual retirement benefits cannot be predetermined. Of course, projections can be made, but many uncertainties are involved in such projections.

Defined Benefit Plans

A **defined benefit plan**, as the name implies, defines the monthly retirement benefit rather than the contribution rate. Formulas are used to establish the amount of retirement benefits employees receive, and the employer is expected to have adequate funds to provide the benefits.

Four basic types of defined benefit formulas exist, but some plans provide benefits based on a combination of these approaches:

1. A *flat amount*. A flat amount formula provides the same dollar benefit to all employees regardless of age, earnings, or length of service. All retired

employees, for example, might be paid $400 per month. It is common for flat amount formulas to include a service requirement, meaning that to achieve the full benefit, an employee is required to participate in the plan for a stated number of years. If this requirement applies, employees with fewer years of service normally receive reduced benefits. Thus, in effect, even a flat amount formula might indirectly recognize years of service. Flat amount formulas are not common, but are used in some union plans. More often, a flat amount formula is used in conjunction with another formula.

2. A *flat percentage of earnings*. A flat percentage of earnings formula is used in many pension plans. Usually, this approach is designed to provide 30 to 60 percent of an employee's earnings. The percentage might apply to an employee's average earnings while participating in the plan (called *career average earnings*), or it might apply to average earnings over the last few years (usually five) prior to retirement (called *final average earnings*) to relate benefits more to the cost of living. Final average earnings can be computed in a variety of ways. For example, earnings can be based on the last five years before retirement, or they can be computed by using the five consecutive years of highest earnings in the ten-year period prior to retirement. Career earnings formulas are likely to provide inadequate benefits during a period of sustained inflation unless the values are updated in some manner. A flat percentage of earnings formula does not consider an employee's length of service, except indirectly. If the service requirement for full benefits is long, and benefits are reduced for less service, the effect is to recognize years of service. Furthermore, because senior employees tend to have higher salaries, this formula might unintentionally discriminate in their favor.

3. A *flat amount for each year of service*. A flat amount for each year of service formula provides a benefit of a stated amount, such as $20 or $25 per month, multiplied by the number of years of service. With a benefit of $20 per month and twenty-five years of service, the monthly retirement benefit would be $500. These plans often specify a minimum number of hours that must be worked in a twelve-month period to receive full credit for a year's service. It is common to require 1,600 to 1,800 hours to meet the requirement. According to ERISA, proportionate credit must be granted to an employee who worked at least 1,000 hours in the twelve-month period. Generally, credit is given to employees who worked for the employer before the pension plan was adopted. This is known as *past service credit*. While the objective is to treat all employees fairly, granting credit for past service causes a number of problems—not the least of which is a funding difficulty.

4. *A fixed percentage of earnings for each year of service.* This type of formula determines benefits as a percentage of earnings for each year of service. In its simplest form, the retirement benefit is equal to a fixed percentage of earnings multiplied by the number of years of credited service. For example, if a plan provides for a 2 percent benefit, an employee who has twenty-eight years of credited service and average monthly earnings of $3,000 would receive a monthly retirement benefit of $1,680 (0.02 x 28 x $3,000).

The more common criticisms of defined benefit plans are voiced by employers:

1. *The variability of contribution amounts.* Because the retirement benefit is defined for each worker, the employer is obligated to ensure that enough funds have been set aside to meet the retirement benefits. The necessary contribution amounts can vary over time with investment results, employee mortality, inflation, employee turnover, employee salaries, and similar factors.

2. *The administration of such plans can be burdensome in time, effort, and cost.* Because the employer must ensure that the contributions will satisfy the amounts needed to pay defined retirement benefits, it must continually evaluate the pension plan assets and benefits promised. In addition, as established by ERISA, most employers offering defined benefit plans must pay premiums to the Pension Benefit Guaranty Corporation (PBGC) in exchange for protection for plan participants in the event that an employer is financially unable to meet its obligations under its pension plan.

Comparing Defined Contribution and Defined Benefit Plans

When comparing the advantages of defined contribution plans and defined benefit plans, several factors are important and are discussed below.

Predictability of Costs   The contributions to a defined benefit plan are whatever amount is needed to fund the promised benefits. An actuarial calculation is required, and the IRS requires that reasonable actuarial assumptions be used. The actual plan experience can differ substantially from estimates, and, as a result, contributions are less predictable than the costs in a defined contribution plan. Note that no dollar limitation applies to contributions to a defined benefit plan. The limit is stated in terms of the benefit that can be funded and deducted.

Defined contribution plans offer an employer a more predictable maximum cost. The employer usually knows that the cost will be no more than a stated percentage of compensation. The cost can even be less than the specified percentage if the forfeitures of terminating employees are used to reduce the employer's cost.

Expense Levels The expenses of operating a defined contribution plan will probably be less than those of operating a defined benefit plan. Actuarial services are unnecessary, and no insurance premiums are payable to PBGC, as are required for defined benefit plans. Perhaps more importantly, a defined contribution plan can be terminated without creating a major corporate liability. When a defined benefit plan is terminated, in some cases the employer will be liable to PBGC for the total of the guaranteed benefits as of the termination date of all plan participants and beneficiaries.

Employees' Planning Considerations One of the primary advantages of a defined benefit plan is that employees can plan for a definite pension benefit at retirement. Using a simple example, a participant might be able to plan for a benefit of 50 percent of his or her final earnings. If the employee assumes that his or her compensation will keep pace with inflation prior to retirement, the pension benefit promised in the future can be calculated fairly accurately many years before actual retirement. The benefit provided by a defined contribution plan is not as easily determined because it is dependent on the amount of contributions, investment results, and inflation.

Impact of Investment Results In a defined benefit plan, favorable investment experience is an advantage to the employer—that is, it reduces the cost of the plan. In defined contribution plans, favorable investment experience benefits the employees by increasing the size of the fund from which benefits will be financed. Of course, since the employer bears the investment risk in a defined benefit plan, unfavorable experience presents a problem for the employer. And, since the employee bears the investment risk in a defined contribution plan, unfavorable experience can harm the employee.

Ease of Understanding Defined contribution plans probably have a certain psychological appeal to employees. Dollar amounts in their individual accounts might have more reality than the accrual of pension credits.

From an employer's point of view, the cost of a defined contribution plan is easy to comprehend because it is expressed as a percentage of payroll. In addition, defined contribution plans are simpler to administer because no actuarial computations are required.

Benefits for Older Employees One of the primary advantages of a defined benefit plan is that it provides larger benefits for older employees more easily than defined contribution plans. As indicated earlier, a defined contribution plan might not accumulate a sizable account for older employees.

Target Benefit Pension Plans

Although not as popular as the types of plans described above, target benefit pension plans are not uncommon. Also referred to as an "assumed benefit" or "variable benefit" plan, such a plan is a hybrid of the two basic types. The benefit formula is the same as that used in a defined benefit plan, at least at the beginning. In other words, a target plan could have a benefit of, say, 40 percent of final earnings. However, the employee's ultimate retirement benefit might increase or decrease depending on the difference between assumed and actual investment results. If a plan assumes an interest rate of 5 percent, larger returns will increase retirement benefits, but returns of less than 5 percent will cause benefits to decline.

Eligibility Requirements of Pension Plans

Within the limits permitted for qualified plans by the IRS, employers generally establish eligibility requirements to determine who can participate in pension plans. Often, certain employees are excluded, on either a temporary or permanent basis, to reduce pension costs. Eligibility requirements can be influenced by employers' overall pension objectives and by union pressures.

Years of Service and Minimum Age

The most common eligibility requirements are based on service, minimum age, or both. Federal law prohibits eligibility requirements that set the minimum age above twenty-one or service requirements longer than one year (unless the plan provides for full and immediate vesting). Generally, an employee must be given credit for one year of service if he or she works at least 1,000 hours in a twelve-month period.

Collective Bargaining Unit

In many companies, the union members participate in a union-sponsored retirement plan, and all other employees are treated separately in another plan. Thus, the law allows union employees to be excluded from a nonunion-sponsored retirement plan when a union-sponsored plan exists with benefits that have been negotiated in good faith between the employer and the collective bargaining unit.

Other Criteria

In the past, it has not been extremely difficult for employers to exclude certain employees based on factors other than age and length of service. For example, "salaried only" plans have excluded employees compensated on an hourly basis. Other plans have excluded employees who work at specific locations. While these types of eligibility requirements have not specifically been prohibited, it now might be difficult to maintain the qualification of a plan that uses eligibility requirements except for those based on age and length of service.

Contributions to the Plan

Employee benefit plans can be financed entirely by the employer (*noncontributory plans*) or by contributions from employees and the employer (*contributory plans*).

There has been a clear trend toward the noncontributory approach for defined benefit plans. In fact, most of these plans are now noncontributory.

Defined contribution pension plans (and many of the defined contribution plans discussed in the following chapter) are more likely to be contributory. The employer's contribution can be set at the same rate as that paid by employees, but it is often larger. Employee contributions can be either mandatory or voluntary. Technically, an employee can never be forced to make contributions, but if an employee chooses to participate in the plan, "mandatory" contributions can be required as a condition for participation.

Vesting

If an employee terminates employment, he or she must receive at least the value in the fund that is attributable to the employee's own contributions. The employee's rights to benefits attributable to the employer's contributions depend on the *vesting* provisions of the pension plan. **Vested pension rights** are those rights in the pension benefits paid for by the employer that belong to the employee, even if the employee terminates employment.

The minimum vesting for employer contributions must be *at least as favorable* to employees as *one* of the following rules:

1. 100 percent vesting after 5 years of service, called **cliff vesting**
2. **"3 to 7" graded vesting** as follows:

Years of Service	Vesting Percentage
3	20%
4	40%
5	60%
6	80%
7 or more	100%

When an employee terminates employment with less than 100 percent vesting, a question arises concerning the disposition of the forfeited funds. As mentioned earlier, forfeitures can be reallocated among remaining participants or applied to reduce future employer contributions in defined contribution plans. Forfeitures *must* be used to reduce employer contributions in defined benefit plans.

Vested benefits to terminating employees can be paid in several forms. In some plans, the employee is entitled to an immediate cash payment, but in other plans, payment is deferred until the normal retirement age. When the benefit is deferred, a person might have a choice of receiving cash or some type of annuity at retirement.

Retirement Ages

Most qualified retirement plans specify a "normal retirement age." The **normal retirement age** is typically defined as the youngest age at which an employee can retire with full pension benefits. The normal age specified in a plan is not necessarily regarded as the expected retirement age. Many participants actually retire earlier or later than the normal retirement age set forth in the plan.

Normal Retirement

In a defined benefit plan, the normal retirement age is needed to determine benefits. In a defined contribution plan, a normal retirement age is needed to determine when participants can begin to receive benefits or to specify when no additional contributions will be required.

The most common normal retirement age is sixty-five, although plans can have a lower or higher normal retirement age. The normal retirement age cannot be greater than the *latest* of the following:

- Age sixty-five
- The fifth anniversary of plan entry, if a participant entered within five years of normal retirement age
- The tenth anniversary of plan entry, for a participant not covered by the preceding five-year rule

For example, if a plan has a normal retirement age of sixty-five, the normal retirement age for a person entering at age sixty-three could be as late as age sixty-eight, and it could be sixty-seven for a participant not covered by the five-year rule who entered at age fifty-seven.

The purpose of allowing these extended retirement ages is to give the employer a reasonable amount of time to fund benefits. Funding benefits over fewer years could be especially expensive in a defined benefit plan.

The accrual of benefits (in a defined benefit plan) and allocations to employee accounts (in a defined contribution plan) cannot generally be reduced or stopped simply because an active employee has reached a specified age. Furthermore, employees hired within five years of the normal retirement age can no longer be excluded from plan participation.

Early Retirement

Many plans contain a provision for **early retirement** (retiring before *normal* retirement age) and can specify an early retirement age. To avoid tax penalties on retirees for early distributions from the plan, the early retirement age must be at least age fifty-five. In a defined contribution plan, the concept of early retirement has little or no meaning because the benefit that is payable is simply the amount accumulated in the participant's account.

Early retirement in a defined benefit plan, however, is entirely different—the early retirement benefit is normally less than the full retirement benefit payable at the normal retirement age. Defined benefit pension benefits are based on the assumption that benefit payments will begin at the normal retirement age and that funds will be invested and earn interest until that date. If an employee retires early, benefits will be payable over a longer period, and there will be a loss of investment earnings. Furthermore, a mortality factor comes into play because early retirement provides a benefit to those who would have died prior to normal retirement. When all of these factors are recognized, the benefits are said to be "fully reduced" or to have a "full actuarial reduction."

In recent years, *early retirement scales* have become increasingly popular. A simple scale might provide a reduction of 1/175 for each month prior to normal retirement age. Thus, a plan with an early retirement age of fifty-nine and one-half and a normal retirement age of sixty-five might have an early retirement payment schedule similar to that in Exhibit 6-12. A scale for early retirement discounts generally reduces benefits less than a full actuarial reduction. Another advantage for employees is that it is easier for them to predict their benefits if they should elect early retirement.

Benefits Provided by Pension Plans

In addition to retirement benefits, a pension plan might provide death and disability benefits. As noted previously, it must also contain *withdrawal benefits* (vested benefits) for eligible participants who terminate employment prior to retirement.

Retirement Benefits

In planning retirement benefits, it is common to assume that combined retirement income from Social Security and a pension plan should be equal to

Exhibit 6-12
Early Retirement Schedule

Year	Age Month	Percent of Normal Retirement Benefit	Year	Age Month	Percent of Normal Retirement Benefit
65	0	100.00%	62	0	79.43%
64	11	99.43%	61	11	78.86%
64	10	98.86%	61	10	78.29%
64	9	98.29%	61	9	77.71%
64	8	97.71%	61	8	77.14%
64	7	97.14%	61	7	76.57%
64	6	96.57%	61	6	76.00%
64	5	96.00%	61	5	75.43%
64	4	95.43%	61	4	74.86%
64	3	94.86%	61	3	74.29%
64	2	94.29%	61	2	73.71%
64	1	93.71%	61	1	73.14%
64	0	93.14%	61	0	72.57%
63	11	92.57%	60	11	72.00%
63	10	92.00%	60	10	71.43%
63	9	91.43%	60	9	70.86%
63	8	90.86%	60	8	70.29%
63	7	90.29%	60	7	69.71%
63	6	89.71%	60	6	69.14%
63	5	89.14%	60	5	68.57%
63	4	88.57%	60	4	68.00%
63	3	88.00%	60	3	67.43%
63	2	87.43%	60	2	66.86%
63	1	86.86%	60	1	66.29%
63	0	86.29%	60	0	65.71%
62	11	85.71%	59	11	65.14%
62	10	85.14%	59	10	64.57%
62	9	84.57%	59	9	64.00%
62	8	84.00%	59	8	63.43%
62	7	83.43%	59	7	62.86%
62	6	82.86%	59	6	62.29%
62	5	82.29%			
62	4	81.71%			
62	3	81.14%			
62	2	80.57%			
62	1	80.00%			

some percentage (such as 50 to 70 percent) of an employee's average earnings prior to retirement. The percentage benchmark can be relatively lower for highly paid employees (perhaps 50 percent of previous earnings) and higher for lower paid employees (such as 70 to 75 percent).

Some plans use benefit formulas or contribution allocation formulas that *do not* recognize Social Security benefits. These arrangements are called **nonintegrated plans.**

Other plans, however, provide **integrated benefit formulas** or **integrated contribution allocation formulas** that *do* recognize Social Security benefits. Furthermore, although a pension plan cannot discriminate in favor of highly compensated employees, a plan might provide benefits that favor the highly compensated employees if the plan is properly integrated with Social Security benefits. This is technically referred to as *permitted disparity*. In other words, because Social Security benefits discriminate *against* highly compensated employers, private pension plan benefits are allowed to *favor* highly compensated employees. The basic concept is that *total* benefits from both sources (the pension plan and Social Security) cannot be proportionately greater for highly compensated employees than for those who earn less.

Death Benefits

In virtually all pension plans, if a person dies prior to retirement, the beneficiaries of the deceased are entitled to a return of the employee's contributions, usually accrued at some rate of interest. In addition, the Retirement Equity Act of 1984 (REA) requires that an employer *must* provide a preretirement spousal death benefit (called a *qualified preretirement survivor annuity* or QPSA) for married participants. This benefit is effective only for the spouses of those employees who die before retirement, and payment of benefits must begin no later than the day on which the deceased would have been eligible for early retirement. The law permits employers to pass along this cost to participants and their spouses through actuarially reduced pension benefits. The benefit must be provided to all employees who have been married at least one year. The benefit is a life income to the surviving spouse and must amount to at least one-half of the benefit the employee would receive if he or she selected early retirement with a joint-and-one-half survivorship annuity. An employee, however, can elect to waive this QPSA death benefit, *provided* the spouse consents to this waiver of the QPSA rights in writing and the consent is witnessed as the law requires.

An employer is not required to provide a death benefit prior to retirement other than as mentioned above. Some employers, however, do provide additional death benefits. This can be accomplished by individual life policies, group permanent life insurance, or cash distributions from the pension plan itself.

After retirement, death benefits depend primarily on the type of annuity provided to the employee. According to REA, pension plan retirement benefits must automatically be available as a joint-and-at-least-50-percent-to-the-survivor annuity (which are called *qualified joint and survivor annuities* or QJSA), provided the employee is married and has been married for at least one year. Married employees can select another option—such as a straight life annuity, a ten-year period certain annuity, or a *modified cash refund annuity* (which guarantees that the retired worker or the beneficiaries will receive at least the amount that has been contributed by the employee)—if they indicate their intention in writing and the spouse provides written consent in the proper form.

Disability Benefits

Some pension plans provide disability benefits. For example, full vesting of all contributions (employer and employee) might be provided to employees who become totally and permanently disabled. Another approach treats a total and permanent disability as an early retirement, typically without actuarial reduction. With this approach, an employee must usually be beyond a certain age (fifty, for example) and must have worked a minimum period of time to be eligible for disability benefits. Separate disability benefits might also be found in a pension plan. In addition, many employers provide disability benefits separate from any such benefits that might be included in a pension plan, such as wage continuation plans, group short-term disability income insurance plans, and, in recent years, group long-term disability plans.

Funding of Pension Plans

When a pension plan is implemented, a funding agency and a funding instrument must be selected. A **funding agency** is an organization (or individual) used to accumulate funds and administer the pension plan. Important funding agencies for pension plans include life insurance companies, banks and other financial institutions, and individual trustees.

Funding instruments are the specific contracts or other vehicles used by funding agencies to provide pension benefits. The selection of the funding instrument often has important implications for the types of benefits, contribution rates, and the security of benefits promised in the plan.

The following types of pension plan funding are discussed below:

1. Trust fund plans
2. Fully insured plans

3. Investment facility contracts
4. Group deposit administration contracts
5. Group immediate participation guarantee contracts
6. Guaranteed investment contracts
7. Individual account contracts
8. Other plans
9. Combination plans

Trust Fund Plans

A **trusteed plan**, or **trust fund plan**, is one in which a trustee *is* the funding agency responsible for the investment of pension funds. Measured in terms of the number of employees covered or aggregate plan assets, trusteed plans are more popular than insured plans.

Interestingly, trust fund plans are especially popular for extremely large plans and very small plans. In large firms, a bank or trust company often serves as trustee. In small firms, the owner (or owners) of the business usually are the named trustee(s). In either case, the major attraction of the trusteed approach is investment flexibility.

In addition to individual trust accounts, banks and other financial institutions manage trust accounts that allow a number of qualified plans to invest in a single, diversified pool of investments. This allows smaller plans to achieve diversification and to attain the advantages of large-scale investing. Although funds are commingled for investment purposes, each trust is administered separately, and of course, assets are accounted for individually.

Trust fund plans are entirely **unallocated**. That is, none of the trust fund is allocated specifically to any particular participants before retirement. Any type of pension benefit formula can be used, because benefits are simply paid from the trust at the appropriate time.

Under trusteed plans, a trust agreement stipulates the responsibilities of the trustee. Generally, these responsibilities include requirements the trustee must satisfy in the receipt, investment, and disbursement of funds. In most cases, the pension plan provisions are separate from the trust agreement. Thus, changes in the provisions of the plan do not directly involve the trustee.

As a general rule, the record-keeping and investment duties of the employer and the trustee are stated explicitly in the trust agreement. Normally, records for employee contributions, earnings, and credited service are handled by the employer, not the trustee. Trustees are held responsible for full accounting of investments and all transactions involving assets in the plan. In other words, employers usually perform the administrative record keeping, while trustees handle investment record keeping.

The investment powers granted to the trustee are set forth in the trust agreement. While the trustee can have considerable investment flexibility, federal law contains a number of requirements for the investment of funds in a trusteed plan. For example, ERISA limits investment in an employer's securities to 10 percent of the fund value (except for stock bonus plans, Employee Stock Ownership Plans (ESOPs), profit sharing plans, and thrift plans discussed in Chapter 7).

Fully Insured Plans

Insured plans use a life insurance company as the funding agency and individual life insurance policies or annuity contracts as the funding instrument. In many plans of this type, a trust is established. Because a trustee is commonly used, these plans are sometimes called **individual policy pension trusts**, or simply **pension trusts**.

In fully insured plans, a separate insurance contract is purchased for each employee. Usually, the trustee applies for individual insurance or annuity contracts for those employees designated by the employer. Contributions are made to the trustee, who in turn pays the premiums on the contracts. Because each individual policy is intended to provide benefits to one specific employee, the policies are referred to as **allocated funding instruments**.

The trust agreement, a legal document, should be drafted or reviewed by the employer's attorney or legal staff. As a practical matter, however, most life insurers provide sample trust agreements for guidance. In fact, many insurance companies have submitted *prototype* trusts to the Internal Revenue Service for approval, and if these forms are used, approval of a specific plan is much easier. In recent years, some life insurers have developed plans that make a trust agreement or trustee unnecessary. In these cases, the insurance company handles the duties that otherwise would have been performed by a trustee.

An important consideration with fully insured plans is the *incidental* life insurance test. Most whole life policies (by themselves) cannot be used to fund the pension benefits because the death benefits are too large in relation to the cash values the policy will develop. To satisfy the IRS requirement, a policy must generate relatively large cash values. Generally, the types of policy that meet the requirement are retirement annuities and retirement income contracts. *Retirement annuities* provide a means of accumulating funds for retirement, but provide no life insurance protection. *Retirement income contracts* differ from retirement annuities in that they contain decreasing term insurance.

Investment Facility Contracts

To compete with the very flexible trust fund pension plans described above, many insurers offer what are referred to as **investment facility contracts**. These contracts are extremely flexible and require that the plan sponsor utilize the investment facilities of an insurance company with the right, but not the mandatory obligation, to buy annuities or other typical retirement plan services from the insurers. Some have referred to this type of contract as enabling a plan sponsor to "rent the investment skills of an insurance company."

Group Deposit Administration Contracts

In **group deposit administration pension plans**, funds are transferred from an unallocated fund held by an insurance company to purchase an annuity from that insurer for an employee only at retirement. The unallocated fund is called by a number of names, such as the *active life fund* or *annuity purchase fund*.

The unallocated fund can either be (1) *commingled* with the other assets of the insurance company, or (2) maintained as a *separate account*. If the unallocated fund is commingled with the other assets of the insurance company, a minimum rate of interest is guaranteed. Any interest earned in excess of the guaranteed minimum rate is generally divided between the plan's account and a *contingency reserve* to compensate the insurer for the minimum interest, mortality, and expense guarantees provided by the contract.

A separate account can be invested in fixed dollar assets, in equity investments, or in some combination of these. If a combination of fixed and variable dollar investments is desired, the employer can choose the proportions to be invested in each. As a general rule, an employer can transfer funds, within limits, from the fixed account to the equity account or vice versa. The flexibility available with separate accounts is a major reason for the recent, rapid growth of deposit administration plans.

Because deposit administration plans are unallocated funding instruments, virtually any type of benefit formula is compatible with a deposit administration plan. Final-pay formulas cause no major problems. Early or late retirement also can be handled rather easily.

If separate account funds have been invested in equities, employees can be given the option of receiving a group variable annuity as the retirement benefit. In some plans, employees may be given the choice between fixed and variable investments, either before or after retirement, or both.

Group Immediate Participation Guarantee (IPG) Contracts

Group immediate participation guarantee contracts, often referred to as **IPG**

contracts, actually are a form of deposit administration program. In a large pension plan, employers might object to the contingency reserve charges applied in some deposit administration plans. With an IPG plan, no interest is guaranteed, and no charge is made to build up a contingency reserve. Only actual benefits and expenses are charged to the unallocated fund.

Guaranteed Investment Contracts

A popular arrangement developed by insurers in recent years is the **guaranteed investment contract (GIC)**. The GIC was developed to attract lump-sum pension, profit sharing, or savings plan funds. Though many different forms of GICs exist, a typical arrangement is for an insurer to offer a fairly high guaranteed fixed interest rate for a certain number of years on the lump-sum deposit. This type of arrangement has proven to be popular because of its relatively high return and other guarantees provided by the insurance companies selling GICs.[5]

Individual Account Contracts

Several types of retirement plans require that separate individual accounts be maintained for each participant in the plan. Profit-sharing plans, thrift or savings plans, and individual retirement accounts (IRAs), all described in Chapter 7, are examples of such plans. Individual account contracts often allow the plan participant to have plan contributions allocated to a fixed or variable funding instrument or often a combination of such instruments. Generally, the insurer will offer a minimum guarantee for the fixed dollar account, with the real rate credited based on the current return being credited, while the variable account would have no guarantees as to principal or interest. Generally, the plan participant is allowed to elect a settlement option in the form of a lump-sum payment or an annuity.

Other Plans

Two other funding arrangements are available: group permanent pension plans and group deferred annuities.

Group Permanent Pension Plans **Group permanent pension plans** use group life insurance as a funding instrument. The principal characteristic of group permanent plans that distinguishes them from individual policy plans is the advantage of group underwriting. Group permanent pension plans attempt to provide both life insurance and retirement income at a reduced cost resulting from use of the group insurance concept.

While group permanent life insurance contracts once were often used to fund pension plans when life insurance was desired, they are not commonly used as pension funding instruments today.

Group Deferred Annuities In their basic form, **group deferred annuities** use single premiums to purchase a fully paid-up deferred annuity annually for each employee in the plan. A life insurer is used as the funding agency and a paid-up annuity as the funding instrument. The amount of the annuity purchased each year depends on the credit earned by the employee during the year. Over time, the annuity benefit increases. When the employee retires, the monthly benefit will be the sum of the benefits provided by all the annuities that have been purchased for that employee. These plans have been largely replaced by the newer types of pension plans described above.

Combination Plans

Combination plans combine fully insured plans, which are allocated funding instruments, with unallocated funding instruments.

Combination plans are used to obtain the advantages of both funding instruments—fully insured plans and unallocated funds. One of the major advantages of fully insured plans is the guarantee available from an insurance company. Because insurance companies pool the experience of a large number of individuals, they guarantee mortality, interest, and expenses. As a result, an employer can be assured that the cost of the insured portion of a pension plan will not exceed the premiums required for the contracts. Another advantage is that combination plans allow an employer to use the administrative experience and expertise of an insurance company. The major advantage of unallocated funds is their flexibility—generally a wide latitude in benefit formulas, investment vehicles, types of benefits, and contributions are available.

A combination plan always uses a trustee. The trustee normally owns the life insurance contracts and might administer the unallocated fund. In many cases, however, the administration of the unallocated fund is handled by a life insurance company.

The types of life insurance policies that can be used with individual policy plans are limited by the "incidental" life insurance test. More types of life insurance can be used when insurance is combined with a trust fund in a combination plan. Basically, the type of life insurance contract selected depends on the balance sought between the individual policies and the unallocated fund. If benefits are to be paid primarily from the unallocated fund, life insurance policies that generate relatively low cash values (straight life contracts, for example) might be used. If life insurance cash values are the primary source of benefits, a policy that generates larger values (an endowment at age sixty-five, for example) might be used. If retirement annuities or retirement income contracts are purchased, a relatively smaller portion of retirement benefits will be provided by the unallocated fund. Evidence of insurability might be required for policies containing larger elements of protection. Most insurers, however, do not require evidence of insurability for life insurance policies up to a specified face amount when used as part of a combination plan.

Almost any type of benefit formula can be used in a combination plan, including final average formulas. If an employee's benefit is larger than the amount that can be financed by the life insurance policies, the deficiency is paid by the unallocated fund. This is possible because money in the unallocated fund is not allocated to specific individuals until retirement.

One of the major advantages of combination plans is that employer contributions to the unallocated funds need not be constant. However, to be tax deductible, the contributions must be within limits established by the Internal Revenue Service. These limits, however, permit considerable flexibility. If an employer has large profits and adequate cash, relatively large contributions can be made to the unallocated fund. When financial results are poor, an employer might make smaller contributions. This type of flexibility in contributions is not possible under an individual policy plan because predetermined premiums must be paid annually.

If contributions to an unallocated fund are determined by the employer, there might be less assurance for employees that the fund will be adequate to provide the promised benefits. This is true even when a life insurance company holds the assets in the unallocated fund. However, if the unallocated fund is placed with an insurance company, the insurer assumes responsibility for maintaining the fund and guarantees a minimum rate of investment earnings. If the fund is completely handled by an insurer, the annuity rates are guaranteed. This guarantee pertains not only to amounts taken from the unallocated fund but also to funds accumulated in the life insurance policies.

Summary

Income planning for retirement is highly desirable. Inadequate planning, limited employment opportunities, longer retirement periods, and inflation can severely cut into income. Investments should be made, and assets accumulated, throughout the working years so that adequate retirement funds will be available. Tax-deferred and tax-deductible investments, when available, are the best ways of accumulating such funds. An individual annuity is a tax-deferred investment. A pension plan also provides tax-deferred income to an employee.

An annuity is paid, not to survivors when the insured dies, but to the insured-annuitant when he or she survives beyond a certain time specified in the contract. The income benefits for annuities are determined by the expected payout period, which is affected by the age and sex of the annuitant. An annuity can be classified according to five criteria—when benefits begin, how premiums are paid, its refund features, the number of lives it covers, and the type of benefit units it agrees to pay (fixed or variable).

A pension plan is an employment-related means of providing retirement income. Pension plans can be qualified by meeting certain complex IRS requirements. Employers who offer qualified pension plans are allowed to deduct contributions to the plans as business expenses, and their employees can defer taxes on the contributions made on their behalf until retirement.

Pension plans are generally either defined contribution pension plans or defined benefit pension plans. In a defined contribution plan, the employer promises to make specific contributions to fund a retirement plan. The contribution level is usually defined as a percentage of the employee's earnings. The level of retirement benefits varies according to the amounts contributed, the length of the accumulation period, and the investment experience of the plan. In a defined benefit plan, the employee is promised a specific retirement benefit. The contributions provided by the employer vary, depending on what is needed to pay the promised benefits. In addition to these types of plans, the target benefit pension plan combines features of defined contribution and defined benefit plans.

Although the specific provisions of pension plans vary, it is possible to generalize about many plan features. The eligibility requirements, for instance, are typically established by the employer. The most common requirements are based on age and years of service; however, some employees can be excluded if they participate in a union plan. Contributions can be made by the employer only (noncontributory) or by both the employer and the employee (contributory). Most plans specify a normal retirement age, usually sixty-five, and many plans contain provisions for early retirement. In addition to retirement benefits, many plans provide death, disability, and withdrawal (vested) benefits.

As mentioned, this chapter classified pension plans into three broad categories. Pension plans can further be defined in terms of how they are funded. All have a funding agency, which is the organization (or individual) that accumulates funds and administers the plan, and a funding instrument, which is the vehicle used by the funding agency to provide benefits.

Chapter Notes

1. 463 U.S. 1073 (1983).

2. Note that while life insurance proceeds paid by reason of the insured's death are normally income tax free to the beneficiary, such is not the case with annuities. For annuities, only the annuitant's investment in the contract is received by the beneficiary income tax free; the remainder of the value received at death is gross income to the beneficiary and is called income in respect of a decedent (IRD).

3. These are contained in Section 72 of the IRC. Under these rules, the annuitant determines the ratio of his or her investment in the annuity (the net premiums paid) to the expected return from the distributions (the periodic annual distribution times the annuitant's expected return multiple). The annuitant excludes this percentage (called the exclusion ratio) of each periodic distribution from his or her gross income for federal income tax purposes as the return of the annuitant's after-tax investment in the contract.

4. This maximum annual dollar limit is, in effect, indexed for inflation since it will equal a limit defined as 25 percent of the dollar limitation for defined benefit plans, which itself is indexed for inflation.

5. The discussion of guaranteed investment contracts is based on material from Everett T. Allen, Jr., Joseph J. Melone, Jerry S. Rosenbloom, and Jack L. VanDerhei, *Pension Planning,* 7th ed. (Homewood, IL: Business One Irwin, 1992), pp. 360-363.

Chapter 7

Planning for Retirement: Other Retirement Plans

This chapter concludes the subject of planning for retirement by discussing a variety of what might be termed tax-favored retirement plans other than the pension plans discussed in the previous chapter. These retirement plans include qualified profit-sharing plans, qualified savings plans, cash or deferred arrangements (CODAs), Section 403(b) plans, simplified employee pension (SEP) plans, qualified Keogh or HR-10 plans, individual retirement accounts or annuities (IRAs), employee stock ownership plans (ESOPs), and supplemental executive retirement plans (SERPs). Any of these plans could be available to help provide for retirement income needs in addition to qualified pension plans or, if purchased, to nonqualified individual annuity policies. Each of these retirement plans has its own characteristics and tax attributes, which makes thorough retirement income planning complex.

Profit-Sharing Plans

A **profit-sharing plan** is a defined contribution plan in which the employer's contributions are based in some manner on the employer's profits. However, it is not actually required that the employer have profits to contribute to the plan—even a nonprofit organization can have a "profit-sharing" plan.

Profit-sharing plans bear a strong resemblance to pension plans. In both pension and profit-sharing plans, the employer contributes money to provide employees with retirement income—and, possibly, with other benefits. The chief distinction between pension plans and profit-sharing plans lies in the approach used to determine employer contributions. With a pension plan, the employer either makes a defined contribution (usually based on payroll) or contributes the sums necessary to provide a defined benefit. With a profit-sharing plan, however, employer contributions can be based on the profits of the corporation. Thus, theoretically, employees have a personal incentive to help their employer earn a profit because they share in that profit through the profit-sharing plan.

Employer contributions to a profit-sharing plan might vary because profits would vary from year to year. In a good year, a profit-sharing plan will likely receive greater contributions from the employer than in a poor year. This flexibility can be advantageous to employers, who need not commit a required amount to an employee retirement program in both good years and bad. However, this variability creates a disadvantage for employees in that it is difficult to predict the amount of funds available at retirement.

The income tax advantages of a qualified profit-sharing plan are essentially the same as those for a qualified pension plan. In both cases, the employer's contributions are deductible, amounts contributed are not currently taxable to employees, and the funds accumulate tax free until distributed. To obtain these tax benefits, both pension and profit-sharing plans must meet generally the same tax qualification requirements. That is, they must be written, communicated to employees, designed for the exclusive benefit of employees, and intended to be permanent. They also cannot discriminate in favor of highly compensated employees.

Eligibility

Even though the minimum eligibility requirements under ERISA and for a qualified retirement plan are the same for pension and profit-sharing plans, employers generally choose more liberal standards in their profit-sharing plans. That is, a broader range of employees is generally eligible for profit-sharing plans than for pension plans. Employers set liberal eligibility standards for several reasons:

1. The purpose of a profit-sharing plan is to encourage all employees, not just long-term employees, to work as efficiently as possible.

2. The employer's cost is normally a function of company profits and is not affected by either the age or the number of employees as is the case with a pension plan. Only the allocation of profits among employees is affected.

3. An employer (or stockholder-employee) can personally benefit from liberal eligibility requirements.

When an employee terminates employment, the plan contributions that have been allocated to that employee and are not yet vested are typically reallocated to the remaining participants in the plan. As a result, the benefits for an employer (or stockholder-employee) are increased.

Profit-sharing plans need not impose a minimum age requirement and might include all full-time employees after they have worked for one year.

Contributions

With a *pension* plan, the employer is generally required to make a contribution each year in an amount specified by the plan. In a *profit-sharing* plan, however, the employer can usually contribute any amount up to the limit allowed in the law and, indeed, can elect to "skip" one or more annual contributions. This flexibility is subject to two general restrictions if the plan is to be acceptable to the Internal Revenue Service for favorable tax treatment:

1. Contributions must be "substantial and recurring" if the plan does not contain a specific contribution formula.

2. Contributions cannot be adjusted (in amount or time) such that discrimination will result in favor of highly compensated employees.

A discretionary approach or a formula approach can be used in determining contributions, or the two approaches may be combined. These approaches are explained below.

The **discretionary method** for determining contributions leaves the decision each year to the company's board of directors. The primary advantage of the discretionary approach is that it provides the employer with a high degree of flexibility. The board of directors can consider a number of factors that a simple formula could not take into account, such as the company's budget for the coming year and the level of expected profits.

The **formula approach** provides for the contribution of a percentage, or other established formula, of company profits to the plan each year. Some companies contribute a flat percentage of all profits, while others contribute a flat percentage of only those profits in excess of a stipulated amount. For example, if a plan requires a 10 percent contribution of profits above $500,000, and the company earns $800,000, the contribution would be $30,000 [($800,000–$500,000) x 0.10].

Another commonly used formula provides for increasing percentage contributions as profits increase. For example, 10 percent might be contributed when profits are less than $100,000, but contributions will be 12 percent when profits are between $100,000 and $200,000 and 15 percent when profits are between $200,000 and $300,000.

Some companies use a *combination* of the discretionary and formula approaches. For example, a formula might establish a broad range for the contributions, but the exact amount might be left to the discretion of the board of directors.

Employer contributions to a qualified profit-sharing plan are deductible if they average 15 percent or less of the annual compensation of participants. However, for taxable years beginning after 1986, if an employer contributes less than the permitted 15 percent to a profit-sharing plan, the employer cannot carry over the unused deductible limit for that year to a succeeding year or years.

Allocation of Contributions

Sometimes contributions are transferred to a trustee who invests and administers the funds on a "pooled basis"—in other words, as a common trust fund. Each person has an individual account in the common fund for record-keeping purposes in this case, or plans can be designed to allow each participant to direct the investment of his or her account. In either case, the ultimate disposition of the individual's share of the fund depends on the benefit provisions of the plan.

The contributions must be apportioned to individual participants by means of a nondiscriminatory allocation formula. Such formulas are often based on a percentage of aggregate compensation but can also use earnings and length of service. Other plans use both age and compensation for allocating employer contributions among plan participants. These are called *age-based profit-sharing plans*.

Percentage of Aggregate Compensation

The most popular method of allocating profits is based on an employee's compensation as a percentage of the aggregate compensation. For example, assume that the total compensation for all participants during the year was $500,000, and Alice earned $50,000. In this case, Alice would be credited with 10 percent ($50,000 divided by $500,000) of the employer's contribution, since she earned 10 percent of the total compensation.

Credit for Earnings and Length of Service

Another type of allocation formula gives credit for both earnings and length of service. To illustrate, a plan might give one point for each $100 of income and two points for each year of service. A ten-year employee who earns $40,000 would receive 400 points (or units) for compensation and twenty points for service, or a total of 420 points. The employee's share of the employer's contribution would then be divided by the total number of points credited to all participants. However, this type of arrangement can encounter problems with the Internal Revenue Service if it discriminates in favor of highly compensated employees.

Benefits

In addition to retirement benefits, profit-sharing plans can be used to provide death benefits, severance benefits, and certain other benefits.

Retirement Benefits

The amount accumulated in a participant's account at retirement depends on the number of years of participation, the amount allocated each year, the investment experience of the fund, and reallocated nonvested forfeitures. Thus, employees with long service tend to accumulate larger amounts than those who have worked a shorter period of time. Consequently, many profit-sharing plans generate a satisfactory level of retirement income for only the employees who have worked a long period of time, perhaps twenty years or more.

Some profit-sharing plans pay retirement benefits for only a fixed period, such as ten years. It is common, however, for trust funds to purchase an annuity for an individual upon retirement if this is desired. In some plans, the person has a choice of a fixed annuity, a variable annuity, or a combination of the two. Retirement benefits under a profit-sharing plan are taxed to the recipient as retirement income is received; the benefits are subject to the same tax consequences as distributions from a pension plan.

Death Benefits

Profit-sharing plans usually provide a death benefit equal to the amount accumulated in a participant's account. Thus, the benefit is smaller in the early years of participation than in later years.

A profit-sharing participant can authorize the trustee to purchase life insurance on an individual basis. Not all participants need to be insured, so long as all employees have the opportunity for insurance. If the funds used to pay the premiums have been accumulated for two years or longer, or if a retirement income or endowment contract is purchased, no limits apply to the amount of insurance that can be purchased (other than the practical limit imposed by the amount of funds in the employee's account). Otherwise, the total premiums cannot be greater than 50 percent of the employee's account.

Severance Benefits

The minimum vesting requirements of ERISA apply to profit-sharing plans as well as to pension plans. Vested benefits belong to the employee whose employment terminates. Nonvested benefits are forfeited.

Forfeitures by terminating employees in a profit-sharing plan can be reallocated among remaining participants on the basis of a participant's compensation or as a proportion of the total compensation of all continuing participants.

Investment of Funds

Pension plans and profit-sharing plans must conform to the investment regulations imposed by ERISA. In general, acceptable investments include mutual funds, real estate (and real estate mortgages), common stocks, bonds, and insurance company products.

Profit-sharing plans frequently make two types of investments that are not common in pension plans. One is investment in the employer's common stock. Though profit-sharing plans, like pension plans, are subject to a 10 percent limitation on the amount of plan assets that can be invested in the employer's securities, this limitation can be changed (increased without limit) if the profit-sharing plan contains a specific provision to do so.

Profit-sharing funds can also be used to purchase key employee life insurance (discussed in Chapter 8). If the profitability of the company largely depends on the efforts of an extraordinary employee, all participants in the plan benefit from that employee's efforts. Obviously, the death of that person represents a loss to the employees, as well as to the employer, because profits will be smaller. To protect itself against this loss, the trust itself can purchase life insurance on the key employee's life.

Distributions and Loans

Distributions or withdrawals from a profit-sharing plan of funds accumulated from employer contributions are permitted by the tax law after the funds have been deposited in the plan (1) for a minimum of two years; (2) as of a stated age; or (3) in the event of an occurrence, such as layoff, illness, disability, death, retirement, or other severance of employment.

The rights of participants to have distributions from a plan are determined by the terms of the profit-sharing plan. Participants can take only distributions from a plan that are permitted by the terms of that plan, even though the tax law might permit more liberal distribution rights. Profit-sharing plan provisions concerning in-service withdrawals and other distributions from the plan can vary considerably but are always limited to what is permitted under the tax law.

The taxable portion of any distributions must be included in the participant's (or beneficiary's) gross income for federal income tax purposes. This taxable portion might also be subject to a 10 percent penalty tax on premature distributions when taken prior to age fifty-nine and one-half, subject to certain exceptions. These and other tax considerations might make it preferable for participants to take loans from a plan within the limits allowed by the tax law, rather than taking in-service taxable distributions from the plan, even where such distributions are permitted by the plan.

It should also be noted at this point that additional important tax-law limitations apply to distributions from profit-sharing plans that have a *cash or deferred arrangement* (CODA) under Section 401(k) of the Internal Revenue Code. These are covered later in this chapter.

The disadvantages of taking cash withdrawals before termination of employment are that they are currently taxable as ordinary income to the participant, might result in the 10 percent penalty tax on premature distributions just described, and can prevent the accumulation of funds for retirement. To offset this, many profit-sharing plans (and also the savings plans described next) include a loan provision, which allows a participant to borrow a certain percentage of the vested funds, at a stated interest rate, for a specified period. A loan is normally repaid, so the retirement funding objective has a greater chance of success.

The Internal Revenue Code limits loans to the smaller of 50 percent of the value of the participant's vested accrued benefit or $50,000 per participant and imposes various other conditions on the loan. For example, there must be a reasonable rate of interest, the loan must be adequately secured, and it must be available to all participants on a nondiscriminatory basis. Loans not meeting these restrictions are treated as fully taxable distributions under the plan.

Comparison of Pension and Profit-Sharing Plans

From the employer's viewpoint, the decision of whether to establish a pension plan or a profit-sharing plan (or perhaps a combination of the two) is not always easy. Both provide retirement income to employees without increasing their current income tax liabilities; both can provide life insurance and annuity benefits; and both help attract and retain employees. Despite these similarities, several important differences exist.

Retirement Income

If the primary goal of the employee benefit plan is to provide retirement income (particularly if the plan contains older employees), a defined benefit pension plan is probably preferable to a profit-sharing plan. The value of benefits in a profit-sharing plan increases with participation. This is also true in most pension plans, but defined benefit formulas can be used that place little or no weight on the length of participation in the plan. Older employees, as a result, can achieve a substantial retirement benefit in a short time in a defined benefit pension plan but not in a profit-sharing plan.

Employee Incentive

If one of the objectives of the plan is to stimulate employee productivity, a profit-sharing plan might be preferable, since it provides a more direct incentive than does a pension plan.

Death Benefits

Death benefits can differ in pension and profit-sharing plans. The death benefit in a pension plan can generally be up to 100 times the projected monthly pension plan benefit payment. In a profit-sharing plan, the participants can be allowed to authorize the trustee to purchase life insurance for them as part of their accounts under the plan. Technically, life insurance must be "incidental" in both pension plans and profit-sharing plans.

In profit-sharing plans, if the funds used to pay the premiums have accumulated for two years or longer, no limits exist on the amount of life insurance that can be purchased on a participant's life. For funds accumulated for less than two years, and when only ordinary life insurance is purchased, aggregate life insurance premiums must be less than 50 percent of the total contributions and forfeitures allocated to the participant's account in the plan.

Funding Flexibility

Funding flexibility is often a major consideration in choosing between a pension plan and a profit-sharing plan. Companies that have volatile profits might be ill-advised to assume the relatively fixed obligations of a defined benefit pension plan. More contribution flexibility is available with profit-sharing plans, since contributions must only be "substantial and recurring."

Limitations on Contributions

The maximum amount of employer contributions that can be deducted might be higher in a pension plan than in a profit-sharing plan. An employer can deduct an average of only 15 percent of total compensation in a profit-sharing plan. For defined contribution pension plans, up to 25 percent of total compensation is deductible. No percentage limitations apply to the deductibility of contributions in a defined benefit pension plan. However, contributions must be actuarially justifiable and reasonable.

Savings Plans

A **savings plan** is a contributory, defined contribution plan—employees must make contributions to participate in the plan; the employer might then make "matching" contributions, which usually are a percentage of the employee contributions. The primary purpose of savings plans is usually to encourage employees to save, but savings plans can also play an important role in retirement income planning and in the retention of valuable employees. Savings plans are also called "thrift plans," "thrift-savings plans," "investment savings plans," or similar names.

For purposes of tax treatment and regulation, savings plans are considered to be the same as profit-sharing plans. Thus, the qualification requirements that apply to profit-sharing plans apply to savings plans as well.

Eligibility and Contributions

Since savings plans are always contributory arrangements, eligibility is limited to employees who choose to make contributions to the plan. These contributions can be determined in a variety of ways and are sometimes made with after-tax dollars. (Savings plans allowing contributions with pre-tax dollars are discussed later in this chapter, under CODAs.) In a typical approach, all participating employees can contribute up to a certain percentage (say, up to 5 percent) of their compensation, and a *matching contribution* is made by the employer. The employer's contribution sometimes matches the employee's contribution dollar for dollar. More commonly, however, the employer contributes a reduced amount, such as 50 or 75 percent of the employee's contribution.

If savings plans were not regulated, a plan's employee contribution level could be set so high that only more highly paid employees could afford to participate. This would create discrimination in favor of the highly compensated employees. The current Internal Revenue Code provides formulas that are used to determine whether or not a plan is discriminatory in this regard.

Benefits

As noted, a primary objective of savings plans is usually to encourage employees to save money for future needs. In keeping with this purpose, savings plans usually have liberal vesting schedules. The vested portion of an employee's account is paid to (or on behalf of) an employee upon retirement, death, disability, or termination.

A savings plan can have provisions for in-service employee withdrawal of funds. Many plans now provide for plan loans while the employees are actively employed for the reasons just described.

Investment of Funds

In most cases, employees are allowed to specify how their account balances will be invested. For example, a given plan might have four or more separate investment vehicles, such as the following:

- A fixed dollar investment account (such as a guaranteed investment contract (GIC))
- An equity fund (composed of either individual common stocks or a mutual fund)
- A balanced account (combining equity and fixed dollar investments)
- A bond fund
- An account containing the employer's stock

Under some plans an employee can use a portion of the account to purchase life insurance or an annuity.

When a plan offers investment alternatives, employees are generally given the right to split the account into two or more funds and to change from one fund to another periodically. The plan can have reasonable restrictions on the number of changes permitted to keep employees from using the savings plan to "play the market" and also keep down administrative costs. Regulations govern the number and kinds of investment choices an employer should offer the participants. These regulations allow for participant choice but also allow the employer to be protected from potential liability for employee investment losses.

Distributions

Distributions from qualified savings plans are made on generally the same basis as just described for qualified profit-sharing plans. However, today many savings plans are structured to provide a CODA under Section 401(k) of the tax code (described in the next section). When this is so, the rules regarding distributions from Section 401(k) plans apply to these savings plans.

Comparison of Savings Plans and Profit-Sharing Plans

From a practical viewpoint, the objectives, benefits, eligibility requirements, and investment policies of savings plans are similar to those of profit-sharing plans. However, some important differences exist:

- Savings plans are contributory, but profit-sharing plans generally are not.
- Unlike profit-sharing plans, savings plans are rarely used as the sole vehicle for accumulating retirement funds—usually they supplement a basic pension plan.
- Savings plans are more common than profit-sharing plans.

From an employer's viewpoint, a difference lies in the cost of the plans. All else being equal, a savings plan will normally be less expensive for an employer— in part because a savings plan requires employee contributions for those who choose to participate.

CODAs (Section 401(k) Plans)

A **CODA** (cash or deferred arrangement), also referred to as a **Section 401(k) plan**, is a qualified profit-sharing plan (including qualified savings plans), a qualified stock bonus plan, or a pre-ERISA money purchase pension plan[1] that meets the rules set forth in Section 401(k) of the tax code. The outstanding characteristic of CODAs is that they give participants the option either to receive taxable cash compensation or to have before-tax dollars flow into the CODA, where it is not taxed until it is withdrawn.

Eligibility

The coverage requirements generally applicable to qualified plans apply to CODAs. However, in a CODA, no more than one year of service can be required before employees are eligible to participate. Other qualified plans can impose a two-year waiting period for entry into a plan with 100 percent vesting.

Because it is argued that more highly paid employees can better afford to shift income into the plan than employees who are paid less, CODAs have some special nondiscrimination requirements. These complex nondiscrimination requirements are known as "actual deferral percentage (ADP) tests" and are beyond the scope of this text.[2]

Contributions

Three principal types of CODAs, each with its own approach to employer/employee contributions, exist:

- *Pure salary reduction plans.* A **pure salary reduction plan** is a CODA that is funded entirely with **elective deferrals**, which means that employees *choose* to reduce their pre-tax salary by a specified amount, and, instead of providing immediate taxable income, the specified amount flows to the CODA.

- *Bonus 401(k) plans.* A **bonus 401(k) plan** operates by having the employer make a contribution to a *bonus fund* for employees. Each participating employee then has the option of taking his or her share of the bonus in cash or contributing all or part of the bonus to the CODA.

  This approach requires a cash contribution from the employer. The bonus approach is sometimes used as a supplemental feature to an existing qualified plan.

- *401(k) savings plans.* A **401(k) savings plan** allows participants to elect salary reductions with the employer making matching contributions to the plan. This approach can be used to transform a traditional savings plan, with its after-tax contributions, into a CODA. This is the most common approach to creating a CODA.

An annual limit on elective deferrals for each participant was adopted by the Tax Reform Act of 1986. The limit was initially set at $7,000, with an annual adjustment for inflation to be made. By 1993, the annual limit was $8,994. This limit applies to the combined total of all elective deferrals under all available 401(k) plans. For example, suppose an employee has two jobs, and one employer offers a pure salary reduction plan and the other employer offers a bonus 401(k) plan. In 1993, an employee may have elected to defer a total of $8,994 between the two plans—such as $5,000 under the pure salary reduction plan and $3,994 under the bonus plan.

As a general rule, contributions by an employer to a qualified plan do not incur Social Security and federal employment taxes. This is not the case for elective contributions to CODAs. Specifically, the employer must pay FICA (Federal Insurance Contributions Act) and FUTA (Federal Unemployment Tax Act) taxes on amounts contributed to a 401(k) plan that are subject to an employee election to defer income, and the employee will continue to pay FICA taxes on that amount.

Elective deferrals must be 100 percent vested immediately. Of course, any employee contributions made with after-tax dollars must be fully and immediately vested. Employer contributions must meet one of the normal vesting requirements for qualified plans.

Distributions and Withdrawals

In addition to the points noted previously with regard to distributions and withdrawals from profit-sharing plans and savings plans, the tax law requires that there be certain restrictions on distributions and withdrawals from a "qualified" CODA before such a qualified CODA can be eligible for the tax advantages of Section 401(k) of the tax code. Thus, elective deferrals (and investment earnings on such amounts) in a qualified plan with a CODA might not be distributable to employees or their beneficiaries before the following circumstances occur:

1. Attainment of age fifty-nine and one-half

2. Separation from service

3. Death

4. Disability

However, withdrawals of elective contributions are permitted in the event of the "hardship" of the employee as defined in IRS regulations, which include certain medical expenses, the purchase of a principal residence, the prevention of foreclosure or eviction, and the payment of college tuition. With respect to this hardship exception, only the amount of the elective contributions themselves can be withdrawn by plan participants as in-service hardship distributions; any investment earnings on the elective contributions must remain within the CODA.

Distributions from a qualified CODA under these special rules are subject to regular income taxation like any other taxable distribution from a qualified retirement plan. In addition, they might be subject to the 10 percent penalty tax on premature distributions from qualified retirement plans if made before age fifty-nine and one-half, subject to certain exceptions. Proper plan loans are not considered taxable distributions for income tax or penalty tax purposes. Thus, many qualified retirement plans that have qualified CODAs allow loans from the plan that meet the requirements for such loans.

Advantages and Disadvantages of CODAs

The basic advantage of a CODA to employees is its favorable tax treatment: Employee before-tax contributions accumulate on a tax-sheltered basis until they are distributed at some later date. If an existing savings plan funded by after-tax contributions is converted to a CODA, the employees will experience an increase in take-home pay because of the decrease in income tax deductions.

From the employer's standpoint, CODAs provide the same basic advantages as any qualified retirement plan. Another possible advantage is that the employer might receive favorable employee reactions for increasing employees' take-home pay by converting an existing savings plan to a CODA. In addition, the availability of a CODA might reduce pressure on the employer to provide other benefits.

Probably the only significant disadvantages of a CODA from the employee's perspective are the limitations on distributions and withdrawals and on contributions. Employees, especially lower paid ones, might be reluctant to participate in a CODA because of the possibility of currently needing the funds. On the other hand, some employees might want to contribute more than the contribution limit allows.

From the employer's perspective, the major disadvantage of a CODA lies in the complex tax rules and possibly in administrative procedures.

Section 403(b) Plans

Section 403(b) plans are tax-favored retirement plans for employees of certain nonprofit organizations and public school systems. At one time, many employees of nonprofit organizations had no opportunity to participate in employer-sponsored retirement plans. Since they are tax exempt, nonprofit organizations had no tax incentive to provide a qualified plan. This problem was officially recognized in 1942 when the Internal Revenue Code was amended to give employees of tax-exempt organizations the opportunity to establish a tax-sheltered retirement plan. Specifically, amounts contributed by employers or by employees (within limits) are excluded from employees' current gross income for federal income tax purposes.

Originally, only annuities could be used to fund these tax-advantageous plans, so the plans were referred to as "tax-deferred annuities" (TDAs) or "tax-sheltered annuities" (TSAs). Since funding instruments other than annuities can now be used, the terms "tax-deferred annuity" and "tax-sheltered annuity" might be misleading. This text will refer to them as 403(b) plans, a term that relates to the relevant section of the Internal Revenue Code.

Eligibility

Only public school systems and organizations that qualify under the terms of Section 501(c)(3) of the Internal Revenue Code can offer 403(b) plans to their employees. More specifically, those in the latter category are nonprofit corporations, funds, community chests, and foundations that are organized and operated exclusively for religious, charitable, scientific, testing for public safety, literacy, or educational purposes, or for the prevention of cruelty to children or animals.

To qualify, an organization *cannot* do any of the following:

1. Divert any of its net earnings to an individual
2. Devote a substantial part of its activities to political purposes
3. Participate in political campaigns

Most churches and private schools qualify as 501(c)(3) organizations. State colleges and universities normally qualify. Organizations that are subdivisions of, and entirely owned by, local and state governments, such as a state hospital, can qualify.

However, some nonprofit organizations and tax-exempt organizations do not qualify as 501(c)(3) employers. To qualify, an organization must obtain a determination letter from the Internal Revenue Service stating that it is tax exempt under Section 501(c)(3). State, county, and city governments are not organized and operated *exclusively* for Section 501(c)(3) purposes and therefore cannot provide 403(b) plans.

To be eligible for participation in a 403(b) plan, a person must be a bona fide employee—not an independent contractor.[3] Furthermore, an individual in an elected or appointed position is not an employee, for purposes of the 403(b) plan laws, unless he or she has been trained for or is experienced in that particular field. For example, an attorney who is elected to the local school board would not be considered an employee. However, the local school superintendent appointed as the chairperson of the school board might be considered an employee.

Before 1989, the participation and coverage requirements of ERISA had little, if any, practical significance for 403(b) plans. This is no longer the case. Currently, if any employee elects to have contributions made to a 403(b) plan with a salary reduction agreement, the employer must allow any other employee the right to participate.[4] Plans that provide contributions by means other than a salary reduction must meet the participation and coverage requirements of ERISA.

Limitations on Contributions

Basically, three types of limitations apply to the amounts of allowable contributions to a 403(b) plan. These limitations are discussed below.

Overall Limit

The first limitation is an overall limit that applies to all qualified retirement plans. In this regard, 403(b) plans are treated as defined contribution plans. As such, the annual contributions to all plans cannot exceed either $30,000 (indexed for inflation) or 25 percent of compensation, whichever is less.

Limit on Elective Deferrals

If the plan permits salary reductions, a $9,500 limit applies to the annual amount contributed by each participant. This is a limit for each employee for all salary reduction agreements. Thus, the $9,500 limit applicable to elective deferrals to a 403(b) plan is reduced by any amounts contributed by deferrals to a CODA, a simplified employee pension (SEP) plan (discussed later in this chapter), or any other 403(b) plans. The limit does not apply to employer contributions.

Maximum Exclusion Allowance

The third limitation on 403(b) plan contributions is called the *maximum exclusion allowance*. As long as an employer's contributions to a 403(b) plan on behalf of an employee do not exceed the employee's maximum exclusion allowance, the employer's contributions are not taxable income for that employee. The allowance is determined according to a three-step formula that is beyond the scope of this text.[5]

Investment of Funds

403(b) plans can be funded with annuities or mutual funds. One of several types of annuity can be used—including single or flexible premium, deferred, and fixed or variable contracts. The annuity cannot contain more than an "incidental" amount of life insurance. The IRS uses the general rule that death benefits cannot be greater than 100 times the monthly retirement benefit. If the contract contains a greater amount, the whole contract fails to satisfy the law, and the entire amount paid as premium is taxable. Also, premiums paid for waiver of premium or disability income benefits represent taxable income.

Investments in mutual funds or closed-end investment company shares can be made through a custodian. Many mutual fund organizations have established relationships with banks to meet this requirement.

Distributions

As with the plans previously discussed, distributions from a 403(b) plan are usually fully taxable as ordinary income. Furthermore, distributions from a 403(b) plan can incur an additional 10 percent penalty tax unless the distribution is handled in one of the following ways:

1. It is made on or after the date the employee reaches age fifty-nine and one-half

2. It is made after the employee's death or disability

3. It is part of a series of substantially equal periodic payments based on the life or life expectancy of the employee (or the employee and the beneficiary) starting after the employee separates from the service of the employer

4. It is made to an employee after reaching age fifty-five and separating from service by early retirement[6]

An employee who receives a distribution from a 403(b) plan might be able to postpone tax on the amount by rolling it over to either an IRA (discussed later in the chapter) or another 403(b) plan. A rollover into a qualified pension or profit-sharing plan is not permitted.

Keogh (HR-10) Plans

Keogh (HR-10) plans, named after the Congressman who sponsored the legislation creating them, are *qualified* retirement plans for self-employed businessowners and professionals (sole proprietors and partners). They might also be referred to as HR-10 plans. Until recently, they were much more restrictive than corporate retirement plans, but now there are only a few important differences. Keogh plans now have virtual parity with corporate plans in terms of contribution limits, eligibility provisions, vesting, and the like.

Although a Keogh can be set up as a traditional defined benefit or defined contribution pension plan, most are defined contribution arrangements. In addition, a Keogh can be designed as a profit-sharing plan.

Eligibility

To be eligible for a Keogh plan, a self-employed person must contribute services to and have earned income from the business. Earned income does not include dividends, interest, royalties, and rental income (unless substantial personal services are provided). Earned income is the proprietor's or partner's share of the net earnings of the company after taking business deductions and is considered to be comparable to the compensation received by employees. A Keogh plan can also be established by a person who is self-employed on a part-time basis.

Contributions

The same contribution limits that apply to corporate qualified retirement plans also generally apply to self-employed persons and employees of a partnership or sole proprietorship in Keogh plans—that is, 25 percent or $30,000 (in a defined contribution plan). However, since the 25 percent limit (or the 15 percent limit for a profit-sharing plan only) applies to the *net* earned income (that is, income after the deduction of amounts contributed to the plan on behalf of the self-employed person and one-half of the person's self-employment taxes), the percentage limits are effectively reduced for self-employed persons.

Benefits

The benefits in a Keogh plan are essentially the same as those in a corporate plan. One exception, however, concerns loans from the plan. In a Keogh plan, loans to owner-employees (a sole proprietor or partner who owns more than 10 percent of a business—measured either by capital contribution or by share of the profits) are considered prohibited transactions. The ability to borrow from the plan, therefore, is an important distinction between Keogh and corporate plans.

Investments

The investments in a Keogh plan need not be different from those in other plans. Nonetheless, special rules are involved if a Keogh plan places funds in a life insurance contract. The law still does not allow some of the tax advantages to self-employed persons that are permitted for corporate owners for certain types of employee benefits, such as nondiscriminatory group life insurance and group health plans. As a result, no deduction is allowed in a Keogh plan for the portion of an insurance premium that is allocable to pure life insurance protection. Thus, if cash value life insurance is purchased by a Keogh plan, no deduction is available for the pure insurance cost, but the remainder of the premium is treated as a plan contribution and is deductible.

Distributions

Since Keogh plans are qualified retirement plans, the principles with regard to distributions from them are generally the same as for other qualified retirement plans. However, because Keogh plans cover self-employed persons as well as those employed by others, a few special rules apply to distributions from them. For example, a distribution to a self-employed person only because of the person's separation from service is not considered a "distribution" for favorable income tax purposes, while such a distribution to an employee could be so considered.

Individual Retirement Accounts and Annuities (IRAs)

Despite the widespread popularity of pension and profit-sharing plans, many individuals are not covered by a qualified retirement plan. In 1982, to encourage savings and investment in the economy, Congress made individual retirement accounts (IRAs) available to all employees with earned income. In 1986, however, in order to increase tax revenues by reducing tax deductions or deferrals, IRA eligibility again was restricted.

Individual retirement accounts and **individual retirement annuities** (both referred to as IRAs) are tax-favored retirement plans established and handled by employees—without any necessary involvement on the part of their employers. However, an employer, labor union, or employee association can become involved by sponsoring an IRA for its employees or by offering a payroll deduction plan.

Funds placed into an eligible person's tax-deductible IRA are deductible on his or her current tax return, thus reducing income taxes for the current year. In any case, for both tax-deductible IRAs and nondeductible IRAs, the internal buildup of earnings under an IRA incurs no current tax liabilities. However, interest and principal that were not previously taxed are taxable when withdrawn—generally during retirement, when one's income tax rate might be reduced. Premature withdrawals can also incur a 10 percent tax penalty.

Eligibility

Any employee or self-employed person who receives compensation or earned income can have an IRA even if he or she is already covered by a tax-qualified plan, a government plan, or certain annuities. Both spouses can establish an IRA if both are employed. An IRA can also be established for a nonemployed spouse of a person who receives compensation or earned income. However, as explained later, not everyone who is eligible to have an IRA will receive the same tax advantages.

Except for nonemployed spouses, a person must receive compensation or earned income to be eligible to establish an IRA. Taxable alimony and compensation from self-employment are considered eligible compensation. However, compensation does not include some forms of income, such as passive income and profits from property (interest, rents, and dividends), disability payments, or income from pensions and annuities.

Contributions

Tax deductible contributions can be made by individuals who are not *active participants* (and whose spouses are not active participants) in a qualified retirement plan. An individual is considered to be an **active participant** if money is added to his or her individual account or if he or she is eligible to earn retirement credits. Vesting of benefits is not necessary for one to be considered an active participant. However, a contribution cannot be made to an IRA in any year in which the individual is age seventy and one-half or older.

If an individual (or spouse) is not an active participant in a tax-qualified plan, the maximum deductible contribution (subject to further limitations described below) is (1) 100 percent of the individual's gross income or (2) $2,000, whichever is less. If an employer provides an IRA for its employees, but contributes less than the maximum, an employee can make up the difference and take the tax deduction. If one spouse receives no compensation or earned income, then the maximum deductible contribution for the *couple* is either (1) 100 percent of the employed partner's gross income or (2) $2,250, whichever is less.

Active participants in a qualified plan who have "adjusted gross income" (AGI), as computed on a federal income tax return, below a certain amount—called the **threshold level**—can make fully deductible IRA contributions to the maximum allowable deduction. The threshold level is $40,000 for married couples who file a joint return and $25,000 for single persons.

The amount by which the AGI exceeds the threshold level is called the **excess AGI**. If an individual's excess AGI is $10,000 or greater, a deduction will not be available for an IRA. In other words, a married couple filing a joint return can take no deduction if their AGI is $50,000 or more.

However, if the excess AGI is less than $10,000, a partial deduction is available. The formula for calculating the partial deduction limit is

$$\frac{\$10,000 - \text{Excess AGI}}{\$10,000} \times \text{Maximum allowable deduction} = \text{Deduction limit}$$

If the calculated deduction limit is between $0 and $200, the actual deduction limit is $200.

For example, suppose a husband and wife file a joint tax return showing a combined adjusted gross income of $46,000. Each spouse earns more than $2,000, and one spouse is an active participant in an employer-maintained retirement plan. Each spouse would have the following IRA deduction limit:

$$\frac{\$10,000 - \$6,000}{\$10,000} \quad \times \quad \$2,000 \quad = \quad \$800$$

Exhibit 7-1 indicates the deductions available for individual taxpayers and for married taxpayers filing separately.

Exhibit 7-1
IRA Deduction/Compensation Limits
(Assuming the taxpayer or spouse is an active plan participant)

	Adjusted Gross Income Range		
	Full IRA[1] Deduction	Reduced IRA[2] Deduction	No IRA Deduction
Individual	up to $25,000	$25,000 - 34,999.99	$35,000 or over
Married Couple (Joint Return)	up to $40,000	$40,000 - 49,999.99	$50,000 or over
Married (Filing Separately)	not available	$.01 - 9,999.99	$10,000 or over

1. Full IRA deduction for an individual is $2,000. Full IRA deduction for a married couple filing jointly is $2,250.

2. The formula for determining the reduced deduction is as follows:
$$\text{deduction unit} = \frac{\$10,000 - \text{excess AGI}}{\$10,000} \times \text{maximum deduction allowed}$$

Contributions to an IRA can be made at any time prior to the due date for the individual's (or the couple's) filing of the federal tax return for the taxable year in which the deduction is taken. Therefore, contributions can be made as early as January 1 and before knowing how much will be tax deductible. However, a person who overstates the amount of deductible contributions on his or her income tax return is subject to a possible penalty for each overstatement.

Spousal IRAs

A spouse with income is entitled to, but not required to have, his or her own IRA. The spouse can use the spousal IRA provision—in effect, choosing to be treated as though he or she had no income.

Nondeductible Contributions

Individuals can make *nondeductible* contributions up to the individual's regular contribution limits and to the extent that they are ineligible for deductible contributions. The advantage is that *earnings* on nondeductible contributions are not subject to income taxation until they are withdrawn.

Excess Contributions

Contributions that exceed the limits described previously are **excess contributions** and are subject to a nondeductible excess contribution tax of 6 percent. If the funds from the excess contributions remain in the plan, the 6 percent tax is imposed on the funds each year. One way of eliminating the penalty tax is to reduce contributions in the year following the excess contribution. However, this is a "one-way street." A person who contributed less than the maximum amount allowed in previous years cannot subsequently make an excess contribution to take advantage of deductions that were lost in the past.

Investment of Funds

Individuals can shelter retirement savings in two ways: (1) individual retirement accounts or (2) individual retirement annuities. Both are referred to as IRAs, but each is a different savings vehicle with distinct characteristics.

Individual Retirement Accounts

To open an individual retirement account, a person enters into an agreement with a trustee or a custodian and can invest the funds in a wide variety of assets (other than life insurance). Some financial institutions also provide accounts with investments individually directed by the participant.

Many types of financial institutions—including banks, savings and loan (S&L) associations, life insurance companies, mutual funds, and credit unions—offer individual retirement accounts. These organizations normally have preapproved prototype plans involving minimal administrative effort by the individual investor.

Individual retirement accounts can be invested in one or more of the following investment vehicles, among others:

1. Mutual fund shares (with various investment objectives)
2. Bank savings accounts
3. Bank certificates of deposit
4. Common stock

5. Savings and loan shares

6. Savings and loan certificates of deposit

7. Bonds

8. Credit union accounts

9. Real estate investment shares

As a general rule, IRA funds cannot be invested in collectibles. An exception allows investments in certain U.S. minted gold and silver coins.

Individual Retirement Annuities

If the retirement plan is funded with annuities only, a trustee or custodian is not necessary. Contributions can be placed with a life insurance company to purchase a flexible premium deferred annuity contract.

Insurance companies have prototype plans and specialized contracts designed for the individual retirement annuity market. Individual retirement annuities issued since 1978 must have flexible premiums. Participating or nonparticipating contracts can be used, and dividends can be used to decrease future premiums or to increase benefits.

Selecting a Funding Instrument

In selecting a particular account or annuity, a person should consider investment risks, expected returns, flexibility, simplicity, and special services that may be provided. No matter which funding instrument is chosen, the funds must be nontransferable and nonforfeitable.

Distributions

IRAs are generally intended to provide retirement income. However, it also is possible to make preretirement withdrawals, but they might be subject to certain tax penalties.

Premature Distributions

A person who takes a distribution from an IRA before age fifty-nine and one-half incurs a 10 percent penalty tax on the entire amount withdrawn. This penalty is in addition to current income tax on the distribution itself. However, the penalty tax will not be imposed on distributions of the following types:

1. Those made to a beneficiary (or to the individual's estate) on or after the individual's death

2. Those attributable to the individual's total disability
3. Those that are part of a series of substantially equal periodic payments (not less often than annually) made for the life or the life expectancy of the individual or the joint lives or the joint life expectancies of the individual and his or her beneficiary
4. Those that are part of a qualified domestic relations order

It might be noted that a premature distribution occurs if the individual borrows from the plan or uses the assets as security for a loan.

Retirement Benefits

Even if the owner of an IRA has not retired, he or she must begin to take distributions no later than April 1 of the calendar year following the year when the owner reaches age seventy and one-half. If all distributions are derived from deductible contributions, all the distributions will be taxable as ordinary income. If nondeductible contributions have been made, each distribution will consist of a taxable and nontaxable portion.

The law requires certain *minimum* distributions. The general idea is that a person must take at least the amount required to exhaust the funds evenly over his or her life expectancy (or over the joint life expectancy of the person and his or her beneficiary, subject to certain limits). A severe penalty tax, equivalent to 50 percent of the difference between the minimum required distribution and the actual distribution, is imposed on insufficient distributions.

IRA Transfers and Rollovers

A **rollover** is the transfer of funds from one type of account to another type. Using a so-called "rollover" provision, an individual is allowed (under certain conditions) to transfer money from and to an IRA without incurring any tax liability.

IRA-to-IRA Rollovers and Transfers

In this category are rollovers and direct transfers that permit IRA owners to make tax-free exchanges of one IRA for another.

In an *IRA-to-IRA rollover*, three major conditions are required to achieve a tax-free rollover:

1. A person must transfer the funds to the new plan no later than the sixtieth day after the funds were received. Funds not transferred to the new IRA within sixty days of being distributed from the existing IRA to the individual are taxed as part of that person's gross income for the year.

2. If property other than money is transferred, the same property must be shifted to the new plan. (Although a life insurance contract cannot be rolled into an IRA, it is possible to have a tax-free rollover of the cash value of a life insurance policy.)

3. Rollovers are permitted only once per year.

In addition, tax-free *direct IRA transfers* can be made. These involve the transfer of IRA assets directly from one plan sponsor to another without those assets going into the hands of the IRA owner. The tax law does not limit the number of such direct transfers that can be made in any one year.

Rollovers From a Qualified Retirement Plan

In this category of rollovers, participants in qualified retirement plans can elect to have certain taxable distributions from these plans either transferred or rolled over to an IRA or to another qualified plan that will accept such transfers or rollovers and thus defer the income tax on the distribution. Therefore, the participant can choose one of two options:

1. Have his or her employer *transfer directly* or *directly roll over* all or any part of the taxable distribution to the participant's IRA or to another employer's qualified retirement plan that will accept such transfers

2. Have the distribution paid to the participant who then *rolls over* all or any part of the taxable distribution to the participant's rollover IRA or to another employer's qualified retirement plan that will accept such rollovers within sixty days of the participant's receipt of the distribution

The technical distinction between these choices is that in the case of the direct transfer or direct rollover there effectively is a trustee-to-trustee transfer of part or all of an eligible rollover distribution to an eligible retirement plan (such as the participant's rollover IRA). But, for the rollover alternative, the eligible rollover distribution is first paid to the participant, who then rolls over part or all of the distribution to an eligible retirement plan (such as the participant's rollover IRA) within sixty days of receiving the distribution.[7]

The Unemployment Compensation Amendments of 1992 established a requirement on employers, effective for distributions after December 31, 1992, of a mandatory 20 percent income tax withholding for eligible rollover distributions *unless* the distributee of the eligible rollover distribution elects to have the distribution directly transferred (or directly rolled over) to an eligible retirement plan, such as the distributee's rollover IRA. In effect, then, a rollover is subject to mandatory 20 percent withholding, while a direct transfer (or direct rollover) is not. To avoid further penalty, the employee who receives a distribution must roll it, including an amount equal to the 20 percent withheld (in other words, the full amount distributed), into an eligible retirement plan within sixty days. The employee can then apply for a refund of the 20 percent withheld on the current year's federal income tax form. Most people believe that this provision will strongly encourage direct transfers (or direct rollovers) over rollovers in which the participant actually receives the money or other property first and then rolls it over. The policy objective for these changes in rollover rules was to encourage keeping qualified retirement plan distributions in the retirement plan system.

When a surviving spouse of a deceased participant in a qualified retirement plan receives a distribution that qualifies as an eligible rollover distribution as the death beneficiary named by the participant under the plan, the surviving spouse also can directly transfer or roll over all or any part of the distribution to the surviving spouse's own IRA under generally the same rules as a participant. Note, however, that a surviving spouse cannot transfer or roll over such a distribution to the spouse's own employer's qualified retirement plan. This tax-deferred rollover treatment applies only to a surviving spouse; no other death beneficiary (such as a trust for the surviving spouse, for example) can utilize this generally favorable tax treatment.

Simplified Employee Pension (SEP) Plans

A **simplified employee pension (SEP) plan** is a retirement plan that closely resembles an IRA, but has higher annual contribution limits and is sponsored by the employer. An employer can sponsor a SEP plan in addition to a qualified pension or profit-sharing plan. SEPs are popular with small employers, especially sole proprietors, because they are easy to set up and do not involve much of the paperwork required for Keoghs.

Eligibility

The employer must include in a SEP every employee who has done the following:

1. Attained age twenty-one
2. Performed services for the employer during the current calendar year
3. Performed services for the employer during at least three of the preceding five calendar years
4. Received at least $3,000 compensation from the employer for the calendar year

The law allows the employer to exclude union employees and nonresident aliens under the usual rules applicable to pension plans. However, an employer cannot restrict participation to those who consent to participate or make contributions to the plan.

Contributions

The maximum amount an employer can contribute to a SEP for an employee is $30,000 or 15 percent of the employee's compensation—whichever is less. Sole proprietors or partners are treated as employees for contribution purposes but can contribute only 13.043 percent of their net profit.

Employees in certain small plans might be able to elect (choose) to have the employer make contributions to the SEP or to receive the amounts as cash compensation. These elective salary reduction arrangements under SEPs have the same annual limit on elective deferrals as under the Section 401(k) arrangements discussed previously. The option to elect SEP contributions or cash is available only in certain situations:

*   When at least 50 percent of the employees elect to have salary reduction amounts contributed to the SEP
*   When the employer has had twenty-five or fewer employees at any time during the preceding year
*   When the deferral percentage of each "highly compensated employee" does not exceed 1.25 times the average deferral percentage for all nonhighly-compensated employees

Amounts contributed for an employee and the elective deferrals (if any) are excludable from the participant's gross income. In other words, there is no current federal income tax liability on money contributed to the SEP.

The plan document must contain a definite, written allocation formula for employer contributions. Employer contributions cannot discriminate in favor of highly compensated employees or self-employed persons.

Distributions

The employee has nonforfeitable access to the account funds. Thus, deferred vesting is not permitted. In fact, the plan document for a SEP must contain a statement that the employer imposes no restrictions on the participant's rights to withdraw funds. Furthermore, funds in a SEP must be nonassignable and nontransferable by participants. Rollovers, however, are permitted.

Because a SEP is a type of IRA, most of the IRA rules pertaining to withdrawals, transfers, rollovers, and taxation apply. These are explained in the section on IRAs.

Employee Stock Ownership Plans (ESOPs)

An **employee stock ownership plan (ESOP)** is a qualified retirement plan based on the use of stock in the employer corporation as a funding instrument. It provides a method by which employees receive employer stock and through which the employer raises funds. Most ESOPs serve two purposes:

1.   To provide financing to a corporation
2.   To provide an employee benefit

Over the years, ESOPs have attracted a great deal of attention. Although the number of these plans is relatively small compared with the number of other plans that provide retirement benefits, their use has grown.

ESOPs as a Financing Technique

Many ESOPs are *leveraged*, which means that the ESOP borrows money from a financial institution and that cash is traded for stock that is issued by the company. Exhibit 7-2 illustrates how this arrangement might provide funds to a company.

First, notice that three organizations are involved in a typical leveraged ESOP—a corporation (the employer), a lender (which can be a bank or another type of financial institution), and the ESOT (an employee stock ownership *trust*).

Line 1 in the illustration depicts a loan made by the lender to the ESOT. The trustee invests the amount borrowed in newly issued corporate stock at its fair market value (see line 2). At this stage, the company has raised funds by selling new common stock, and the ESOT has invested in the company's securities.

Line 3 indicates that a note is given to the lender. Line 4 represents the fact that the company guarantees the satisfactory fulfillment of the provisions of the note in the event that the ESOT fails to fulfill its obligation.

The annual contributions to the ESOT (line 5) can be used by the ESOT to pay the installment payments on the debt (line 6). Subject to the limits in the law, these payments are tax deductible by the corporation as contributions to a qualified trust.

The results of these transactions, listed below, can be attractive to all parties.

*   The lender makes a loan that is guaranteed by a corporation with earning power as well as by a note from the ESOT.

Exhibit 7-2
Illustration of an ESOP

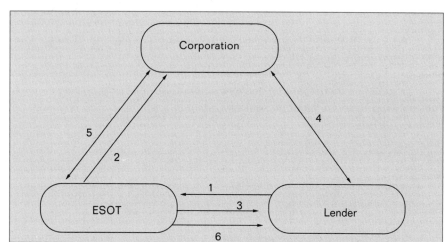

- The employees accumulate common stock in the company on a tax-favored basis.
- The corporation raises funds in an efficient manner, and the payments to the ESOT (for both principal and interest) are tax deductible. Furthermore, employees are likely to become more productive and dedicated as they gain an equity position in the company.

The ESOP described above is referred to as a **leveraged ESOP,** since it relies on borrowed money. Not all ESOPs use debt. Plans that do not rely on debt (often called **basic** or **ordinary ESOPs**) operate in much the same way but without the lender. The employer contributes funds to the ESOT, which invests in the common stock of the employer.

ESOPs as an Employee Benefit

As an employee benefit, ESOPs closely resemble profit-sharing plans. The ERISA rules for employee participation and vesting apply to ESOPs, and the requirements concerning the allocation of funds to employees are the same. In addition, the limits imposed on the maximum amounts that can be deducted by the employer are the same.

One important difference between ESOPs and profit-sharing plans is that ESOPs are designed to invest primarily in the securities of the employer. A profit-sharing plan is permitted to invest up to 100 percent of the plan assets in company stock under certain circumstances, but it is unusual that a profit-sharing plan would actually do this. ESOPs, however, are not exempt from the rules regarding prudent investments, and the trustee(s) must act solely for the benefit of employees and their beneficiaries.

Confining investments primarily to the employer's securities can have advantages and disadvantages for employees. If the company prospers, the stock might appreciate. If the company does not perform well, an employee could lose his or her job at the same time the invested funds are declining in value. Also, when a company issues new stock, the increasing number of shares will cause dilution of already outstanding stock and might cause earnings per share to decline.

An issue for ESOPs (and a general difference from profit-sharing plans) is valuation of the employer's stock. ERISA stipulates that the price paid for company stock cannot exceed "fair market value." When securities are purchased in an active market, there is little problem. ESOPs, however, have special appeal to small- and medium-sized companies. If the stock of such closely-held companies is not actively traded, a qualified appraiser must be used to establish the fair market value.

The allocation of benefits to employees in an ESOP is usually based on compensation, as it is in a profit-sharing plan. However, employees might not be entitled to receive shares that are pledged as collateral for a loan. If an employee retires, for example, and becomes entitled to a distribution, only the unencumbered shares might be available. At a later date, when the stock is released from the assignment, the additional shares become available.

Supplemental Executive Retirement Plans (SERPs) and Nonqualified Deferred Compensation Plans

Qualified retirement plans have substantial tax advantages for both the employer and the employee. In return for these advantages, a plan must not discriminate in favor of "highly compensated employees." Consequently, for this reason and other tax law requirements, an employer might want to supplement the retirement income of certain more highly paid employees.

Methods of providing larger benefits to such highly paid employees exist through the establishment of **supplemental executive retirement plans (SERPs)** and **nonqualified deferred compensation plans**.

These plans can also be used for a variety of purposes in addition to providing benefits for highly compensated employees. Such plans can be used to recruit and retain important or key employees as well as to meet any special circumstances of the employer and/or employee.[8]

Many different types of SERPs and nonqualified deferred compensation plans exist, ranging from very simple to extremely complex arrangements. The basic difference between SERPs and nonqualified deferred compensation plans stems from whether the key employee has already earned the benefit in question.[9]

If additional retirement benefits are provided, the plan is called a SERP. Many different defined benefit and defined contribution approaches can be used by the employer to provide additional retirement benefits to selected executives.[10] For example, a SERP can be used for the following:

1. To restore benefits that have been limited because of maximum limits under qualified retirement plans
2. To provide incentives for key executives
3. To provide unreduced benefits at an early retirement age

Nonqualified deferred compensation arrangements, on the other hand, are provided primarily to save federal income taxes on current executive compensation and to defer that compensation to the future. Such deferred compensation plans can also be used to even out the effect of executive bonuses, to tie the executive to the firm for a specified period, and to provide for the executive to be available for consulting work on behalf of the employer after retirement.[11]

Both SERPs and nonqualified deferred compensation plans can be an important part of an employer's and employee's planning to meet the retirement exposure. Such plans should be enacted only after carefully establishing the objectives to be served by such plans in total employee benefit and compensation planning.

A nonqualified deferred compensation plan can provide significant tax advantages to an employee by postponing the payment of income and income taxes until the employee might be in a lower tax bracket. In contrast, a raise might have marginal appeal because of the associated large tax liability. Moreover, the person might be more concerned about retirement income than about additional current income. Furthermore, such a plan would provide additional income to the executive when it is needed—after retirement.

Summary

This chapter described a number of sources of retirement income other than Social Security, income from capital accumulations, annuities, and pension plans. Each was discussed generally in terms of eligibility, contributions, benefits, and investment of funds. Tax status and distribution procedures were also discussed when appropriate.

In profit-sharing plans, the employer contributes to a fund for employees' retirement income. Employer contributions for any one year are usually based on the profits of the corporation for that year.

A savings plan is a form of profit sharing. Employees must make contributions to participate, and the employer often matches these contributions, sometimes dollar for dollar but more often at some reduced percentage of the employee's dollar. The employee is typically allowed to decide how to invest his or her account balance.

A CODA is a profit-sharing plan that meets the rules in Section 401(k) of the tax code. Contributions can be made by the employee, by the employer, or both. Funds accumulate on a tax-sheltered basis until they are distributed. Withdrawals can be made without a significant penalty only under restricted conditions.

Section 403(b) plans are tax-favored retirement plans for employees of certain nonprofit organizations. Employees are eligible only if they work for public school systems or organizations that qualify under the terms of Section 501(c)(3) of the Internal Revenue Code. Contributions to this plan are limited by an overall limit, a limit on elective deferrals, and a maximum exclusion allowance.

Keogh plans are qualified retirement plans for self-employed persons. To be eligible, the owner must contribute services to, and earn income from, the business. As in other plans, the contribution limit is 25 percent of compensation or $30,000, whichever is lower.

Individual retirement accounts (IRAs) can be established by an individual, without any involvement on the part of his or her employer. Any employee or self-employed person can have an IRA. Those who meet certain requirements can invest up to $2,000 per year into an IRA on a tax-deferred basis. Any unpaid taxes on principal, and all taxes on interest, must be paid when funds are withdrawn during retirement. Penalty is due for early withdrawal.

A simplified employee pension (SEP) plan is a nonqualified pension plan that closely resembles an employer-sponsored IRA but has higher annual contribution limits.

An employee stock ownership plan (ESOP) is a qualified retirement plan based on the use of stock in the employer corporation as a funding instrument.

These plans can function both as a financing technique for the employer and as a benefit system for the employee. They are similar to profit-sharing plans in terms of ERISA rules for employee participation, vesting, the allocation of funds to employees, and the limit on the maximum amounts contributed by the employer. However, ESOPs must be primarily invested in the securities of the employer.

A supplemental executive retirement plan (SERP) provides larger benefits to highly paid employees whose benefit levels are otherwise limited by the law. Nonqualified deferred compensation plans delay the receipt of income that has been earned, and therefore defer tax liabilities.

Chapter Notes

1. A pre-ERISA money purchase pension plan is a defined contribution pension plan that was in existence on June 27, 1974, and which, at that time, included a salary reduction arrangement. Thus, this is a rather narrow category of "grandfathered" pension plans. As noted previously, most CODAs are in qualified savings plans.

2. For further information on ADP tests, please see Everett T. Allen, Jr., Joseph J. Melone, Jerry S. Rosenbloom, and Jack L. VanDerhei, *Pension Planning*, 7th ed. (Homewood, IL: Business One Irwin, 1992), pp. 234-235.

3. Generally, an employee is defined as a person who acts for another under a contract of wages with the employer and whose activities are controlled by the employer. An independent contractor might have a contract for wages or other remuneration, but only the results to be achieved are under the control of the other party. The independent contractor controls the methods and means of doing the work.

4. The right to participate must include those who want a salary reduction of more than $200 and does not include individuals covered under certain other plans, resident aliens, students who work fewer than twenty hours per week, and employees of churches.

5. If further information is required with respect to the formula for calculating the maximum exclusion allowance, see Allen, Melone, Rosenbloom, and VanDerhei, *Pension Planning*, pp. 462-463.

6. Two other exceptions are (1) a "qualified domestic relations order" and (2) distributions less than the amount allowable as a medical deduction.

7. The definition of an **eligible rollover distribution** for this purpose is any taxable distribution to a participant other than distributions consisting of substantially equal periodic payments over the lifetime of the participant (and his or her designated beneficiary) or distributions for a specified period of ten years or more and certain other distributions.

8. For a more complete discussion of executive retirement plans, see Garry M. Teesdale and Bernard E. Schaeffer, "Executive Retirement Benefit Plans," in

Handbook of Employee Benefits, ed. Jerry S. Rosenbloom (Homewood, IL: Dow Jones-Irwin, 1988), 3rd ed., pp. 897-914; and Allen, Melone, Rosenbloom, and VanDerhei, *Pension Planning*, Chapter 26.

9. Allen, Melone, Rosenbloom, and VanDerhei, *Pension Planning*, p. 475.
10. Teesdale and Schaeffer, *Handbook of Employee Benefits*, pp. 899-903.
11. Teesdale and Schaeffer, *Handbook of Employee Benefits*, pp. 903-904.

Chapter 8

Estate Planning and Business Continuation Planning

This chapter deals with the two important topics of estate planning and planning for the continuation of various kinds of closely held business interests in the event of the death or disability of an owner or owners. The issues arising out of both of these topics often involve the purchase of life insurance, annuities, and disability insurance to solve the various tax and other problems involved. In fact, estate planning and business continuation planning frequently call for the purchases of substantial amounts of life insurance because the property values (and taxes) involved are so large. Therefore, an understanding of both of these rather complex subjects can be of considerable importance to insurance professionals.

Estate Planning

The term **estate planning** refers to arrangements for the efficient transfer of property, during lifetime or at death, from one person to another person (or persons).

Virtually everyone has an **estate**, which is a person's accumulated wealth. Estate planning should not be limited to those with large estates. In fact, estate planning can be more important for the owner of a small- or medium-sized estate than for a wealthy person because improper estate planning can have a proportionately greater effect on those without large estates.

Estate planning is done mainly *during* one's lifetime. Risk management is part of the estate planning process, when viewed broadly, because it helps a person to increase the value of his or her estate by preventing loss and reducing the consequences of loss. Managing one's investment program is also part of the estate planning process, when viewed broadly, because it also helps to increase the value of the estate by increasing one's wealth. However, these processes are only indirectly related to the transfer of property. An estate plan deals directly with the distribution of property.

An estate plan exists for every person, even those who haven't actively made a plan of their own, since assets will be distributed at death according to state intestate law in the absence of a consciously prepared will or other arrangement. (Wills and dying intestate are discussed later in this chapter.) However, many people have ill-conceived estate plans. An improper plan might distribute assets contrary to the wishes of the estate owner or might result in unnecessary taxes and estate administration costs.

Efficient estate planning has the following results:

1. *It distributes assets according to the desires of the estate owners.* Many people want to specify which heir receives particular pieces of property or amounts of their estates.

2. *It minimizes estate and inheritance taxes.* **Estate taxes** are imposed on the right to transfer property at death, while **inheritance taxes** are imposed on the right of beneficiaries and heirs to receive property from a decedent. Thus, estate taxes can reduce the value of an estate, while inheritance taxes reduce the value of one's inheritance.

3. *It minimizes income taxes.* During a person's lifetime, estates can be built through tax-deferred or tax-free means. In addition, arrangements can be made to transfer estates to heirs without the heirs being subjected to income taxes on their inheritance.

4. *It minimizes probate costs.* **Probate** refers to the transfer of property by will or *intestate laws* (which apply if a person dies without a will). Costs involved in probate proceedings include costs to distribute the estate and costs to defend against challenges to a will.

Conflicts often arise among these four basic objectives. For example, conflict might occur between tax savings and the distribution of property to the desired persons in appropriate amounts at the desired time. If Sam, an estate owner, wants to pass property to his children at his death, the property might be subject to tax as part of his estate. However, if Sam leaves the property to his wife, who then gives it to his children at some future date, the property is not subject to estate tax when Sam dies. If such a conflict exists, the estate owner must decide which objective is more important and how the objectives should be balanced.

Estate planners regularly recommend life insurance as a means of financing estate planning objectives in case the client dies before accumulating adequate investments to finance his or her postmortem objectives. Life insurance is one of the best ways to create available cash at the time of death. It is an ideal way to provide funds to pay estate taxes, fund the transfer of business ownership, provide cash for estate administration, and provide funds to surviving family members for both immediate needs and long-term support.

Parties Involved in Estate Planning

Designing and implementing an efficient estate plan can be simple or complex, depending on circumstances. If a property owner has many types of property and a large estate, a substantial amount of expertise in several areas might be needed. Few financial advisers are competent to handle all aspects of a sophisticated case. What frequently is needed, in complicated cases, is a *team* of advisers.

Normally an estate planning team consists of an attorney, an accountant, a trust officer, an investment counselor, and a life insurance specialist. An attorney is needed for legal advice concerning the overall plan and for drafting and reviewing wills and other legal instruments. An accountant is needed to provide technical advice on taxes and financial statements. A trust officer might be necessary if a trust is used to implement an estate plan. Furthermore, an investment counselor can provide advice for maintaining and increasing the estate's value.

A life insurance specialist often provides two vital functions to the estate planning team. First, he or she might be the one to initiate an estate plan (or a review of an existing plan). Second, he or she is the most knowledgeable person to select the proper insurance product to be used for an estate plan.

Overview of Estate Planning

Generally, estate plans are developed in a series of five steps called the **estate planning process**:

1. Gather facts
2. Evaluate the existing estate plan

3. Formulate and test a new estate plan
4. Execute the new estate plan
5. Periodically review and revise the estate plan

Gather Facts

The first step in making an estate plan is to obtain facts about the estate owner's present and anticipated estate and how he or she prefers to have the estate distributed. Normally, a standardized questionnaire is used rather than an informal method of collecting the information.

Knowing the names, ages, health, income, occupation, and residence of all close family members is essential to beginning an estate plan, as is a complete description of the estate owner's assets and liabilities. Each asset should be identified and valued, and the legal ownership of each should be determined. It should be clear, for example, whether a savings account in a bank is individually owned or in some form of joint ownership. Included in the gathered facts should be the estate owner's status in any employee benefit plans and the Social Security program. Anticipated changes in the person's and family's financial condition should be considered to the extent to which they can be foreseen. The existing estate plan should be described completely, and questions about the estate owner's will, any trusts in effect, and any gifts the estate owner has made should be noted.

The estate owner's desires for transfer of the property at death should be ascertained. The person must indicate to whom he or she wants the property to be distributed, when the distribution should be made, and in what amounts. An estate owner might want a charity or an educational institution to receive some of the property. The estate owner might believe children should not have complete access to the property until they reach a certain age.

These questions can be complicated by business interests. For example, if a small business is to be transferred to a child, the child might not have the necessary qualifications to manage the company. Furthermore, if one child takes over the business, the other assets must still be divided and the estate balanced among other children or family members. These are just a couple of examples of the types of problems that can be involved in distributing the estate according to the estate owner's desires.

Evaluate the Existing Estate Plan

The second step in the estate planning process is an analysis of the existing estate plan. It can be tested by determining how the property would be distributed if the estate owner were to die immediately. Starting with this assumption, property must be classified (normally by an attorney) according to whether it would be included or excluded from the **probate estate** (the property passed to others by will or intestacy law) and the **gross estate** (probate property as well as property transferred by other means, such as by a beneficiary designation on a life insurance policy) for federal estate tax purposes. Next, the amount of estate shrinkage that will occur when the person dies must be estimated. **Shrinkage** is a decrease in the value of an estate and is normal because of creditors' claims, estate administration costs, and taxes.

If the estate owner is married, these calculations should be made under several assumptions. One calculation should show the effect on the estate if the husband dies first; another computation should be based on the wife's dying first. In addition, the costs of successive estate transfers (assuming the second spouse dies shortly after the first) should be estimated.

An analysis of the existing estate plan helps determine the need for cash at the estate owner's death to (1) pay debts, estate administration costs, and taxes, and (2) make cash transfers to beneficiaries. The plan should be designed so that involuntary liquidation of any estate assets is not necessary.

The legal instruments used in the existing plan should be reviewed to see whether they distribute assets according to the estate owner's wishes. They should also be checked to determine whether they are up to date in view of prevailing legal and tax practices. Recent changes in tax law, for example, might not be reflected in the existing plan.

Formulate and Test a New Estate Plan

The third step in the estate planning process is to develop and test a revised estate plan to be certain that it overcomes the weaknesses of the existing plan.

Execute the New Estate Plan

After the new estate plan is developed, it must be implemented. Often, this requires the purchase of additional life insurance, the drawing up of legal documents, or the making of gifts.

Periodically Review and Revise the Estate Plan

Estate planning is a continuing process. Laws, legal concepts, planning techniques, and the personal and financial circumstances of most individuals change over time. Therefore, estate plans should be reviewed periodically (perhaps annually) and adjusted as necessary.

Tax Issues

Tax planning should not dominate the estate planning process. However, careful consideration should be given to the tax consequences of any estate plan. Federal estate taxes, state death taxes, federal gift taxes, and possibly even the federal generation-skipping transfer tax can substantially erode an estate. However, sound estate planning can substantially increase the amount of money that escapes taxation and is instead passed to heirs. The following discussion explains the nature of these various taxes and briefly describes some estate planning approaches that can reduce their impact.

Federal Estate Tax

A **federal estate tax** is imposed on the privilege of transferring property at death. It is levied on the estate itself, not on the beneficiaries or heirs who receive the property. Depending on the circumstances, this tax can be the largest tax involved in an estate planning situation.

Four basic steps are followed in the computation of the estate tax:

1. Determining the *gross estate*
2. Subtracting allowable deductions to arrive at the *taxable estate*
3. Applying federal estate tax rates to the taxable estate to determine the *tentative tax*
4. Subtracting credits to arrive at the *tax payable* (if any)

Gross Estate

An individual's gross estate includes all interests (tangible and intangible) in real and personal property, wherever the property is situated. The value of each asset is measured at its fair market value.

The executor must select as a valuation date either the date of death or the date six months later. The same date applies to all property, with the exception of property distributed, sold, or exchanged during the six-month period, which is valued as of the date of the transfer.

Property owned by a decedent is included in the gross estate. Examples include a home, business interests, real estate investments, bank accounts, stocks, bonds, mutual funds, household furnishings, jewelry, professional tools and equipment, and autos. The gross estate also includes accrued but unreceived income.

Jointly Owned Property Jointly owned property is subject to the following rules when determining the amount to include in a decedent's gross estate:

1. *Fractional interest rule*. Property owned jointly with a *spouse* is included in the gross estate of the first spouse to die, according to the **fractional interest rule**. This rule treats property as belonging *half* to each owner; however, it applies only to property owned with spouses as joint tenants with rights of survivorship or as tenants by the entireties. (Under either form of ownership, when one spouse dies, the full ownership of the property is given to the surviving spouse.) Suppose, for example, that Al and his wife, Bev, invest in a mutual fund, as joint tenants with rights of survivorship, using $10,000 of Al's money and $5,000 of Bev's money. Suppose their interest in the fund is worth $30,000 at the time of Al's death. Exactly $15,000 of this asset—half its current value—will be included in his gross estate.

2. *Consideration furnished rule*. Jointly owned property not held by a husband and wife as joint tenants with right of survivorship is subject to the **consideration furnished rule**. According to this rule, if the surviving joint owner can *prove* he or she contributed to the original purchase price of the property, only the proportion contributed by the deceased owner will be included in the decedent's estate. Surviving joint owners often have difficulty proving they contributed to the original purchase price. Without such proof, the entire value is included in the deceased's gross estate.

    Suppose, for example, that Tricia and her daughter Lynn, as joint tenants with right of survivorship, own common stock that has a present value of $30,000. Assume that Tricia originally contributed $10,000 and Lynn originally contributed $5,000 to the purchase price of the stock. In the event of Tricia's death, two-thirds of the total $30,000—$20,000—will be included in her gross estate because she contributed two-thirds of the original purchase price. However, if Lynn cannot prove she contributed $5,000 of the purchase price, $30,000 will be included in Tricia's estate.

Life Insurance Life insurance in which the insured has any *incidents of ownership* at the time of his or her death is included in the insured's gross estate, regardless of beneficiary designation. **Incidents of ownership**, as examples, include the power to do the following:

1. Designate or change the beneficiary on the life insurance policy
2. Surrender the policy
3. Assign or borrow the cash value of the policy

However, the payment of premiums is not regarded as an incident of ownership.

If a person possesses *any* incidents of ownership in life insurance on his or her life, the full amount of the insurance proceeds will be included in his or her gross estate. If the policy is jointly owned, the full proceeds will be included in the decedent's estate, less any premium payment amounts furnished by the surviving joint tenant when the joint tenants are not married. Furthermore, if an individual *indirectly* possesses an incident of ownership, the proceeds might be included in his or her gross estate. For example, a life insurance policy owned by a corporation of which the insured owns more than 50 percent will be included in the insured's estate to the extent that someone other than the corporation is named as beneficiary. In addition, if the insured dies within three years of transferring the incidents of ownership of life insurance on his or her life, the full amount of the death proceeds will be brought back for inclusion in his or her gross estate for federal estate tax purposes at the insured's death.

Policyowners are often advised to keep life insurance policies out of their gross estates for tax purposes. However, it is important to consider the loss of control and possible loss of the asset when incidents of ownership are relinquished to keep the insurance out of the estate.

When desired, life insurance proceeds can be kept out of an insured's gross estate by making certain the insured possesses no incidents of ownership at death. This can be accomplished in the following ways:

- At policy inception, someone other than the insured can be named as owner of the policy. For example, a son can apply for a policy on the life of his mother and possess all ownership rights. At the mother's death, the proceeds will not be included in her gross estate. If the son dies before his mother, only the cash value of the policy will be included in his estate.

- For an existing policy, it is possible to remove the proceeds from the insured's estate by absolutely assigning all incidents of ownership to another person or an irrevocable trust more than three years before the insured's death. However, the transfer might have gift and income tax consequences that should be carefully examined.

Estate tax laws and regulations generally are not organized according to traditional types of life insurance and related plans. However, some generalizations can be made as to their estate tax treatment based on the just described general principles of the estate taxation of life insurance:

- *Group life insurance.* Group life insurance is included in an insured employee's estate if he or she possessed any incidents of ownership, such as the right to name the beneficiary. In recent years, most states have specifically authorized (and many group policies have permitted) the transfer of an employee's ownership rights in his or her group term life insurance if the employee wishes to relinquish his or her incidents of ownership in this type of coverage.

- *Key employee life insurance.* If a key employee life insurance policy (discussed later in this chapter) is properly arranged, the employer possesses all incidents of ownership and the proceeds will not be included in the insured employee's estate.

- *Split dollar.* In split dollar plans (discussed later in this chapter), the insured generally possesses at least some incidents of ownership, and the insured's beneficiary receives the face amount less the indebtedness to the employer. It can be argued that only the amount payable to the employee's beneficiary is included in the deceased employee's estate. However, steps might be taken to remove all incidents of ownership from the employee. One method is to place all incidents of ownership with the employer and the employee's beneficiary. If the employee's beneficiary is given the ownership rights normally given to the employee, no part of the proceeds should be included in the beneficiary's estate if he or she should predecease the insured.

- *Annuities.* The gross estate of an individual includes any annuity values that exist at the time of death. If death occurs before benefit payments begin, the accumulated value of the contract is included in the estate. If death occurs after benefits have been started, the present value of all future payments, if any, will be included in the estate.

- *Social Security.* Social Security benefits, including the lump-sum death benefit and the value of monthly survivor benefits, are *not* included in a person's estate.

- *Nonqualified deferred compensation arrangements.* For estate tax purposes, nonqualified deferred compensation benefits are treated in the same fashion as annuities. The present value of any post-death benefits is included in the employee's estate. This is true even if benefits in the plan might be forfeited prior to the employee's death.

Taxable Estate

The second step in calculating the estate tax is to subtract allowable deductions from the gross estate's value to arrive at a **taxable estate**. These deductions are summarized below.

Funeral and Administrative Expenses

Allowable funeral expenses include the costs of the funeral service and burial, a cemetery plot, and a monument or headstone. Administrative costs include attorney's fees, accountant's fees, executor's fees, appraisal costs, court costs, and necessary expenses to maintain (but not improve) estate property. Deductible administrative expenses are not limited to expenses associated with the probate estate but include expenses incurred to administer assets outside the probate estate.

Debts   Allowable deductions include claims against the estate, such as personal obligations of the decedent that exist at the time of death. Obligations incurred after the decedent's death are not deductible.

Losses   Casualty and theft losses during estate administration are deductible from the gross estate to the extent that they are not compensated for by insurance.

Marital Deduction   If a person is married at the time of death, the full amount of the property included in the gross estate that passes (or has passed) to a surviving spouse is deductible (subject to certain requirements explained below). This **marital deduction** is limited to the value of property that actually passes to the spouse. If, for example, the decedent has an estate of $800,000 but only $600,000 passes to the surviving spouse, then the marital deduction is limited to $600,000.

Most transfers from one spouse to another qualify for the marital deduction, including property transferred by a will, without a will, by joint ownership, by a trust, or by insurance. In fact, the method of transfer in itself is unimportant—with one exception found in the terminable interest rule.

The **terminable interest rule** requires that, except for qualified terminable interest property trusts (also known as Q-TIP trusts), the survivor's interest in the property must not terminate or fail because of (1) the passage of time or (2) the occurrence or nonoccurrence of a certain event. Suppose property is left to a wife for ten years, with the remainder of the property going to the children. The wife's interest is terminable—it ends after ten years. Therefore, this property does not qualify for the marital deduction.

The terminable interest rule ensures that property will not escape estate taxation. Without it, property could be left to a surviving spouse and then transferred to others without being taxed in the surviving spouse's estate

Charitable Contributions   Contributions to charitable and religious organizations are deducted after the marital deduction, whether contributions were made before or at the decedent's death.

Tentative Tax and Tax Payable

After all deductions have been taken, the **tentative tax** is determined by applying the rates in Exhibit 8-1 to the value of the taxable estate. The tentative tax is then reduced by any applicable credits to arrive at the **tax payable**.

Exhibit 8-1
Unified Transfer Tax Rate Schedules

If the amount is:		Tentative tax is:			
Over	But not over	Tax	+	%	On Excess Over
$ 0	$ 10,000	$ 0	18		$ 0
10,000	20,000	1,800	20		10,000
20,000	40,000	3,800	22		20,000
40,000	60,000	8,200	24		40,000
60,000	80,000	13,000	26		60,000
80,000	100,000	18,200	28		80,000
100,000	150,000	23,000	30		100,000
150,000	250,000	38,800	32		150,000
250,000	500,000	70,800	34		250,000
500,000	750,000	155,800	37		500,000
750,000	1,000,000	248,300	39		750,000
1,000,000	1,250,000	345,800	41		1,000,000
1,250,000	1,500,000	448,300	43		1,250,000
1,500,000	2,000,000	555,800	45		1,500,000
2,000,000	2,500,000	780,000	49		2,000,000
2,500,000	3,000,000	1,025,800	53		2,500,000
3,000,000	10,000,000*	1,290,000	55		3,000,000

*For amounts in excess of $10 million, an additional tax is applicable.

Unified Credit   The federal estate tax is intended to apply only to sizable estates. Congress has effectively exempted estates of less than $600,000 by permitting a **unified credit** of $192,800 for each individual to be applied to tentative estate tax that is otherwise payable. $192,800 happens to be the estate tax normally applicable to a $600,000 estate; after deducting the credit, no estate tax normally is due on an estate of $600,000 or less.

The credit is *unified* because this one credit applies both to gifts made during one's lifetime and to transfers at death. Therefore, gifts before death can reduce the amount of one's estate that can escape taxation. For example, if a credit of $5,000 was taken on a gift made ten years ago, the unified credit available is now $187,800 ($192,800 – $5,000). Thus for this person, a federal estate tax liability exists if his or her taxable estate is valued at $586,487 or more.[1]

Additional Credits   Additional credits are allowed for death taxes levied by state governments (discussed later in the chapter) and foreign governments and for taxes paid on prior transfers. Thus, it is possible even for estates larger than $600,000 to have no federal estate tax liability.

Illustration

The following example recaps the major points in the federal estate tax computation process and illustrates the value of tax planning.

Max, who is sixty-three years old and married, is interested in estimating the federal estate tax that will be payable if he dies soon. Max's will states that his net estate, after payment of expenses and debts, is to be divided equally between his two sons. This rather unusual (and not necessarily to be recommended) approach is acceptable to Max's wife, Ann, because it is expected that her sons will take care of their mother's financial needs during the remainder of her lifetime. Max has made no gifts during his lifetime that would affect his unified credit. Exhibit 8-2 shows the details of the estate tax computation process involved; $102,300 of estate tax will be payable by Max's estate.

However, under a different and generally more acceptable approach Max's federal estate tax liability can be eliminated or deferred. This approach is illustrated in Exhibit 8-3. Suppose that Max's will provides, in effect, that just enough of his estate will pass to Ann so that the federal estate tax is reduced to zero (or the lowest possible amount). This approach is common in estate planning. It makes effective use of the unlimited marital deduction in the estate of the first spouse to die and the unified credits in the estates of both spouses. In Max's case, $600,000 passes to his two sons and $270,000 passes to Ann so as to qualify for the marital deduction. Now, none of Max's estate is sacrificed to estate taxes.

When Ann ultimately dies as a widow, leaving her remaining assets to her two sons, her estate will not qualify for a marital deduction. However, the first $600,000 of Ann's estate will be eligible for her unified credit. Thus, Max, Ann, and their heirs benefit from the unified credit in both estates.

State Death Taxes

Most state death taxes can be classified as either estate taxes or inheritance taxes—or sometimes both. As noted above, when computing the federal estate tax, a limited credit can be taken for state death taxes paid. The federal estate tax is reduced by the amount paid for state death taxes. The available credit is subject to federally imposed limits that vary according to the size of the estate. In some states, the total state death taxes are greater than the federal estate tax credit and therefore impose an additional burden on estates.

Exhibit 8-2
Estate Tax Computation

Assets (estimated fair market value)	
Residence	$170,000
Savings account	5,000
Automobiles	15,000
Household furnishings	30,000
Other personal property	10,000
Common stock	50,000
Bonds	20,000
Business interest	300,000
Life insurance:	
Individual life	300,000
Group term	50,000
	$950,000
Liabilities	
Mortgage loan	30,000
Personal loan	20,000
Other estimated deductions	
Funeral expenses	10,000
Administrative costs	20,000
	$80,000
Estate Tax Computation	
Gross estate	$950,000
Debts, funeral expenses, and administrative costs	80,000
Taxable estate	870,000
Tentative tax (from Exhibit 8-1)	295,100
Unified credit	192,800
Federal estate tax payable (without regard to other credits)	$102,300

Estate Taxes

State estate taxes are generally patterned after the federal estate tax. Many states levy a state estate tax in an amount that will equal the credit for state death taxes available under the federal estate tax law. This is sometimes referred to as a **pickup** or **sponge tax** because it absorbs the amount of the federal credit.

Inheritance Taxes

Some states impose an inheritance tax on the right of beneficiaries to receive property from a decedent. This tax is imposed on each beneficiary's share, not on the estate as a whole.

Exhibit 8-3
Estate Tax Computation With Marital Deduction

Assets (estimated fair market value)	
Residence	$170,000
Savings account	5,000
Automobiles	15,000
Household furnishings	30,000
Other personal property	10,000
Common stock	50,000
Bonds	20,000
Business interest	300,000
Life insurance:	
Individual life	300,000
Group term	50,000
	$950,000
Liabilities	
Mortgage loan	30,000
Personal loan	20,000
Other estimated deductions	
Funeral expenses	10,000
Administrative costs	20,000
	$80,000
Estate Tax Computation	
Gross estate	$950,000
Debts, funeral expenses, and administrative costs	80,000
Net estate	870,000
Marital deduction	270,000
Taxable estate	$600,000
Tentative tax (from Exhibit 8-1)	192,800
Unified credit	192,800
Federal estate tax payable (without regard to other credits)	$0

Federal Gift Tax

People make gifts for many reasons. One financial motivation is the desire to reduce the size of their estate, thereby reducing federal estate and state death taxes. However, those who give gifts might incur a federal gift tax.

The federal gift tax is imposed on donors, not recipients (donees). A donee does not incur an income tax liability upon receiving a gift, and a donor does not receive an income tax deduction for the amount of a gift (other than in the case of charitable contributions).

The federal gift tax law applies to all transfers, whether the gift is direct or indirect, of real or personal property, in trust or otherwise, tangible or intangible.

Annual Gift Tax Exclusion

The federal gift tax is not intended to tax ordinary, small gifts, such as Christmas, birthday, anniversary, or graduation presents. Therefore, the law contains an **annual gift tax exclusion** for gifts of a present interest. This exclusion is allowed for each donee and is available each year.

Gifts of a Present Interest   To qualify for the annual exclusion, a gift must be a gift of a present interest and cannot be a *gift of a future interest*. This means that the use, possession, or enjoyment of the property by the donee cannot be postponed until the future.

Annual Limit   A person can give $10,000 or less to each of any number of individuals—family members or others—and not incur a gift tax liability. However, as noted, a $10,000 limit applies for each individual donee.

Suppose, for example, a father gives $8,000 to his son and $12,000 to his daughter in the same year. He could exclude the entire gift to the son, but only $10,000 of the $12,000 gift to the daughter could be excluded.

The amount a donor can give is not limited by this exclusion, but gifts in excess of the annual exclusion will be subject to federal gift taxation, like the $2,000 of the gift to the daughter in the example just given. However, the donor can apply his or her unified credit to any gift taxes actually payable.

Gift-Splitting Privilege   The gift-splitting privilege allows a married person to double the annual exclusion by assuming that a gift is made equally by the husband and wife. Thus, a married couple can effectively give up to $20,000 each year to each donee with no gift tax consequence. Of course, both spouses must consent to the gift. In the above example, if the father *and* mother give $12,000 to their daughter, the entire amount is excluded from federal gift taxes.

Charitable Donations

Gifts for certain public or charitable purposes are fully deductible for federal gift tax purposes. The donor is not taxed on these gifts, regardless of their size. Gifts to individuals—regardless of their need—cannot qualify for the charitable deduction.

Marital Deduction

An unlimited marital deduction is available for gifts to spouses. Other than for Q-TIP trusts, the gifts from one spouse to the other must meet the *terminable interest requirements*. In general, this means the gifts must meet the same requirements that apply to the estate tax marital deduction.

Relation of Federal Gift Tax to Estate Taxes

The underlying philosophy of the federal estate and gift tax law is that property should be taxed in the same manner, whether it is transferred at or before death. In effect, the estate tax is merely a tax on a person's last gift.

Illustration

Assume Dianne has made no previous gifts and in 1994 gives her daughter, Jill, $200,000 in securities with her husband Ralph joining in the gift. Because Dianne's husband consents to join in the gift, half of the gift is presumed to have been made by Dianne and the other half by Ralph. Thus, Dianne will be deemed to have made a taxable gift of $90,000 to Jill in 1994. This is true even if legally Dianne owned all of the gift property in her own name before the gift was made. This is the effect of the gift-splitting provision of the gift tax law.

Dianne and Ralph are each entitled to a $10,000 gift tax annual exclusion for each donee, so each is entitled to deduct this amount from her or his half of the total gift ($100,000 – $10,000 = $90,000 taxable gift for each). The gift tax on a $90,000 taxable gift is $21,000 (from Exhibit 8-1). Dianne and Ralph, however, are not required to pay a gift tax because they can each use up a portion of the $192,800 unified transfer tax credit. Dianne's remaining unified credit is $171,800 ($192,800 – $21,000), and Ralph's remaining unified credit is also $171,800. Dianne's and Ralph's use of a portion of their unified credits while they are alive will reduce the credit available to their estates after their deaths. As an estate planning matter, it would have been preferable for Dianne to have made this $200,000 gift to Jill over a period of years (say, $20,000 per year for ten years) to stay within her and Ralph's annual exclusions each year. In this way, they would not have used up any of their unified credits.

Planning Considerations

Three aspects of the estate and gift tax law are particularly important for estate planning purposes:

1. Gifts might actually exhaust all of the unified credit, with the result that federal estate taxes payable later might be higher than they would have been without such gifts.

2. Periodic gifts are taxed at increasingly higher rates because the gifts are cumulative over life. When the gift tax is calculated, all previous gifts are considered, and the latest gift is taxed using the appropriate marginal tax rate shown in Exhibit 8-1. For example, if a $20,000 taxable gift is made in one year, it is subject to a $3,800 federal gift tax. If, two years later, another $20,000 taxable gift is made, it is subject to a $4,400 federal gift tax because the tax bracket is now $20,000 to $40,000, not $10,000 to $20,000, because the total gift given is $40,000.

3. As noted previously, the proceeds of an existing life insurance policy given by the insured to another person within three years prior to the insured's death will be included in the insured's gross estate.

Despite these limitations, federal estate taxes can be reduced by making gifts.

Use of Annual Exclusion   Estate taxes can be reduced by taking advantage of the annual gift exclusion. If a couple has three children, the couple can reduce its estates by $60,000 each year by making annual gifts of $20,000 to each child. Over time, a married couple can substantially reduce their estates with such annual gifts.

Gifts of Property Likely To Appreciate   A second tax-reduction possibility, besides the annual gift tax exclusion, is to make gifts of property likely to increase in value. Suppose a married couple owns a small apartment building worth $250,000. If the husband and wife give the building to their daughter, the gift will be valued at $250,000—its fair market value at the time of the gift. If, instead, they retain ownership of the building and die years later, the value of the building—for estate tax purposes—might be much higher.

Gifts to Spouses   The unlimited federal gift tax marital deduction facilitates making gifts between living spouses for estate planning purposes. The value of property given to a spouse within the restrictions of the marital deduction escapes—or, at least, postpones—federal estate taxation.

Generation-Skipping Gifts

Each generation tends to pass an inheritance to the next generation. For example, Matthew's estate passes to his son Alex, and an estate tax is paid. When Alex dies, his estate passes to his daughter Laura and again estate taxes are paid.

In the past, it was common for wealthy people to avoid taxation by the use of generation-skipping gifts. For example, Matthew might leave his estate in trust with only a life income to Alex and with the remainder going to his granddaughter Laura at Alex's death. In this case, although Matthew's estate would incur a tax liability, Alex's estate would not be involved with these particular funds and hence would be *skipped* for federal transfer tax purposes.

However, the value of large generation-skipping gifts has been substantially reduced by a **generation-skipping transfer tax (GST tax)**. This tax is on generation-skipping transfers as defined in the tax law. It would generally become due when a gift is made to a donee who is more than one generation removed from the estate owner. Thus, in the previous example, if Matthew had made a direct gift to his granddaughter Laura, the amount of the gift would be subject to the GST tax.

The GST tax is applied at a flat rate equal to the *highest* federal estate tax marginal rate (currently 55 percent) and is payable *in addition to* any other estate or gift taxes that apply to the transfer. Therefore, it is generally to be avoided in estate planning if possible. It should be noted, however, that each person has a $1 million lifetime GST tax exemption so this tax applies, in effect, only to gifts in excess of $1 million per donor. Thus, significant generation-skipping planning is still possible, using this GST tax exemption for both spouses, when desired and applicable.

Executing an Estate Plan

Wills and trusts are of primary importance in implementing the desires of many individuals when planning their estates. These planning tools are discussed below.

Wills

A **will** is an important legal expression of a person's wishes as to the disposition of his or her property upon death. To be valid, a will should be in writing, signed by the creator of the will, and signed by at least two witnesses as verification of the creator's signature.

A person who dies *with* a valid will is said to die **testate**. Many people have no will. If a person dies *without* a valid will—**intestate**—the property is transferred according to state laws of distribution. These laws establish the order in which the deceased's surviving family members, dependents, and others are entitled to the deceased's estate. The pattern of distribution varies from state to state, and it would be only through sheer coincidence that property would be distributed according to the property owner's desires.

Contrary to common belief, a will is needed by many small estate owners as well as by those who have large estates. Furthermore, a will should be written by an attorney since improperly drawn wills often cause estate settlement problems. Many state statutes limit the effectiveness of oral wills and wills that are not properly witnessed. A will should be reviewed and updated periodically with the aid of an attorney.

Intestacy Statutes

The following rules based on the District of Columbia intestacy statute provide examples of how property might be allocated if a person dies without a will:

1. If children and grandchildren are living, the surviving spouse takes one-third and the children and children of any deceased child split the remaining two-thirds.
2. If no children or grandchildren exist, the surviving spouse takes one-half and the decedent's father and mother split the remaining one-half.
3. If the mother and father are not living, the surviving spouse takes one-half, and the decedent's brothers and sisters or their descendants split the remaining one-half.
4. If no children, grandchildren, father, mother, brothers, sisters, or descendants of brothers and sisters exist, the surviving spouse takes all of the real and personal property.

Numerous variations exist in the intestacy statutes of states. Many have homestead (principal residence) exemptions and family allowances that differ greatly in amounts. The portion provided to a surviving spouse varies among the states, and special situations, such as adopted children, illegitimate children, posthumous children, and children of half blood, are handled differently in the various states.

Advantages of a Will

Wills, as noted above, are useful in disposing of a decedent's estate according to his or her wishes. However, having a will provides additional advantages:

1. *The ability to provide income to surviving family members while the estate is going through the estate administration process.* The process can take many months or even years. During this period, surviving family members might be unnecessarily strained financially unless it is stipulated in the will that a certain income is to begin immediately after the property owner's death and is to continue until the estate has been distributed.
2. *The ability to name the person desired to serve as the executor or executrix of the estate.* This selection is important since it is the executor's responsibility to collect the assets of the deceased, determine and pay legal claims against the estate, and distribute the remaining assets to the proper individuals.

Without a valid will (or with a will that does not name an executor), the probate court will appoint an administrator or administratrix. Use of an inexperienced administrator might result in (1) an unnecessary decrease in value of the estate and a (2) delay in the distribution of assets.

3. *The ability to minimize problems arising from distributions to minor children.* Without a will, minor children might become entitled to property they do not have the legal capacity to manage. A guardian must then be appointed by the court, which can result in unnecessary expenses and delays. Furthermore, the appointed guardian might not be the person the decedent would have selected to manage his or her estate.

4. *The ability to include information about specific property and advice for its management.* Such information and advice can be incorporated in the will or in papers associated with the will. By placing this type of information in the will, the estate owner is assured that it will be read and its importance will be emphasized.

5. *The ability to minimize estate shrinkage.* A will accelerates the settlement process and reduces delays that can cause estate values to decline. Furthermore, a properly drawn will can minimize taxes. If a person, for example, wants to take maximum advantage of the marital deduction, the will should specify the spouse's share and the terms of the bequest.

6. *The ability to make gifts and establish trusts.* A will can be used to make gifts to whomever and for whatever the estate owner chooses. Similarly, a person can establish a testamentary trust or trusts at death by means of the will (discussed later in this chapter).

Coordination of Wills With Other Methods of Distribution

It is important in estate planning to coordinate a will with other methods of distributing a person's property at death, such as life insurance or trusts. Coordination problems often arise because a will controls only the disposition of property that passes through probate. Life insurance, for example, unless payable to the insured's estate, is not controlled by a will but rather by the beneficiary designation in the contract. Or, when property is co-owned with right of survivorship, the property passes automatically to the surviving owner when the other owner dies. For example, if a wife is the life insurance beneficiary and also, as a joint owner, receives the family residence, this can affect the best allocation of the probate property. The amounts provided to the wife in the will should recognize the amounts provided to her by other means.

Trusts

A **trust** is an arrangement by which one person or organization holds legal title to property for the benefit of another person or persons. Trusts serve a variety of purposes in estate planning. Because of legal and tax complications, trust instruments should be drawn up by an attorney. The following section should familiarize the reader with the basic nature of trusts and with how each type of trust accomplishes certain objectives.

Ingredients of a Trust

Five essential ingredients are needed for a trust to be valid:

1. *Grantor.* A **grantor**, also known as a **settlor** or **creator**, is the property owner who establishes a trust.
2. *Trustee.* The **trustee** is the individual or organization that holds legal title to property provided by the grantor.
3. *Property.* A trust must have property (also known as the *corpus* or *res*); otherwise it is a *dry trust* and invalid.
4. *Beneficiary.* A trust must exist for the benefit of some person, persons, or organization. Secondary or contingent beneficiaries of a trust may exist.
5. *Terms.* A trust must have a purpose; otherwise, a trustee cannot know how to administer the trust.

Responsibilities of a Trustee

Trustees, by statute, have a responsibility to fulfill the following obligations:

1. Administer the trust solely for the interest of the beneficiary (or beneficiaries)
2. Not delegate the administration of the trust
3. Keep and provide accurate records
4. Furnish information to the beneficiary
5. Exercise reasonable care and skill in administering the trust
6. Take, keep control of, and preserve trust property
7. Keep trust property separate from other property, although the terms of the trust and state law might allow a trustee to commingle trust funds with other funds (in *common* trust funds)
8. Make trust property productive
9. Deal impartially with beneficiaries
10. Cooperate with cotrustees
11. Submit to the control of others who have the legal authority to direct the trustee

The terms of the trust agreement can also confer upon the trustee a number of powers that are not listed above. As long as the trust agreement does not violate the law, a grantor can direct the trustee to engage in a wide variety of practices. For example, the trust agreement might allow a trustee discretionary powers to incur expenses that are reasonable and necessary to handle the trust property, and the trustee might be allowed to sell, pledge, mortgage, or lease trust property.

Selecting a Trustee

The trustee selected by the grantor can be an individual or a corporate entity. Four factors should be considered in selecting a trustee:

1. *Experience*. The amount of experience the potential trustee has had in managing the type of property that will comprise the trust corpus and in handling the other expected functions should be considered.

2. *Stability and life expectancy*. The stability and life expectancy of the potential trustee should be evaluated. The trust might be effective for a long time, and the death or poor health of an individual trustee might cause problems. By way of contrast, the life expectancy of a corporate trustee is infinite.

3. *Personal factors*. The trustee's personal characteristics, such as his or her personal knowledge of and personal interest in the beneficiary's welfare, should be considered. Corporate trust departments are sometimes considered to be impersonal, while an individual trustee might be a close family friend who is knowledgeable about the beneficiary's needs.

4. *Size of the trust*. The size of the trust should be taken into account. Many corporate trustees will not handle a trust unless the value of the trust property is in excess of a certain figure, such as $100,000. Corporate trust fees, however, are not necessarily higher than those charged by individuals. Sometimes, individual trustees will serve without a fee.

Types of Trust

Trusts can be divided into two basic types: living trusts and testamentary trusts.

-   A **living trust** or *inter vivos* **trust** is created and becomes operative during the lifetime of the grantor. It can be irrevocable or revocable. It can also be funded or unfunded.

-   **Testamentary trusts** are created by the grantor's will and do not become operative until his or her death. With this type of trust, a person maintains full ownership and control of the trust property until death. The fact that a trust has been established in the will does not interfere with the management of the property during lifetime at all. In fact, the trust can be terminated at any time prior to the grantor's death.

Revocable Living Trust   A grantor who establishes a **revocable living trust** transfers property to a trust but maintains his or her rights to change or revoke the terms of the trust. The grantor allows the trust to manage the property, but can reclaim the property at any time. Because the grantor retains this control of the property, his or her estate value is not reduced by the value of the property in the trust. A revocable living trust becomes irrevocable at the grantor's death or when the grantor makes it irrevocable.

Irrevocable Living Trust A grantor who establishes an **irrevocable living trust** makes an absolute gift and relinquishes all rights to terminate, revoke, or change the terms of the trust. One advantage of this type of trust is that it provides a method of transferring property without having it go through the public disclosure associated with probate. Since wills are public documents, they can be read by anyone. Furthermore, the delay and costs of probate are avoided, but this advantage is partially offset by the cost involved in establishing the trust.

Use of an irrevocable trust can reduce income taxes if several rules are followed to ensure that the grantor has given away the property without retaining any prohibited property rights. Generally, if the rules are followed, the income from the trust property will be taxable not to the grantor but rather to the beneficiary, if distributed, or to the trust itself, if not.

A common reason for establishing irrevocable trusts is to reduce federal estate taxes. The property will not be included in the grantor's estate, and if arranged properly, the property will not be taxed in the trust beneficiary's estate. Since this would constitute a gift for federal gift tax purposes to the beneficiaries of the trust, however, a gift tax might be payable unless the gifts to the trust can be kept within the grantor's annual gift tax exclusions (and possibly the grantor's spouse's annual exclusions in the case of split gifts). However, a GST tax might apply in this type of situation.

An irrevocable trust might be preferable to making a gift outright if the grantor (donor) wants the advantages of a gift but wishes a trustee to exercise some control over the beneficiary's use of the gift. For example, if a father wishes to make a gift to his son to save estate and possibly income taxes but is concerned that the son does not have the necessary ability to handle the property, it might be wise to establish an irrevocable trust. This accomplishes the tax objectives, and the trustee can be empowered to manage the property for the son according to standards established in the trust agreement and at the trustee's discretion.

As just noted, one disadvantage of an irrevocable trust is that it represents a gift of property and therefore is subject to gift tax laws. The $10,000 ($20,000 for a married couple) annual gift tax exclusion is available for gifts of present interests, and the exclusion applies to each trust beneficiary as a separate donee. The trust itself is not regarded as the donee.

Testamentary Trust   If a trust is not needed until the grantor's death, a testamentary trust might be appropriate. A testamentary trust is established under the grantor's will and becomes operative upon the grantor's death.

A common method of minimizing estate taxes at the death of each spouse is to establish two testamentary trusts: a *marital deduction trust* and a *nonmarital trust*. Other common terminology referring to this two-trust concept is *marital and family trusts* or *A-B trusts*.

- The **marital deduction trust** is often structured to take advantage of the marital deduction by placing enough of the grantor's estate in it, through a formula clause in the will, so that the amount of the grantor's taxable estate will be reduced to the point at which the tax on that estate will be entirely eliminated by the unified credit and other credits available to the estate.

- The remainder of the grantor's estate, which is the amount on which estate taxes will be entirely eliminated by the unified credit and other credits, is placed in the **nonmarital trust**.

The terms of the marital deduction trust must meet the marital deduction requirements and depend upon the type of marital deduction trust selected. In a **general power of appointment trust**, the surviving spouse must have the right to all the trust income during his or her lifetime and the power to direct the trust property to anyone he or she wishes during his or her lifetime, at his or her death, or both. In a **Q-TIP trust** (qualified terminable interest property trust), the surviving spouse must have the right to all trust income for his or her lifetime, but the grantor can specify who will receive the trust corpus upon the surviving spouse's death. Any property remaining in the marital deduction trust at the death of the surviving spouse is included in his or her gross estate and, thus, can be subject to estate taxes at that time.

The basic objective of the nonmarital trust is to give the surviving spouse some rights in the property, but not enough rights to make the property includable in the surviving spouse's estate. Thus, the surviving spouse might be given several significant rights, including the right to receive some or all the income from the trust; the right to withdraw at his or her sole discretion the greater of $5,000 or 5 percent of the trust property each year (noncumulative); and, under certain conditions, the right to receive additional amounts of principal.

It often is best to place assets that tend to lose value in the marital trust and appreciating assets in the nonmarital trust. This allows the value of the property that will be included in the surviving spouse's gross estate to decrease, hopefully to the point at which it will not be subject to estate taxes. If the income from the marital trust is not sufficient for the spouse to live on, it might be best to exhaust the marital deduction trust corpus before entitling the spouse to touch the income from the nonmarital trust. The surviving spouse can then live on the income from the nonmarital trust, yet the property in the nonmarital trust will not be subject to estate taxes upon the death of the spouse.

Special Trusts Virtually all trusts can be classified into one of the basic types discussed above. However, many trusts have a unique characteristic or an important provision, and these trusts are known by specific names. The following three trusts are important examples of special trusts:

1. A **pour-over trust** receives assets from a will or another trust and consolidates them under professional management into a logical, integrated plan. While these trusts might be either revocable or irrevocable, or living or testamentary, most are living, revocable trusts. Pour-over trusts are useful in minimizing taxes when a person has no incidents of ownership in a life insurance policy, but when the proceeds are payable to his or her estate. Proceeds payable to a pour-over trust will not be included in the gross estate for tax purposes.

2. The corpus of a **life insurance trust** is life insurance that is held by the trustee, payable to the trustee, or both held by and payable to the trustee. These trusts can be revocable or irrevocable, and their tax treatment follows their basic characteristics. Life insurance trusts might provide the following:

   - Greater flexibility than that obtainable with life insurance settlement options

   - Restrictions and limitations on the use of funds

   - Alternatives to the appointment of a guardian for minor beneficiaries

   - Avenues to avoid subsequent estate taxes when trust beneficiaries die

   - Investment management

   - Consolidation of assets

   - Estate liquidity in the form of loans to the estate or purchase of assets from the estate

3. A **sprinkle trust** is a trust that contains a *sprinkling clause*. With a **sprinkling clause**, the trustee can have the right to use discretion in determining the proper payments of trust income to the different beneficiaries as their needs vary over time. For example, the trustee might increase the income of a beneficiary when a special need, such as medical expenses or college education, exists.

Gifts in Trust

Donors might decide to make lifetime gifts in the form of a trust rather than outright to the donee or donees under the following circumstances among others:

- The gifts are relatively substantial in amount.
- The gifts are part of a planned giving program.
- The donees are minors.
- The donors want the property held for and managed for the donees rather than allowing them complete control over it.

Gifts in trust have the advantage of allowing the grantor to set the terms of the trust, within certain limits, under which the gift property will be administered by the trustee for the donees as trust beneficiaries. Trusts can also be used for generation-skipping purposes within the planning framework that is still available under the GST tax rules.

A problem involved in making gifts to trusts is that, depending on the terms of the trust, the donor might not be able to take advantage, or full advantage, of the $10,000 (or $20,000 for split gifts) federal gift tax annual exclusion. This is true because, by the very nature of the trust device, at least part, and frequently all (depending on the terms of the trust), of any gift in trust is going to be a gift of a future interest. As previously explained, a gift of future interest does not qualify for the gift tax annual exclusion. This often is a serious issue in making gifts to trusts because the donor normally wants full use of the federal gift tax annual exclusion in making such gifts.

To solve this problem to a large extent, estate and tax planners use **Crummey powers** in trusts. The fundamental purpose of including these powers is to allow the whole amount of gifts to trusts (up to certain limits) to be gifts of a present interest and hence qualify for the gift tax annual exclusion. When the trust agreement provides each donee (or trust beneficiary in the case of gifts in trust) with a Crummey withdrawal power over his or her share of each year's gift to the trust made by the donor, each donee is considered to have a present interest in the whole amount of his or her share of each year's gift up to the dollar limit stated in the Crummey power. The effect is for the donor to be making gifts to the trust of present interests at least up to the combined dollar limits of the Crummey powers for all the donees who have such powers. Hence, the donor's gifts fall within the gift tax annual exclusions for the donees. Since the real purpose of using Crummey powers in trusts is to qualify gifts to the trust for the gift tax annual exclusion, it is expected that the donees will never actually exercise their Crummey rights. However, they can legally do so.

Business Continuation—Sole Proprietorships

Business continuation planning is a process by which business owners determine how to deal with the loss of the (or an) owner. More *sole proprietorships* (businesses owned by one person) exist than any other form of business enterprise. Sole proprietorships are vulnerable to major losses caused by the death or disability of the owner—this often marks the death of the business as well. Without sound planning, there can be a substantial reduction in the value of the decedent's estate, with financially disastrous results for the heirs. Life insurance can be used to address this potential problem.

Loss Exposure

A sole proprietorship is often built around the talents and contributions of its proprietor. If the proprietor dies or becomes disabled, the business is hurt by the loss of this most valuable asset for several reasons.

First, the loss of valuable management ability might be only partially replaceable. The disabled or deceased proprietor's spouse often assumes responsibility for operating the business, but the business will suffer if the spouse is not both trained in the business *and* capable of managing it. If a capable manager is hired, the cost of the manager can be an additional financial drain.

The disability or death of a proprietor can also affect employee morale. Employees become concerned over the fate of the company and their own job security. If the ability of the owner's replacement is questioned, employees might seek other jobs, compounding the problems facing the business.

Liquidity needs and the loss of credit present other problems. The disability of a sole proprietor creates a need for liquidity because of medical expenses and the continuation of personal maintenance expenses. The death of a sole proprietor creates a need for liquidity because of probate costs, other estate administration expenses and debts, and death taxes. No legal distinction exists in a sole proprietorship between business assets and the owner's personal assets. All assets, regardless of type, are immediately subject to the claims of creditors, yet forced liquidation of business assets is generally undesirable. Furthermore, long-time creditors might refuse to lend additional money to a firm with an uncertain future.

The value of a business might be significantly reduced if business assets must be liquidated on short notice. The very survival of the business might be uncertain. Moreover, the number of potential buyers might be very limited, and these buyers might be in an excellent bargaining position. As a result, a seller might receive much less for the business than he or she thinks it is worth.

Inventory often loses value because some items are out of season or out of style by the time the assets are sold. Used furniture and fixtures normally have little value in a forced sale. Goodwill, based on the owner's efforts, might evaporate with the loss of the owner. Fixed assets, such as a building, might or might not decline in value, but they are not necessarily a major item on the balance sheet of sole proprietorships.

Those who inherit the business assets of a sole proprietorship might not be interested in using them to operate the business. If the assets must be sold, it often is desirable to sell them to someone who can use them all in continuing to operate the business. The business assets are worth more to someone who can manage them as a business than they are to anyone lacking the experience, knowledge, and skills to make them productive. Key employees are often potential buyers. With proper advance planning including the agreement of the proprietor, they can arrange life insurance on the proprietor as a way of funding the purchase of business assets when the owner dies.

There is a synergy in the value of business assets if they can be used collectively as an ongoing organization. The assets generally constitute a proper mix of items necessary to carry on that particular business. If such assets are sold separately, and each buyer purchases one or a few items, the unit is broken up into less valuable segments. Most business assets are liquidated for less value than they would have in an ongoing situation. Because of collection difficulties, accounts receivable normally bring 20 to 40 percent of their previous value.

The owner's disability can be a worse threat to a firm's survival than death, because of the medical expenses and the continuation of personal maintenance expenses. Furthermore, if the spouse must care for the disabled proprietor, he or she will be unavailable to manage the business.

Plans To Avoid or Minimize Losses

Financial losses can be minimized by continuing the business after the sole proprietor's death or disability. Expected profits should be sufficient to warrant business continuation. These results depend on how the business is continued, which include the following methods:

1.   By someone without proper authority

2.   By a court order

3. By an action initiated by the proprietor alone prior to death (that is, without developing an agreement with others)

4. By a trust agreement

5. By a buy-sell agreement

Business continuation in the event of the sole proprietor's death is discussed below, while continuation in the event of the sole proprietor's disability is discussed later in the chapter.

Continuation by Someone Without Proper Authority

In many situations, a sole proprietor dies without leaving express authority to someone to continue the business. The proprietor might have had no plans for business continuation, or might have assumed or agreed orally that a son, daughter, or someone else would take over the business. Under these circumstances, it is likely that the person who assumes control does so without proper legal authority.

Unless specific plans have been made to the contrary, all assets and liabilities (including business assets and liabilities) must pass through the estate administration process. In the usual situation, the executor or administrator of the estate must settle the estate as quickly as possible. This normally involves selling estate assets to pay debts, taxes, and estate administrative expenses, and then distributing the remainder of the estate to the heirs. The distribution can be made according to the terms of the deceased's will or, if no valid will exists, by the laws of intestate distribution.

Anyone who continues the business without proper authority is inviting legal problems. The law generally provides that losses from the business will be borne by the person assuming control but that profits will benefit the estate and heirs. Obviously, this is a personally hazardous and thankless position— especially since the business might be much more difficult to operate profitably after the sole proprietor's death.

An heir who attempts to gain authority to continue the business by obtaining the consent of the other heirs will probably have difficulties for three reasons:

1. The consent of all heirs is required, and it might be difficult to identify and locate all of them.

2. Minors are not legally competent to give their consent.

3. Any heir can withdraw consent at any time.

In short, an informal or oral plan to continue a sole proprietor's business is an ineffective arrangement. Generally, heirs should liquidate the estate, includ-ing the business, regardless of the losses incurred.

Continuation by Court Order

Most states have laws that give the executor or administrator authority to continue a business temporarily. These statutes are designed to avoid or minimize losses to heirs. Some statutes allow continuation until the inventory is sold in the ordinary course of business. Others permit continuation for a *reasonable* period until the business can be sold as a going concern. However, the term "reasonable" is not expressly defined. These statutes do not solve all problems since they are not designed to handle unique or specific situations.

Continuation by Proprietor-Initiated Action

While a sole proprietor's oral statements directing someone to continue the business are not effective, it is possible to bequeath the business by will. This approach can eliminate concerns over authority to continue the business and can also alleviate some of the financial problems that follow the owner's death. The existence of a trained and legally designated successor should eliminate the uncertainty in the minds of employees and creditors over the future success of the business. Liquidity problems might arise because of the need to settle an estate, but in most cases, this need can be met by life insurance on the sole proprietor. Consequently, it might not be necessary to liquidate the business.

It is important for the success of the business that the will provide an inheritance for any surviving spouse of the sole proprietor—at least according to the minimum state distribution requirements. Otherwise, he or she might be allowed to take this distribution against the estate. All plans specified in the will could then fail or be made more difficult, and the business might have to be sold. This problem can be handled by life insurance or a prenuptial agreement. The business can be given to whomever the proprietor chooses, and other assets (including life insurance) can be given to other surviving family members or other survivors.

Even if it is planned for a business to be sold after the sole proprietor's death, it might still be wise to arrange the will in such a manner that an heir will have at least temporary ownership of the business. An heir might be able to avoid liquidation losses by continuing the business until it can be sold as a going concern. If so, life insurance would normally be needed to meet liquidity needs.

Trust Agreements

Sometimes a sole proprietor wants to leave the business to a family member, but the family member (a minor child, for example) is not yet ready to own and manage the business. Other times a proprietor simply wants the business held as an investment for the family. In these situations, the proprietor, in his or her will, can leave the business to a trust, with the trustee responsible for managing the business (1) for the family or until a family member can take over or (2) until it can be sold at a good price. Some banks and trust companies offer this kind of trust service to business owners.

In trusteed business continuation agreements, the responsibility of the trustee is that of a fiduciary. The trustee, as a fiduciary, is expected to oversee the operation of the business prudently and to make decisions that best meet the interests of the beneficiary of the trust. The trust should include a provision permitting the trustee to hire an adviser to carry on the business while the trustee has control of the business. The trustee will then be compensated for services and will compensate those engaged on behalf of the trust.

Buy-Sell Agreements

Sole proprietors can use **buy-sell agreements** to handle the financial losses and legal problems that accompany death. This approach requires the following steps:

1. Finding a person (or persons), such as a relative, employee, or creditor, before the proprietor's death who is interested in buying the business when the proprietor dies

2. Developing a legally binding agreement that obligates the owner to sell and the interested buyer to purchase the company at a mutually agreeable price when the sole proprietor dies. The buy-sell agreement should be drawn up by an attorney to ensure that it is in proper form and that it conforms to the wishes of the parties involved. A formal written agreement assures each party that the transaction will occur and allows each to plan accordingly.

Most buy-sell agreements are funded by life insurance owned by the purchaser on the life of the owner. Life insurance is the ideal funding instrument since it automatically supplies funds at the time they are needed, upon the proprietor's death. Often, it is desirable to set up a trust so that a trustee will receive the life insurance proceeds and make sure the business is transferred properly. In addition, the trustee can maintain the life insurance policies and expedite settlement after the proprietor's death.

First Offer Provision

Most buy-sell agreements include a **first offer provision** that requires a sole proprietor who decides while he or she is still alive to sell the business to offer it first to the other party to the buy-sell agreement at the price specified in the agreement. Because a sole proprietor's business assets are not legally separate from personal assets, it is important to describe the assets and liabilities (if any) that will be transferred to the buyer.

Valuation Clause

A **valuation clause** establishes the method that will be used to determine the price of the business. A valuation clause should always be included in a buy-sell agreement for the following reasons:

1. Without an agreed price or method of determining the price, neither party would regard the agreement as reliable.

2. With a previously agreed on valuation method, the heirs of the sole proprietor will not be placed in a difficult bargaining position after the sole proprietor's death.

3. If the valuation is reasonable and proper (that is, it is an arm's length transaction) and meets certain other conditions (such as those contained in Chapter 14 of the Internal Revenue Code, when applicable[2]), the Internal Revenue Service will accept it as the value of the business for estate tax purposes.

Several valuation approaches are possible:

- *Negotiation.* The price can be determined by negotiation, and the agreed dollar value can be used in the agreement. The advantage of this approach is that the parties involved are in the best position to place a value on the business. The value should be recomputed periodically to reflect changing conditions. Most agreements that use this approach state that the value will be determined by some specified method if the business has not been revalued within a certain period, such as two or three years.

- *Appraisal.* Appraisers can be used *after* the sole proprietor's death. Often, the sole proprietor's heirs select one appraiser, the buyer selects another, and the two appraisers select a third. The value they decide on is *binding* on the parties to the buy-sell agreement. A problem with this approach is that the purchase price is not established prior to the proprietor's death. This makes it difficult for the buyer to fund the agreement, and the uncertain purchase price can cause estate planning problems for the proprietor.

- *Use of a formula.* A formula can be used to value the business at the time of the proprietor's death. Although the actual valuation is not known until the proprietor dies, it can be approximated by applying the formula while the proprietor is alive.

One common formula approach adjusts book value to reflect goodwill.[3] This can be done by determining the adjusted book value (which adjusts the value of the firm's assets and liabilities to current market value) and net profits of the company, perhaps as an average over the previous five years. A reasonable percentage of the net profits can be attributed to earnings on book value, and the remainder can be attributed to goodwill. The amount traceable to goodwill can then be capitalized (given a "tangible" asset value by multiplying by a factor such as two, three, or four), and the capitalized goodwill is added to the company's book value. To illustrate this approach, assume that a company has a book value of $100,000 and average net profits of $30,000. If 12 percent earnings on book value is reasonable and the goodwill should be capitalized at a multiple of three, the value of the company would be as shown in Exhibit 8-4.

The adjusted book value formula suffers from two major disadvantages. First, book value might not accurately reflect the company's assets and liabilities. Second, the formula does not account for future changes in the value of the company. One approach to overcome this disadvantage is to assume that net profits will continue to increase at the same rate that occurred during some past period.

Exhibit 8-4
Hypothetical Adjustment of Book Value To Reflect Goodwill Value of Firm

Facts:	
1. Adjusted book value	$100,000
2. Average net profits	30,000
3. Capitalization multiple	3
Average net profits	30,000
Less 12% of book value	12,000
Difference attributable to goodwill	18,000
	x 3
Capitalized goodwill	54,000
Plus book value	100,000
Value of the company	$154,000

Termination Provision

A termination provision is important in a buy-sell agreement. Usually, this provision allows the agreement to be terminated under the following circumstances:

• Either party becomes bankrupt.
• The buyer dies or becomes permanently disabled.
• The buyer voluntarily terminates his or her employment with the company.

Premium Payments

Since the buyer is purchasing the business, it is logical for the buyer to pay for the insurance. This might present a financial problem for the buyer unless the proprietor either lends the buyer money or, if the buyer is an employee, increases the employee's salary enough to pay for all or part of the premiums. A split dollar arrangement (discussed later in this chapter) with the proprietor's being the insured might be desirable if the proprietor pays a portion of the premium.

Beneficiary Designation

Many authorities believe a trustee should be named as the beneficiary of insurance used to fund a buy-sell agreement so that the trustee can collect the proceeds and can promptly and efficiently arrange the transfer of the business. A trustee is unbiased and is usually experienced in these matters.

An alternative is to name the purchasing party as the beneficiary since the buyer has paid the premiums and must have proceeds to discharge his or her obligation to buy the business. To gain legal ownership of the business, the buyer must pay the proceeds to the proprietor's estate.

It is normally considered unwise to designate the proprietor's estate or the proprietor's spouse or other heir as the beneficiary. Since the estate receives the proceeds and is legal owner of the company, the seller's heirs and the buyer are not then in equal positions. The proprietor's spouse or other heir might misunderstand the purpose of the buy-sell agreement. He or she might claim both the insurance proceeds and the business.

Tax Aspects

The life insurance premiums used to fund a buy-sell agreement are not deductible for federal income tax purposes. If a sole proprietor increases an employee's salary to pay the premiums, the entire salary is still deductible by the employer as a business expense but is still taxable income to the employee. However, the proceeds of the life insurance policy will be received by the employee income-tax-free.

The value of the business is included in the estate of a deceased proprietor and is subject to federal estate taxes. If the purchase price determined in a buy-sell agreement is an "arm's length" transaction, and certain other conditions are met, that price will be the valuation of the business that is included in the deceased's estate.

Other Provisions in a Buy-Sell Agreement

It is common to state that only the buyer and seller have the power to alter the agreement. The buy-sell agreement should provide that the sole proprietor's heirs and the buyer are bound by the agreement. Furthermore, the buyer should be given the power of attorney to continue the business immediately after the proprietor's death until the transfer in ownership is formally made.

Advantages of an Insured Buy-Sell Agreement

Both the proprietor and the buyer of a business derive certain advantages when the agreement is funded by life insurance.

Advantages to the Proprietor With an insured buy-sell agreement, the proprietor and his or her heirs are assured of receiving the full, going-concern value of the company, thus eliminating the losses that result from forced liquidation. In addition, the proprietor's estate can be settled promptly. Without such an agreement, business problems might delay the settlement of the estate for years. Furthermore, negotiations with the IRS over the value of the business can be avoided.

An insured buy-sell agreement has advantages in addition to those benefits occurring after the death of a proprietor. If an insured agreement is in force, the proprietor's business will have additional solidity. Creditors, suppliers, and customers might be more inclined toward long-term relationships. Employees, too, are likely to feel more secure and dedicated to the company. Furthermore, the proprietor's business responsibilities might be less if the buyer is eager to work closely with the owner.

Advantages to the Buyer Assuming that the buyer is an employee of the proprietor, an insured buy-sell agreement provides the buyer with more job security and a better idea of what to expect in the future. This helps the buyer plan his or her business and personal estate with more certainty. Even before the business is purchased legally, the buyer will begin to feel more like an owner than an employee.

Business Continuation—Partnerships

Like sole proprietorships, partnerships are vulnerable to major losses caused by the death or disability of an owner. Surviving business partners, however, are more likely than sole proprietors to understand the types of losses that can occur when one of the partners dies or is disabled, since each partner can see the contributions of the others and can easily imagine the problems created by the death or disability of one of them. Since the continuation problems confronting proprietorships were discussed in the preceding section, emphasis here is on how partnership exposures and solutions differ from those in a sole proprietorship.

Loss Exposure

A general partnership is automatically dissolved when a partner dies, since that kind of partnership is a voluntary, contractual relationship in which each partner's actions impose unlimited liability on the other partners. Accordingly, no person can choose a partner for someone else, and a person cannot be obligated to become a partner of another.

Unless the partners have an agreement to the contrary, the death of a partner terminates the survivors' authority to continue the partnership except to wind up the company's business. The surviving partners legally become *liquidating trustees* and are obligated to complete outstanding business, collect the assets and liabilities of the company, and pay the amount of the deceased partner's interest to his or her estate. They cannot enter into new business contracts on behalf of the partnership.

In general, the types of losses that occur when a partner dies or becomes disabled are the same as those involved when a sole proprietor dies. In both cases, the company may (1) lose management talent, (2) have problems with employees, (3) have acute liquidity needs, (4) suffer from a loss of credit, and (5) be forced to liquidate the business.

Of course, some of the losses have a different impact in the case of a partnership. For example, a surviving partner might be liquidating his or her own job when the partnership is terminated. Moreover, the survivor will be required to pay the firm's debts if the estate of the deceased partner becomes insolvent.

Reorganizing a Partnership

Although a partnership is dissolved when a partner dies, it can be reorganized. One method of reorganizing and continuing the business is for the surviving partners to accept the heirs of the deceased as general partners. This is not desirable if the heirs are inexperienced and are able to contribute little to the operation of the company. Furthermore, the surviving partners and the heirs might have different business goals. For example, the former might want growth and expansion, while the latter favor current income.

Another possibility is to accept the heirs as limited partners who do not participate in the management of the company. This is usually impractical because they will receive their share of company profits without contributing to the business. Furthermore, a court will generally require that the interest of minor heirs be liquidated.

A third approach to reorganizing a partnership is for the surviving partners to accept a buyer of the heirs' interest as a partner. This provides the heirs with cash and allows the partners to continue the business. However, unless a buyer is found prior to the partner's death or disability, it can be difficult to find someone with the requisite experience who will pay a reasonable price for the partnership interest.

Fourth, the surviving partners could sell their interests to the heirs if the heirs are interested in and financially capable of buying the business. However, this is seldom done since heirs normally need cash, and surviving partners usually want to continue the business.

Finally, the surviving partners could purchase the interest of the heirs unless one or more of the following problems is insurmountable:

1. The surviving partners do not have the cash needed to buy the deceased's portion of the business.
2. A purchase price cannot be agreed to by all parties.
3. The purchase of the interest in question is difficult to arrange through the deceased's executor or administrator who is unfamiliar with the business.

As with a sole proprietorship many problems are eliminated if an insured buy-sell agreement exists for a partnership. The buy-sell agreement, the insurance to fund the plan, and the benefits of such a plan are basically the same for a partnership as they are for a proprietorship. However, buy-sell agreements are often easier to arrange for a partnership because a buyer need not be searched for. Partners are usually eager to buy the share of the business owned by another partner.

Arranging Partnership Buy-Sell Agreements

Two common types of partnership buy-sell agreements are the cross-purchase plan and the entity plan. (The discussion below focuses on the death of a partner. Business continuation in the event of a partner's disability is discussed later in the chapter.)

Cross-Purchase Plan

Under a **cross-purchase arrangement**, the other partners *must* purchase the interest of the deceased partner, and the deceased partner's estate *must* sell the business interest to the surviving partners. The partnership itself is not a party to the plan; rather, each partner is the owner, premium payer, and beneficiary of life insurance policies on the other partners.

To illustrate a cross-purchase plan, assume that partners Cindy and Bruce each own 50 percent of the $200,000 partnership. Each partner insures the life of the other for $100,000. Thus, Cindy purchases a $100,000 life insurance policy with Bruce as the insured and herself as the beneficiary, and Bruce purchases a $100,000 life insurance policy on Cindy's life with himself as the beneficiary. If Bruce dies, Cindy receives $100,000 in cash to purchase Bruce's share of the business and vice versa.

If four equal partners exist—Dave, Tom, Chris, and Mindy—and the business is worth $200,000, $50,000 worth of life insurance must be purchased on each partner. Dave should have $16,667 of insurance each on Tom, Chris, and Mindy; Tom should have $16,667 each on Dave, Chris, and Mindy; and so on. If, for example, Tom dies, the other three receive $16,667 each (a total of $50,000), and Tom's share of the business can be purchased in equal shares by Dave, Chris, and Mindy.

When a partner dies, the policies owned by the deceased partner on the other partners' lives can be handled in two ways:

1. If the cross-purchase agreement is to continue among the surviving partners, they can purchase the policies on the other surviving partners' lives from the deceased partner's estate to help them fund the continuing agreement.

2. The policies can be surrendered for cash by the estate.

In either case, the cash value is included in the estate of the deceased partner.

Entity Plan

In an **entity plan**, the partnership is the owner, premium payer, and beneficiary of life insurance policies on each partner's life. When a partner dies, the partnership receives the cash needed to liquidate the deceased's share of the business. The partnership then records the changes in ownership interests among the surviving partners according to agreement or on the basis of the capital accounts.

To illustrate, assume that a business is worth $200,000 and that Alice owns 50 percent of the company, Dick and Lou each own 20 percent, and Fran owns 10 percent. The partnership will purchase $100,000 on the life of Alice, $40,000 each on Dick and Lou, and $20,000 on Fran. If Dick dies, for example, the partnership receives $40,000, which is used to liquidate Dick's interest. Since the firm is still worth $200,000, Dick's $40,000 interest must be divided among the three remaining partners. If the same proportions of ownership are maintained, Alice will own 62.5 percent of the company, Lou will own 25 percent, and Fran will own 12.5 percent. The amount of insurance on each partner should be increased after one of the partners dies to ensure that sufficient funds will be available to buy out the interest of yet another deceased if necessary.

Cross-Purchase Versus Entity Plans

In choosing between a cross-purchase and an entity plan, several factors should be considered. For instance, the cross-purchase plan becomes awkward as the number of partners increases. With four partners, twelve policies are required; when six partners exist, thirty policies are necessary.[4]

Another factor to consider is the fairness or equity between the premium burden and the benefits of the plan. In a cross-purchase plan, each person purchases insurance in the amount of the business he or she will buy. Consider the case in which Vivian, who is fifty-five years of age, owns 70 percent of the company, and Lance, only thirty years of age, owns 30 percent. If the business is worth $200,000, Vivian will buy a policy on Lance's life in the amount of $60,000. Since Lance is young, the premium should not be too burdensome. On the other hand, Lance must buy a $140,000 policy on a much older person. Thus, while cross-purchase plans equitably divide plan benefits, an unequal heavy financial burden is a common problem. Lance must pay a larger premium, but he has a better chance than Vivian of acquiring the business, and he stands to gain a larger portion of ownership than Vivian.

An entity plan might not be as equitable as a cross-purchase arrangement. If wide differences in age or large variations in the proportions of the partnership owned exist, an entity plan favors the younger partners and those who have smaller interests. Since the partnership pays the premiums, the premium payments reduce the share of income available to the partners in proportion to their ownership interest. However, since premiums are not a deductible expense, the payments made by the partnership actually constitute income that is taxable to the partners. Consequently, an older partner with a larger partnership interest is paying a disproportionately large segment of the buy-out funding.

One solution to this inequity is to adjust the purchase price of the various interests. An older partner who owns a relatively large portion of the company might be willing to bear some inequity if the other partners are willing to increase the amount paid to the older partner's heirs.

Other Aspects of Partnership Insurance

After a decision is made between a cross-purchase or entity plan, most of the other decisions are analogous to those discussed in a sole proprietor situation. For example, the general approaches to and concerns of valuing a partnership correspond with those of a sole proprietorship. Three issues, however, important in partnership insurance differ from sole proprietorship insurance—uninsurable partners, beneficiary designations, and tax aspects.

Uninsurable Partner

If one of the partners is uninsurable and cannot obtain life insurance at any reasonable price, some other funding arrangement can be employed to ensure that sufficient funds are available to reorganize the partnership when that partner dies. One solution is to establish a sinking fund to cover the uninsurable partner's interest. One method of building a sinking fund is for the other partners as individuals to purchase an annuity on the life of the uninsurable individual.

Another procedure is to increase the permanent coverage on the insurable partners enough to cover the insurance not purchased on the uninsurable partner. The additional cash values will provide a sinking fund that can be used to purchase a portion of the uninsurable individual's interest or that can be used as collateral to finance the purchase.

Beneficiary Designation

Whether a cross-purchase plan or an entity plan is used, it might be desirable to name a trustee as the beneficiary of the policies. This places the execution of the buy-sell agreement in the hands of an experienced, unbiased party who can monitor premium payments and warn partners if any portion of the plan is not fully funded.

As with sole proprietor arrangements, one approach that should be avoided is to name the spouse or other heir of the insured partners as the beneficiary since he or she might misunderstand the purpose of the buy-sell agreement and claim both the insurance proceeds and the deceased's share of the business. In addition, creditors of the estate might interfere with the desired use of the proceeds. If the assets in the estate are inadequate to meet creditors' claims, they might be able to satisfy their claims from the insurance proceeds.

Tax Aspects

The taxation of partnerships is a very complex subject and this book only presents some basic concepts regarding the tax aspects of buy-sell agreements. First, the life insurance premiums paid to fund a partnership buy-sell agreement are not deductible for income tax purposes whether they are paid by the individual partners or by the partnership itself. Second, life insurance death proceeds normally are not subject to income tax when received by the beneficiaries upon the insured partner's death.

Upon a partner's death, the value at death of his or her share of the partnership will be included in his or her gross estate for federal estate tax purposes. When a properly drawn buy-sell agreement covers the partnership interest, the purchase price (valuation) set in the agreement will normally determine the partnership interest's value for federal estate tax purposes, provided the special requirements of Chapter 14 of the Internal Revenue Code are met, if applicable, and the other case law requirements regarding valuation are also met. This can be an important advantage of a properly drawn buy-sell agreement.

Business Continuation—Closely Held Corporations

A **closely held corporation** typically is a small company that is owned and controlled by a small group of stockholders who often also work for and manage the company. In many respects, these corporations more closely resemble a partnership than a public corporation.

When a stockholder of a publicly held corporation dies, any adverse financial effects are minimal, since a ready market is available for the heirs who need or desire to sell their shares. Consequently, insurance for business-continuation purposes is unnecessary for the heirs.

The situation is entirely different when a stockholder in a closely held corporation dies. Since these organizations usually are small and directly managed by the stockholders, the income provided by the business might be all or a large portion of their income. Furthermore, the stockholders are likely to have a large part of their wealth tied up in the company. Therefore, their death has adverse financial consequences for both the corporation and the heirs.

Types of Closely Held Corporations

In terms of federal and often state income tax treatment, corporations can be classified as (1) taxable C corporations and (2) nontaxable S corporations.

C Corporations

C corporations are taxable for corporate income tax purposes under Subchapter C of the Internal Revenue Code. The shareholders of C corporations thus might be subject to double taxation of corporate profits—once at the corporate level under the corporate income tax and potentially again at the individual shareholder level if the corporation pays dividends to its shareholders.

In the case of closely-held C corporations, their controlling shareholders often attempt to avoid the effect of double taxation by having their corporations not pay dividends, or pay relatively low dividends, and then have their corporations pay them high salaries as employees.

While publicly traded corporations are C corporations, only some closely held corporations are. In the case of many closely held corporations that qualify, their shareholders have elected S corporation status for them.

S Corporations

An **S corporation** is a corporation that meets certain eligibility requirements (described below) and whose stockholders all elect under Subchapter S of the Internal Revenue Code not to be taxed as a corporation. In this case, an S corporation is taxed essentially like a partnership, with its profits (and losses) passing through directly to its shareholders to be taxed to them on their individual income tax returns. Thus, a double tax problem does not exist for these business entities.

Before an S election can be made for a corporation, the corporation must meet the following eligibility requirements:

1. Be a domestic corporation
2. Have no more than thirty-five shareholders
3. Generally, have only individuals, estates, and certain kinds of trusts as shareholders
4. Have only one class of stock
5. Not have a nonresident alien as a shareholder
6. Not be a member of an affiliated group of corporations

Furthermore, *all* stockholders must initially consent to an S election for a corporation. However, once the election is made, it requires a *majority* of the shares to vote to revoke the election. But, if S corporation stock is transferred to or otherwise falls into the hands of an ineligible shareholder, the S election is terminated. If an S election is revoked or terminated, the corporation becomes a taxable C corporation, and, in general, an S election cannot be made again for the corporation for five years, with some exceptions.

Loss Exposure

The death of a stockholder of a closely held corporation does not dissolve the firm. The corporation continues to exist, and the interest of the deceased stockholder is transferred first to the estate of the deceased and then from the estate to the heirs. However, the company normally does lose a valuable member of the management team, which may affect employee morale, credit, or confidence. Furthermore, both the firm and the heirs of the deceased stockholder usually have great liquidity needs. Thus, the basic problems are the same as those encountered when a sole proprietor or partner dies.

Reorganizing Closely Held Corporations

Heirs of a deceased stockholder have three choices:

1. Take an active role in the corporation

2. Remain inactive and hope the business will meet their needs
3. Sell their interest in the business

Heirs who own a minority interest have limited rights. They can attend meetings, vote, and receive their share of dividends. In some instances, minority stockholders have been successful in suits to force the company to pay larger dividends. However, in general, the majority stockholders control the firm, and their interests usually are different from those of the heirs; namely, heirs are generally interested in receiving large dividends, while surviving stockholders are more interested in growth.

If the heirs are majority stockholders, they can control corporate policy. This can be detrimental to the health of the company if the heirs are inexperienced and incompetent. They might distribute too much of the corporate income as dividends and weaken the firm or even force its dissolution.

If the heirs and surviving stockholders own equal interests, each stockholder group has equal rights so that neither faction actually controls the corporation. Disputes, therefore, often cannot be reconciled. One solution to this dilemma is for the heirs to stay out of the active operations of the company.

Since many heirs need cash, they choose to sell their shares in the organization. If prearranged plans for selling the stock do not exist, problems can arise. Other stockholders might not have immediate access to the necessary funds since credit sources might not be available. Moreover, it might be difficult to determine a price acceptable to both the heirs and the surviving stockholders since stock of a closely held corporation is not actively traded. The heirs might search for other buyers, but they might be scarce or nonexistent if the shares represent a minority interest. A majority interest is more marketable, but then the surviving stockholders (and probably the employees) would be in a vulnerable position.

Most, if not all, of these problems can be solved by a buy-sell agreement similar in concept to those used for partnerships. Each stockholder enters into a legally binding agreement to sell his or her shares to the other stockholders or the corporation at death, and the other stockholders or the corporation is bound to purchase them. The heirs are assured of receiving a fair price without delay, and the surviving stockholders are assured of maintaining (and perhaps gaining) ownership and control of the corporation. The funds needed are provided by life insurance proceeds. Haggling over the price to be paid is not necessary, and all parties can plan their futures with more certainty. Such buy-sell agreements are commonly used for both closely held C corporations and S corporations.

Arranging Closely Held Corporation Buy-Sell Agreements

Buy-sell agreements for closely held corporations can be established on a cross-purchase basis or a stock redemption (stock retirement) basis.

- *Cross-purchase plan.* With the **cross-purchase plan**, the stockholders individually agree to buy the stock of the deceased, and each stockholder agrees that his or her interest in the corporation will be sold in the event of his or her death. Life insurance policies are purchased by each stockholder, with himself or herself as beneficiary, on the lives of the other stockholders. The proceeds of the policies can be used to purchase the shares of deceased stockholders.

- *Stock-redemption plan.* Under a **stock-redemption plan** or a **stock-retirement plan**, the stockholders agree to sell their shares to the corporation, which is obligated to buy the shares. The corporation purchases and is the beneficiary of life insurance policies on each stockholder's life. When a stockholder dies, the death benefit can be used to purchase his or her shares.

Factors to be considered in deciding between a cross-purchase plan and a stock-retirement plan are somewhat different from those involved in a partnership case. The first factor to consider is whether the corporation has the ability to buy its own stock. Some states have restrictions or prohibitions that prevent a corporation from buying company stock. In these states, there might be no choice except to use a cross-purchase plan.

A second factor to consider is the impact of federal income taxes. This is not a factor for a partnership since it is not a taxable entity, and all taxes are paid by the partners. However, in the case of a C corporation, which is a taxable entity, the tax question might be an important consideration. Since life insurance premiums are not tax deductible, the effective tax rates of the corporation should be compared to the tax rates of the stockholders. If the corporation is in a higher tax bracket than the stockholders, the stockholders might wish to pay the premiums under a cross-purchase plan. If, on the other hand, the stockholders are in a higher bracket, it would be less expensive to use a stock-retirement approach.

A stock-retirement plan can involve other income tax problems. Corporate-owned life insurance policies held by C corporations are now potentially subject to the federal corporate alternative minimum tax to the extent that 75 percent of the corporation's adjusted current earnings exceed its taxable earnings. In addition, in the case of partial redemptions, the IRS might tax the redemptions as dividend payments to the stockholder by the corporation under certain conditions.

If many stockholders exist, a stock-retirement plan (if permitted) can be simpler and more practical than a cross-purchase plan. Only one life insurance policy on each stockholder will be required, while a cross-purchase plan will involve many policies. However, if the stockholders vary widely in ages and percentage of ownership in the corporation, a stock-retirement plan might not be as equitable as it would be when stockholders own an equal number of shares of the corporation or are about the same age. With a stock-retirement approach, the premiums are paid in proportion to the stockholders' ownership in the company. Those with the larger interests are paying larger portions of the premium, even though they do not have as much to gain as those with smaller interests.

Another factor to be considered is the existence of creditors' claims against the corporation. If a stock-retirement plan is used, insurance proceeds might have to be used to pay creditors. With a cross-purchase plan, the proceeds are paid to stockholders, so corporate creditors cannot attach them.

In general, the other considerations involving the purchase of insurance to fund a business-continuation plan for a closely held corporation are similar to those in the case of partnerships. The buy-sell agreement must cover essentially the same points. The valuation process and beneficiary designations are similar, and the problem of uninsurable stockholders must be viewed in the same way.

As with sole proprietorships and partnerships, life insurance premiums on policies used to fund such agreements are not deductible for federal income tax purposes. Correspondingly, life insurance death proceeds on the death of an insured stockholder are normally received by the policy beneficiary income-tax-free. Finally, the value of a decedent's stock interest is included in his or her gross estate for federal estate tax purposes, subject to the rules of the Internal Revenue Code's Chapter 14 for family businesses.

Disability and Retirement in Buy-Sell Agreements

As noted in the preceding discussion, the main loss exposure normally covered in buy-sell agreements for all types of business entities (corporations, partnerships, and proprietorships) is the death of a business owner or owners. However, a buyout of a business interest might also be desired in the event of an owner's prolonged (and presumably permanent) total disability or when the owner retires. Thus, a buy-sell agreement might deal with the loss exposures of disability and retirement, as well as with that of death.

When disability is covered in the buy-sell agreement, important considerations include determining an appropriate definition of disability and determining when a disability buyout should begin. Disability income policies on the lives of the owners can be used to fund or partly fund a disability buyout. In this case, the definition of disability used in the insurance policies might also serve as the definition for buyout purposes. The periodic disability income benefits from the policy or policies on a disabled owner's life can be used to effect or help effect an installment buyout of the owner's business interest. Some insurers also sell disability policies that provide lump-sum disability benefits for business buy-sell situations.

When retirement is covered, or when retirement otherwise occurs, the cash values (if any) of the life insurance policies that were intended to fund a buyout in the event of the insured business owner's death can be used to help finance the purchase (or the redemption or liquidation) of the owner's interest upon retirement. Policy loans can be taken against the life insurance policies, or the policies can be surrendered for cash. The purchase or redemption of a retiring owner's business interest can be done in installments over more than one year to ease the financial burden on the buyer and to spread out any capital gain to the retiring owner over more than one year.

Key Employee Insurance

The most valuable asset of many business firms is not listed on a balance sheet. Companies list their inventory, accounts receivable, buildings, and other assets, but they do not show the value of employees to the organization. Yet, many business firms would have substantial financial problems if one or more of their important, or "key," employees died, became disabled, or terminated employment.

Astute management recognizes the importance of key employees to the company's financial health. Loss of a key employee could mean a loss of revenue, because customers demand that their work be performed by that person only or because no other employee has the skills to do a particular kind of task. Sometimes the value of the key employee is a result of his or her efficiency, which dramatically reduces production costs and gives the firm a price advantage. Whatever the reason, key employees make a special contribution to business income that can be counted on as long as they remain active employees of the firm.

Losses when key employees resign are generally uninsurable, but these losses can be prevented through appropriate employee compensation and employee benefit programs (such as well-designed employee stock or incentive plans). Key employee insurance helps an employer to protect against the loss of key employees because of death or disability.

Identifying Key Employees

A **key employee** can be described as a person who possesses an unusual skill, talent, or ability and whose death, disability, or termination of employment would probably cause a substantial financial loss to the company.

A number of factors might be considered to identify key employees. These factors include a person's title and position, decision-making authority, and salary. In addition, some people are considered key employees for the following reasons:

- They have developed *personal contacts* that bring the company business, and these contacts might be lost if these key individuals die, become disabled, or resign.

- They provide a *source of capital or credit* not otherwise available. Small businesses, particularly, have difficulty obtaining capital inexpensively and securing loans at favorable rates and on acceptable terms. A key employee might be able to arrange a favorable rate because of who he or she knows.

- They possess *special talents*, such as the ability to invent new products or to be technically responsible for the company's efficient operations.

Key employees are common in companies having one or more of the following characteristics:

- The business has been built (or is being developed) by a small number of people.

- The company does not have many individuals who can move quickly to a higher position.

- The company is growing rapidly, it does not have abundant working capital, and credit is obtained through personal contacts.

- The product or service offered by the company is unique—or, at least, unusual.

- Severe competition exists or rare training is needed.

Although few companies have all these features, this list generally describes small firms that owe their success to one or a few key employees. Large companies might have many executives and other "important" employees, but, unlike key employees, these people can sometimes be replaced with relative ease.

Estimating Key Employee Losses

Even when a company knows an individual is a key employee, it is difficult to estimate the loss that might be associated with his or her death or disability. Nevertheless, some estimate must be made in order to determine an amount of life insurance that might compensate for a key employee's loss. Methods of estimating value of the loss that might be caused by a key employee's death or disability include the following:

- When a key employee has been in charge of a project that must now be discontinued since he or she is irreplaceable, the amount lost is the amount invested in the project that cannot be recovered, plus the profit that would have been realized from the project.

- When a key employee is a salesperson responsible for a large share (for example, 25 percent of sales are attributed to one of ten salespersons) of the company's profits, the amount lost is the amount of decline in profits. If profits are adversely affected, estimates must be made for the size and duration of this decline.

- When a key employee can be replaced, only the additional costs of replacing the key employee should be considered. These expenses include any fees paid to an employment agency, the new employee's moving expenses, and the difference between the new and old employees' salaries, assuming the new employee is paid more than his or her predecessor or that it takes more than one new employee to do the work of the key employee. Education and training expenses might be applicable if a new person must be prepared because no one else currently possesses the skills of the key person.

- Some life insurance companies provide formulas for estimating the value of a key employee. Some formulas are based on the present value of the lost income attributable to the key employee, while others simply use a multiple of annual salary. It is important that the formula be reliable or representative of the employee's actual value to the firm. Formulas based on book values or asset values of the firm rarely have a realistic relationship with the employee's true worth.

Key Employee Life Insurance Arrangements

Key employee life insurance does not require any special type of insurance policy. Moreover, while a key employee must authorize the purchase of life insurance on his or her life, no formal agreement is required between the company and the key employee.

Term insurance can be purchased if the sole purpose of the arrangement is to reimburse the company for losses caused by the key employee's death. However, a policy that accumulates a cash value might be appropriate. The cash value can provide a source of funds for paying deferred compensation benefits, and the level premium structure eliminates the need to pay rapidly increasing premiums for term insurance at older ages. Cash value can also be used to fund temporary replacement personnel if the employee is disabled or to provide cash to the employer if the employee terminates employment.

A company has an insurable interest in the lives of its key employees—and consequently can buy life insurance on their lives—if their deaths would be financially detrimental to the company. A key employee must consent to the purchase of insurance on his or her life and must affirm the information contained in the application. As a further underwriting safeguard, many insurers require that a corporation's board of directors pass a resolution stating the purpose of the insurance. The resolution is then attached to the application. Normally, the company (employer) is the applicant, owner, premium payer, and beneficiary.

Insurable interest is required in life insurance only at policy inception. When a key employee's employment is terminated, the firm can continue to pay the premiums and keep the insurance in force, surrender the policy for its cash value, or sell the policy to the insured. The last approach is particularly advantageous for individuals who have become uninsurable.

Tax Aspects of Key Employee Life Insurance

The Internal Revenue Code prohibits an income tax deduction by the employer for key employee life insurance premiums. Correspondingly, key employee life insurance premium payments by the employer are not treated as taxable income to the key employee.

If a cash value policy is carried on the life of a key employee, the annual increase in the cash value is generally not subject to income taxation—either to the employer or to the key employee. If the employer surrenders the policy and the cash value exceeds the total net premiums paid, the gain is taxable as ordinary income to the employer.

As noted previously, a provision introduced into the Internal Revenue Code in 1986 subjects the annual increase in the cash value and the net death proceeds of life insurance owned by C corporations to potential taxation as part of the corporate *alternative minimum tax (AMT)*. The AMT calculation can be complex, and its details are beyond the scope of this text.

As a general rule, life insurance death proceeds received by an employer are not subject to federal income taxes. This rule is valid whether the beneficiary is an individual or an unincorporated business. Similarly, life insurance death proceeds paid to a corporation as beneficiary do not constitute gross income for regular corporate income tax purposes to the corporation. However, if these amounts (now general assets of the corporation and no longer life insurance proceeds paid by reason of the insured's death) are then paid by the corporation to its stockholders, they can be treated as dividends subject to taxation as income. That distribution is not deductible by the corporation. Also, as just noted, although life insurance death proceeds received by a C corporation are not included as regular income for federal income tax purposes, they do become part of the AMT calculation.

Split Dollar Life Insurance

Split dollar life insurance refers to the use of cash value life insurance policies in situations where two parties take the following two actions:

- Share the cost of paying premiums
- Divide the cash value and death benefits in a manner consistent with the sharing of the premiums.

Split dollar plans are most common in business situations where the employer and an employee share the cost of the coverage. Split dollar policies are also used in estate planning.

Split dollar plans provide many advantages:

- Since these plans are not qualified employee benefits and do not enjoy special tax treatment, they can be provided to employees whom the employer wants to favor.
- The employer can provide life insurance coverage at a lower out-of-pocket cost than would be required for employer-pay-all coverage. Moreover, the basic split dollar plans provide for the employer to recover premiums paid for the employer's portion of the split dollar coverage.
- The employee gains the advantage of life insurance at a lower cost than would be required for an individual policy totally funded by the employee. In addition to the death benefit payable to the beneficiary of the employee, these cash value policies can be used to help provide deferred

compensation to the employee and his or her family. Moreover, many split dollar plans allow the employee to own the life insurance policy outright after the split life insurance agreement is terminated with the employer.

Types of Policies Used

Term insurance policies cannot be used for split dollar plans because term insurance lacks the cash value needed to provide a predeath benefit to the employer sharing the premium costs. Thus, split dollar life insurance plans require cash value life insurance policies. When participating traditional whole life policies are used, dividends are often applied to purchase paid-up additions to enhance the death benefit payable to the beneficiary. Split dollar plans are often designed with limited premium paying periods. Some designs use policies that would be paid up by normal retirement age. Other plans require premiums only for the first eight or ten years of coverage.

Types of Split Dollar Life Insurance Plans

Split dollar plans are essentially an agreement between two parties (usually an employer and employee) as to how each will share the premiums, claims for death proceeds, and cash surrender values of a life insurance policy. Split dollar plans can be configured in many ways. The two general methods are the endorsement method and the collateral assignment method.

Endorsement Method

The following is true when the endorsement method of split dollar life insurance is used:

- The employer owns the life insurance and, thus, has maximum control over the policy and its cash values before the death of the insured.

- The employer generally pays the premiums and is reimbursed by the employee for the employee's share.

- The employee designates the beneficiary to receive the death benefit in excess of the employer's portion of the death benefit.

Collateral Assignment Method

There are differences under the collateral assignment split dollar plan:

- The employee owns the life insurance.

- The employee makes a collateral assignment to the employer of that portion of the cash value allocated to the employer—usually the aggregate amounts of premiums that have been paid by the employer.

Termination of Split Dollar Plans

Split dollar life insurance plans are often designed for the employer to cease to participate in the coverage at some specific future date. When an endorsement plan has been used, the most common procedure is for the employer to borrow the policy cash value in an amount equal to the employer's interest in he policy. The employer can then transfer the policy, with the outstanding indebtedness, to the employee.

If a collateral assignment plan has been established, the employee uses the policy loan proceeds to pay the employer an amount equal to its interest in the policy. This payment entitles the employee to a release of the employer's interest in the policy cash value and death benefit.

The final result in either case is that the employee owns the policy outright, becomes responsible for further premium payments, if any, and has control of the policy cash values and death benefit.

Summary

This chapter briefly discussed the principles of estate planning and summarized some of the issues involved in business continuation planning for sole proprietorships, partnerships, and closely held corporations.

Estate planning involves arrangements for the efficient transfer of one's estate to others, using an established process: gathering facts, evaluating the existing estate plan, formulating and testing a new estate plan, executing the new plan, and periodically reviewing and revising the estate plan. An important goal of many estate plans is to minimize the effect of estate taxes, state death taxes, and federal gift taxes. Devices used in estate planning include gifts, wills, and trusts.

Business continuation is a concern for sole proprietors, partners, and closely held corporations. It is desirable to develop a plan to continue or transfer the business and its assets upon the death or disability of a proprietor, partner, or stockholder. Such a plan can help preserve the decedent's assets for the sake of his or her heirs. A business continuation plan also enables surviving partners or stockholders to maintain or expand each survivor's interest in the business. Life insurance can play an important role in business continuation plans by providing the money necessary to carry them out.

Businesses can also be severely threatened by the death, disability, or termination of a key employee. Key employee insurance can protect an employer against such losses. Although term life insurance can be used to reimburse an employer when a key employee dies, cash value life insurance should be considered if the employer seeks protection against a key employee's death, disability, or termination. With a cash value key employee life insurance policy, the employer has access to the policy's cash value in the event the key employee is disabled or terminated and will receive death benefits if the key employee dies.

Split dollar life insurance can be used for estate planning or to favor particular employees. As the name implies, two parties—usually an employer and an employee—share the cost of purchasing a cash value life insurance policy on the employee's life. They then split the cash value and death benefit in a manner consistent with the sharing of premiums.

Chapter Notes

1. By using the unified transfer tax rate schedule in Exhibit 8-1, the following equation can be solved to determine the value of an estate that will be subject to federal estate tax if the available unified credit is $187,800:

$187,800 = (x - 500,000) \times 37\% + 155,800$

$x = 586,486.48$

Thus an estate valued at $586,487 or more will be subject to federal estate tax.

2. Chapter 14 of the Internal Revenue Code provides special valuation rules for federal gift and estate tax purposes with regard to certain transfers of interests among family members. The purpose of Chapter 14 is to prevent older generations in family businesses from being able to set unrealistically low valuations on their business interests for federal estate and gift tax purposes by entering into buy-sell agreements (and other arrangements) with younger generations that use low valuation provisions.

3. Book value itself is often inappropriate because it is based on historical costs and ignores the company's profitability as a going concern.

4. The number of policies required in a cross-purchase plan is always $n(n-1)$, where n is the number of partners.

Chapter 9

Case Study

This chapter presents a detailed, extensive case that illustrates the application of information presented in the text to the entire set of circumstances faced by one family. The major focus will be on analyzing the family's present position and identifying specific alternative ways in which the family's objectives can be achieved. The development of an overall risk management plan will be discussed in more general terms. The discussion at the end of the chapter will, however, consider the costs of the alternatives mentioned throughout the chapter and analyze the family's ability to pay for the recommended measures. *The case is designed to bring out the many issues that affect the development of such a plan rather than to arrive at an overall plan.*

The risk management process and the financial planning process are illustrated in this chapter. Before beginning the risk management process, an individual or family should establish personal objectives. The risk management process, which consists of the following steps, can then be used to establish an appropriate risk management plan:

- Identifying and analyzing loss exposures
- Examining alternative risk management techniques
- Selecting the best risk management techniques
- Implementing the risk management plan
- Monitoring and revising the risk management plan

Financial planning is an important part of risk management. In determining a family's or individual's financial plan, the following steps are recommended:

- Gather the necessary financial information
- Establish financial objectives
- Analyze the current financial position and identify alternatives
- Develop and implement a financial plan
- Periodically review and revise the plan

Four observations about risk management should be mentioned before the case analysis begins:

1. *Risk management is an integrative process that looks at the overall risk and financial situation of a family, rather than at separate objectives independently.* In some cases, one solution can solve several problems. For example, the purchase of property insurance can protect the property owner from loss when a piece of property is damaged and also protect the property owner's capital accumulation for his or her child's education. In a similar vein, the purchase of universal life insurance might be appropriate when a person has both a need for protecting dependents against his or her death and a desire to accumulate funds for his or her retirement. Likewise, contributions to an IRA might be suggested to someone who wants to accumulate retirement funds and to minimize current federal income taxes.

2. *It might be impossible to develop a risk management plan that will meet all stated risk management objectives.* For example, a husband and wife might not have adequate resources both to buy needed health insurance and to fund fully the future college expenses of their children. The couple will need to revise its objectives or to modify its lifestyle so that additional resources are available.

3. *The goal of personal risk management is to meet the objectives of the individual or family without unacceptable trade-offs.* This is related to observation 2 above. While it might be impossible to meet all stated risk management objectives, the goal of risk management is to meet as many objectives as possible without creating unacceptable trade-offs. For example, the husband and wife in the example in 2 above want to purchase health insurance *and* fully fund their children's college education but are not financially able to do so. The couple might not be willing to forgo health insurance to fund their children's education fully. For them it might be better to purchase health insurance with a deductible, partially fund their children's college education, and either encourage their children to excel in school so that they might earn scholarships or explain to them that they might have to work their way through school.

4. *Perhaps most important, often no single answer exists to a particular risk management case or problem.* Usually several possible alternative solutions

are available, as will be demonstrated where appropriate in the case analysis.

The Case Facts

The following data have been obtained on the family used for this case analysis. The information is presented in a narrative form, but in practice a risk manager or financial planner would have gathered much of the information through a questionnaire. Some of the data would also have been ascertained during interviews with the family.

Carol and Paul Claude ("PC") Ulrich, age forty-one and forty-four respectively, have been married for four years. Each has two children from a prior marriage, all of whom live with the Ulrichs. Carol's two children, Betsy and Eric, are ages twelve and eight. PC's twins, David and Wendy, are age nine. Carol receives a $300 monthly child support payment from her former husband, who visits his children on a regular basis. PC's ex-spouse pays $250 monthly as child support. Since she lives more than 1,000 miles away, her visits with the twins are limited to summer vacation time.

The Ulrichs reside in a metropolitan area with a population of about 250,000. PC bought the home seven years ago for $115,000. His basis in the property at that time was $50,000 from a rollover of his share from the sale of a home owned jointly with his former spouse. After Carol and PC were married, they added an addition to the house, costing $75,000, which provided more space to meet their needs. Carol paid for the addition. PC then jointly titled the home with Carol. The current mortgage balance is $66,990. PC and Carol estimate that the current market value of the primary residential property is $250,000, although the current market value of the dwelling (excluding the value of the land) is estimated at $220,000 and its replacement cost at $230,000. The residence is insured with a Homeowners 3 Special Form (HO-3) endorsed with an inflation guard that values the replacement value of the dwelling at $240,000. The HO-3 also includes $100,000 worth of personal liability insurance. The standard $250 deductible applies to property losses.

Carol owns some antique porcelain that is on display in a cabinet in their living room. Her collection cost $8,500 to assemble. A friend, who is an avid collector of these items, estimated that Carol's collection is worth at least $20,000. In addition, Carol's engagement and wedding rings and other jewelry (which she would like her daughter to receive when Carol passes away) are valued at $10,500. Household furnishings, clothing, appliances, toys, and hobby paraphernalia, acquired at various times before and after Carol and PC's marriage, amount to $50,000 actual cash value.

When PC's aunt died two-and-a-half years ago, PC inherited her furnished summer home, located on a river about 150 miles from their primary residence in the same state. When the summer property was distributed from the estate two years ago, it was valued at $125,000, including its furnishings and the land. The Ulrichs do not believe that the summer home's value has increased since that time. They have since acquired a twenty-foot motorboat powered by a 125-horsepower outboard motor and a trailer to haul the boat from the summer home to the boat ramp five miles away. When not in use, the boat, motor, and trailer are stored in a shed on the riverfront property.

PC is a freelance reporter for a local newspaper and receives assignments on a somewhat regular basis. Last year, he earned $15,000 (net of taxes and expenses) as a reporter. In addition, he writes children's storybooks for a major publisher. These books are popular, and he receives royalty income from the publisher on a quarterly basis. His current royalty income amounts to $35,000 per year.

PC maintains an office in the primary residence, where he writes the newspaper articles and books. The office, equipped for desktop publishing with two computers, a laser printer, two modems, and appropriate software and supplies, is also used by PC to meet with the illustrator of his books and with representatives of both the newspaper and the book publisher. The illustrator for his books frequently collaborates with PC in this office.

Two years ago PC established "PC's Books for Kids," a catalog business that specializes in high-quality children's books that he personally selects. The inventory, which averages $35,000 at cost, is kept in a self-storage facility where once or twice a week he, often assisted by Carol, packages and ships orders. Most sales are made by accepting the major national credit cards. An answering service takes telephone orders over an 800 line, Carol and PC handle the paperwork for mail orders, and a local CPA firm performs the billing, bookkeeping, and inventory management for the business. Last year, PC netted $18,000 from this business, and he expects profits to grow at least 6 percent each year. The most recent Statement of Financial Position for PC's Books for Kids is shown in Exhibit 9-1.

Carol is a commissioned sales representative for a firm specializing in direct-mail advertising material. As with any such sales position, her monthly income varies, although her average annual income is $25,000. Although Carol has been with the firm for six years, she would like to have a position that would provide more time to be with the children, particularly in the summer months when school is not in session. She needs about thirty credit hours to complete her bachelor's degree in education and would like to do so

Exhibit 9-1
PC's Books for Kids Statement of Financial Position December 31, 199X

Assets		Liabilities and Net Worth	
Cash	$ 5,000	Accounts payable	$ 8,000
Accounts receivable	7,000	Bank loan	9,000
Inventory	35,000		
Mailing supplies	500	PC's equity	30,500
		Total Liabilities and	
Total Assets	$47,500	Net Worth	$47,500

as a full-time student rather than spend several years attending night school. The Ulrichs have examined their finances and feel confident that they can manage their living expenses on PC's income for the year that Carol needs to finish her degree. However, PC and Carol are quite concerned that should Carol leave her current position, the family would no longer have health insurance, since Carol, PC, and all the children are adequately covered under Carol's employer's group health insurance plan.

Regardless of their concern over health insurance, the Ulrichs are planning for Carol to complete her education and find a teaching position within commuting distance from their primary residence. If this plan comes to fruition, they will be able to spend their summers on the river, since PC could write at the river house and also could return to the city each week to handle his freelance newspaper assignments and to attend to the mail-order business.

Should Carol leave her current employer, she would have to roll over or withdraw her accumulation in the firm's 401(k) plan, since the plan does not permit continued participation after termination of employee status. The value of Carol's interest at this time, divided equally between a guaranteed investment contract (GIC) and an open-ended long-term bond mutual fund, is $30,000. This sum represents both her and her employer's tax deferred contributions as well as the accumulated investment earnings.

Until PC and Carol were married, PC contributed $2,000 annually to a tax-deferred IRA. He ceased making these payments when he and Carol were married because the contributions no longer were tax deductible since Carol participated in a qualified retirement plan and their aggregate income exceeded (and still does) the limits for making tax deductible contributions. PC's IRA contributions totaled $10,000, and the value of the IRA, invested in certificates of deposit (CDs) at the local bank, is $21,000. The annual rate of return on his several CDs currently averages 5.1 percent.

PC owns a one-year-old minivan, which he uses for work and personal use. His average annual mileage is about 20,000, 4,000 of which represents travel to and from his work for the newspaper and 5,000, travel for his mail-order business. Carol's four-year-old sedan is driven for personal use (about 10,000 miles annually), except when her company-supplied vehicle is being serviced. Both vehicles are insured under a personal auto policy (PAP) that has a liability limit of $100,000, a medical payments limit of $5,000, and an uninsured motorists limit of $100,000. The collision deductible is $250 and the other than collision (OTC) deductible is $100. In addition, PC is covered for his business use of the minivan under the PAP.

Seven years ago, PC bought a $75,000 universal life insurance policy on his life. When he married Carol, he made her the primary beneficiary and the twins equal contingent beneficiaries. The annual premium is $900. Carol has a $50,000 group term life insurance policy that is provided and fully paid for by her employer. PC is the primary beneficiary, and her children from her previous marriage are the contingent beneficiaries.

Shortly after their marriage, Carol and PC drew up new wills. Each has named the other as the recipient of his or her separate property, with the exception that Carol's jewelry is to be distributed to her daughter.

The Ulrichs currently have a balance of $18,000 in a noninterest-paying checking account; $5,000 in a savings account earning 2.3 percent interest compounded monthly; and $8,500 in CDs, yielding an annual average of 4 percent. During the last two years, PC and Carol have begun acquiring shares in a balanced mutual fund that has averaged a rate of return of 11.5 percent over the two-year period but is currently generating a 10.5 percent return. They started this investment with a $3,000 deposit and have contributed $100 monthly since then. All dividends and capital gains are automatically reinvested in additional shares. Their investment in the mutual fund is currently valued at $6,500.

The Ulrichs' two major financial concerns are the education of their children and their retirement. While Carol's 401(k) and PC's IRA are currently their only means for accumulating retirement funding, Carol and PC have purchased Series EE bonds for the children's education funds. Shortly after PC and Carol were married, they began periodically purchasing $50 face amount Series EE bonds for each child and have titled the bonds in the child's name. Each child currently owns a total of $1,900 face value of these bonds. The bonds most recently acquired earn 4 percent until redeemed. The other bonds earn at least 6 percent annually if held for at least five years. The Ulrichs are concerned that their current funding will fail to provide the needed education funds, currently estimated to be $10,000 per year for each year of college, particularly with college costs currently rising at 5 percent per year.

Exhibit 9-2 shows the Ulrichs' assets and liabilities, and Exhibit 9-3 summarizes their income for the most recent year.

Exhibit 9-2
Ulrichs' Assets and Liabilities as of December 31, 199X

Assets		Liabilities	
Bank accounts		Mortgage	$66,990
Checking	$ 18,000	PC's auto loan	10,800
Saving	5,000	Carol's auto loan	1,500
CDs	8,500	Boat loan	8,100
Other financial assets		Credit cards	3,400
Balanced fund	6,500	Property taxes	4,200
PC's IRA	21,000	**Total Liabilities**	$94,990
Carol's 401(k)	30,000		
Life insurance cash values	5,200		
Personal assets			
Primary residence	250,000		
Porcelain	20,000		
Furnishings-primary residence	60,000		
Jewelry	10,500		
Summer residence	115,000		
Furnishings-summer residence	10,000		
PC's auto	12,000		
Carol's auto	7,000		
Boat	18,000		
Trailer	2,250		
Desktop publishing equipment	3,000		
Business net worth	30,500		
Total Assets	$632,450		

Personal Objectives

Without a clear understanding of an individual's or family's personal objectives, it would be impossible for a risk manager or financial planner to develop

Exhibit 9-3
Ulrichs' Net Income for 199X

Earned Income		
PC's newspaper earnings	$15,000	
PC's royalties	35,000	
PC's mail-order business	18,000	
Carol's earnings	25,000	
Interest (savings and CDs)	455	
Balanced fund	649	
Total earned income		$ 94,104
Other income		
Child support for PC's children	3,000	
Child support for Carol's children	3,600	
Total other income		6,600
Total Net Income		$100,704

proper recommendations. Furthermore, a person who has not thought through his or her objectives might not make the most appropriate decisions.

Risk managers and financial planners usually aid clients in formulating explicit objectives. The information provided in data-gathering questionnaires is one source of information for this task. In fact, many questionnaires specifically ask clients to identify objectives and to rank their importance. Other objectives evolve from discussions with clients. Regardless of how objectives are formulated, they should be clearly stated in writing. This process provides an opportunity for individuals to think about what their objectives actually are. By quantifying their goals, families and individuals can determine whether they seem to be realistic. The process also minimizes the possibility that objectives are overlooked. Finally, it provides a framework within which future decisions can be made.

The Ulrichs have explicitly identified several personal objectives:

- Carol would like to be employed as a teacher so that she can spend more time with her children.

- Carol wants to return to school full time for one year to complete her bachelor's degree in education.

- Carol wants school and work to be within commuting distance of her current home.

- Carol wants her jewelry to pass to her daughter when Carol dies.
- Carol and PC want to fully fund each of their four children's college education.
- Carol and PC also want to save for a comfortable retirement.

These are the objectives on which the Ulrichs' risk management process focuses. The following sections (1) analyze the loss exposures—both nonfinancial and financial—faced by the Ulrichs, (2) evaluate their impact on the family's objectives, (3) consider the risk management alternatives available to the Ulrichs, and (4) discuss an overall risk management plan for the family.

Analyzing Loss Exposures and Identifying Alternative Treatments

The data for the Ulrichs have been gathered, and the family's explicit objectives have been identified. It is now possible to analyze the loss exposures the Ulrichs face and determine their impact on the family's objectives. The family's current treatment of the exposures can be considered in order to determine whether their objectives are being met by the existing risk management plan. If they are not, alternative approaches for achieving the objectives must be considered.

Property Loss Exposures

Loss from real and personal property damage can result from a wide variety of perils. Some of the more prevalent are fire, lightning, windstorm, hail, explosion, smoke damage, water damage, damage by or to an auto, vandalism, theft, and glass breakage. The property owned by the Ulrichs, which is summarized in Exhibit 9-4, column A, is subject to these and other perils.

The potential financial severity of direct property damage loss is essentially the maximum loss that could be sustained by the property. This loss potential can be measured in several ways, although for property loss sustained by individuals and families the most commonly used methods are *actual cash value* (ACV) and *replacement cost* (RC). RC valuation measures the cost to fully replace the lost property with similar property and is typically used to evaluate loss exposures involving residential real property. ACV valuation, used primarily for personal property, accounts for obsolescence and age of the lost property and can be measured as the market value of the property prior to the loss or as the replacement cost of the damaged property less any depreciation. The RC and ACV for the Ulrichs' property is shown in columns B and C, respectively, of Exhibit 9-4.

Exhibit 9-4

Ulrichs' Property

(A) Property	(B) Replacement Cost	(C) Actual Cash Value
Primary residence (dwelling only), in which PC maintains an office, in a metropolitan area	$230,000	$220,000
Antique porcelain	20,000*	20,000*
Jewelry, including Carol's engagement and wedding rings	10,500	10,500
Various other personal property	60,000	50,000
A summer residence (dwelling and shed only) located on a river about 150 miles from their primary residence	110,000	105,000
The furnishings of the summer home	10,000	8,500
A 20-foot motorboat with a 125-horsepower outboard motor stored at the riverfront property	18,000	16,000
The boat trailer, also stored at the riverfront property	2,250	2,000
Desktop publishing equipment used by PC for his freelance reporting and writing children's books	4,500	3,000
Mail-order business inventory	35,000	35,000
PC's one-year-old minivan, used for business 45 percent of the time [(4,000 + 5,000)/20,000]	15,000	12,000
Carol's four-year-old sedan, sometimes used for business	12,500	7,000
*Estimated value		

The potential severity of direct property damage can be greater than the economic loss for various reasons, such as an individual's mental anguish at the loss of a cherished family heirloom or a family's lost sense of security following the burglary of its home. Risk management often focuses on the financial aspects of direct loss of property—it is important to consider noneconomic consequences of loss as well. For example, for sentimental reasons, Carol's engagement and wedding rings are probably worth more to her and PC than their financial value.

The Ulrichs are also subject to loss consequences beyond those resulting from direct damage reducing the value of property. For example, if the residence becomes uninhabitable when it is heavily damaged by fire, the Ulrichs might incur additional living expenses if they must move to a rental apartment or move to the summer home and commute to the city. Or, if Carol's sedan is damaged in an auto accident, she might have to rent another vehicle until the sedan can be repaired or replaced.

Some of the potential consequences of the Ulrichs' property loss exposures could prevent the family from achieving its objectives, at least for a period of time. For example, if the primary residence is destroyed, the family might not be able to afford Carol's return to school until the family is resettled and is once again financially stable. Such a loss could also keep Carol and PC from funding their children's college education and saving for a comfortable retirement because they would have to pay for a new home.

Other potential loss consequences of the Ulrichs' property loss exposures are less severe. For example, if Carol's jewelry is stolen during a robbery of the primary residence, the loss, though emotionally draining, is not likely to keep Carol from returning to school or to keep Carol and PC from saving for the children's college education and a comfortable retirement. The jewelry is not essential and can be replaced piece by piece over time. If the Ulrichs want to replace the jewelry soon after the loss, however, the family might experience some delay in achieving their personal objectives. Their savings would be depleted, and Carol might not be able to afford to return to school. Thus, the family's plans to save for the children's college education and Carol and PC's retirement could be delayed.

The financial aspects of the Ulrichs' property loss exposures are currently dealt with through personal insurance and retention. The family has an HO-3 with $240,000 of coverage on the primary residence and the standard deductible of $250. The family also has a PAP that provides both collision coverage, with a deductible of $250, and OTC coverage, with a deductible of $100, for PC's van and Carol's sedan. In addition to the deductibles, the family retains all property exposures not covered by these insurance policies as identified in column B of Exhibit 9-5. Thus, if Carol's jewelry is stolen, she will receive only $1,000 to cover the $10,500 loss, because jewelry is subject to a special internal policy limit in the HO-3.

Exhibit 9-5
Inadequacies of and Recommended Changes for the Ulrichs' Property Risk
Management Plan

(A) Property Exposure	(B) Inadequacy	(C) Recommendation
Antique porcelain	Not covered for breakage; covered on an ACV basis	Scheduled personal property endorsement to HO-3
Jewelry	Subject to a $1,000 limit if stolen; covered on a broad named perils, ACV basis	Scheduled personal property endorsement to HO-3
Desktop publishing equipment	Subject to a $2,500 limit as business property; covered on a broad named perils, ACV basis	Consider purchasing coverage for business personal property with RC, "all-risks" coverage
Mail-order business inventory	Subject to $250 limit as business property off-premises; covered on broad named perils basis	Purchase business personal property coverage
Other personal property	Valued on an ACV basis; covered on a broad named perils basis	Endorse RC coverage and special personal property coverage to HO-3
Summer home	Not covered by any property insurance	Purchase a dwelling policy with RC, "all-risks" coverage; consider a flood policy
Furnishings of the summer home	Not covered for theft while the Ulrichs are not staying at the summer home; covered on a broad named perils, ACV basis subject to internal 10 percent limit	Include under the dwelling policy on the summer home; RC, "all-risks" coverage under either policy; consider flood coverage
Motorboat and trailer	Subject to a $1,000 limit; not covered for theft; not covered for windstorm unless in fully enclosed building; covered on a broad named perils, ACV basis	Purchase a boatowners or yacht policy
Primary residence	Policy limit of coverage on dwelling exceeds replacement cost of dwelling	Adjust limit of coverage to more accurately reflect current replacement cost; discuss inflation guard index with insurance company
HO-3 and PAP deductibles	Might be too low	Increase

The antique porcelain and the jewelry should be insured under a schedule. The porcelain and the jewelry would then be covered for "all-risks," including breakage of the porcelain and theft of the jewelry. In addition, the Ulrichs should have the porcelain appraised by a professional appraiser (and most likely would be required to have such an appraisal if they were to insure it).

The scheduled value of the porcelain should accurately reflect its appraised value, and the scheduled limit of the jewelry should be set at $10,500. The ISO homeowners policies do not cover loss to personal property that is specifically insured under another insurance policy or endorsement. Thus, the porcelain and the jewelry must be listed at their full value on the schedule for the Ulrichs to receive full coverage in an event of total loss of the scheduled property.

With respect to the desktop publishing equipment, the Ulrichs might be able to continue to retain the $2,000 RC property loss exposure not covered under their HO-3. However, they might consider a business property policy or endorsement if the premium for the coverage is reasonable with respect to the additional property protection provided. Business personal property insurance can be purchased on a replacement cost and "all-risks" basis.

The mail-order business inventory is also business personal property, and it is located off the residence premises. The HO-3 provides only $250 of coverage for business personal property when it is located off the residence premises. PC's business cannot retain a $34,750 loss without severe financial hardship. PC's earnings would be drastically reduced, and the family might not be able to support itself without Carol's working. Business personal property insurance should be purchased to cover loss to or of the inventory.

The Ulrichs should add a personal property replacement cost endorsement to their HO-3. If a total loss to their personal property occurs, they will receive only $50,000 of the $60,000 they will need to replace their property. If the Ulrichs do not need to replace all of their personal property immediately following such a loss, the $10,000 difference could possibly be retained by the Ulrichs. Otherwise, this $10,000 difference cannot be retained by the Ulrichs without delaying achievement of their personal objectives. The replacement cost endorsement would provide them with full coverage in the event of a covered loss.

The Ulrichs should also endorse "all-risks" personal property coverage to their HO-3. Under their current coverage, if their personal property is damaged by a peril not listed in their policy, such as damage caused by rain coming in through an open window, they will have to retain the exposure. Depending on the size of the loss, this could delay Carol's return to school or could interfere with the family's plans to fund the children's college education or Carol and PC's retirement. A special personal property coverage endorsement would provide them with "all-risks" coverage on their personal property.

A glaring omission in the Ulrichs' property insurance is the lack of property insurance on their summer home. Because it is an additional residence not located on the residence premises, it is not covered under the Ulrichs' HO-3. Furthermore, any property usually located at the summer home, including the boat and its trailer, is subject to an ACV limit equal to 10 percent of the HO-3's Coverage C limit—or, $12,000 with the current $240,000 of insurance on the dwelling. The boat and trailer are further subject to the $1,000 special limit of Coverage C. As for loss due to theft, the boat and trailer are not covered, and the other personal property located at the summer home is not covered for theft while the Ulrichs are not staying at the summer home. Furthermore, the boat and trailer are not covered for windstorm damage unless they are inside a fully enclosed building at the time of the damage. All of this means that if, for example, the summer home and all the personal property located at the summer home, including the boat and trailer, are destroyed by fire, the Ulrichs will collect a total of $9,500—$8,500 for the actual cash value of the personal property usually located at the summer home and $1,000 for the boat and trailer. They are currently retaining a $130,750 (replacement cost) property loss exposure. If the Ulrichs intend to replace the summer home and its furnishings, they must purchase insurance because they will not be able to cover the loss without jeopardizing all of their personal objectives.

To cover the summer home and its furnishings, the Ulrichs should purchase a dwelling policy that includes $110,000 replacement cost coverage on the summer home and $10,000 replacement cost coverage on the furnishings. The property should be insured on an "all-risks" basis with a theft endorsement. If the summer home is in a designated and eligible flood zone, the Ulrichs should consider a flood insurance policy on the summer home and its furnishings. For any coverage purchased, the Ulrichs should consider a sizable deductible, such as $500 or $1,000. They are financially able to retain this deductible amount, and the premium savings should, in the long run, more than cover any resulting loss payments that are within the amount of the deductible.

The outboard motorboat, its motor, its equipment, and its trailer, should be insured under a separate boatowners or yacht policy. The boat and its motor and its equipment should be insured for replacement cost, if acceptable to the insurer. This policy should provide "all-risks" coverage including coverage for losses caused by perils of the sea, such as sinking or capsizing. Again, the Ulrichs should consider a large deductible.

Another problem with the Ulrichs' property insurance involves the amount of coverage on the primary residence—the inflation guard on the Ulrichs' HO-3 appears to be working too well. The Ulrichs are carrying $240,000 of insurance on their home, which they believe would only cost $230,000 to replace. They should have the home inspected to get an accurate replacement cost for the dwelling. If the coverage limit exceeds the replacement cost, the Ulrichs should reduce the amount of their dwelling coverage to the appropriate level. They should also discuss with their insurer the possibility of modifying the inflation factor to more accurately reflect the growth in their home's replacement value. However, because home values can change at faster or slower rates than any index on which the inflation guard might be based, the Ulrichs must periodically review their HO-3 dwelling insurance limit.

Along with the deductibles mentioned above, the Ulrichs should consider the deductibles on both their HO-3 and their PAP. They have adequate resources to assume relatively large deductibles. In the long run, any losses assumed under the deductibles should be more than offset by premium savings. The $250 deductible on their HO-3 might be increased to $500 or $1,000.[1] The $250 collision deductible on their PAP could be increased to $500 or $1,000, and the OTC deductible could be increased to $250 or $500.[2] The Ulrichs must consider the frequency of loss in their decision to increase their deductibles. If auto theft is a concern in their area, they might prefer a $250 OTC deductible to a $500 deductible.

Column C of Exhibit 9-5 summarizes the recommended changes to the Ulrichs' property risk management plan. In determining which of these recommendations to follow, the Ulrichs must consider their ability to retain certain loss exposures and the cost of the additional insurance. The family does not want to purchase insurance for a loss exposure it can easily retain, nor does it want to forgo insurance on loss exposures that it cannot retain without interference in achieving its personal objectives. Lastly, the Ulrichs do not want to trade dollars with an insurance company. They need to make sure that the premium they pay is reasonable with respect to the severity of the loss exposure they are transferring to the insurer. For example, if the premium the family pays for its HO-3 is reduced by only $10 a year by increasing the deductible from $250 to $500, the family might decide it is worth the extra $10 in premium each year to maintain a $250 deductible. However, if the family could save $30 a year by increasing their deductible to $500, it might choose to make the change.

The above discussion focused on the Ulrichs' risk financing. The Ulrichs can also use risk control to treat their property loss exposures, if they are not already doing so. Risk control activities have a potential for saving both trouble and money. For example, the family could remove the personal property stored at the summer home or reduce the amount to a level that can be retained. This would allow them to include adequate coverage for the personal property under their HO-3 and require them to purchase additional property coverage for only the summer home. Furthermore, they could store any personal property remaining at the summer home on its upper level to control flood damage. This could allow the family to retain any flood loss to personal property.

The risk control techniques available to the Ulrichs include the obvious, such as (1) smoke detectors in both residences to warn residents of fire or (2) deadbolt locks on all external doors to prevent unlawful entry to the primary residence and the summer home. Avoidance is also an alternative that can eliminate some exposures, but, from a practical standpoint, this technique is inappropriate for the Ulrichs. For example, the family might avoid loss to its summer home and motorboat by selling the property. However, the family might prefer to keep this property, and thus, must control these exposures in another manner. Other risk control techniques include the following:

- Storing unworn jewelry and other valuables in a safe deposit box
- Installing fire extinguishers and security systems in both houses and both autos
- Storing the motorboat at a moorage rather than at the summer home

Risk control measures are important to insurance programs. Many property insurance companies provide premium reductions or discounts to individuals and families who use specific risk control measures. For example, many insurers provide a 5 to 10 percent premium discount to people who install and use security systems in their homes and in their autos.

Liability Loss Exposures

Personal liability can result from an act of negligence or from contractually assuming the liability of others. It is essential that possible loss exposures be identified. For the Ulrichs, possible sources of liability loss exposures include the following:

- Carol and PC's ownership and use of real property
- Carol and PC's ownership and use of autos and a boat
- The family members' personal activities
- Carol and PC's business activities
- Carol's use of an auto supplied by her business

Liability actions can result in severe economic problems and have become an increasingly troublesome area of personal risk management. Judgments might involve monetary damages far in excess of the family's total asset value or net worth. The probability of liability losses is not easily determined, but the severity can be catastrophic and can keep the family from achieving any of its personal objectives. Therefore, adequate risk control and financing of the liability loss exposure is a necessity.

Controlling liability loss exposures involves taking care of the family's surroundings and the family's behavior. Avoidance, as mentioned above, is not of much practical use for the Ulrichs. Safe behavior by all members of the family, however, can help to keep liability losses from occurring, as well as reduce the severity of any liability losses. For example, if the primary residence is properly maintained, it is unlikely that a visitor will be injured by a falling light fixture. If Carol and PC supervise the children's use of the motorboat, the chance of its injuring a water-skier through carelessness is reduced. If Carol's sedan is periodically serviced, it is less likely that the brakes will fail and cause Carol to hit another motorist at a stop sign.

Because of the potential for catastrophic liability loss, personal liability loss exposures should be insured. The Ulrichs have $100,000 personal liability insurance under their HO-3 and $100,000 auto liability insurance under their PAP. All other liability loss exposures are currently being retained by the Ulrichs. Unfortunately, as stressed in column B of Exhibit 9-6, the Ulrichs' liability loss exposure financing leaves them in serious jeopardy of catastrophic loss.

The summer home is not an insured location because it is not currently listed as such on the HO-3 policy. Therefore, the Ulrichs are not insured against general personal liability arising out of their ownership and use of the summer home. The Ulrichs should add the summer home to the HO-3 policy for liability coverage so that the policy will apply to general personal liability loss exposures associated with the summer home even though the property loss exposures are covered under a dwelling policy.

The liability limits on both the Ulrichs' HO-3 and PAP are grossly inadequate for the family's level of wealth and apparent level of income. The Ulrichs should purchase a personal umbrella liability policy with at least $1 million worth of coverage—even a policy with coverage worth $2 million or more would not be unrealistic. Without such coverage, one liability claim could easily cause the loss of the assets that the Ulrichs have accumulated over the years.

The liability coverage limits on the HO-3 and the PAP should be maintained at the level required for underlying limits by the Ulrichs' personal umbrella liability policy. Depending on the insurer's requirements, the current $100,000 provided by each policy probably will not be sufficient, so the Ulrichs might be required to increase each of the liability limits to $300,000 (or more).

Exhibit 9-6

Deficiencies of and Recommended Changes for the Ulrichs' Liability Risk Management Plan

(A) Liability Exposure	(B) Deficiency	(C) Recommendation
General personal liability	Inadequate limit under HO-3; not covered if arises out of summer home	Purchase personal umbrella liability policy; increase HO-3 liability limit to satisfy underlying coverage requirement; name summer home to HO-3 or purchase personal liability insurance to limit needed to meet umbrella's underlying requirement
Personal auto liability	Inadequate limit under PAP	Purchase personal umbrella liability policy; increase PAP liability limit to satisfy underlying coverage requirement
Personal watercraft liability	Not covered by HO-3	Purchase boatowner or yacht policy with adequate liability limit to meet umbrella's underlying requirement
Personal auto liability for Carol's business auto	Not covered by PAP	Endorse extended non-owned auto coverage to PAP with sufficient limits to meet underlying requirement of umbrella
Carol and PC's business liability	Not covered by HO-3	Consider purchase of business liability policy for Carol; purchase business liability policy and a commercial umbrella liability policy for PC
Personal injury liability	Not covered by HO-3	Purchase personal umbrella liability policy

Liability arising out of the ownership, use, or maintenance of the motorboat is not covered by the HO-3 because the 125-horsepower rating of the outboard motor exceeds the maximum horsepower level permitted for coverage under the policy. If the Ulrichs purchase the boatowner or yacht policy as recommended above, the liability coverage under the policy will apply to the boat's ownership, use, and maintenance. The liability limit for the boat should be set at the limit required by the personal umbrella liability policy (typically $100,000 to $300,000), assuming such liability is included under the umbrella.

The company car provided to Carol presents an exposure that raises some serious issues. Since the car is furnished for her regular use, it is excluded from the Ulrichs' PAP. Presumably, she has liability protection under a commercial policy carried by her employer. However, the amount of coverage might be inadequate, and certain suits involving fellow employees are probably excluded. Coverage for PC if he drives Carol's company car might also be inadequate. To insure this exposure properly, the Ulrichs should add extended nonowned auto liability coverage to their PAP. This coverage will likely also be required by the personal umbrella liability insurer as one of the underlying coverages. As with the other liability coverages, the Ulrichs should carry the underlying limit required by the personal liability umbrella policy.

Both Carol and PC are subject to business liability. Carol, as a sales representative, might face the exposure of being sued, along with her employer, for false advertising, misrepresentation, or similar activities that could arise out of her business dealings. If the amount of coverage provided by her employer is inadequate, some additional business liability coverage might be necessary. PC definitely needs to purchase business liability insurance. Any injury arising out of his business activities is not covered under the HO-3. The Section II personal liability coverage specifically excludes such coverage. Furthermore, many personal umbrella liability policies do not cover business liability even if it is covered by underlying insurance. PC should also purchase a commercial umbrella liability policy (and, in fact, he might be able to purchase a combined personal and commercial umbrella liability policy at less than it would cost to purchase each coverage separately). If PC does not purchase the appropriate business liability insurance, he might be forced to retain the following losses:

- Liability for bodily injury to an illustrator of one of his children's books that occurred while the illustrator was visiting PC at his home office
- Liability for damage to the property of a tenant at the self-storage premises resulting from a fire caused by PC's negligent maintenance of his storage unit
- Liability for slander arising out of one of PC's freelance reports to the newspaper
- Liability for failing to meet a publisher's deadline, resulting in the loss by the publisher of thousands of dollars in advertising

One final loss exposure that must be mentioned is liability for personal injury such as defamation of character. A business liability policy should cover such liability exposures as they pertain to Carol and PC's business activities. But both Carol and PC are also exposed to personal injury liability loss on a personal level. The personal umbrella liability policy should provide coverage for such liability exposures. However, the personal umbrella might require that underlying coverage for such losses also be purchased before it provides coverage for personal injury loss. Thus the Ulrichs might also need to add a personal injury endorsement to their HO-3.

The recommendations with respect to the Ulrichs' liability loss exposures are summarized in column C of Exhibit 9-6. In this area, the Ulrichs should make all the recommended purchases. Liability exposures can be catastrophic and should not be retained.

Illness and Injury Loss Exposures

The Ulrichs face several types of financial loss in the event of illness and injury, particularly if Carol or PC becomes disabled:

- Loss of current income and future income potential
- Extra costs and obligations—such as medical expenses, long-term care expenses, and costs to replace household services
- Loss of business values
- Loss of credit rating from circumstances such as the inability to repay debts

Medical expenses of any family member, not just of Carol or PC as the wage earners, can have an adverse financial effect on the family. The severity of the disability exposure can be more significant than that of the death exposure for either PC or Carol because, in addition to the loss of income, support must be provided for the disabled family member and catastrophic medical and reha-bilitation expenses can be incurred. If catastrophic medical expenses or disability losses are not insured, the family might become bankrupt. The Ulrichs' illness and injury exposures, with the current inadequacies of and recommended changes to their risk management plan, are listed in Exhibit 9-7.

Medical Expenses

Currently, the medical expense coverage of the Ulrichs is adequate. Until Carol leaves her position as a commissioned sales representative, the family is covered by group health insurance. When Carol does leave her job, the family can purchase individual family health insurance coverage that includes, at the minimum, major medical expense insurance, or it can continue its current health insurance coverage for up to eighteen months under the requirements of COBRA. However, purchasing individual family health coverage is the recommended alternative

Exhibit 9-7
The Ulrichs' Illness and Injury Loss Exposures and Their Treatment

Loss Exposure	Current Treatment Inadequacy	Recommended Treatment
Medical expenses	Benefits provided by Carol's current job	Purchase at least major medical expense insurance
Disability	Neither PC nor Carol insured against disability	Purchase long-term disability income insurance on both PC and Carol
Long-term care	Neither PC nor Carol insured for long-term care	Purchase coverage for both PC and Carol; could postpone purchase for a couple of years

Under the COBRA extension the Ulrichs will have to pay for the coverage, possibly at a rate of up to 102 percent of the usual group premium (including any portion that the employer used to pay). While this premium is likely to be lower than the cost of individual family health insurance, COBRA benefits expire after eighteen months. If Carol has not found another job or if her new employer does not provide health insurance benefits, the family will need to purchase individual family health insurance anyway. Furthermore, if a severe medical problem has arisen during the eighteen-month COBRA extension—such as one of the children's being diagnosed with leukemia or Carol's being diagnosed with breast cancer—individual family health insurance might be unaffordable or unavailable to the Ulrichs.

To protect their insurability as well as their health loss exposures, the Ulrichs should purchase, at the minimum, a major medical expense insurance policy. The family could retain less severe illness and injury loss exposures, such as treatment for a child's broken leg or medication for strep throat, but if a severe or catastrophic illness or injury occurred, the family would experience severe financial problems. For example, if PC had a heart attack and required open-heart surgery, his medical expenses would amount to more than $100,000. The family cannot retain this amount. The Ulrichs must make sure that they have at least their catastrophic and severe illness and injury loss exposures insured. If they want and can afford the premiums for basic medical expenses insurance or a comprehensive medical expense policy, they can purchase such coverage.

Disability

Assuming medical expenses are adequately covered by insurance, the disability income needs of the Ulrichs are essentially equal to their projected net income for any given year. In the case of long-term disability, their income needs might drop slightly, since certain costs associated with work—such as transportation, clothing, and income and Social Security taxes—will cease.

The Ulrichs currently have only the disability benefit provided under Social Security covering PC and Carol. They are retaining any loss exposure above the benefit for which they qualify under Social Security. Thus, if PC is totally disabled and cannot work for a year, the family would lose approximately $33,000 in annual income ($2,750 a month)—his royalties of $35,000 per year would probably continue for the year, but he would not earn income from the newspaper or from the mail-order business. Social Security benefits will not begin until the end of the fifth month of the disability *only* in the event that he cannot earn income in any position and could provide approximately $1,198 per month for the remaining seven months—or, $8,386 for the year.[3] Thus, the net drop in the family's income will be at least $24,614 for the year. The family's expenses would likely decrease due to a reduction in PC's business expenses. However, at the same time, the family's expenses would increase because of the care needed for PC in addition to the usual household costs—such as food, clothing, electricity, and mortgage payments. The situation would be particularly catastrophic if Carol has returned to school and the family has been supported totally by PC before his disability.

In the short-term, the Ulrichs have enough savings to offset the loss of income resulting from the disability of either Carol or PC. Unnecessary expenses—such as for trips to the summer home or boating excursions—could be eliminated and the family could reduce its necessary living expenses by purchasing store-brand foods and shopping for clothes at discount or second-hand clothing stores. With these risk control measures, the family could probably retain two to three months worth of income loss with only a short delay in attaining their financial objectives.

Based on this analysis, the Ulrichs should consider purchasing long-term disability income insurance with a two- to three-month elimination period on both PC and Carol. As indicated above, the Ulrichs should be able to retain the loss of either PC's or Carol's income for the duration of the elimination period. However, if either PC or Carol becomes disabled for more than a year, the family would suffer a catastrophic loss. With a short elimination period on a long-term disability income insurance policy, the Ulrichs can meet their disability income needs without also having to consider short-term disability income insurance. This will keep their costs lower.

Disability income policies are often designed to provide a level of income equal to about 65 to 75 percent of the current income level (or maximum percent allowed by the insurer and affordable by the family). Thus, the disability income insurance coverage on PC should replace 65 to 75 percent of his current income ($3,142 to $3,625 per month), and the disability income insurance covering Carol should replace 65 to 75 percent of her current income ($1,354 to $1,563 per month). However, since PC's royalties will continue, the Ulrichs should consider replacing 65 to 75 percent of the income *lost* if PC were disabled—that is, 65 to 75 percent of $33,000 or $1,788 to $2,063 per month.

Because of the strictness of the Social Security definition of total disability, PC and Carol should not count on receiving Social Security disability benefits and should not consider the benefit amounts in determining the amount of disability income insurance to purchase. If either PC or Carol suffers an illness or injury that satisfies Social Security's requirements for receiving disability benefits, the Social Security administration will ensure that the total disability income received by the disabled worker and his or her dependents does not exceed 80 percent of the worker's predisability average earnings. If it does, the Social Security disability benefits will be reduced to the level that satisfies this 80 percent limit.

The disability income planning for PC can be particularly complex. The longer he is disabled, the greater the loss of income, because he will begin to lose his royalty income. The Ulrichs will need to carefully and frequently review their disability income insurance plan to ensure that they have met their disability income needs.

Long-Term Care

Illness and injury can result in the need for long-term care at home, in a nursing home, or in another long-term care facility. The expenses associated with long-term care can be catastrophic and are not covered by medical expense insurance or disability income insurance. If either PC or Carol were to require long-term care, the wealth that PC and Carol had accumulated for their children's education and their retirement could be depleted in a couple of years (even with offsetting income provided by long-term disability income), leaving the family in severe financial straits. Therefore, the Ulrichs should consider purchasing such coverage on both PC and Carol.

The Ulrichs must determine the type and amount of coverage they want and compare the premiums of various policies. They should consider a deductible to keep their premiums low. Furthermore, long-term care insurance is *relatively* inexpensive when purchased at younger ages, and premiums do not increase much if this insurance is purchased between the ages of forty and fifty. Carol and PC could postpone the purchase of this insurance for a few years.

Life Insurance Planning

Financial loss occurs upon the death of any person who provides income or services on which others depend. Numerous types of financial loss can occur. Many of these consequences are similar to those that might be experienced following an illness or injury loss:

- Loss of current income and future income potential
- Extra costs and obligations, such as funeral expenses, estate and inheritance taxes, and loss of household services
- Loss of business values
- Loss of credit rating because of the inability of survivors to repay the deceased's debts

In addition, tax advantages—such as filing joint income tax returns, gift-splitting for federal gift tax purposes, and use of gift and estate tax marital deductions—can be lost.

In the case of the Ulrichs, the death of either PC or Carol would create financial hardship for the family. To estimate the severity of the loss, it is necessary to analyze the surviving family's income and cash needs, assuming death were to occur in the immediate future.

Insurance Needed on PC's Life

According to the level of income earned in the past year, PC is the primary breadwinner for the Ulrich family. For this reason, the amount of life insurance required to meet the family's cash and income needs in the event of PC's immediate death is considered before the amount needed in the event of Carol's death.

Cash Needs

Based on the information provided by the Ulrichs, Exhibit 9-8 lists the family's *cash needs* in the event of PC's death and the resources currently available to meet these needs.

The current cash needs cannot be met with the available resources. An additional $122,335 worth of life insurance is needed on PC's life to meet all of the family's cash needs. Two points, however, must be made about this procedure. First, mortgage redemption and the repayment of other outstanding debt are sometimes considered to be income needs rather than immediate

Exhibit 9-8
Ulrichs' Life Insurance Cash Needs and Resources

Cash Needs		Available Cash Resources	
Funeral expenses	$ 6,500	Social Security death benefit	$ 255
Estate settlement costs	5,700	Universal life policy	75,000
Extra expense fund	20,000	Bank accounts	31,500
Education fund*	160,000	Balanced fund	6,500
Mortgage redemption	66,990	PC's IRA balance	21,000
Auto loan repayment	10,800	Business net worth	30,500
Boat loan repayment	8,100	Total available resources	$164,755
Business loan repayment	9,000		
Total cash needs	$287,090		

* Assuming that the death proceeds for the education fund would be invested
in an investment vehicle that would earn at least 5 percent to keep the education
fund balance in line with the rising costs of college education.

cash needs. That approach is appropriate if the interest rate on the debt is lower than the current rate of return that could be earned by investing the insurance proceeds (or other assets) for the survivors. Second, PC's business net worth has been listed as an asset currently available to meet the family's needs. This approach is appropriate only if the business interest can indeed be converted to cash at the same value. As discussed later in this chapter, a properly designed business continuation plan can address this problem.

Income Needs

Now consider the monthly income needs of the family upon PC's death. Future income needs are difficult to analyze because of the impact of future inflation. Perhaps the best way to approach the analysis is to assume *initially* that there will be no inflation in the future. Under this premise, assume that the family will have the *monthly income needs* identified in Exhibit 9-9 in the event of PC's immediate death.

If PC were to die immediately, Carol would need the following income amounts:

- From age forty-one to fifty-one, $4,500 per month. During this time period Carol will be supporting at least one child full time as well as maintaining her lifestyle.

- From age fifty-one to fifty-five, $4,000 per month. By the time this period begins, all the children are expected to be in college full time. Thus Carol will still be supporting at least one child, but on a part-time basis. She will also be trying to maintain her lifestyle.

• From age fifty-five to sixty-seven, $3,500 per month. Once this period is reached, all the children are expected to be on their own, so Carol will have only herself to support.

• From age sixty-seven until Carol dies, $3,100 per month. Carol plans to retire at age sixty-seven. At that time she will no longer need to cover the expenses associated with working and thus can live on a lesser amount.

Exhibit 9-9
The Ulrichs' Monthly Income Needs and Income Sources

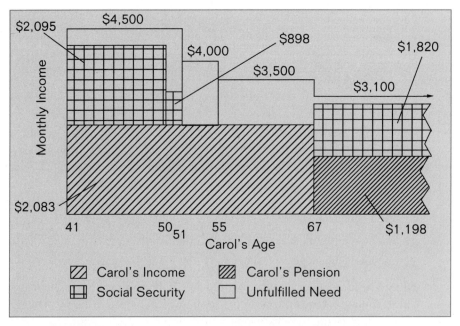

Various considerations were made in determining the amounts needed. The family desires to maintain its current standard of living following PC's death. Thus money will have to be available to buy food, clothing, and other personal items to which the surviving family members are accustomed. In addition, although most outstanding debts are assumed to be paid off with lump-sum death benefits, Carol will still have her auto loan and credit cards. She will also need to replace her auto at some point. Furthermore, the family's maintenance expenses, such as electric, water, and phone service payments, will still have to be met.

Aside from the expenses that will continue after PC's death, other uses of income will also arise. Since PC was the spouse who worked at home and was able to provide child care and to maintain the household, Carol will probably have to hire a cleaning service a couple of times a week and might have to enroll the children in after-school programs during the school year. During the summer, Carol might have to hire a full-time nanny or enroll the children in summer camp. To be conservative, extra funds are planned in case an emergency is not met by the emergency or extra expense fund set aside under the cash sum needs.

The future resources available to meet these income needs are also identified in Exhibit 9-9. Assuming that Carol continues to work at the direct-mail advertising firm until she retires at age sixty-seven (and continuing to ignore inflation), her monthly net income is estimated at its current level of $2,083. The following Social Security survivor's benefits will also be available to the family:[4]

- Until Carol is fifty, $2,095 per month.[5]
- While Carol is between ages fifty and fifty-one, $898 per month.[6]
- Once Carol retires at age sixty-seven, $1,198 per month.[7]

Carol also participates in a 401(k) plan through her employer. Assuming that, were PC to die immediately, she will no longer make contributions but will rely only on the employer's contributions to the plan on her behalf, the 401(k) plan will provide approximately $1,820 of monthly income to Carol once she retires.

As Exhibit 9-9 indicates, the Ulrichs have unfulfilled income needs in the event of PC's death. These income needs can be summarized by the amount required at different periods, measured by Carol's age, as done in the timeline in Exhibit 9-10.

Exhibit 9-10
The Ulrichs' Unfulfilled Monthly Income Needs

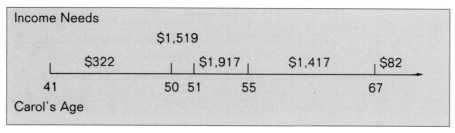

Taking into account inflation and growth rates for Carol's net income and Social Security benefits, and using the programming method and complex calculations not shown here, it is possible to determine that the approximate amount of life insurance needed to fund these income needs is $254,000.[9] The resulting estimate takes into account the investment return that can be earned between the time the proceeds are paid at PC's death and the time the funds are needed, as well as the impact of inflation on both the Ulrichs' needs and their income sources.

Suggested Amount of Insurance on PC's Life

This estimate of the amount of life insurance required to fund the Ulrichs' income needs is added to the amount required to fund the family's cash needs to determine the amount of life insurance the family might purchase on PC's life. Thus, the Ulrichs should purchase an additional $376,335 worth of life insurance on PC's life.

The programming approach used thus far to determine the appropriate amount of life insurance assumes that the Ulrichs' assets will be liquidated to provide income for Carol and the children. A capital need analysis approach could also be used. It would result in a somewhat higher amount of necessary life insurance, because it assumes that the life insurance proceeds and other assets will be conserved as invested assets and that the survivors will consume only the interest earnings on those investments. This approach might be desirable if the Ulrichs plan to preserve the estate for the children.

In addition to estimating the proper amount of life insurance for PC, two other important questions must be answered with regard to his life insurance. First, the type of life insurance to be purchased must be selected. Second, the distribution of the policy proceeds must be considered.

Type of Life Insurance Needed

The Ulrichs' life insurance needs in the event of PC's death can be categorized as temporary needs or permanent needs. The family's temporary needs include the following:

- The education fund
- Mortgage redemption
- Auto, boat, and business loan repayments
- Income to support the children

The family's permanent needs are as follows:

- Funeral expenses
- The estate settlement fund
- The extra expense fund
- Income to support Carol

The traditional recommendation for PC would be to purchase a combination of term life insurance and whole life insurance. However, since PC already has a universal life policy in force and its face amount is sufficient to meet the family's permanent life insurance needs, only term insurance need be purchased by the Ulrichs. Since the additional amount of life insurance required by the family is estimated to be worth $376,335, the Ulrichs should purchase $376,335 worth of term insurance (or as near as they can get to that figure).

The Ulrichs will need to review their life insurance needs periodically. Both their permanent and their temporary needs can change. For example, the amount needed to fund the children's education will increase with the cost of such education until the oldest child graduates and then will decrease to $0 when the youngest child graduates. However, by purchasing a combination of term life insurance and universal life insurance, the family will have the flexibility it needs to make most of the required adjustments. Thus, to handle the increased cost of education, the Ulrichs can increase the amount of term life insurance (subject to proof of insurability) on PC's life at each renewal. Once the amount required for education begins to decrease, the amount of term life insurance carried on PC's life can be decreased at each renewal.

Maintaining the universal life coverage on PC also provides additional benefits that would not have been possible with whole life insurance:

- The Ulrichs might be able to skip a premium payment if the cash value in the universal policy can cover the mortality and expense charges for the period.
- If emergencies arise that cannot be met with other savings, partial withdrawals can be made from the policy without a reduction in the death benefits payable.

Furthermore, if the need for permanent insurance declines in later years, the policy could then be converted to an annuity to provide supplemental retirement income to that provided through Carol and PC's retirement planning.

Distribution of Policy Proceeds

Currently, the policy proceeds of PC's universal life insurance policy will be paid to Carol upon PC's death. If Carol dies before PC, the policy proceeds will be paid to PC's children. An alternative to this distribution plan is to name a trust as the contingent beneficiary. In this case, if Carol is not alive when PC dies, the policy proceeds will be placed in a trust that would then provide income to the children. The advantages of the Ulrichs' using a trust in this manner are as follows:

- PC can designate a trustee that he has faith in to administer the trust funds.

- Professionals can be hired to assist trust administrators by providing investment advice and investment management services.

- Distributions can be made according to the children's needs while they are minors.

- A lump-sum distribution can be made to each child once he or she reaches the age of majority (when a person is mature enough to handle the funds)

Although PC could designate a trust as the primary beneficiary, rather than Carol, the Ulrichs probably prefer that Carol receive the lump-sum distribution. She will have the flexibility at PC's death to manage the funds in the manner she prefers, including the election of settlement options or the use of a trust.

Insurance Needed on Carol's Life

A similar procedure to that used to estimate the life insurance needs for PC could be used to estimate Carol's life insurance needs. Her contribution to family finances is currently lower than PC's contribution. Also, PC is more likely to be able to overcome the loss of Carol's income than Carol would be in the case of PC's death. In addition, since PC is the primary care provider of the children and the house during the week while Carol is at work, he might need to hire a cleaning service only once a week and to enroll the children occasionally in after-school programs or summer camp. Thus, the amount of additional life insurance on Carol's life is lower than that required on PC's life. A comparable programming (or need) analysis assuming Carol dies immediately indicates that the amount of additional life insurance needed on Carol is $226,145.[10]

As with PC's situation, many of the needs brought about by Carol's death would be temporary—such as paying off the mortgage and establishing an education fund. However, the family also has permanent needs for life insurance to pay for Carol's funeral expenses and estate settlement as well as provide for an extra emergency fund. It is estimated that, of the additional $226,145 worth of life insurance recommended for the Ulrichs, their temporary needs amount to $186,145, and their permanent needs amount to $40,000. The Ulrichs should, therefore, for reasons similar to those discussed for PC, purchase $186,145 worth of term life insurance on Carol's life and purchase a $40,000 universal life policy on Carol's life.

The primary beneficiary for Carol's existing group term life insurance is PC, with her children as the contingent beneficiaries. The same suggestion made for PC with respect to setting up a trust as the contingent beneficiary, with the children as the beneficiaries of the trust, applies to Carol's situation.

One item that the Ulrichs must consider is the loss of Carol's group term life insurance if she should quit her job and return to school for a year. It is likely that when Carol returns to the work force, she will receive group life insurance as an employee benefit. The Ulrichs might consider purchasing an additional $50,000 worth of individual term life insurance on Carol's life for the period of time that she is in school and searching for a new job.

Investment Planning

Proper investment planning considers the needs and desires of the investor for preserving capital and maintaining liquidity while also generating the highest possible level of return. In addition to having general financial objectives common to many people, such as being able to meet emergencies, the Ulrichs have two principal financial objectives that must be dealt with through investment planning: achieving a comfortable retirement and fully funding the children's education. Although both involve investment planning, the retirement objective will be dealt with in the section on retirement planning, and the educational funding will be discussed in the following section. This section covers the overall investment strategy of the Ulrichs.

The Ulrichs currently have the following general investments:

- $18,000 in a noninterest-bearing checking account

- $5,000 in a savings account earning 2.3 percent annually, compounded monthly

- $8,500 in CDs earning, on average, 4 percent annually

- $6,500 in a balanced mutual fund earning, on average, 10.5 percent annually

- $5,200 in cash value in PC's universal life insurance policy

Financial advisors recommend that families maintain an emergency fund to pay for uninsured contingencies such as unemployment, unreimbursed medical bills, or a new roof for the house. Most financial experts suggest that this fund should be equal to three to six months of the family's after-tax income and that the fund should be invested in marketable and liquid investments. These types of investments have a relatively low yield. The Ulrichs earn approximately $7,750 per month after taxes, but this income could fluctuate sizably from one period to another. However, the Ulrichs currently hold $43,200 in liquid investments, with $18,000 earning no interest at all. This is a poor investment plan. The amount in liquid investments, especially the amount in the noninterest-bearing checking account, is too high. In addition, the rates of return for the savings account and the CDs are relatively low.

The Ulrichs should consider the following alternatives for maintaining an emergency fund:

- Maintaining approximately $5,000 in interest-bearing checking account.
- Looking for a savings account and CDs with higher rates of return
- Considering moving some funds into a short-term bond mutual fund to earn a slightly higher yield with little interest rate risk and low liquidity risk
- Maintaining liquid investments of approximately $30,000, continuing to invest the $5,200 in the universal life policy's cash value (as discussed earlier in this chapter), and investing the remaining $8,000, currently in short-term, liquid investments, in longer-term investments with higher return potential—such as a long-term bond mutual fund or a growth stock mutual fund—to meet long-term needs

A few comments can be made concerning the Ulrichs' investment in mutual funds. In the broad spectrum of investments, a balanced mutual fund has moderate potential for capital appreciation and income stability and a moderate degree of investment risk. This type of mutual fund is appropriate for meeting the Ulrichs' emergency fund needs, but they should consider switching some of their funds to a somewhat more aggressive mutual fund, such as a mutual fund that invests in good quality growth stocks. In the long run, the potential exists for a greater return, although it is accompanied by a greater degree of risk. Whichever funds the Ulrichs choose to invest in, they should recognize that there are many such funds, each performing differently over time. The family should determine whether a different balanced mutual fund would be more appropriate *and* carefully consider in which mutual fund(s) to invest. The family should reconsider its mutual fund investments periodically to ensure that each is meeting the family's needs. However, if a decision is made to switch from one fund to another, the Ulrichs might incur taxes on the capital gains from their mutual fund investment.

A possible plan for the Ulrichs' investment management program might be to distribute their money as follows:

- $5,000 in an interest-bearing checking account earning at least 2.3 percent
- $5,000 in an interest-bearing savings account earning at least 3 percent
- $7,500 in CDs earning at least 5 percent
- $12,500 in the balanced mutual fund earning 10.5 percent
- $5,200 in the universal life insurance policy on PC's life
- $8,000 in a growth stock mutual fund earning at least 12 percent

At some point the Ulrichs might want to consider their income tax situation. The family faces a situation that confronts many families: a large portion of their gross income goes to pay federal and state income taxes—$4,173 per month at their assumed tax rate is 35 percent. If taxes are reduced, a larger portion of the family's income can be devoted to achieving financial goals. However, the Ulrichs must keep in mind the following comments concerning tax planning:

- *Tax planning should not be done at the expense of other objectives.* Taxes are only one of many factors that should be considered in financial planning.
- *Tax planning might require that the taxpayer give up something,* such as the ability to have complete control over the use of certain investments.
- *Tax laws and family circumstances change.* Taxpayers should retain a degree of flexibility over their investments, but this flexibility might be severely limited by some tax-planning techniques.

Tax issues will be raised when appropriate in the remainder of the chapter.

Educational Funding

The Ulrichs have purchased $50 EE savings bonds amounting to $1,900 for each child, in the particular child's name. These bonds earn between 4 and 6 percent, depending on their date of purchase.

The Ulrichs must reconsider their investment planning for the education fund. The EE savings bond program has both advantages and disadvantages associated with it. Although the bonds can accumulate tax-deferred interest earnings, the interest income will be taxable income to the children when they cash in the bonds, unless their total earned income is below income tax thresholds. In addition, the interest earned, particularly on the most recently purchased bonds, is minimal and fixed. Inflation in education costs is greater than the after-tax interest earned on the bonds. Furthermore, because the children are the owners, Carol and PC are not guaranteed that the bonds will be used to finance the children's college education.

The Ulrichs have a variety of alternatives available to them for financing their children's education. To identify the best education funding arrangement, the family must consider certain questions, such as, for reasons discussed below, whether naming the children as owners of the education funds is appropriate and which types of investment are appropriate.

Children as Owners of the Investments

The decision to name the children as owners of the investments made to fund their education revolves around two issues: control and taxes.

Control Issues

If the children are owners, Carol and PC cannot be sure that the funds will actually be used to fund the children's education. This is a problem that the family currently has with their investments in EE bonds. However, even if Carol and PC retain the ownership of the investments, they cannot be sure that the investments will be used to fund the children's education. An emergency might arise that cannot be adequately met with their emergency fund, or they could be tempted to use the funds for other purposes, such as purchasing a new car.

The family could resolve this problem with the use of a trust, such as a Section 2503(c) trust (as found in the Internal Revenue Code). Education funds can be maintained in this trust until the child reaches age twenty-one, regardless of the age of majority established by state law. The fund can also be paid out before that time, as needed. A separate trust must be established for each child, however, and the cost to set up each trust can range from $500 to $1,000. In addition, annual costs for trust administration, such as preparing annual income tax forms, will be incurred. Yet these costs could be offset by potential tax savings, as discussed next.

Tax Issues

If Carol and PC retain ownership of the education fund investments, the investment income will be subject to income tax at their marginal tax rate. Of course, tax-free investments could be used if appropriate.

Carol and PC can make outright annual gifts, free of any gift taxes, of up to $20,000 per year (if both make gifts to their individual gift maximum of $10,000 per year) to each of their children. Each child's funds can then be invested in that child's name. This will often involve (but might not require) the appointment of a guardian for the children. However, this alternative can result in the possibility that the children will be taxed on the investment income earned on the gifts. In addition, the children might use the money for something other than to cover the costs of college.

An alternative to outright gifts is to provide gifts under provisions of the Uniform Gift to Minors Act (UGMA). The act requires only that a custodian of the gift, who can be the parent who gave the gift, be appointed. This custodian has full powers over the gifted property and its income on behalf of the child. However, if the parent is both the transferor of the property and its custodian, the amount of the account will be included in the parent's estate for estate tax purposes. Furthermore, if one parent is the transferor and the other parent is the custodian, the account balance could be included in the parent-custodian's estate because he or she exercises control over the funds and is the spouse of the transferor. In addition to these tax issues, the custodianship terminates at the age of eighteen (or the state's age of majority, if different from age eighteen). At that time, full control of the funds passes to the child, who can use them for any purpose. The principal benefit of a UGMA is the ability of the custodian to control the funds until the child reaches the age of majority.

By making gifts, whether or not through the UGMA, federal income taxes on the earnings of the education fund will be minimized. In general, if the child files his or her own tax return, the first $1,200 of earnings for each child will be tax free, and the remainder will be taxed at either (1) the parent's marginal tax rate unless the child is at least age fourteen, or (2) the child's tax rate (usually 15 percent) if the child is age fourteen or older. If the child is included under the parent's tax return, the first $1,000 of earnings for the child will be tax free and the remainder will be taxed at the parent's marginal tax rate.

For the Ulrichs, making a gift, as they are currently doing, is a viable alternative for funding the children's education. Due to the $1,000 and $1,200 thresholds, it is not likely that the Ulrich children will be subject to federal income tax before they complete their college education.

As mentioned above, a Section 2503(c) trust can be used to hold gifts for the children. For federal income tax purposes, the trust income is taxable to the trust as long as it is retained in the trust. Federal income taxes applicable to trust income are determined according to the following schedule as stated in the Revenue Reconciliation Act of 1993:

- 15 percent tax on income of $1,500 or less.

- When the income is greater than $1,500 but not greater than $3,500, the tax payable is equal to $225 plus 28 percent of the excess over $1,500.

- When the income is greater than $3,500 but not greater than $5,500, the tax payable is equal to $785 plus 31 percent of the excess over $3,500.

- When the income is greater than $5,500 but not greater than $7,500, the tax payable is equal to $1,405 plus 36 percent of the excess over $5,500.

- When the income is greater than $7,500, the tax payable is equal to $2,125 plus 39.6 percent of the excess over $7,500.

Thus, a Section 2503(c) trust is not likely to provide as advantageous tax benefits to the Ulrichs as those available through the use of outright gifts. In addition, the Ulrichs would have to pay up to $1,000 per child—or $4,000— to set up the trusts. The Ulrichs should continue to make outright gifts to the children.

Types of Investment

The Ulrichs' planning horizon extends from six years for the oldest child to ten years for the youngest child. Thus, medium- to long-term investments are appropriate. The Ulrichs could stay with the EE bonds or similar investments that offer safety of principal, liquidity, and low returns, but as pointed out above, these investments are not maintaining returns that match or exceed the expected inflation of college education costs. Common stock or common stock mutual funds could be used, but they might be too risky for the Ulrichs. However, the Ulrichs might consider putting some of the education funds into a blue chip common stock mutual fund that would provide increased returns at relatively lower levels of risk.

Bonds might be the most appropriate investment for the Ulrichs' education fund. The Ulrichs could purchase high quality corporate bonds with maturities that roughly match the time the funds will be needed. These bonds should provide a return that is greater than that available through the EE bonds with less risk than that associated with stock. As an alternative to individual bonds, the Ulrichs could invest in a bond mutual fund.

The Ulrichs could reduce the amount of income taxes they pay by purchasing municipal bonds or shares in a municipal bond mutual fund. These will allow the family to match the maturity of the bonds with the time the funds are needed, yet achieve an after-tax investment return comparable to that on corporate bond investments. Furthermore, the Ulrichs will not be required to pay federal income taxes on the interest earnings of these bonds. However, if the Ulrichs purchase shares of a municipal bond mutual fund, they will have to pay income taxes on any *capital gains* realized by the fund.

Another tax-advantaged investment is zero-coupon bonds. As with the bonds previously mentioned, zero-coupon bonds can be purchased with maturities that match the timing of the Ulrichs' needs for college funds. However, since zero-coupon bonds do not pay interest until their maturity or until they are sold at a profit, the income tax payable on any investment income is deferred until the bonds mature or are sold at a profit. Furthermore, if the children are owners of the bonds when income taxes become due, they are likely to pay less tax than if Carol and PC were owners, since the children will be in a lower tax bracket. Thus, the Ulrichs can minimize the impact of income taxes on the accumulation of an education fund for the children.

Amount Needed

The final consideration in the decision regarding educational funding is to determine when the funds should be invested and how much should be invested. The oldest of the Ulrichs' children will begin to require funds in six years, the twins will need college funds beginning in nine years, and the youngest child will require funds beginning in ten years. The current cost of college for each child is around $10,000 per year, and this cost is expected to grow at 5 percent each year. The required funds and the time they will be needed are shown in Exhibit 9-11.

Exhibit 9-11
Annual Contributions to Education Fund

Years From Now	Number of Children in School	Annual Expected Cost per Child	Total Cost Per Year
1	0	0	0
2	0	0	0
3	0	0	0
4	0	0	0
5	0	0	0
6	1	$13,401	$13,401
7	1	14,071	14,071
8	1	14,775	14,775
9	3	15,514	46,542
10	3	16,289	48,867
11	3	17,104	51,312
12	3	17,959	53,877
13	1	18,857	18,857

As mentioned earlier, it is recommended that the Ulrichs continue to make gifts of the education funds to the children. However, the investment of these funds should not be in Series EE bonds. The Ulrichs must decide whether to invest in a corporate bond fund yielding 9 percent before taxes, in a tax-free municipal bond fund yielding 6.5 percent, or in zero coupon bonds yielding 9 percent before taxes. The amount that the Ulrichs must annually invest in each alternative for each of the next twelve years to fully fund their children's education is as follows:

- $17,284 per year if a corporate bond fund is used
- $16,113 per year if a municipal bond fund is used
- $20,477 per year if zero coupon bonds are used

These figures are based on the following assumptions:

- The $7,600 currently invested in Series EE bonds will be reinvested in the selected alternative.

- The children will file their own tax returns once they reach age fourteen.
- Upon reaching college age, their effective income tax rate will be 22 percent (after allowable deductions).

The amount required for the Ulrichs to fully fund their children's education is high. Unless the Ulrichs can free up enough financial resources to meet these funding requirements, they will need to revise their objective to fully fund the children's education.

Alternatives for the Ulrichs to consider include the following:

- Investing the child support income of $6,600 for the children's education. Carol and PC can cover the children's everyday needs with their disposable income. The use of the child support payments for education funding can ease the financial strain of meeting their objective.
- Using the $8,000 invested in the stock fund for educational purposes. This would alleviate some of the front-end funding concerns and increase the base on which to earn investment income.
- Transferring some of the emergency fund savings into an investment for education funding. For example, $5,000 of the amount invested in the balanced fund could be transferred to the stock fund or to the bond fund earmarked for education. This would also alleviate some of the front-end financial burden and increase the base on which to earn investment income.
- Using low-interest education loans to finance a portion of each child's education.

Regardless of the amount invested, the Ulrichs should select the municipal bond mutual fund. The required yearly investment for full funding of the children's education is less for the municipal bond fund than for the corporate bond fund or the zero-coupon bonds. Furthermore, the Ulrichs will not have to pay income taxes on the fund's interest earnings although they might have to pay income taxes on the fund's capital gains.

Retirement Planning

The goal of retirement planning is to accumulate savings sufficient to replace the annual employment income that a retiree will no longer receive during retirement. The Ulrichs indicated that they would like to maintain a standard of living similar to that enjoyed before retirement. They currently have four sources of retirement income—Carol's pension, PC's IRA, Social Security retirement benefits, and savings and investments.

The amount often mentioned as necessary for retirees to maintain a lifestyle comparable to the one they had before retirement is 70 percent of preretirement income. This percentage, however, has been creeping up because up to 85 percent of Social Security benefits received can now be taxable. At first glance, the 70 percent preretirement income figure would seem to be appropriate for the Ulrichs. Social Security taxes will no longer be payable, their mortgage loan and the boat loan will be paid off (retirees often maintain auto loans), and the ordinary living costs will diminish as the children become self-sufficient.

However, one factor might make the 70 percent figure too low for the Ulrichs. This factor is the possibility of financial emergencies, such as an uninsured catastrophic illness. Retirees often feel they have adequate funds for these financial emergencies but realize too late that, when these funds are used for that purpose, the retirement income generated by the remaining funds is no longer adequate or, in some cases, no longer exists. The Ulrichs should plan to purchase health insurance to supplement their Medicare coverage and should plan to establish an extra emergency fund to meet their needs if an uninsured catastrophic illness occurs. For these reasons, assume the Ulrichs' objective is a retirement income equal to 80 percent of their preretirement income.

The difficulty for the Ulrichs is determining their preretirement income. Generally an individual's earnings can be assumed to grow at the estimated rate of inflation. Sophisticated retirement planning programs account for the increase in future earnings attributed to upward mobility in one's occupation as well as potential job or career changes and their effect on income level. For the Ulrichs, the situation becomes quite complex, since both PC's and Carol's incomes are subject to a high degree of variation. In addition, their annual income will most likely increase with inflation and growth in PC and Carol's earning power.

To avoid complication, yet to adequately discuss the issues, several assumptions are made:

- The retirement planning process will be based on the current level of Carol and PC's income. Adjustments to the retirement plan can be made as the Ulrichs' situation changes.

- PC's current newspaper income is expected to increase at an average annual rate of 3 percent to account for growth in the local economy. PC's royalty income and Carol's earnings are expected to grow at an average annual rate of 5 percent to account for both inflation and increase in earning power. PC's mail-order business income is expected to increase at an average annual rate of 6 percent to account for inflation and business growth. If these expectations are inaccurate (PC's royalties and business income could grow much more rapidly) or if other conditions change (such as Carol's employment), the Ulrichs can review and revise their retirement plan as needed.

- The Ulrichs will both retire when Carol reaches age sixty-seven (PC will be age seventy). Thus, they have a twenty-six-year retirement planning horizon.

- Given family longevity, Carol and PC each expect to live for twenty years of retirement.

By the time Carol reaches age sixty-seven, the Ulrichs' estimated annual income will be $327,579, as calculated in Exhibit 9-12. Thus, in their first year of retirement, Carol and PC hope to replace 80 percent of this income, or receive $262,063. This amount will need to increase with inflation to maintain the standard of living desired by the Ulrichs. Assuming a 3 percent average annual rate of inflation throughout the Ulrichs' retirement years, the annual retirement income desired is shown for certain years in column (2) of Exhibit 9-13.

Exhibit 9-12
The Ulrichs' Expected Income

Income Source	Current Net Income Level	Annual Growth Rate Over 26-Year Period	Income Level When Carol Is Age 67
PC's newspaper income	$15,000	3%	$ 32,349
PC's royalties	35,000	5%	124,449
PC's business income	18,000	6%	81,889
Carol's income	25,000	5%	88,892
Total Income	$93,000		$327,579

Both PC and Carol will be eligible for Social Security retirement benefits. It is assumed that Carol and PC's combined retirement benefits will be $59,911 for the first year.[11] These benefits will continue to increase with the cost of living (assumed to be, on average, 3 percent per year) and are shown in column (3) of Exhibit 9-13 for certain years of the Ulrichs' retirement.

Exhibit 9-13
Desired Retirement Income Levels

(1) Year of Retirement	(2) Desired Retirement Income	(3) Social Security Retirement Benefits	(4) Unfulfilled Retirement Need
1	$ 62,063	$ 59,911	$202,152
5	294,954	67,430	227,524
10	341,933	78,170	263,763
15	396,394	90,621	305,773
20	459,529	105,054	354,475

The Social Security retirement benefits do not fulfill the retirement income needs of the Ulrichs, as can be seen in column (4) of Exhibit 9-13. If it is assumed that the Ulrichs will earn 7 percent per year (after taxes) on their retirement funds once they reach retirement, the Ulrichs must accumulate $2,695,022 by the time Carol reaches age sixty-seven to fund the retirement income levels they desire.

The Ulrichs currently have $21,000 in an IRA owned by PC and $30,000 in Carol's 401(k) plan. The IRA is invested in bank CDs that are averaging an annual return of 5.1 percent. Carol's 401(k) funds are invested in a long-term bond fund and a GIC. The Ulrichs should consider more growth-oriented investments for both of these retirement funds. They are both young enough to invest in more aggressive investments than they are currently using. PC can roll his IRA directly into another IRA invested in a growth stock mutual fund earning, on average, 12 percent per year. Carol should consider a similar move, whether she stays with the employer and her current plan or rolls over the 401(k) funds into an IRA. In both PC's and Carol's cases, the rollovers must be directly made from one vehicle to another so that Carol and PC avoid a withholding tax of 20 percent and a potential penalty tax of 10 percent of the amount withheld.

If the Ulrichs follow these recommendations, by the time Carol reaches age sixty-seven, PC's $21,000 IRA will be worth $399,842 and Carol's $30,000 retirement fund will be valued at $571,202, and they will need to accumulate $1,723,979 of additional retirement funds. If the Ulrichs use an investment that earns 12 percent per year over the twenty-six-year retirement planning period, they will need to invest $11,468 per year in a tax-deferred, tax-deductible investment to meet their financial objective of a comfortable retirement.

To keep their annual investments to a minimum, yet to save sufficiently for retirement, the Ulrichs must consider investments for their additional retirement fund that will enable them to defer taxation on current income and interest earnings and that will allow them to make their contributions with pre-tax dollars. While Carol is still working, they will not be able to make tax-deductible contributions to an IRA. However, they do have some choices:

- PC can establish a Keogh and make tax-deductible contributions from all three income sources.[12] The investments backing the plan should earn 12 percent. The earnings of the plan would be tax deferred until distributions must be taken or PC retires.

- PC and Carol can make after-tax annual contributions of $2,000 to an IRA funded by an investment, such as a growth mutual fund, earning 12 percent. The interest and capital gains will accumulate free of current taxation even though the contributions are not tax deductible. Choosing such an alternative, however, will require the Ulrichs to increase their total retirement investment because the $11,468 annual contribution rate assumes that the contribution is tax deductible.

- Carol can increase her tax-deductible contributions to the 401(k) while she is still employed with her current employer. The additional contributions should be invested in a growth mutual fund earning at least 12 percent. She will need to check with the plan's administrator to make sure she does not over-contribute to the 401(k) and incur a 6 percent excess contribution tax.

Probably the most appropriate alternative for the Ulrichs is to have PC establish a Keogh. This would allow the retirement fund contributions to be made with pre-tax dollars as well as defer taxes on the investment earnings of the plan. However, the contributions cannot exceed 15 percent of the net income earned by PC. Currently, that means the contributions cannot exceed $10,200. Because the Ulrichs need to invest $1,468, this is a concern at the current time. The Ulrichs will need to invest the excess amount of $1,268 (for the first year) in another vehicle. As PC's business income increases, he and Carol will be able to place more of their retirement into PC's Keogh.

Estate Planning

Some estate planning for the Ulrichs was covered in the earlier section on life insurance, when the amount of additional life insurance was determined for both PC and Carol. This calculation took into account costs associated with death and the creation of an education fund for the children. However, additional estate planning is necessary for several reasons:

- To ensure that their wills are in order
- To minimize estate taxes
- To plan for the children if PC and Carol should die simultaneously

Checking Their Wills

PC and Carol were married relatively late in life. Each has acquired personal property from before their marriage and has children from a previous marriage. Currently their wills transfer all property, with the exception of Carol's jewelry, to the surviving spouse. Thus, assets that they might have assumed would be passed to their respective children might not be. For example, PC's will leaves the summer home to Carol, although it was left to him by his aunt and he might really want the home to go to the twins upon his death, so that it stays with his side of the family. The Ulrichs need to review their wills to make sure that the property they held before their marriage passes to the heirs they truly intend it to go to. The desired results can be arranged with the proper will provisions.

In addition, any property acquired after their marriage might be considered jointly owned, depending on state law. If PC and Carol want to leave property to their respective children, they must consider the legal constraints established by their state's laws, and plan accordingly to ensure that the desired property goes to the intended heir. For example, Carol might want to be sure that her children have ownership rights to the portion of the house that she paid for. She and PC might have to establish separate ownership of the house, perhaps by the amount each contributed (although this will create problems as to the division of the unpaid mortgage) before Carol's children from her previous marriage can inherit a portion of the house.

Minimizing Estate Taxes

The Ulrichs' wills currently leave their estates to each other. In the absence of planning, this could result in the payment of estate taxes that otherwise could have been avoided, particularly upon the second spouse's death.

If either PC or Carol were to die in the near future, their gross estates would be as shown in Exhibit 9-14. These calculations assume that most of their property is jointly owned. However, PC owns the summer home and its furnishings, his businesses, his IRA, and the life insurance policies on his life. Carol owns the porcelain and jewelry, her 401(k), and her life insurance policies. Notice that the life insurance amounts include those additions that have been recommended for the Ulrichs.

Exhibit 9-14

The Ulrichs' Gross Estates

PC		Carol	
Real property	$240,000	Real property	$125,000
Personal property	62,125	Personal property	77,625
Business property	52,000	401(k)	30,000
IRA	21,000	Life Insurance	226,145
Life insurance	376,335		$458,770
	$751,460		

Assume that PC predeceases Carol. If he leaves everything to her, no estate taxes will be payable because of the unlimited marital deduction. However, Carol's gross estate would increase by approximately $750,000, ignoring funeral expenses and estate settlement costs. If Carol were to die shortly after PC, she would have a gross estate of approximately $1,210,000. After subtracting debts, funeral expenses, and estate settlement costs, her taxable estate would still exceed $1,100,000 and be subject to an estate tax of over $190,000.

This tax could largely be avoided if PC were to rewrite his will so that $600,000 of his estate would pass upon his death to a trust for his children. However, Carol would have the right to the trust income for her lifetime and the right to receive a portion of the trust principal if needed to support her or the children. The remainder of PC's estate would then be left to Carol also in trust. Although Carol might be capable of handling financial affairs, a trust for this portion of the estate would be able to provide her income even if she were to become incapacitated. The trust could be arranged so that Carol can have access to the property held in trust and can make changes with the help of the trust management as her needs change. Under this two-trust arrangement, the amounts left in trust to Carol would qualify for the marital deduction, and the amount left in trust to the children would use the full amount of the unified credit, thus making PC's estate free of estate taxation. At Carol's later death, the children would also receive her estate with less or, possibly, no estate tax payable, if she is able to spend down or give away some or all of the value of her estate. Since many of PC's assets consist of property jointly owned with Carol, the assets left to the children's trust should probably consist of property he owned outright plus life insurance proceeds.

If Carol predeceases PC, her estate (other than the assets that pass directly to PC because of joint ownership) could be left to a trust for the children. However, Carol's estate is much smaller than PC's, so the potential estate tax savings is significantly less.

Simultaneous Death of Carol and PC

The possibility always exists that Carol and PC would both die before the children are adults. Anticipating this possibility, the Ulrichs should make provisions in their wills for the children's inheritances to be left to trusts through which the assets could be properly managed. Since their estate would be relatively large, they might also wish to provide that all or some of the trusts' assets be retained by the trust until the children are no longer minors.

The use of trusts for the children helps Carol and PC in another way. Both Carol and PC apparently assume that their former spouses will take care of the children if both PC and Carol should die while the children are below the age of majority. This might not be the case. Establishing trusts for the children ensures that they will be taken care of financially if PC and Carol die while the children are still minors.

However, the Ulrichs still need to make some provisions for guardians for the children until they reach majority. Carol and PC must determine whether their former spouses should and will become their respective children's guardians if both Carol and PC die while the children are minors. If this is not the best solution, Carol and PC can name alternate guardians in their wills. The ultimate selection, however, will be determined by the courts, which will give considerable weight to the desires of the parents.

Business Continuation Planning

The Ulrichs apparently have not given much thought to the continuation of PC's mail-order business. Carol helps PC run the business and might desire to take it over if PC is disabled or dies and cannot continue the operation himself. In addition, the children might want the business when they are older. If either situation occurs, PC must provide express authority in his will as to who should continue the mail-order business operation. If the children are interested, PC might establish a trust to operate the business until the children are able. Furthermore, Carol could run the business for the trust until the children take over.

If neither Carol nor the children are interested in operating the business, but the family wants to continue receiving income from it, PC can arrange for a trust to operate the business. PC will need to establish the authority in his will and should make all the preparations before his death. However, evidence suggests that businesses do not perform well when management is distanced from the operation, as in a trust arrangement. Thus, this might not be a viable alternative for PC.

If the previous courses of action are not acceptable to the Ulrichs, PC should make other arrangements. For example, he could arrange a buy-sell agreement with an interested buyer—such as one of his book suppliers. This would benefit the family by providing them a guaranteed source and amount of income from the disposal of the business. This would help to avoid the loss that usually accompanies the forced liquidation of business assets. Furthermore, if PC wants to dispose of the business due to disability or retirement, he will have a willing buyer, and, here also, will avoid the losses associated with a forced liquidation of the business assets.

If a buy-sell agreement is arranged by PC, it should be funded by insurance. The use of insurance helps to ease the transfer of the business by making the funds readily available with which to make the purchase. Care should be taken to ascertain a reasonable value to meet IRS requirements and adequately reflect the value of PC's businesses. In this way, the family will be assured of receiving the value of the business in a timely manner and the buyer will not have to worry about arranging finances at the time of PC's death.

Unemployment

The peril of unemployment can lead to the loss of income and the liquidation of assets to provide financial support to a family. Except in very bad economic times, the duration of unemployment rarely exceeds one-to-two years. Most wage earners are covered under unemployment compensation programs that on average provide up to six months worth of benefits. However, these programs usually require previous work experience before an individual can qualify for benefits, and benefits are subject to a maximum weekly amount, which typically replaces only about 50 percent of lost income. Private insurance is unavailable to supplement these social insurance benefits. Therefore, serious financial consequences can result from unemployment for any family that does not have an adequate emergency fund.

The Ulrichs have reasonably adequate resources if Carol is unable to find a job soon after completing her education or if she becomes unemployed at some point. However, the family might have to cut back on expenses, such as travel, and their ability to meet their financial objectives might be seriously limited depending on the length of Carol's unemployment. The situation would be more troublesome if PC were unemployed, but this contingency seems unlikely, since he is self-employed with three sources of income. Both of his businesses would have to fail at the same time, and his freelance income would also have to cease.

A Plan That Meets Objectives Without Unacceptable Trade-Offs

The next step in the risk management process is to develop and implement an overall plan that meets as many of the family's objectives as possible. This might be the point at which it is first realized that some of the desired objectives are either not attainable or will take longer to achieve than had been hoped.

As mentioned at the beginning of this chapter, there is no *one* "right" risk management plan. Any of several alternative plans might be appropriate for a given set of circumstances. As stressed throughout the chapter, the Ulrichs will need to consider each of their objectives carefully and determine which recommendations are most appropriate for them.

The remaining discussion in this section reviews the solutions suggested for the Ulrichs and ties them together. The decisions remaining for the Ulrichs will be emphasized; no one plan will be recommended. As indicated at the beginning of the chapter, the purpose of this case is to bring issues into focus rather than provide a complete set of answers for the hypothetical Ulrichs.

The recommendations made throughout the chapter must be carefully considered by the Ulrichs, since it is not likely that they will be able to implement all of the suggested risk management and financial planning devices. The family will have to (1) determine how the implementation, or the lack thereof, will affect their objectives and (2) choose to implement those techniques that are most efficient and cost effective for their needs.

For example, the loss exposures that could have the most catastrophic effect on the family's current finances are the loss of health, the death of either PC or Carol, and the possibility of liability. Thus, the family should purchase the additional life insurance, the disability insurance, the medical expense insurance (when Carol leaves her current employer), and the recommended liability insurance, and PC should establish a business continuation plan.

However, in order to determine which suggestions to implement, the Ulrichs should first prioritize their objectives. In this manner, the family will ensure that the more important objectives are adequately dealt with before those of lesser importance. This will help the family to, in effect, prioritize the suggestions. The Ulrichs can then implement as many of the suggested risk treatments as they can afford in order of highest to lowest importance.

For example, the Ulrichs might develop the following list of objectives, in order from those of highest importance to those of least importance:

- Ensure that liability losses will not cause severe and catastrophic financial harm to the Ulrichs.
- Organize the Ulrichs' estate plans. Otherwise, the state's intestacy laws might prohibit property passing to minor children.
- Arrange for adequate life insurance on PC to protect Carol and the children in the event of his death.
- Arrange for adequate life insurance on Carol to protect PC and the children in the event of her death.
- Arrange for adequate health insurance coverage on the family to protect it from severe and catastrophic financial loss exposures.
- Arrange for adequate protection against severe and catastrophic property loss exposures.
- Fully fund the children's education and provide for a comfortable retirement for Carol and PC.
- Arrange for the continuation of PC's businesses.
- Arrange for adequate protection against any remaining loss exposures.

Given this list of priorities, the Ulrichs can begin to consider the suggested risk treatments. The recommendations can be prioritized, and their cost can also be considered. The family will then be able to select the most effective measures that they can afford to implement.

To estimate what amount the Ulrichs can afford to pay towards additional risk management techniques, the Ulrichs' usual income and expenditures must be considered. Exhibit 9-15 provides the Ulrichs' net income and expenditures for the previous year. The exhibit indicates that the Ulrichs had a $21,803 surplus of income over expenditures that could be used to implement selected risk treatments. With this estimate, the Ulrichs can determine which risk treatments can be implemented, in order of priority.

The first area of concern for the Ulrichs is that of their liability loss exposures. Unlike the family's other loss exposures, a liability loss could occur at any time and literally wipe out the family's total wealth. The analysis of their current risk management plan indicated that there were several areas in which the family was retaining severe and catastrophic liability loss exposures. The following additions to the family's liability insurance were recommended:

- Increase liability coverage on their homeowners policy from $100,000 to $300,000—$9 in additional premium per year.

Exhibit 9-15

The Ulrichs' Income and Expenditures for 199X

Earned income (net taxes)			
PC's newspaper earnings	$15,000		
PC's royalties	35,000		
PC's mail-order business	18,000		
Carol's earnings	25,000		
Interest (savings and CDs)	455		
Balanced fund	649		
Total earned income (net taxes)		$94,104	
Other income			
Child support for PC's children	3,000		
Child support for Carol's children	3,600		
Total other income		$ 6,600	
Total net income			$100,704
Expenditures			
Ordinary living costs		$40,500	
Loan payments:			
Mortgage	$10,200		
PC's auto	3,000		
Carol's auto	2,100		
Boat	3,000		
Credit cards	5,250		
		$23,550	
Insurance			
Homeowners	$ 799		
Personal auto	952		
Universal life on PC	900		
		$ 2,651	
Home maintenance		2,100	
Property taxes		4,500	
Educational funding		1,900	
Investment in balanced fund		1,200	
Retirement funding		2,500	
			$ 78,901
Excess of income over expenditures			$ 21,803

- Increase liability coverage on their personal auto policy from $100,000 to $300,000—$60 in additional premium per year.
- Purchase an extended nonowned endorsement to their personal auto policy—$30 in additional premium.
- Add the summer home to the liability coverage on their homeowners policy—$6 in additional premium per year.
- Purchase a personal injury endorsement to their homeowners policy—$13 in additional premium.
- Purchase a personal umbrella policy—$215 per year.
- Purchase business liability insurance—$250 per year. (Property loss exposures are addressed below.)
- Purchase liability coverage for the boat—$285 per year. (Property loss exposures are addressed below.)

The total cost of these recommendations is $868. As shown in Exhibit 9-16, the Ulrichs can afford to purchase the recommended liability coverages.

The second item of importance is that of the estate plans for Carol and PC. Carol and PC want to ensure that their wills are in order and that the children are provided for in the event that one or both of them should die. This will require a one-time fee of $325. Exhibit 9-16 indicates that the Ulrichs can afford to do this.

The Ulrichs have indicated that their third priority is to purchase the additional $377,000 worth of term life insurance recommended on PC's life. The cost of this insurance is $1,190 per year. Again, as shown in Exhibit 9-16, the Ulrichs can afford to purchase life insurance on PC.

As their fourth priority, the Ulrichs want to make sure that Carol's life is also adequately insured so that PC and the children are protected from financial loss if she dies. An additional $186,000 worth of term life insurance was recommended on Carol's life, with a cost of $415 per year. A $50,000 universal life policy was also suggested at a cost of $500 per year. In addition, if Carol quits her job to return to school, her $50,000 group term policy should be replaced with a $50,000 individual term life policy that would cost $112 per year. If each of these policies is purchased, the total cost will be $1,027. As indicated in Exhibit 9-16, the Ulrichs are able to purchase all three policies on Carol's life.

The next priority is the Ulrichs' concern for their health loss exposures. Although the family is currently and adequately insured under a medical expense policy provided through Carol's employer, the coverage will be lost when Carol returns to school. Furthermore, neither PC nor Carol are covered by disability income insurance. It was recommended that, when Carol returns

Exhibit 9-16
A Running Balance of the Ulrichs' Available Resources

Excess of income over expenditures for 199X	$21,803
Cost to purchase liability coverages	868
Remaining resources	20,935
Cost to put the estate in order	325
Remaining resources	20,610
Cost to purchase term life insurance on PC	1,190
Remaining resources	19,420
Cost to purchase universal life and term life insurance on Carol	1,027
Remaining resources	18,393
Cost to purchase major medical expense insurance and PC's disability income insurance	9,600
Remaining resources	8,793
Net cost to make property insurance changes	558
Remaining resources	$ 8,235

to school, the Ulrichs should purchase at the minimum a major medical expense insurance policy. The cost of such a policy would be $7,200 per year. It was also suggested that long-term disability income insurance be purchased on both PC and Carol. If Carol returns to school, such insurance will not be available since she will not be earning income. Therefore, the Ulrichs might decide to purchase a long-term disability insurance policy with a three-month elimination period on only PC. The cost for this policy is $2,400 per year. The total cost to fulfill this objective is $9,600, which, according to Exhibit 9-16, the Ulrichs can afford to do.

The sixth priority identified by the Ulrichs is the need to arrange adequate protection against severe and catastrophic property loss exposures. The Ulrichs face two potentially catastrophic loss exposures that have not been dealt with—the summer home and PC's inventory are not insured for property damage. The summer home can be insured under a dwelling policy with replacement cost "all-risks" coverage and a $1,000 deductible for $464 per year. PC's inventory can be insured under a business property policy for $195 per year. The other property loss exposures identified as inadequately insured are not considered severe or catastrophic. If the Ulrichs can afford to purchase the recommended coverages for these exposures, they will do so after considering the children's education fund, PC and Carol's retirement funding, and PC's business continuation plan.

However, since the Ulrichs' concern is to arrange for adequate protection of severe and catastrophic property loss exposures, the deductibles on the homeowners and personal auto policies, and the limit of coverage on the primary dwelling can be considered at this time. As indicated in the analysis of the Ulrichs' property loss exposures, the family can afford to increase the deductible on their homeowners policy from $250 to $500 (for a savings of $31 in premium per year). The family can also afford to increase the deductibles on their personal auto policy—from $250 to $500 for collision and from $100 to $250 for other than collision (for a savings of $53 per year in premium). The Ulrichs should also reduce the limit of coverage on the primary residence from $240,000 to $230,000, since the replacement cost of the dwelling is $230,000. (This will result in a savings of $17 in premium per year.) Thus the net result for this objective is an increase in the cost of the Ulrichs' property insurance of $558 ($464 + $195 – $31 – $53 – $17). The Ulrichs can afford to make these changes, as is seen in Exhibit 9-16.

The next item of importance to the Ulrichs is the funding for their children's education and for PC and Carol's retirement. As discussed earlier in the chapter, the Ulrichs need to invest $16,113 in a municipal bond fund for each of the next twelve years to fully fund their children's education. They are currently investing $1,900 a year in Series EE bonds; thus, they will need to increase their investment by $14,213 per year. In addition, to afford a comfortable retirement, the Ulrichs must invest $11,468 in a Keogh and possibly a nontax-deductible IRA (although tax-deferred) each year for the next twenty-six years. Since Carol is currently contributing $2,500 a year to her 401(k) plan, the Ulrichs will need to increase their annual retirement plan funding by $8,968 per year. The total increase in funding requirements to fulfill this objective is $23,181. According to Exhibit 9-16, the Ulrichs *cannot* afford to meet this funding requirement. After fulfilling the higher-priority objectives, the Ulrichs have only $8,235 to contribute to their education and retirement funds.

At this point the Ulrichs will have to reconsider their objectives and their order of priority. They do not have the resources to fulfill the education fund and retirement fund objective, the business continuation objective, and the remaining property protection objective if they meet the funding requirements of the higher-priority objectives. The Ulrichs will have to determine whether they want to assign a higher priority to the education and retirement funding or whether they want to modify this objective and higher-priority objectives. For example, the Ulrichs might decide to put off their retirement plan until they can afford to meet the funding requirements and, instead, devote all remaining resources to the children's education fund. Or they might decide to arrange for the continuation of PC's businesses and then split any remaining resources between the children's education fund and PC and Carol's retirement fund.

The choices to be made by the Ulrichs are many. However, with the help of a personal risk manager or financial planner, they should develop an overall plan that will meet their needs.

Periodically Reviewing and Revising the Plan

The final step in the risk management process is to establish procedures for the periodic review of the risk management plan and for its possible revision. A properly developed risk management plan is by necessity based on certain circumstances and assumptions. When these circumstances and assumptions change, the plan should be reviewed and revised as required. In the case of the Ulrichs, many unexpected events might occur, such as a divorce, death or disability of a family member, Carol's inability to find a job close to home, or PC's loss of freelance writing opportunities because the newspaper he contributes to ceases operation. Changes in economic conditions can also have a significant effect on the achievement of financial objectives. For example, a drop in interest rates might require the Ulrichs to increase the annual amount of retirement funding.

In general, risk management plans should be reviewed at least once a year. However, a new plan, such as the one that will be established for the Ulrichs, should probably be reviewed after a shorter period, such as six months, to see that it has been implemented properly and is actually meeting their risk management and financial objectives. Reviews should also take place as soon as possible following a drastic and sudden change in the family or financial environment, such as when Carol returns to the work force.

Chapter Notes

1. The deductible amount, however, will have to be approved by the mortgage holder. Many mortgagees do not allow deductibles greater than $500.
2. The deductible amount will have to be approved by the lienholders of both autos. Many lienholders will not allow deductibles greater than $500.
3. The disability benefits for a disabled worker are based upon the worker's average indexed monthly earnings (AIME). The case does not provide enough information to determine PC's AIME, so it is assumed that his AIME is $3,700. The

disability benefit estimate provided in the text is based on the highest disability benefit any family could receive in 1993 at the assumed AIME level. Thus, based on PC's actual AIME, the Ulrichs could receive less than $1,198 per month. And, if the benefits began in a year later than 1993, the Ulrichs could receive slightly more than $1,198 per month.

4. As was done with the Social Security benefits discussed earlier, PC's AIME is assumed to be $3,700. The benefits are given at 1993 levels.

5. During this period each child is eligible for survivor's benefits until he or she reaches age eighteen. However, the maximum family benefit is $2,095 per month, which is equal to the benefit for three children. Thus until the *twins* reach age eighteen, the children's benefits of $2,095 per month are available. Carol is also eligible to receive benefits as PC's surviving spouse until the last child reaches age sixteen. However, because of her earned income, her benefit amount is reduced to $0.

6. During this year, the youngest child, Eric, will be the only child younger than eighteen. Thus he qualifies for a survivor's benefit, which amounts to $898 per month for one child.

7. Technically, Carol, as PC's surviving spouse, is eligible for survivor's benefits once she reaches age sixty. However, Carol's income from age sixty until she retires completely eliminates her survivor's benefits. Once she retires, Carol's survivor's benefits are paid because she is no longer earning income that causes her benefits to be reduced.

    Upon retirement Carol qualifies for both her own retirement benefit and her survivor's benefit. However, she is eligible to receive only the larger of the two, which is $1,198 per month of survivor's benefits.

8. This is based on the assumptions that the employer will contribute $2,100 per year to the 401(k) on Carol's behalf and that an average rate of 7 percent is earned on the contributions.

9. The annual rate of inflation is assumed to be 3 percent. The annual growth rate in Carol's net income is assumed to be 5 percent, and the annual growth rate for Social Security benefits and Carol's retirement benefit from her employer is assumed to be 3 percent.

10. This figure assumes that PC will use the death proceeds to pay off the mortgage (if feasible at the time) and establish an education fund and an extra expense fund, as well as to purchase health insurance, among other things.

11. The retirement benefits for a retired worker and his or her spouse are based on the worker's average indexed monthly earnings (AIME) as calculated by the Social Security Administration over the worker's active working life. The case does not provide enough information to determine PC's AIME at retirement; thus, it is assumed that by retirement age, his AIME will be $4,800. At current benefit levels, PC and Carol would receive a monthly benefit of approximately $2,315. Assuming that the current benefit levels grow, on average, 3 percent per year for the next twenty-six years, the amount of Social Security retirement benefit payable to PC and Carol at the start of their retirement is $59,911 per year.

12. Actually, tax law would require PC to set up a Keogh for each business and make contributions to each Keogh with the income from that particular business. To simplify the discussion, however, only a single Keogh is mentioned.

Bibliography

Allen, Everett T., Jr., Joseph J. Melone, Jerry S. Rosenbloom, and Jack L. VanDerhei. *Pension Planning*. 7th ed. (Homewood, IL: Business One Irwin, Inc., 1992).

Bests Insurance Reports. (Somerville, NJ: A. M. Best Company).

Blue Cross Association. "Questions and Answers About the Blue Cross Organization," mimeograph, 1984, p. 1.

Blue Cross Special Report. "The New Look at Long-Term Care" (1991), p. 34.

Cohen, Marc A., et al. *Long-Term Care Financing Proposals: Their Costs, Benefits and Impact on Private Insurance*. Health Insurance Association of America, January 1991.

Corliss, Gary L. "The Evolution of Long Term Care Insurance." *Resource*, vol. 16, no. 2, February 1991, p. 12.

Morrissey, Joanne S. "Long-Term Care or Long-Term Disaster?" *National Underwriter*. Life & Health/Financial Services, June 25, 1990, p. 39.

1993 Life Insurance Fact Book Update. (Washington, DC: American Council of Life Insurance, 1993).

Slafsky, Neal. "Carving a Niche in the LTC Market." *Best's Review*, March 1991, p. 35.

Teesdale, Garry M., and Bernard E. Schaeffer. "Executive Retirement Benefit Plans." *Handbook of Employee Benefits*. 3d ed. Edited by Jerry S. Rosenbloom. (Homewood, IL: Dow Jones-Irwin, 1988).

Van Gelder, Susan, and Diane Johnson. *Long-Term Care Insurance: A Market Update*. Health Insurance Association of America, January 1991, p. 7.

Index

C

F

N